NEW LIGHT ON POPE

ALEXANDER POPE

WITH HIS DOG BOUNCE

From the painting by Jonathan Richardson at Hagley Hall, Stourbridge

NEW LIGHT ON
POPE

WITH SOME ADDITIONS TO HIS POETRY HITHERTO UNKNOWN

By

NORMAN AULT

LONDON: 1949
METHUEN & CO., LTD.

First published in 1949

CATALOGUE NO. 5109/U

THIS BOOK IS PRODUCED
IN COMPLETE CONFORMITY WITH
THE AUTHORIZED ECONOMY STANDARDS

PREFACE

THE present volume is the outcome of some twenty years' inter-mittent exploration of the by-ways of eighteenth-century litera-ture, for the most part in an endeavour to track the footsteps of Pope, and his friends and enemies, hither and thither on their lawful—and unlawful—occasions.

The resultant 'discoveries'—a few of which have already been published in various periodicals—will be seen to affect in a greater or lesser degree many aspects of Pope's life, character, and works, hitherto regarded as established beyond question, and to necessitate, in consequence, a reconsideration of much current opinion. They may even add an impetus to the move-ment—long needed but now at last becoming perceptible—towards a new appreciation of his poetry, which must inevitably follow a better understanding of the man behind the poet.

In addition to the 'new' poems here attributed to Pope, some of them now printed for the first time, the recovered material is of many kinds, textual as well as critical, bibliographical as well as biographical, the more important of which are enumerated, and their significance in Pope's life summarized, in the opening chapter. And if it cannot be pretended that this work has reached the ultimate truth on all the subjects discussed, on some at least it may justly be claimed to have travelled further from the accepted untruth than any previous inquiry.

A book of this kind could hardly have been begun, much less completed, without its author receiving more help and con-sideration than one has any right to expect. First I must grate-fully acknowledge my indebtedness to the private, but public-spirited, owners of manuscripts and copyrights, who have most kindly allowed me to examine, transcribe, and print verse or prose from original autographs or texts in their possession; namely, His Grace the late Duke of Portland, and the late

Marquess of Bath, for the use of the Oxford papers at Welbeck and Longleat respectively; the late Mr E. Riddell-Blount, for the use of the Mapledurham letters and library; and Mr D. F. Hyde of New York, for the Strafford letters; and also to public bodies for similar permission, viz. the British Museum and the Bodleian libraries, the Harvard College Library, and the Pierpont Morgan Library, New York, for the use of manuscripts referred to in the footnotes.

For help of other kinds I have much pleasure in thanking my friends the Professors of English Literature, at various universities, as follows: John Butt of Durham, D. Nichol Smith of Oxford, James R. Sutherland of Queen Mary, London, Geoffrey Tillotson of Birkbeck, London, and H. O. White of Trinity, Dublin—all eighteenth-century 'specialists'; and also Miss Edith Sitwell, Mr C. G. Long, Mr Francis Needham, Mr C. H. Wilkinson, and Mr Harold Williams, for valuable criticisms or suggestions, collations or transcriptions, and unfailing encouragement; Professor George Sherburn of Harvard, for news of certain Pope items treasured at Longleat (including the unprinted poem, 'The Six Maidens'), which led to my own fruitful search of several days there amongst the Portland Papers; and lastly, the Hon. Mrs Hugh Wyndham, from whom I first learnt of the existence of Bounce's portrait, and Viscount Cobham, her brother, who has generously permitted me to include Richardson's portrait of Pope and Bounce, at Hagley, as my frontispiece—this being the first reproduction ever made of the whole picture showing Bounce in the foreground.

Oxford, 1948.   N. A.

CONTENTS

The 'Cupid' ornament on the title page is reproduced from a tailpiece used by Pope in the quarto edition of The Works, *1717.*

NEW LIGHT ON POPE

CHAPTER I

NEW JUDGEMENT

I. THE ANONYMOUS POEMS

'DESCEND, in the name of God, to some other amusements, as common mortals do. Learn to play at cards, or tables, or bowls; get talking females . . .'—Thus Swift once implored Pope, in an attempt to lessen his habitual concentration on his work. If only he had succeeded, it would have saved the writing of many books—including the present volume. But the Dean's alternatives were not, it seems, attractive enough; and Pope's unresting pen moved satirically, or moralizingly, or even merrily, on.

This devotion to his craft had many consequences which can be seen in his life and his work. Chief amongst them obviously is the exquisite and unique distinction of his verse, which brought him greater fame, both contemporary and posthumous (if the continuous reprinting of a poet's works is any criterion[1]), than has rewarded any other English poet except Shakespeare. With this in mind, and remembering also, that, as editor followed editor throughout two hundred years, the works themselves have been submitted to an intensive study hardly matched outside Shakespearean criticism; and furthermore, that no other poet's 'life' has been told and retold so often and so diversely—it will probably be thought by many that there can be nothing left to say.

The truth, however, is that so strangely compounded was Pope's personality that he has been misunderstood and misjudged more consistently than any of the major poets; while as a satirist of society he made so many enemies (both before and since his death), and conducted his verbal warfare with such elusive and unpredictable movements, that his work still abounds in numerous unsolved problems of text and date and allusion, and his life in as many apparent contradictions of character, and secrecies of motive.

One of the most striking and persistent characteristics of Pope's

[1] Between 1744 and 1900, not counting separate works or the smaller collections, no less than eighty editions of Pope's Works, or Collected Poems, were published, an average of one every two years; and no decade passed without at least one. They represent the labours of some thirty known editors, many of them scholars of note, besides much anonymous work.

activity as an author was his practice of anonymity. Not counting the
Homer translations, the greater part of his work, both in prose and
verse, was first published without his name. Moreover, many of the
occasional and miscellaneous pieces first printed anonymously were
afterwards left unacknowledged for one reason or another, or simply
forgotten, and have only since his death been attributed to him, some
of them quite recently. And although to these must now be added yet
others identified for the first time in the following chapters, we still
cannot be sure that the whole of his 'unofficial' verse, in all its surprising variety of form and style and bizarre occasion, has even yet
been recovered. For when it is remembered, on the one hand, that he
was immobilized in great measure and for long periods at a time by
'the natural imbecility of his body' (his word for his feeble physique);
and, on the other, that he was endowed with senses alert and acute
beyond the normal, and a restive and brilliant mind ever demanding
employment—it will perhaps seem scarcely an exaggeration to say
that Pope was always writing.

Swift, for instance, not infrequently complained that Pope never
had any leisure for conversation, was inattentive in company, and
loved solitude; that, in short, when Swift wanted to sit and talk, 'Pope
walks, and courts the Muse'.[1] Thus, at times, the Dean would break
out into half-serious, half-humorous expostulation, as already seen;
and at other times would explain such strange behaviour to his friends
by saying that 'Mr. Pope . . . hath always some poetical scheme in his
head,'[2]—a habit of mind for which there is ample evidence in their
correspondence and verse. On more than one occasion Pope reveals
his own attitude to the pursuit of poetry, but never more significantly,
perhaps, than when writing to the poet Fenton, he said:

> I am a little scandalized at your complaint that your time lies
> heavy on your hands, when the muses have put so many good
> materials into your head to employ them.[3]

This, however, only repeated a generalization of his own experience,
which had appeared earlier in one of his *Spectator* letters, thus: 'Whoever has the Muses . . . for his Companions, can never be idle enough
to be uneasy.'[4]

Pope refers to this constant preoccupation with poetry again and
again in his works. It filled so much of his life as to make him wonder
and question—

[1] See *Dr Swift to Mr Pope*, in *Miscellanies* [IV], 1732.   [2] Ball, v, p. 19.
[3] *Letters*, 4to, 1737, p. 186.
[4] *The Spectator*, June 16, 1712; see Pope's *Prose*, I, pp. xxxiv, 42.

> This subtle Thief of Life, this paltry Time,
> What will it leave me, if it snatch my Rhime?
> If ev'ry Wheel of that unweary'd Mill
> That turn'd ten thousand Verses, now stands still. [1]

At other times he spoke as if it had brought him some ease in a world of pain and infirmity, or was even a method of self-preservation, as it all too certainly was: 'The Muse but serv'd ... To help me thro' this long Disease, my Life.' [2]

There were moments when he wearied of his pen and spoke loudly against its tyranny ('Heav'ns! was I born for nothing but to write?') [3]; and others when he would pretend his verses were poured forth with effortless ease ('Take it as you find it, yᵉ Production of half an hour 'tother morning') [4]; and yet other occasions when he would protest against the idea that he had given up all for poetry ('Those who think I live in a study, and make poetry my business are ... mistaken'). [5] But all such denials of his habitual absorption in poetry were like wind flurries on a river, momentarily ruffling the surface of his consciousness but with little or no effect on the deep-flowing current of his being.

Indeed, only eighteen months before he died, William Murray wrote to George Grenville: 'Pope is at Bath, perched upon his hill, making epigrams and stifling them in their birth.' [6] And barely two years earlier (as Dr Johnson tells us in the well-known story), [7] 'Lord Oxford's domestick ... in the dreadful winter of Forty ... was called from her bed by him [Pope] four times in one night, to supply him with paper, lest he should lose a thought.' Full well had he weighed the consequences of his 'ruling passion' years before, both for himself and those about him, in a world that has little use and less patience for such a strange devotion. One of his early sayings about poetry was: 'No man can be a true Poet, who writes for diversion only' [8]; and four years later we have: 'No man ever rose to any degree of perfection in writing, but thro' obstinacy and an inveterate resolution against the stream of mankind.' [9] And, ten years later still, he elaborated the idea thus:

> To write well, lastingly well, immortally well, ... must not one be prepared to endure the reproaches of men, want, and much fasting, nay martyrdom in its cause? It is such a task as scarce leaves a man

---

[1] Hor. Ep. ii, ii, ll. 76–9. [2] *Epistle to Arbuthnot*, ll. 131–2.
[3] *Ibid.*, l. 272. [4] Rawl. letters 90, f. 46 v. [5] Polwhele, i, p. 321.
[6] *Grenville*, i, p. 16. [7] Johnson, iv, p. 155.
[8] *Correspondence*, i, 1735, p. 303. [9] *Ibid.*, p. 69.

time to be a good neighbour, an useful friend, nay to plant a tree, much less to save his soul.[1]

Such evidence of his application to his art could be multiplied; but enough has perhaps been cited to suggest, that, with 'man' as his 'study', with the urge, the ability, and the endless opportunity to write, and—still more to the point—with the almost complete repression or limitation of a man's normal physical activities and distractions, the real problem is, not that Pope wrote so much, but that he did not write more. And that problem, once stated, in turn suggests not only that Pope wrote more than has yet been recovered (which is perfectly true), but also the probability that, although some pieces have —like his juvenile epic, *Alcander*—been destroyed, there are others still awaiting identification.

Yet much of this verse was never intended for cold print at all, still less for inclusion in *The Works of Mr. Alexander Pope*. For although in one of the recovered poems, *The Capon's Tale*,[2] he advised Lady Mary Wortley Montagu, at the beginning of their quarrel, to 'own' as well as 'hatch' her poetical 'chicks', he was very far from following his advice with his own occasional pieces. On the contrary, he usually took such pains to conceal his connection with them, that if, with the eager assistance of the piratical bookseller, Curll, a few of his own chickens did somewhat embarrassingly come home to roost in his lifetime,[3] it is certain that he never dreamt of the day when they would return in such a flock of wild fowl as in the present volume.

The reasons for Pope's desire for anonymity were probably almost as numerous and diverse as the poems themselves, and only a few can be glanced at. It was not at that time unusual for writers to withhold their names from political and topical contributions to the periodicals and miscellanies where so many of Pope's unofficial pieces first saw the light: anonymity was accepted as 'part of the game'. Another reason for not acknowledging his work on publication could have been—at least as regards some of the major poems—a desire to obtain unbiased critical opinions, which would have been impossible had his name been subscribed to them originally. (It is certain that he followed this course sometimes in his letters, and submitted to friends unsigned pieces for criticism.)[4] In other instances anonymity might be explained by a wish to test the weight of opposition, or reprobation, which certain ethical pieces would probably arouse, and thus be prepared to deal with it, when, after acknowledgement of authorship, it

[1] Oxford MSS. (EC, VII, p. 399).   [2] See *post*, p. 244.
[3] A lamentable example will be found in Chapter VIII.   [4] See *post*, p. 62.

came to be directed against himself; while with some of his satires he may have thought it would be in every way desirable if the first resultant howls of execration and anger were dissipated on a nameless author before it became known that he himself was responsible for them.

But the chief and abiding cause of his withholding his signature from the majority of the unsponsored pieces is, beyond question, to be found in his life-long ideal of poetical craftsmanship, that conception of correct and flawless verse, which had dominated his mind ever since those early conversations of his, when he was 'about fifteen', with the poet and critic, William Walsh. As the oft-told anecdote[1] goes, it was his old friend's reiterated advice—that the only way left of excelling as a poet was the unceasing pursuit of classic correctness of versification—which so impressed the ambitious young poet that he ever afterwards made it his 'study and aim'. Thus, as the years passed, this craving of his, or rather, this fundamental need of his soul—'To write well, lastingly well, immortally well'—grew to be the 'ruling passion' of his life, and, more than anything else, compelled him relentlessly and consistently to refuse his name to every poem that in any way fell short of that ideal.

It would seem, however, that no explanation hitherto propounded has yet reached the heart of the problem and told us why Pope's inner eye became so unwaveringly, so devotedly, fixed on the shining ideal, that, in effect, his whole poetic life may be said to have resolved itself into an Augustan version of the quest of the holy grail.

Pope himself never realized it to the full, nor did he perceive that his need for perfection, in the one sphere where for him it was attainable, was more deeply rooted in his being than the seed of Walsh's early sowing. His half-sister, Mrs Racket, once told Spence:

> I believe nobody ever studied so hard as my brother did, in his youth.—He did nothing else but write and read.[2]

From other remarks Pope made occasionally, it appears that before he knew Walsh his 'early Bent to Poetry', as he called it, was already inducing him to study with a concentration beyond his years and strength. Frail and feeble from boyhood, he suffered much pain from constantly recurring bouts of headache and sickness; and in his letters there is frequent reference to 'my almost continual illnesses'. According to Sir Joshua Reynolds, even when full-grown, he was barely four and a half feet high,[3] and deformed at that, with spinal curvature

---

[1] Spence, p. 280. [2] *Ibid.*, p. 267. [3] Malone, p. 429.

which grew worse with the years. Sensitive and perceptive beyond the ordinary as Pope was, it is only too likely that his desire for perfection sprang up and drew its miraculous growth from his bitter realization, during the formative years of adolescence, of how much he was doomed to be deprived of a man's rightful heritage, not only of health and strength and physical endurance, but also—and more tragically —of ordinary human stature and human shape.

Small wonder if, with such an experience at the most impressionable age, he early became obsessed with the idea of flawless perfection. If that were so—and there is much evidence to prove it—then Walsh did no more than confirm him in his resolve to excel in the only way possible—in his poetry—at whatever cost of drudgery and application. The cost was paid—paid in aches and pains and weariness beyond telling, and a very definite worsening of his already fragile bodily health—but the world has his poetry for ever. Surely he could be excused if he thought of himself when he praised a certain prince as one—

Whose little body lodg'd a mighty mind.[1]

But it was not only the poems which had fallen short of the ideal Pope had set before himself, that he so steadfastly refused to acknowledge, or admit into his *Works*. As already suggested, he also wrote pieces of a very different kind; and however delightfully witty, wicked, or absurd, we may think them, 'classic perfection' was obviously the last quality they aimed at, and the last phrase ever to be associated with them. For as there was never poet who studied more assiduously the perfection of his verses than he, so there was never one who at the same time wrote with so different a pen such ribald and frequent poems in comment on the contemporary scene. Psychologists doubtless have a word for these two reciprocating phases, and would explain them as compensatory in effect—a continual unconscious readjustment for the preservation of a sane mental balance. Noteworthy instances of these alternating moods are remarked, in passing, on subsequent pages, where some piece of rhymed absurdity is shown to be not less authentically Pope's for having preceded or followed the making of some noble poem perfectly expressed.

With all these diverse influences at work to inspire his pen or govern its performances, it is not very surprising after all that so many of Pope's miscellaneous poems should lack his signature. Nevertheless it may astonish many readers to learn that a number of his best-known occasional poems cannot be proved to be his at all—that they are

[1] *Iliad*, v, l. 999.

nothing more than 'attributed pieces'. Such a once famous (or notorious) thing as the 'Worm-Powder' poem, for example, was never acknowledged by him; nor was it incorporated in his *Works* until he had been dead some years, at which time (1751) the charming but unacknowledged trifle, *On a certain Lady at Court*, was similarly accepted as Pope's. Stranger still, the ever-delightful but authorless *Farewell to London* was not printed before 1775, or found in the *Works* before 1779; while the better-known but unclaimed pieces, *The Court Ballad* (sometimes called 'The Challenge') and *Sandys's Ghost*, were not included in the canon until 1797 and 1824 respectively; not to mention a dozen others still more tardily recognized—all perfect things of their kind, though a few of them, perhaps, could not be regarded by some of us, any more than by Pope, as quite 'correct', if for different reasons. When we add to all those unacknowledged pieces the burlesque version of *The First Psalm*, which Pope seemingly repudiated by public advertisement, it becomes apparent that neither the original, nor the continued, anonymity of many of his miscellaneous poems can be used as an argument against his authorship.

Because successive editors of Pope throughout two centuries have automatically repeated some otherwise unsupported attribution to him of this or that poem, the poem itself has not in fact been made more authentic thereby. Conversely, an attribution now first made in this volume and supported by evidence should not be suspect simply because the ascription has not been parroted for two hundred years.

As might have been expected, different degrees of probability attach to the attribution to Pope of these pieces written on such different occasions throughout the poet's life; for the evidence that is still extant after so many years naturally varies in quantity and conclusiveness from poem to poem. It is believed, however, that no piece has been included in the following pages unless the weight of evidence is in favour of Pope's authorship; or, in other words, unless its rejection would raise greater difficulties than its acceptance. As each poem is accompanied by the evidence for its ascription to Pope, and none ascribed by mere assertion, it will perhaps be allowed that the attributions in this volume have been more carefully made than many in the distant past, and some (a few of which are noticed in this work) more recently. For the reader, the counsel of perfection regarding all the attributed poems, new and old alike, is to be swayed neither by familiarity nor by novelty; but, after weighing all the available evidence, to judge each ascription separately on its merits, and decide accordingly.

b

II. PORTRAIT OR CARICATURE?

One of the most important results of a general survey of Pope's 'new' occasional pieces—and of the incidental discoveries made during the search for them—is the information they afford about the man himself. From Pope's day down to the present century, his character progressively suffered more misrepresentation (wilful or not) at the hands of his editors and biographers, than that of any other writer in our literature. Recently, however, owing in great part to the sympathetic championship of Edith Sitwell,[1] and the patient researches of George Sherburn,[2] the popular portrait of Pope with its slightly Satanic expression is, as it were, gradually fading on the canvas, and a recognizably human countenance is beginning to peer out through the age-old caricature. Furthermore, the work of the scholars on the 'Twickenham Edition' of Pope's poems (in course of publication) is also largely helping to a juster appreciation of the man as well as the poet. The discoveries described in the present volume throw new light on several much debated questions of the poet's conduct in certain connections or events, for they not only prove the integrity of his friendships, and justify in great measure his warfare with his enemies, but also reveal little-known aspects of his character, as well as his work, the total effect of which can only be still further to humanize that legendary, many-sided, unaccountable creature called Pope.

Pope the pastoralist, Pope the critic, Pope the translator, Pope the moralist, Pope the satirist, nay, also (as some have thought him) Pope the hypocrite, and even Pope the Devil; and, master and servant of them all, Pope the model of 'correct' versification and faultless style—*that* man, whether execrated or praised, has been a familiar figure in literary history for two hundred years. What is now emerging from this collective examination of the news-sheets, miscellanies, journals, correspondence, pamphlets, manuscripts, and pictures of the period, and the resultant new additions to his poetry (not to mention a fresh survey of the whole Pope canon), is that two further aspects of his work and character await recognition. The first is that his study of art was so much more sincere than has hitherto been supposed, and affected his poetry so much more vitally, that 'Pope the painter' must now be added to his many 'sides'; the second, not less important, being the revelation of his gust for sheer irresponsible fun, which, in different circumstances, or under physical handicaps less embitter-

---

[1] *Alexander Pope*, by Edith Sitwell, 1930.
[2] *The Early Career of Alexander Pope*, by G. Sherburn, 1934.

ing, would have justified yet another epithet—'Pope the clown!'

That he allowed no hint of the clown to stain the classic perfection of *The Works* is perhaps understandable after reading the foregoing pages. Nevertheless, there it was; and it now becomes an aspect of his complex personality that can no longer be overlooked. The knowledge that somewhere deep within him there sprang a fount of bubbling good-humour will not surprise readers familiar with such pieces as *The Court Ballad*, or *Sandys's Ghost*, which are so happily compacted of it. What will astonish many people, however, is that the new attributions are lacking in those spiteful or scurrilous qualities which have been regarded so long—too long—as Pope's peculiar distinction amongst the poets. His sense of fun is now seen to comprise the whole gamut of wit and humour, from the keenest satire to the tenderest raillery, from pedantic quips to broad burlesques, not excluding nonsense that veils at times more meanings than his puns, and is as free of all inhibitions. As he once explained in a whimsical apology 'for all this buffoonery' in a letter to his old friend Cromwell: 'I may as well throw out what comes uppermost, as study to be dull'.[1] Whatever Pope's sins were, that, at least, was not one of them.

Besides laughing at the foibles of mankind in general, Pope could also laugh at himself—which is pre-eminently the hall-mark of sanity. Obviously, no one as sensitive as he could help being stung to the quick occasionally by the brutal descriptions and mockery of his size, shape, and bodily infirmities, put about by Dennis, Gildon, Curll, Cibber, and a score of other enemies named and nameless. Normally, however, he was capable of making fun (if, at times, a little wryly) even of his physical shortcomings; and numerous instances could be cited both in his prose and verse. He could smile as he likened himself to a dozen things, animate and inanimate—to a dog,[2] a spider,[3] a windmill,[4] a frog[5] (but—was it too bitter a draught?—he seems rarely or never to have likened himself to an ordinary human being). He jested at his size—'For Gay can well make two of me'[6]; at his deformity—'One does not like your looks, nor tother my Shape'[7]; while jokes about his aches and pains and weaknesses abound in his writings—'They all say 'tis pitty I am so sickly, & I think 'tis pitty They are so healthy.'[8]

Another aspect of Pope's character illuminated by these discoveries

[1] Rawl. letters 90, f. 29.
[2] *Ibid.*, f. 17.
[3] Pope's *Prose*, I, p. 125.
[4] *Ibid.*
[5] Rawl. letters 90, f. 28 v.
[6] *The Court Ballad*, stz. 6.
[7] Add. 28618, f. 9 v.
[8] Rawl. letters 90, f. 22.

is his practice of mystification, which is now seen to be less frequent and more innocent than is commonly supposed; and even the admittedly dubious affair of the *Letters* when considered (as in the following section) from a new point of view, such as Pope's, seems to take on a tinge no longer diabolically black but a very human grey. Thus the well-known misquotation, that Pope could not even drink tea without a stratagem, is after all no truer to the facts than such sayings tend to be. As later pages show, concealment in literary matters, for example, was frequently forced on him by the actions of others—by friends as well as enemies. If, like one of his own Homeric heroes, he sometimes made his way 'dark thro' paths oblique', it was, more often than not, a quite blameless ramble. And if, at times, his liking for mystification was titillated by the publication of his unowned pieces, that, as we have seen above, was not his reason for leaving them unacknowledged.

Nevertheless, for such a famous man as Pope to achieve anonymity for his pen was not quite as simple as the phrase, 'leaving them unacknowledged' might suggest. In many instances it was an active rather than a passive business, and called for both trouble and ingenuity to accomplish; the simple reason being that for approximately the last eighteen years of his life what Pope wrote was 'news' as well as poetry. In common, therefore, with many famous people, before and since, he doubtless felt himself entitled to some measure of privacy, and supposed, as most people would, that he was justified in going to whatever lengths were necessary to obtain it.

Clearly it would not have been much use for Pope to have withheld his name from his unofficial verses, if they had been written in his usual heroic couplets and finger-printed with his characteristic mannerisms. Even so, his own opinion, whether or not his work could be recognized by his style, seemed to vary from time to time. Spence records him once as saying:

> There is nothing more foolish than to pretend to be sure of knowing a great writer by his style. [1]

At another time when speaking of Wycherley's *Posthumous Works*, he said:

> Those verses that are published, are a mixture of Wycherley's own original lines, with a great many of mine inserted here and there, (but not difficult to be distinguished). [2]

And again, in the *Epistle to Arbuthnot*, after talking of people who mistake other writers' work for his, he breaks out—

---

[1] Spence, p. 168.   [2] *Ibid.*, p. 151.

Poor guiltless I! and can I chuse but smile,
When ev'ry Coxcombe knows me by my *Style*?[1]

It is, however, suggestive that the majority of his unacknowledged
pieces were written in metres other than the heroic couplet; the common street-ballad of the four-line stanza being one that he was particularly successful with, both as regards its verisimilitude and the
safe-keeping of his anonymity. (Incidentally, it is worth remarking
that the various forms of these miscellaneous pieces are themselves a
refutation of the old gibe that Pope was a poet of only one tune.) There
can be no question that their unlikeness to Pope's known verse,
together with the absence of his name, explains why so many of them
escaped contemporary identification.

It should not be forgotten that Pope was the first man to make
poetry 'pay'; that is, the first poet without patron or place, to live—
far from penuriously—on the proceeds of his work; for that, too, was
not without its bearing on his opportune practice of mystification. A
considerable amount of reticence on his part in literary affairs is therefore not only understandable but was actually necessitated by the
conditions of the time. There were pirates like Curll, and the nameless
compilers of the cheaper miscellanies, continually on the look-out for
any publishable trifle that might 'blow' their way:

To seize his papers, *Curl*, was next thy care;
His papers light, fly diverse, tost in air:
Songs, sonnets, epigrams the winds uplift . . .[2]

Besides which, there were always the 'Grub-street Verse-Writers',
often the hirelings of the two political parties, ready, as Swift warned
Pope, to pick up any chance scribblings of his, and—

Sell them to *Curl* for Fifty Pound,
And swear they are [their] own.[3]

With so many and such various external reasons accounting in
great measure for Pope's frequent recourse to concealment and secrecy, there was always present the still stronger personal urge (too
often forgotten by his critics) which derived ultimately from his
lamentable physical constitution. This was the instinctive defence
mechanism by which a hyper-sensitive soul attempts to avoid or
mitigate the rougher contacts of a society not too considerate of its
weaker members. With Pope the practice probably dated from early

[1] *Epistle to Arbuthnot*, ll. 281-2.   [2] *Dunciad* A, ii, ll. 105-7.
[3] *Advice to the Grub-street Verse Writers*, ll. 19-20.

youth, a period when some secret knowledge or concealed action often brings with it a sense of power or superiority—about the only power attainable by one so constituted. If, later on, he found the art of judicious concealment useful at times in dealing with the world out-side—that was no more than he saw to be the practice all round him (but with far less excuse) of friend and foe alike. Thus it would seem—with so many of his friends in politics practising secrecy professionally, and so many of his enemies making anonymous attacks on him from behind screens and covers—that Pope cannot after all be accused of any abnormality, or even singularity, in his use of mystification, especially when so much of it was only another, and sometimes politer, way of saying, 'Mind your own business!'

III. 'PATHS OBLIQUE'

Propensity—idiosyncrasy—foible—many an act or habit that in another person would be passed over with a smile, was charged against Pope as misrepresentation or stratagem of the deepest cun-ning. Take, for example, what have been called 'Pope's mischievously erroneous dates'. Every student of the poet soon learns that he used frequently to misdate former occurrences in his life when referring to them in retrospect: such as the year when this or that poem of his was written or published, or other literary events happened—not to men-tion incidents of personal, or even public, concern. In subsequent chapters statements by Pope about his early poems will be found, which seem boastfully, or pathetically (much depends on one's sym-pathies), to overstress his undoubted precocity in poetry. Such a gift for versification is very flattering in remembrance, and the poet seems to have been peculiarly conscious of it. His father is thought by some to have encouraged him to make verses too early and too continuously; but it is evident that the youngster did not need much driving: 'I lisped in numbers for the numbers came.'

Pope was no longer young when this craze for early dating over-took him; there had been one example in the 1717 volume of *The Works*, but it becomes most noticeable from 1736 onwards, when he was beginning to reprint the contents of that volume, and was taking the opportunity so provided of printing other early pieces for the first time. But, although he had still 'a good memory' for the printed word, which, as Spence reports,[1] lasted his lifetime, his memory for figures

[1] Spence, p. 285.

was becoming untrustworthy several years before his death. This is seen very clearly when there is a definite, verifiable date connected with the particular poem referred to. For example, on reprinting *Windsor Forest* in 1736, he inserted a note saying that the portion of the poem celebrating the Treaty of Utrecht 'was not added till the year 1710, in which it was publish'd.' Now, according to contemporary newspapers, the poem was not published until the spring of 1713.[1] This not only disproves Pope's statement that it was published in 1710, but reflects doubt upon the date of composition—doubt that is justified by his untouched, unedited correspondence with his old friend, John Caryll, which proves that he was working on the additions to *Windsor Forest* during the winter of 1712–13,[2] that is, on the very eve of the Peace Treaty.[3]

The same note of Pope's says, further, that the early part of the poem was written in 1704 'at the same time with the Pastorals'; which is not impossible, if by 'written' he meant the first youthful sketch of the poem. But it is virtually certain that Pope, tireless corrector and polisher as he was, would never print in 1713 an untouched poem of 1704. A case in point is *The First Book of Statius his Thebais*, which is dated on the half-title 1703, but which on the following page (in 1736) has a note saying, 'This piece . . . was made almost in his Childhood. But finding the Version better than he expected, he gave it some Correction a few years afterwards.' Indeed, as far as it has been possible to ascertain, he rarely if ever sent a poem to press without having found something to correct in, or add to, the last previously printed text, or transcription; the extent of such alterations seeming— at least with some of the earlier pieces—to have varied with the time that had passed since his last revision of them.

Another reason why Pope's late notes on the dates of the early poems are a little suspect is that they leave so many years when he apparently wrote nothing! Thus, if the ascribed dates are to be taken literally, it would mean that 1704–5 were wonderful years in which he wrote the four *Pastorals*, two-thirds of *Windsor Forest*, *January and May*, and *To a Young Lady*; after which he rested until 1708–9, in which years he wrote the *Ode for Musick* and *An Essay on Criticism*; then nothing again until *The Temple of Fame* in 1711, and so on. But the chief difficulty about compiling such a chronology would, of course, be the dating of those dozen or more poems which, on different oc-

---

[1] Published March 7, 1713; see *The Evening Post* of that date.

[2] For further detail, see *post*, p. 32.

[3] The Treaty was signed March 30, 1713.

casions, he stated were written at different times. The strangest example of this is his *Epistle, To Mr Addison*,[1] to which, after a lapse of some twenty years, he ascribed four different dates at four different times—all of which, incredible as it may seem, are probably correct.[2]

Unquestionably such muddles as these cannot be the result of a planned 'stratagem'; nor—one would think—could they have been caused intentionally by any rational being. It is thus more than probable that, where *our* misunderstanding, or ignorance, of the facts is not the cause, many of Pope's alleged misrepresentations, with their seeming deceptions, contradictions, and concealments, for which he has been so hotly censured any time these two hundred years, are due to no greater sins than an unreliable memory and a very human carelessness about details. Such details could hardly have appeared to him, when adding these notes, very important for his work, either in retrospect or in prospect. It is certain, however, that, while he was preparing new editions of his poems and dreaming about immortal verse and undying fame, he little anticipated that future editors and readers would be greatly troubled by such varying details, and would —being English and for the most part Protestant—account such discrepancies as proofs of a grave moral defect in his character, if not his religion, rather than as evidence of a deficiency in his physical make-up, which too often allowed patience to lose the never-ending battle with pain and fatigue, or (on good days) with fatigue only.

Much the same error of judgement which led to Pope's careless dating of his poems, probably accounts, at least in part, for his perplexing treatment of his letters before publication—treatment which in the past has led to words like falsification and forgery being used to describe it. On this count also, there are many who think that Pope has been judged much too harshly. Although, since C. W. Dilke's articles in *The Athenaeum* of 1854, there has been no doubt that Pope remodelled some parts of his correspondence before publication, correcting, re-writing, conflating two or three letters into one, re-addressing letters to different persons, and so on; the heinousness of such crimes has been exaggerated out of all proportion even to the motives suggested for them. A more reasonable, and therefore more probable, explanation of the unquestioned facts, which will also cover many, if not most, of the charges, is that Pope looked at his letters with different eyes from ours. It cannot be too emphatically repeated that the supreme compulsion of Pope's life was his passion for literary correctness, style, and polish (about which something has been said on

---

[1] See *post*, pp. 120–1.　　　　[2] See *post*, pp. 121–4.

an earlier page); and this motive should never be forgotten in any discussion about his printed correspondence, because it supplies the chief clue that leads to the heart of that labyrinth.

In brief, when Pope came to publish his letters (which he had been reclaiming from correspondents over many years), there is much reason to believe that he regarded them as prose compositions, causeries, essays—anything rather than as historical documents, which in his eyes at that juncture they obviously were not. Indeed, there is definite evidence that he thought of his letters as the raw material of literature rather than the finished product. When, on the discontinuance of *The Spectator*, Steele wanted him to contribute to its projected successor, *The Guardian*, he immediately wrote to Caryll asking for the return of his letters, which, he explained, 'may be of Use to me in a Design I am lately engaged in'.[1] And, still more to the point, when he had received his letters back he found numerous 'Faults' in them—'many things that would give me Shame ... many things freely thrown outt ... Thoughts just warm from the Brain without any polishing or Dress, the very Deshabilée of the Understanding'.[2]

Pope was an author by vocation; and in 1735, professionally speaking, he had on his hands an accumulation of possible literary material written over a period of nearly thirty years, and, for that reason, to his experienced mind and eye, very uneven in quality and unequal in interest. Two problems therefore confronted him: the first, with the letters of Voiture in his mind, was how to lick that inchoate mass of good, bad, and indifferent correspondence into impeccable literary 'copy' for publication above his signature; and the second, what arrangements to make with the booksellers to ensure the author a profitable publication.

How Pope achieved the first is known to most students, if only by the diatribes of Dilke, and, later, of Elwin. But his drastic handling of the letters is of recent years beginning to be placed in a more reasonable and convincing light by scholars whose pleas for a less censorious attitude towards Pope in this matter are based on both evidence and sympathy. Thus, if Pope 'edited' his letters before printing them, he did not differ (except possibly in degree) from the majority of those of his century who thus exhibited selected aspects of what purported to be their private life to the public eye. Nevertheless, however much he corrected or polished, abridged or expanded, divided or combined this literary material, as wit, or taste, or discretion prompted, it has been recently stated that 'it is doubtful if Pope has so falsified his letters

[1] Add. 28618, f. 10 v.   [2] *Ibid.*, f. 11.

as to change the story fundamentally'—at least as regards his correspondence with Addison and Wycherley.[1] This assertion is appositely illustrated in the present volume.[2] Pope must have had much correspondence with Steele and Addison, for example; but in those early days he was not keeping letters or copies (the backs of them were, to his thrifty mind, too useful for scribbling verses on, as the Homer MSS. testify). On the other hand, he had an abundance of his letters returned by the Carylls, some of them written *at the same time* as the lost letters to Steele and Addison, and therefore presumably touching on at least some of the same subjects, such as his current work, etc. Pope, for instance, must have remembered writing to Steele as well as to Caryll about the Hadrian verses, for there is the *Spectator* letter[3] as well as the Caryll transcripts[4] as witness. But Steele of course never returned his letters; and so, when Pope wanted to include a letter to Steele in a series about the Hadrian poems, he transferred from one of his reclaimed letters to Caryll a paragraph which probably said much the same thing in much the same way, and corrected its context to what he thought he might have said, had it been written to Steele in the first place. That some such proceeding really did happen in connection with the Hadrian poems is shown on a subsequent page.[5] It is therefore possible, even probable, that we have here a specimen explanation of the way in which some—if not most—of the 'concocted' letters (which after all are relatively few in number) came into being; and also the kind of motive which occasionally caused other letters to be printed with address or date differing from the original.

Nevertheless, there is something to be placed on the credit side of the balance sheet. For example, Dr Johnson said of these much criticized writings, that, in them 'there is nothing but liberality, gratitude, constancy, and tenderness'[6];—not a bad achievement for 'wicked forgeries'. Nor need it be always forgotten that the poet, Thomas Gray (himself a famous letter-writer), would seem to have justified Pope's long editorial labours on his 'Letters' by the statement that 'they were not good letters, but better things'.[7] Such opinions were typical of the century.

Lastly, it should be noted, that, although we may still wish that Pope had acted otherwise (his editors for example would have had an easier task), the 'documentary' damage to the letters was not as wide-

---

[1] Sherburn, pp. 20–21. [2] See *post.*, pp. 60 ff. [3] See *post*, p. 61.
[4] Add. 28618—Copies of Pope's letters made by the Caryll family before returning the originals.
[5] See *post*, p. 64. [6] Johnson, IV, p. 152. [7] Nicholls, p. 37.

spread as is generally supposed; for much, indeed most, of his correspondence has not been affected. Fortunately, some of the more important groups of letters (such as the two series to Cromwell and the Blount sisters) have survived in autograph, others (like the Caryll transcripts) in careful contemporary copies; while a large number of letters were never returned to him, or were written later, and so escaped even the risk of revision. Thus it follows that references to the letters, to illustrate or prove some point of chronology, authorship, or text, in the following pages, need not necessarily be regarded with suspicion, as by far the largest number of references are to letters in the Cromwell, Caryll, and Blount collections.

Turning now to the second problem, the publication of the letters, with which we left Pope confronted: there is a considerable amount of evidence to show that he had something of a flair for business transactions; and we also know that besides the eminently successful conduct of his trade as an author, his friends, on occasion, were only too glad for him to look after the business side of their publications—often very much to their profit, as they afterwards found.[1] As regards his second problem, then: to judge by the result, he seems to have conceived the idea of anticipating the official publication of his letters[2]—indubitably a literary event of considerable importance—by an apparently unauthorized issue of much the same (but never identically the same) material beforehand. Such a proceeding would not only act as an advertisement of the authorized edition, but, being also a foretaste of delights to come, would itself be eagerly bought; and, moreover, being carefully incomplete, and therefore faulty, it would provide an excuse (if one were needed) for the publication of a correct, authoritative edition later. But in addition to the unprinted letters, Pope also had on his hands the remainder sheets of an edition of his correspondence with Wycherley, which, having found few purchasers in 1729, he had bought from the publisher; and these too he thriftily purposed getting rid of. Thus it came about that arrangements to compass these ends were secretly made with Curll, whose piratical raids on literary property were notorious, and who in 1726 had acquired and published without Pope's consent the original Pope-Cromwell correspondence above mentioned. The story is still far from clear. There was much secret coming and going, much manœuvring for position between unnamed people called 'P.T.' and 'R.S.', on

---

[1] See *post*, p. 232 n.

[2] See C. W. Dilke's *Papers of a Critic*, I, pp. 287 ff.; EC, I, pp. xxvi ff.; and Straus, pp. 154 ff.

one side, and Curll on the other. And when at last the 'surreptitious' editions began to appear on May 12, 1735, the House of Lords intervened and impounded the books, only to release them three days later; after which, publication proceeded merrily, some editions having Curll's name in the imprint and some having none.

In passing, it may be remarked that if in this business Pope appears to have acted with more than one end in view (which in human affairs is neither so rare nor so censurable as some of his critics seem to imagine), and if in what has been called 'the plot against Curll' the rascally old bookseller had happened to suffer some small inconvenience or even slight damage (which has yet to be proved), it could have been regarded as a piece of tardy poetical justice for the manifold wrongs he had done Pope from time to time over a score of years. However, what really happened was that Curll attempted to seize the copyright, and was stopped; and about the same time Cooper's name began to appear in the imprint as a publisher of the letters, with Pope's connivance,[1] and, presumably, as part of his counter-stroke. Nevertheless, Curll continued to add volume to volume in what became a series, which he called *Mr. Pope's Literary Correspondence*, but which contained decreasingly less, from little to nothing, of Pope's unprinted material.

Long before 'Volume the Fourth' (not to mention 'Volume the Fifth') of Curll's hotch-potch appeared, it must have become clear that something had gone wrong with the obscure and shabby plan; for it is impossible to believe that Pope had envisaged such a proliferation of editions as sprang into being. No less than twenty separate editions or variant issues, claiming to be either his 'Literary Correspondence' or his 'Letters', were published between May 12 and December 31, 1735[2]; and there were at least three more before the publication of his long-awaited, much advertised, authoritative edition, in folio and quarto, on May 19, 1737.[3] And because Pope, who in 1735 had started to reprint his poetical works in various editions and with various booksellers, began in 1737 to include the Letters in his *Works* as separate volumes, it is obvious that still more editions of the *Letters* must be added to those already mentioned, to make up the extraordinary total published within the last nine years of his life. Such in brief is the story of Pope's *Letters*, and, when told without rancour or self-righteousness, is seen, happily, to form not nearly so large or so disgraceful an episode in his life as was formerly supposed.

---

[1] Polwhele, 1, p. 322.   [2] See Griffith, 1, ii, pp. 292–328.
[3] See *The London Evening Post* of that date.

In any true portrait of the poet, while it is essential that such shadows be present, they should be present only in proportion to their significance in his life, and not allowed to darken the whole picture, and thus falsify the likeness. As Pope's real character becomes more clearly seen, the truth of what appears to be Spence's final judgement is only the more firmly established. Spence is sometimes said to be, in a smaller way, Pope's Boswell; from 1728 to the poet's death in 1744, he knew him intimately and made innumerable notes of his conversation, formal and informal. And Spence, after Pope's death, 'meditating the posthumous publication' of his own volume of *Anecdotes*, with nothing to gain by fair words, wrote on the first page of his completed folio manuscript, as follows:

> All the people well acquainted with Mr. Pope, looked on him as a most friendly, open, charitable, and generous-hearted man; —all the world almost, *that did not know him*, were got into a mode of having very different ideas of him: how proper this makes it to publish these Anecdotes after my death. [1]

IV. ENEMIES AND FRIENDS

A large part of a man's character is revealed in his human contacts— in his attitude to his foes no less than to his friends. In both these relations Pope has been greatly maligned in the past; and epithets like 'false friend' and 'treacherous enemy' have been all too freely and unjustly hurled at him, and repeated without reference to all the ascertainable facts, and so have added their contribution to the general denigration of the poet.

Now the present chapter does not pretend to be more than introductory to the subsequent discussions of a number of poetical, biographical, and bibliographical 'discoveries' bearing on Pope and his work, made by the writer in recent years. So far from attempting a sketch of the poet's life, it has to do only with those episodes, encounters, and circumstances which are affected by this new knowledge. Nevertheless, even this means that several considerable sections of his biography must in future be re-orientated, if not largely re-written; not least important amongst them being those chapters which deal with his enemies and his friends.

In view of the old libels still current about Pope, the outstanding fact about the new material is that in neither of these connections has

[1] Spence, p. xiii (with no italics).

anything been found in the least treacherous, or false, or otherwise discreditable to him; but, on the contrary, some unlooked-for acts of generosity to his enemies, and to his friends a loyalty and love beyond the common. The documented story, for example, of the quarrel, or rather discord, between Addison and Pope, very positively shifts the lash of censure from the youthful poet's crooked shoulders to the upright back of the man who was old enough, if not wise enough, to have acted differently. Possibly Addison had been worked on by those of his friends who were Pope's enemies; but that could not entirely excuse him. He was a man of the world, a recognized arbiter of conduct and of morals; one who not only 'taught us how to live' (according to his friend, Tickell),[1] but also 'how to die'[2]; and who, before that happened, was assured—if not quite sure—of his position 'in the highest rank of wit and literature',[3] and whose constant pose declared himself above mean acts of petty jealousy—of which the new evidence convicts him.

Pope's well-known quarrel with Dennis was quite another matter. It began earlier than the Addison affair, and ended many years later. And though more than one benevolent act on Pope's part towards that irascible old critic now comes newly into the story,[4] Dennis himself—if the evidence is to be trusted—'never, never reached one generous thought', at least as far as Pope was concerned. Here again, the fresh material not only 'excuses' but removes 'some un-courtly stains' from Pope's portrait, which have hitherto helped to make it a caricature.

But when we find two such enemies as Dennis and Curll in conjunction against Pope—which occurred at least once, and possibly twice, in the earlier years—strange developments might well be expected. This curious encounter, so far as can be ascertained, has not only never been explained, but seems never to have been so much as mentioned since it happened. Curll in his latter days we have already met; in this incident we catch a glimpse of him not long after the publication of Pope's second lampoon[5] against him, which also contains

[1] In his elegy on Addison's death prefixed to the four-volume edition of Addison's works, 1721.

[2] Edward Young tells how, when Addison was dying, he sent for his rakish step-son, Lord Warwick (for whom, see Biog. Notes), and said to him: 'See in what peace a Christian can die.' Young's *Conjectures*, 1759, pp. 101 f.

[3] Johnson, II, p. 395.   [4] See *post*, pp. 294 ff.

[5] *A Further Account of the . . . Condition of Mr Edmund Curll . . .* was published about the end of November 1716. See Pope's *Prose*, I, pp. xcviii, and 273, for date and text.

several amusing references to Dennis, two of them in obvious anti-cipation of his criticism of Pope's *Iliad*. The first overt move in this new episode, however, was a newspaper announcement, by Curll, of Dennis's forthcoming attack on Pope's great translation. This had been long threatened by the critic, and even longer expected, it would seem, by Pope, not without apprehension; for he never forgot the revolting treatment he had received (as he had much reason to believe) at Dennis's hands some nine months earlier in *A True Character of Mr. Pope*. The new attack was announced in *The Post-Man*, on Tuesday, February 26, 1717, thus—'Next Thursday will be pub-lished, Mr. Dennis's Remarks upon Mr. Pope's Translation of Homer; . . . Printed for E. Curll.' In spite of the repetition of this announcement in at least two other papers[1] on Thursday, under the heading, 'This Day is publish'd', something seems to have happened between the 26th and 28th, though the first news of it was not heard until the following Tuesday morning (March 5), when *The Flying-Post* displayed this extraordinary advertisement:

> Whereas Mr. Dennis's Remarks on the Senseless Popish and Jacobite Translation of Homer, were design'd to be publish'd on Thursday last, This is to give Notice to the Publick, That no such Book is to be expected. For the Popish and Jacobite Translator having got the foresaid Remarks into his Possession on Wednesday last, which was the Day before the intended Publication, made a smart, a surprizing, and a knock down Answer to them; that is, He immediately gave Orders to Bernard Lintott, to buy up the whole Impression.

But a set-back like that (if it happened at all) could not stop Curll. It would seem that he pocketed the money and immediately rushed another 'Impression'—probably a very small one—through the press; and so was able to advertise in an evening paper[2] of that same day, March 5: 'This Day is publish'd, Mr. Dennis's Remarks . . .' and all the rest of it. This time he seems to have succeeded, because two days later he began to advertise the work as 'Just publish'd'.[3]

So the book, which was little more than a pamphlet 'Price 1s. 6d.', was published after all; and Pope's 'knock down Answer' (if indeed he took any steps in the matter) brought him no more than a few days' respite. It is difficult to see how he could have expected more, and, for that reason, difficult to believe the story exactly as it was told. It does

---

[1] *The Daily Courant*, Feb. 28, 1717; and *The Evening Post*, Feb. 26–28.
[2] *The Evening Post*, March 2–5.   [3] *The Post Boy*, March 5–7.

however suggest, if there is a modicum of truth in the advertisement, that Pope was not so indifferent to Dennis's brutal attacks on his work, his religion, and his physical disabilities, as he sometimes pretended to his friends to be. [1]

Although Pope's quarrel with Dennis exceeded in offensiveness and duration his quarrel with Addison, they were at least alike at the end, insomuch that Pope was again moved to make offers of reconciliation to his enemy. The famous quarrel with Colley Cibber was direly different: it lasted much longer, and piled up to the bitterest of climaxes, and was ended only by Pope's death. It was more a state of being than a quarrel. It began in shame, and culminated in such hatred as drove Pope in the last year of his life to undertake the incredible task of changing the whole aim and application of the already published *Dunciad*, in order to pillory Cibber as mankind's supreme dunce. The real story of the quarrel, which includes some newly attributed poems, is told in detail for the first time in a subsequent chapter. [2]

Other of Pope's enemies are encountered in the present work: Horneck, Duckett, Gildon, Baker, Jacob, and Moore-Smythe—tiny, obscure figures in the long story of our literature, who, like minor characters on a darkened stage, are seen only when they come within the bright spot-light circle focused on Pope. Him they attacked and fought, usually without provocation or genuine cause; and now to him alone owe their rare momentary escapes from oblivion. The 'new light' is not for them; they appear and disappear in these pages, and hardly anything fresh is to be said about them, except perhaps Gildon, whose *New Rehearsal* is now shown to belong to the Pope-Addison imbroglio. Frequenters of Grub-street and its purlieus, hack-writers in and out of Curll's employ and unlucky either way, titled poetasters, and literary pretenders, and scribbling coxcombs of all kinds—most of Pope's enemies were authors of sorts; a fact which explains the greater part of his quarrels in a word. For with Grub-street's jealousy of one who lived so well by his pen, on the one side, and, on the other, an impatience amounting at times to an almost rabid intolerance of bad writing, who can wonder, with such provocative causes of friction ever present, that conflict was endemic between them. Thus while Pope could never have mistaken bad style and bad matter for other than what they are, the bad writers only too frequently mistook his attacks on their bad work for attacks on themselves as private individuals; not perceiving that it was not a personal

---

[1] See Spence, p. 275.   [2] See *post*, pp. 298 ff.

matter with Pope at the outset, whatever it developed into later. In brief, Pope was all too often misunderstood into strife. It might also be noted, while on the subject of Pope's quarrels, that he was not, as so many of his censurers seem to think, *peculiar* in disliking his enemies. Many people besides Pope found them unlikeable, if not actually offensive: Cibber, Dennis, Curll, even Addison—each had his own ill-wishers in plenty who detested him on personal or political grounds, and not as a partisan of Pope.

Even that striking personage, Lady Mary Wortley Montagu, was no exception; for she, like Pope, had many enemies; and when she and he slipped from friendship to hatred—for reasons which will probably never be known—they simply had each one enemy the more. But though we may never learn the real cause of their quarrel, what seems to have been the first manifest move of Pope's after their estrangement is identified in these pages in the guise of a poem which is now shown for the first time to have been written by Pope (or possibly Pope and Swift) and originally addressed to Lady Mary.

Although Pope's life at this point may begin to appear a long conflict as well as a 'long disease', mention must be made of one other quarrel, as an example of those for which friendship rather than enmity was primarily responsible. When, in 1716, Sir Richard Blackmore, physician and poet, made a violent attack on Swift in his first volume of *Essays*, Pope grew so indignant for his absent friend (Swift being then resident in Ireland) that he straightway took up the cudgels on the Dean's behalf; and afterwards, whenever occasion offered, made fun of the prosy old poet, whose wrath was thereupon transferred to him. As might be imagined, the consequence was that Pope continued the quarrel at first hand; and, in addition to much incidental jesting, he finally produced a choice bit of clownery (only recently identified as his)[1] in which the baronet is awarded another title, 'England's Arch-Poet'.

As one might expect from the incident just mentioned, Pope was never backward in championing the causes of his friends. He regarded their interests as his own, and rushed to their support as the various occasions (not always literary) offered; for the quick flower of his sympathy would burst into brightest bloom when skies were blackest over them, in direct contradiction of the libels which called him fair-weather friend and treacherous. When his friends fell on evil days, and were imprisoned or exiled (like Atterbury), or self-banished (like Bolingbroke), in marital trouble (like Mrs Weston[2]), or financial

[1] See *post*, pp. 248 f.   [2] Add. 28618, f. 8 v.

c

straits (like Deane,[1] and Savage,[2] and Dodsley[3]), in sickness and pen-
ury (like Mrs Cope[4]), or bereavement (like Caryll[5]), Pope was ready
with succour, comfort, pity, or aid, to do for them everything he could.
And when the first Earl of Oxford and Mortimer, after a long im-
prisonment in the Tower, was living in retirement and disgrace in the
country, Pope characteristically chose exactly that time and those
circumstances in which to speak out for him publicly, and call him
friend. The original autograph of the great 'Epistle' which Pope sent
to Lord Oxford is still in existence at Longleat. It contains many
interesting differences from the published version, especially in the
last few lines which show the gradual desertion of the fallen statesman by various classes of people one after another, and which are believed to be printed now for the first time. They testify, even more
poignantly than the revised text, to Pope's emotion when writing
them.

> Tho' Int'rest calls off all her sneaking Train,
> Tho' next the Servile drop thee, next the Vain,
> Tho' distanc't one by one th' Oblig'd desert,
> And ev'n the Grateful are but last to part;
> My Muse attending strews thy path with Bays,
> (A Virgin Muse, not prostitute to praise).
> She still with pleasure eyes thy Evening Ray,
> The calmer Sunsett of thy Various Day;
> One truly Great thro' Fortune's Cloud can see,
> And dares to tell, that Mortimer is He.
>
> *A. Pope.*

Such examples of Pope's loyalty to his friends, with others too
numerous to mention, have received little enough consideration in the
past. While as for his alleged treachery to them—the other point of the
popular two-pronged libel—the long chapters in this work on Gay,
and Swift, and Rowe, and Martha Blount, and, pre-eminently, the
story of Pope's unbroken friendship with Henrietta Howard, later
Countess of Suffolk, in which he is completely acquitted of the old
charge of double-dealing[6]—all witness to his unswerving fidelity to
those he loved.

With his love for his friends there existed a keen knowledge and
appreciation of their characters, which could regard even their
idiosyncrasies with affection, as a number of the 'new' poems delight-

---

[1] Add. 28618, f. 68.   [2] Roscoe, I, pp. 534 ff.   [3] Johnson, IV, p. 160.
[4] Add. 28618, f. 68 v.   [5] *Ibid.*, f. 54.   [6] See *post*, pp. 267 ff.

fully show. We see him, for instance, fondly poking fun at Swift's long sermons, at Gay's secretaryship, at Teresa Blount's dislike of books, or at Argyle's modesty, and we cannot help liking both him and them all the better for it. As he once wrote to Cromwell:

> I find I value no man so much, as he in whose sight I have been playing the fool. [1]

But with his friends it was not of course all play: Pope honoured them and they him by discussing the work they had on hand, and their plans for the future.

It is not therefore surprising that they should have collaborated from time to time in various combinations of two or three, Pope invariably being one of them; or that, with Pope and Gay being so much together, the public should have fancied it could discern Pope's hand so frequently in Gay's verses.

Once, and once only, was multiple authorship formally admitted by them, and that was when Gay acknowledged the help of 'two of my friends' on the third page of that extraordinary farce, *Three Hours after Marriage*. [2] But although Gay had carefully left his friends unnamed, they were very generally known to be Pope and Arbuthnot, even during the short time the play ran. This is shown by an undated, anonymous broadside in the British Museum, hitherto unrecognized, which doubtless helped to spread the news. The farce was produced on January 16, 1717, and although it made a great stir was withdrawn after seven days. The play was published on January 21; and on January 22 [3] appeared the broadside, entitled, *The Drury-Lane Monster*, identifying the three collaborators beyond question, and apportioning to each his share in the play. The play was called a 'Monster', because it was a 'three legged Beast' produced by 'three Mongrels' 'in Triple Alliance'—which would seem to be a sufficient reason. As satire the lampoon is a feeble effort, only wishfully strong in its intent to hurt Pope and his friends, who are portrayed thus:

> Near the Hundreds of *Drury* a Monster was shown
> For five Days together, the Talk of the Town . . .
> And such are the Marks of this wonderful Creature,
> Each Parent is seen in each odd sort of Feature.
> By his Crump, and his Paunch, and his Belly reclining,
> By Bawdy and Blasphemy, Hand in Hand joining,

[1] *Letters*, 4to, 1737, p. 68.
[2] For further details of this play, see *post*, pp. 298 ff.
[3] See *The Evening Post* of that date.

The first of them dealt in a Greek kind of Metre,
Tho' he ne'er saw the Language and knew not a Letter;
(For *English* translated from *French* is much better.)

By his Airs, and his Folly, and Gestures Fantastick,
By Conundrums, and Puns, and Quibbles Elastick,
The Second, of Pattens and Fans is a Chimer,
And of Childish Play-things, a paultry sad Rhimer.

But by the low Wit and the awkward Grimace,
By the false Terms of Art, and the clumsy dull Face,
The third and chief Parent 'tis easy to trace,
Who gang'd up to Toon without Muckle to eat,
With scarce Plod to his Back, or Shoon to his Feet,
A famous Physician as ever was seen,
Who once had a Patient, and she was a Queen.

Pope, as usual, was the hardest hit of the three friends—he was such a figure of fun—for those who liked that sort of fun—that he could never hope to escape even in a crowd, much less as one of three.

Other pieces, in the writing (or planning) of which Pope probably collaborated with Swift, and with Gay, are found on subsequent pages; and it may be remembered that he himself told Spence that he had written other things with other friends, such as Arbuthnot, Pulteney, and Parnell. But the most famous collaborations of all were the discussions of the Scriblerus Club; for although most of their literary projects ended up as works of single authors, at least they began as collective ideas. It may also be noted that even the Club invitations in verse to guests were ostensibly written by several members. Occasionally, however, they appear to be by Pope alone; and one of the latter is printed for the first time in the present volume.

In conclusion, before we leave Pope's friends, one word must be added about the most affectionate and least exacting of them all, and a place be found here—as always at his fireside—for his dogs. For the closing chapter shows the poet to have been their life-long champion, not only in his letters and in numerous passages in his prose and verse, but also in the 'new' poem, *Bounce to Fop*. And with this brief reference to the last and best-loved of all his dogs, Bounce, and to the long 'heroick epistle' her master wrote in her name, this introductory chapter—lest the tale be told twice over—abruptly stops.

CHAPTER II

POPE'S FIRST MISCELLANY

I. POET AS EDITOR

Pope's ostensible scorn of the ubiquitous poetical collections of his period was expressed in a number of passages in his works as well as in his correspondence. For example, he wrote to Wycherley:

This modern custom of appearing in miscellanies, is very useful to the poets, who like other thieves, escape by getting into a crowd.[1]

And, in a letter to Henry Cromwell, he said:

Our modern Bards put forth in the Spring time in as great abundance, as Trees do Blossoms . . . Thus the same reason that furnishes Common Garden with those Nosegays you so delight in, supplies the Muse's Mercury's & . . . Jacob's Miscellanies wth Verses.[2]

To-day his contempt of them is chiefly remembered by the lines in *The Dunciad*, in which he satirically discovers their perennial source in the purlieus of Bedlam:

Hence Miscellanies spring, the weekly boast
Of Curl's chaste press and Lintot's rubric post.[3]

More frequent still was his repudiation, explicit and implicit in prefaces, notes, letters, and at least one newspaper advertisement,[4] of any responsibility for the compilation of miscellanies or the inclusion of his poems in them. Nevertheless, Pope, like many another poet, owed his earliest opportunity and encouragement to these despised collections. He appeared in print for the first time with the publication of his *Pastorals* and two other pieces in Tonson's *Poetical Miscellanies*, VI, 1709; and not a few of his better-known poems, *The Rape of the Lock* amongst them, first saw the light in subsequent miscellanies. Indeed, it was mainly due to them that his shorter poems obtained their widespread recognition between the first two authoritative volumes of his collected *Works* in 1717 and 1735. Moreover, from 1727 onwards, he openly collaborated with Swift in the production of the famous series,

---

[1] *Letters*, 4to, 1737, p. 21.
[2] Rawl. letters 90, f. 11.
[3] *Dunciad* B, 1, 39–40.
[4] *The Grub-street Journal*, April 23, 1735.

Miscellanies in Prose and Verse.[1] This opposition of word and act has never been adequately explained. There must have been some reason over and above Pope's intolerance of poor work and the provocation of Curll's piracies to account for all this parade of ridicule and repudiation which ceased only with the poet's life. Curll neither published all the miscellanies, nor limited his attentions to Pope. Why, then, should Pope, alone of his contemporaries, strive so continuously to dissociate himself from these collections?

One of the most censured traits of Pope's peculiarly complex character was his love of mystification in literary matters. What was at bottom the reason for it, is discussed in a previous page[2]: the only tenable conclusion being that there was no one reason, but a dozen reasons which varied in number and combination from occasion to occasion. Recent discoveries, however, show that concealment of both editorship and authorship was practised by him on a far greater scale than has hitherto been suspected; and it is becoming increasingly apparent that his wholesale disparagement of the miscellanies was largely simulated to conceal the fact that he was, or had been, engaged in producing them over a period of many years. The present writer has argued elsewhere that Pope was *entirely* responsible, as the unnamed editor, for a very rare miscellany published by Lintot, entitled *Poems on Several Occasions*, 1717[3]; and that he took the opportunity to include in it anonymously at least twenty-four—and probably more—of his own poems, with which, for various reasons, he did not then wish his name to be identified; the result being that most of them have remained unknown down to the present time. It is the purpose of this chapter, first, to show that he was the editor and compiler of the earlier and better known collection generally called by its publisher's name, 'Lintot's Miscellany'; and, secondly, to prove his authorship of an anonymous poem included in it, which has never hitherto been reprinted or associated with his name.[4]

On May 20, 1712, Bernard Lintot, the bookseller, announced in *The Spectator* the publication of a new miscellany entitled *Miscellaneous Poems and Translations. By Several Hands*, which eventually ran into six editions. The last of them, dated 1732, is of scant interest for us; there

---

[1] See *post*, p. 224.   [2] See *ante*, pp. 10 f.

[3] Reprinted as *Pope's Own Miscellany*, N. Ault, Nonesuch Press, 1935.

[4] The substance of this chapter was written in 1934, and published in *The Nineteenth Century and After*, November 1934, under the title 'Pope and the Miscellanies'. Six years later an article entitled 'Pope's Contributions to the Lintot Miscellanies of 1712 and 1714', by R. K. Root, was printed in *ELH* (Baltimore, U.S.A.), for December 1940, covering practically the same ground as far as 1714.

is little change of contents, and more than one reason for thinking
that Pope's active direction of the miscellany ceased with the fifth
edition of 1726 (reprinted 1727), about which time he left Lintot for
other publishers. Our survey, therefore, is limited to the years 1712–
1726, during which the miscellany changed from an octavo volume
comprising fifty-one poems to two duodecimo volumes together containing ninety-six, of which only eighteen had come down from the
original edition. This gradual transformation obviously could not
have been planned in advance; nevertheless, when the successive
changes which brought it about are examined, they suggest one
increasing purpose throughout, and one only, namely, the enhance-
ment of Pope's fame—grounds enough, in view of the poet's temper-
ament, to create a suspicion that not only was he responsible for the
direction in which the miscellany developed, but also for the management of its contents to achieve that end.

Some seven months before the miscellany was published, an
advertisement appeared in *The General Post* for October 8–10, 1711,
and was repeated some half-dozen times during the rest of the
month, in these words:

> A new Miscellany of Poems, most of which were never printed.
> Four Songs written in 1683 . . . Several Poems written by Mr. Pope;
> as also some Originals by Mr. Butler and Mr. Smith, late of Christ
> Church in Oxford, and other great men. Those who have excellent
> Copies by them, may command a Place in this Miscellany, if sent
> before the 1st of November to B. Lintott[1] at the Cross Keys in
> Fleet-street.

The last appearance of this invitation in the same paper was on
November 2. But on November 12 we find Pope writing to Henry
Cromwell, a common friend of his and Gay's, to ask for a copy of a
poem addressed to Lintot by Gay, which had been mentioned by
Cromwell in an earlier letter. The poem, which was entitled *On a
Miscellany of Poems. To Bernard Lintott*, and was obviously written after
a sight of the above advertisement, arrived in due course; and Pope
acknowledged it on December 21, sending Gay his thanks 'for the
favour of his poem.' He then tells Cromwell:

> His Verses to *Lintot* have put a Whim into my head, which you
> are like to be troubled wth in the opposite page. Take it as you find
> it, ye Production of half an hour 'tother Morning.[2]

---

[1] He spelt his name thus until 1715, and 'Lintot' thereafter.
[2] Rawl. letters 90, f. 46 v.

Pope's poem was entitled, *Verses design'd to be prefix'd to Mr. Lintott's Miscellany*. Both poems were duly inserted in the miscellany. Again, the letters show that in the preceding year Cromwell had sent Pope some translations from Ovid for criticism; they are mentioned several times, and one of them (*Amor.*, eleg. 16, lib. ii) Pope deals with at some length in his letter of July 20, 1710. Pope apparently kept these poems by him, for we find that elegy and another by the same pen included in the miscellany. Yet again, a letter from John Caryll (dated May 23, 1712, but written before he had heard that the miscellany was published) proves that Pope had previously told him of the intention to include Betterton's poems in it; and the same letter also shows Caryll inquiring whether *The Rape of the Lock* would also 'come out' in it, or not. Both Betterton's poems and *The Rape* appear in the first edition.

But any doubt that Pope was concerned in the preparation of the miscellany is settled by Addison, who, when speaking of the 'rising genius' of Pope in *The Spectator* (October 30, 1712), definitely calls our collection 'the late Miscellany published by Mr. Pope'. Addison, if any one, was in a position to know the truth of the matter. Then at the height of his influence and producing with Steele the most celebrated journal of the period, he was situated at the very focus of literary news, and was unlikely to make such a statement on inadequate grounds. Furthermore, Pope had been known personally both to him and to Steele for some time; he contributed to their paper before the miscellany was published, and again after Addison had made that statement; yet he left it undisputed.

In the miscellany—as in the thirty or more newspaper advertisements of it between May 16 and July 21, 1712—no mention is made of editorship; nevertheless, Addison's attribution of it to Pope is confirmed by internal evidence which reveals the characteristic imprint of his personality in a number of ways. Parallels can be perceived between this and his later miscellany, *Poems on Several Occasions*, above mentioned. In both most, if not all, of the living contributors were his friends or personal acquaintances. In both he appropriated to himself the largest share of the volume, amounting to something between one-quarter and one-third of its pages. In both he disguised the preponderance of his poems by partial or complete anonymity. And in both he included work which he subsequently reprinted as his own, and work which throughout his life he would never acknowledge.

A glance at the 'Contents' of our miscellany, Pope's maiden essay at editorship, shows that he ascribed to himself only five poems, namely: *Statius his Thebais, Bk I., The Fable of Vertumnus and Pomona, To a young Lady, with the Works of Voiture, On Silence,* and *To the Author of a Poem, intitled Successio.* Broome has the same number given to him, plus two anonymous pieces; Fenton has four to his name and two without it; Prior three, and the rest of the named contributors one or two each. But of the remaining eleven anonymous poems in English which cannot be attributed to other hands, Pope himself later acknowledged two—the original two-canto version of *The Rape of the Locke,* and the above-mentioned *Verses* on Lintot's Miscellany, while yet another, *The Story of Arethusa,* can be assigned to him (on evidence presently to be adduced) with a certainty that lacks only the final warrant of his signature. In passing, it should be noted that even at the date of our miscellany, anonymity was not a new policy of Pope's: he had withheld his name from the *Messiah* which had appeared in *The Spectator* in the preceding week, and also from the *Essay on Criticism* in 1711.

Further evidence pointing to Pope's direction of 'Lintot's Miscellany' is to be found in the differences between the first and second editions. In the first edition there is an omission of thirty-two pages (pp. 321–352); and, as this gap occurs in every known copy without any trace of mutilation or of hiatus in the text, it is certain that the miscellany was published in this condition. The book is an octavo; the 'signature letters' run consecutively from B to X (pp. 1–320); Y and Z (pp. 321–352) are missing; and a new series starts with Aa, Bb (pp. 353–376, plus eight pages of book advertisements). Thus, as a poem ends on the last page of signature X (p. 320) and another begins on the first page of Aa (p. 353), it is obvious that the signatures Y and Z could have been, and were, withdrawn *before* the book was made up, but apparently *after* the sheets had been printed, for the page numbers following the gap are left unaltered.

The 'Second Edition', dated 1714, is a reissue of the unsold sheets of 1712 with certain clearly defined additions, among which are the signatures Y and Z now inserted in their proper place. These restored pages are entirely occupied by Pope's *Windsor Forest* and *Ode for Musick,* and it has been too rashly assumed that these two signatures are the identical thirty-two pages which were removed from the 1712 edition, and afterwards restored to their original place in the second edition.[1]

All the evidence is against that assumption; for a close comparison of these 'replaced' pages with the pages before and after the gap,

[1] See *A Pope Library,* T. J. Wise, 1931, p. 8; and R. K. Root, *op. cit.,* p. 271.

reveals only too clearly that the Y–Z signatures are not uniform with the rest of the book. For example, their pages are overcrowded, having normally three extra lines to the page, besides which the caption-titles of both poems are crammed into the top quarter of the page, in marked contrast with the titles of similarly important poems in the 1712 setting, which occupy approximately twice the space and are displayed in type roughly twice the size. The difference once pointed out is obvious.

In 1736, Pope first revealed the fact that *Windsor Forest* 'was written at two different times, the first part in the year 1704, at the same time with the Pastorals: the latter part was not added till the year 1710, in which it was publish'd.'[1] Pope's erratic dating of many of his early poems has already been considered, and this particular example discussed.[2] It is therefore sufficient to say here that while 1704 is possible for the first draft of the first part, it is practically certain that the official text of it represents later careful, and probably extensive, revisions; and also, that, as 1710 is demonstrably wrong for the year of publication, it is apparently just as wrong for the date of the writing of the latter part—as is shown both by its subject matter and by Pope's contemporaneous statements about it in his untouched correspondence with John Caryll.

Thus, to begin with, we know from Pope's letter of December 5, 1712, that his old friend had actually seen the early shorter version; Pope's words being—

> The Poem of Windsor Forest has Undergon many alterations, & receved many Additions since you saw itt, butt has not yett been out of my hands to any Man.[3]

And from a later letter (December 21, 1712) it is clear that he is still at work on the 'Additions', for he describes how, while shivering in the midst of winter—

> I am endeavouring to raise up round about me a painted Scene of Woods, and Forests in Verdure and Beauty, Trees springing, fields flow'ring, Nature laughing . . .[4]

And he immediately afterwards says that 'Windsor Forest will come out' before the Temple of Fame, 'butt I do not yett know when'. Then, a couple of months later, he writes again to say: 'I have just sent the Poem of Wind: forest to the Press'; and goes on to remark that he was both 'glad and ashamed' that Caryll 'had more lines than one of y^t

---

[1] *Works*, 1, 1736, p. 67. [2] See *ante*, p. 13.
[3] Add. 28618, f. 11 v. [4] *Ibid.*, f. 13.

Poem by Heart.'[1] There can be no doubt, therefore, either of the separate existence of the shorter early version (which amounted to almost exactly two-thirds of the poem), or that the last third of it was being written in the winter of 1712–13.

Calculations of lines and space show that if the early short version of *Windsor Forest* (amounting, Pope implied, to 296 lines) and the *Ode for Musick* were set up like the rest of the miscellany, they would together exactly fill our missing thirty-two pages. It seems probable, therefore, that the 'copy' supplied by Pope to Lintot for the first edition included the original short version of *Windsor Forest* (incorporating of course the results of Pope's normal, up-to-date revision which usually preceded the printing of his works, early or late), and the *Ode for Musick*, and that the whole book was set up in type. Before going to press, or, more probably, after the sheets were printed, Pope withdrew these two poems, occupying the Y–Z signatures, for separate publication in folio, and the book was issued with the gap found in all copies. But whether they were withdrawn for financial or political reasons (two separate and single publications being probably more profitable, or the moment unpropitious), or, as so often with Pope, for reasons more complex, it should be noted that neither poem could have been easily withdrawn without the other, once they were printed. For although they occupied together two whole sheets, *Windsor Forest*, being much longer than the *Ode*, took up one and a half sheets. Consequently, even if Pope desired to expand only the former (as expand he certainly did), the other had to be withdrawn from the miscellany with it, unless it was to be reprinted on a separate half-sheet, which meant extra expense and delay. Then, or a little later, when the prospect of peace (consummated by the Treaty of Utrecht, March 30, 1713) began to fill all minds, Pope, seeing the possibility of adapting *Windsor Forest* to celebrate the occasion, commenced to work on it; and, as is shown by his letter to Caryll[2] written in November, he was well advanced with his additions when Tickell's poem *On the Prospect of Peace* was published on October 28, 1712. To judge from Pope's correspondence, it was about this time that Caryll was first allowed to read the original version of *Windsor Forest*, not improbably in a copy of the discarded Y–Z signatures; for Pope was then actively employed on the manuscript itself, and we do not know that any duplicate manuscript existed. From his letters it is clear that from November to January he was still at work on it, which seems to indicate that it could not have been, as has been suggested,[3] a mere

---

[1] Add. 28618, f. 37 v.   [2] *Ibid.*, f. 34.   [3] R. K. Root, *op. cit.*, p. 271 n.

correction or revision on which he was so long employed, but rather
the 'additions' celebrating the Peace. The expanded version was published in folio on March 7, 1713, and not long after was followed by
the folio edition of the *Ode for Musick* on July 16. Five months later, in
the second edition of our miscellany (dated 1714, but actually published on December 3, 1713),[1] these two poems, despite an addition
of some 140 lines to *Windsor Forest*, are crowded back into the gap
which, it would seem, their removal had made.

The only accessions to the second edition are five poems, probably
all by Pope: three of these are attributed to him—namely, *Windsor
Forest* and the *Ode for Musick* in the inserted Y–Z signatures, and the
Essay on Criticism at the end; but he withheld his name from the other
two, *Upon a Girl of Seven Years Old*, and *Epigram upon Two or Three*,[2] both
short pieces, and printed there for the first time, though he afterwards
acknowledged the *Epigram*. (In some copies these two poems, which
occupy one leaf with duplicate page numbers, 321–322, have been
cancelled, leaving a stub.) The second edition was provided with a
new title-page on which Pope's name figures. It reads:

> *Miscellaneous Poems and Translations. By Several Hands. Particularly*
> [Nine titles of poems by Pope follow, in two columns of smaller
> type, then—] *By Mr. Pope. The Second Edition. London: Printed for
> Bernard Lintott ... and William Lewis ... 1714.*

Only Pope's name now, and only Pope's poems! There were no poems
mentioned on the title page of the first edition, and no name except
of course the publisher's imprint. The presence of Lewis's name with
Lintot's in the 1714 imprint is due to the inclusion of the *Essay on
Criticism*, of which he held the copyright.

The newspaper advertisements likewise show that Pope's active
connection with the miscellany was still maintained. In those announcements of the first edition which had mentioned any names
at all, Pope's name was placed fourth in a list of eight contributors,
whereas every advertisement of the second edition cites the titles of
eight of his poems, and his is the only name to appear. Final proof (if
proof is still needed) of Pope's editorial responsibility for the miscellany is to be found in the book advertisements which Lintot and Curll
combined to issue early in 1714. One of their joint lists appears at the
end of *The Count de Gabalis* (published April 8, 1714), in which Lintot
gives the whole thing away in these words:

[1] Not December 4 as generally stated: see *The Englishman*, December 1–3, 1713.
[2] The case for Pope's authorship of these two pieces is stated by the present writer
in the forthcoming *Miscellaneous Poems* of Pope (Twickenham Edition, Vol. VI).

VIII. Mr. *Pope*'s Collection of Miscellany Poems. Price 5s.

IX. — — His Rape of the Lock. Price 1s.

There are several other curious features about the second edition of Pope's first miscellany, copies of which may vary. For example, there are the old 1712 title-page and half-title, which are sometimes retained and sometimes not; similarly, an errata leaf may be present or absent; eight pages of book advertisements are not always in the same place, and stubs appear in different positions; and there is one leaf, Y8, which has been cancelled and replaced, and no one, as yet, has been able to find a satisfactory explanation of it.

Six years elapsed before the 'Third Edition' was issued; but midway in this interval Pope anonymously compiled and Lintot published the miscellany, *Poems on Several Occasions*, 1717, previously mentioned. With its third edition, published August 15, 1720, 'Lintot's Miscellany' becomes two volumes in duodecimo; the title-page of the first volume giving the titles of eight of Pope's poems in two columns, and mentioning his name alone, while that of the second volume names ten other authors in two columns. Pope's acknowledged poems, which in 1714 amounted to nine, are now increased to no less than twenty; and, in spite of the fact that he has now excluded his fifty-page translation from Statius, they take up approximately the first two-thirds of the first volume. But these are not all; elsewhere in the volumes are five others lacking his name, two of which had been implicitly acknowledged earlier, the remaining three having recently been ascribed to him by the present writer.[1] Nearly half the poems in the former editions have been discarded, among them most of the anonymous pieces, the few still remaining being now ascribed to their several authors. Among the new contributors, of whom some half-dozen appear in this edition, are Nicholas Rowe and James Ward, who were brought in by the transference of poems from Pope's other collection, *Poems on Several Occasions*, 1717, which had apparently met with little success, to help to fill out the second volume. This procedure, in which fifteen pieces were taken over (three of his anonymous poems among them), points especially to Pope's active connection with the third edition. His hand seems also to be revealed by the inclusion in the first volume of Buckingham's panegyric, *On Mr. Pope and his Poems* (reprinted from the commendatory poems of *The Works*, 1717); for this was the introduction of a new feature in the miscellany which he was later to develop further; and we may note

---

[1] In *Pope's Own Miscellany* mentioned above.

that his portrait from now onwards figures as a frontispiece to the first volume.

The 'Fourth Edition', published November 13, 1722, shows comparatively few alterations, although it has been wholly reset. What changes there are, however, imply that Pope still directed its destinies; for two former contributors of no importance have been displaced and another shorn of a couple of pieces, possibly to make room for two new poems bearing Pope's name.

Between the publication of the fourth and fifth editions other evidences of Pope's control of the miscellany are to be found in his correspondence.[1] On October 31, 1724, he wrote to Broome:

> As to my Miscellany, I hear of nothing like it at present [i.e., no new edition] . . . But whenever times and seasons are so composed as to relish the old and polite arts, no opportunity shall be missed to place your verse in the best lustre I can.

Again, on May 25, 1725, after Broome's decision to withdraw his poems from the next edition in order to print them in a volume of his own works, Pope writes:

> I only could be glad one copy of yours, that which you design to me, as a memorial of our friendship, may appear not only among your own, but attend also upon mine, in the new edition of my things which Lintot is printing, together with the testimonies of some other of my friends.

Writing again to Broome on November 22, 1725, he says: 'I am going to print your verses [i.e., the complimentary poem above alluded to] in a Miscellany'; and yet again, on December 30, 1725: 'I have put your verses to me into a Miscellany, which will come out in two or three months.'

The 'Fifth Edition', to which Pope was referring in the letter just quoted, was published at some date before June 9, 1726,[2] and reprinted in 1727. The title of the collection is changed, and now reads: *Miscellany Poems, Vol. I. By Mr. Pope. The Fifth Edition;—Vol. II. By Several Hands.* And both volumes alike are provided with a half-title

[1] For the following four letters to Broome, see EC, VIII, pp. 87, 97, 104, 109.

[2] According to an advertisement of another book in *The Evening Post* of June 9, 1726, which mentions 'Pope's Miscellany, Vol. I'. The Miscellany is also advertised in a book list in Parnell's *Poems*, published June 14, 1726. Its 'Fifth Edition' was also being advertised widely in December 1726 in *The Whitehall Evening Post* and other papers; and again (this being probably the 1727 reprint) in March 1727.

stating without any ambiguity: 'Mr. Pope's Miscellany.' The first volume opens with forty pages of complimentary poems to Pope (twelve pieces in all, the last being Broome's eulogy, the subject of the letters above quoted); then follow twenty-seven poems by Pope, filling upwards of 200 pages, eight short poems by three other people, two more pieces by Pope, both anonymous; and, to end with, another flattering poem now signed by Broome, and now entitled *To Mr. Pope, On his correcting my Verses*, which had appeared anonymously in the previous editions with the less gratifying title: *To a Gentleman who Corrected some Verses for me*. Moreover, in the second volume are the attributed poems mentioned earlier. But that is not all the evidence that he is still in complete control of the miscellany. Among the dozen commendatory poems marshalled so impressively in the forefront of this edition, he has reprinted from his other miscellany, *Poems on Several Occasions*, 1717, an anonymous panegyric, *To Mr. Pope*, which there is no small amount of evidence to prove—and nothing to disprove—was written by himself (as has been shown in the reprint of that miscellany previously mentioned). He has also inserted for the first time, as a prelude to *Eloisa to Abelard*, an excerpt of eighteen lines from Prior's *Alma* in praise of 'Dan Pope' and his poem; and has included in the second volume yet another poem addressed to himself, *Occasional Verses to Mr. Pope*, the author of which is unknown. Eulogies of each other by the poets of this period are a normal feature of the contemporary miscellanies; and even these tributes of praise might have been passed over without remark, had any other living poet been commended in these volumes. As it is, the inclusion of encomiums of no one but Pope will doubtless be regarded by many people as a final proof of his editorship.

Shortly after this edition had appeared, some question of editorial responsibility seems to have been raised by one of the contributors. The matter is first alluded to at the end of a letter from Christopher Pitt, the poet, to Spence (dated July 18, 1726):

> This is enough in conscience for this time; besides I am desired by Mr. Pope or Mr. Lintot, I do not know which, to write to Mr. Pope on a certain affair.

Pitt's letter to Pope is lost, but, judging from Pope's reply, it seems to have been concerned with the unauthorized inclusion of his poems in the miscellany. Whatever it was, Pope apparently found himself in a rather embarrassing position. His letter (dated July 23), after some compliments on his correspondent's verse, goes on to say:

As to my being the publisher, or any way concerned in reviewing or recommending of Lintot's Miscellany, it is what I never did in my life, though he (like the rest of his tribe) makes a very free use of my name. He has often reprinted my things, and so scurvily, that, finding he was doing so again, I corrected the sheets as far as they went, of my own only. And, being told by him that he had two or three copies of yours, which you also had formerly sent me (as he said) through his hands, I obliged him to write for your consent, before he made use of them. This was all.[1]

One of Pitt's poems figures among the eulogies of Pope with which the first volume opens, four others appearing in the second volume.

This disclaimer of Pope's, for whatever reason made, has generally been taken at its face value to mean that his connection with 'Lintot's Miscellany' was as temporary and slight as it seems to suggest. But on examination it is seen actually to deny only irrelevant things like reviewing, recommending, and some proof-correcting; and the word 'publisher' having several meanings, even at that date, a repudiation of that office in its connotation of bookseller might, if carefully left undefined, seem to cover any or all of the others—editor, author, owner of copyright, or what not. Such a quibble might serve Pope's immediate purpose with a comparative stranger like Pitt; but it can avail little in face of the foregoing evidence, all of which testifies that Pope spoke no more and no less than the truth in his letter to his friend Broome when, referring to the collection known as 'Lintot's Miscellany', he called it simply 'my Miscellany'.

II. 'THE STORY OF ARETHUSA'

Spence, in his *Anecdotes*, reports that Pope when talking about his juvenile verses once said to him:

> In the scattered lessons I used to set myself . . . I translated above a quarter of the Metamorphoses, and that part of Statius which was afterwards printed with the corrections of Walsh.[2]

Now one of the strangest of Pope's many idiosyncrasies, as the present writer has shown elsewhere,[3] was his profound reluctance both to destroy his early poems and to acknowledge them; of which the effect was that he actually published a number of these juvenile pieces with-

[1] Roscoe, VIII, pp. 580 f.   [2] Spence, p. 278.
[3] *Pope's Own Miscellany*, pp. xv ff., xxviii ff.

out his name before he was thirty, and thereafter, while often alluding
to them in such general terms as we have seen, carefully suppressed
(with one or two exceptions) the fact of their publication and all particulars by which they might be identified.

Among Pope's acknowledged poems in the first edition of 'Lintot's
Miscellany', 1712, are two translations—*Statius his Thebais, Book I.*,
and *The Fable of Vertumnus and Pomona* (Ovid's *Metamorphoses*, Book
XIV)—which he subsequently stated 'were selected from many others
done by the Author in his Youth'. When, therefore, in this miscellany
of which he was the concealed editor his acknowledged translation of
Vertumnus and Pomona is found placed next to another translation from
the *Metamorphoses*, which, though unascribed, has much in common
with it, and, moreover, has never been claimed by or for any of his
contemporaries, the possibility that it is likewise by Pope's hand
becomes apparent enough to demand further examination. The
poem, which hitherto seems to have been reprinted only once,[1] runs
exactly as follows:

THE STORY OF *ARETHUSA*,
TRANSLATED
From the Fifth Book of OVID'S METAMORPHOSES.

CEres desires to know the wondrous Cause
  Why *Arethusa* now a Fountain flows.

The Streams their Murmurs hush'd and silent stood,
Whose Goddess strait appear'd above the Flood;
And dry'd the Sea-green Tresses of her Head,   5
And told *Alpheus*' ancient Love, and said.

A Nymph I was, and of th' *Achaian* Train,
That ne'er drew Bow, nor darted Spear in vain:
None bent more eagerly the Toils to set,
To chase the Boar, or pathless Woods to beat.   10
And tho' no Toys, no Dress I made my Care,
Tho' bold; yet was I still reputed Fair.
Our Female Arts I scorn'd, preventing Praise,
And simple, thought it ev'n a Crime to please.

One Day as from *Stymphalus*' Wood I came,   15
Hot with the Chace, the Sun encreas'd my Flame;

---

[1] Namely in *The Nineteenth Century*, in the article aforesaid.

d

Unruffled in its Course a Flood I spy'd,
So calm, so smooth, it scarcely seem'd to glide;
So deep, and yet so clear, that ev'ry Stone,
With borrow'd Lustre, from the bottom shone.   20
The pendent Banks with hoary Willows crown'd
Diffus'd a sweet, refreshing Shade around.
I came, and in the Brink my Foot I dipp'd;
Then to the Knee in dimpling Curls I slipp'd;
Nor cool'd, upon a Bough my Veil I hung: 25
And, on the Bank my airy Garments flung,
Into the bounding Tyde I naked leap;
And as I frisk'd and wanton'd in the Deep,
Amidst the bubbling Flood surpriz'd I hear
A hollow gurgling Noise, and struck with Fear   30
I shriek'd, and rushing made the nearer side,
When rising from his Waves *Alpheus* cry'd,
Oh! whither, *Arethusa!* dost thou fly?
Whither! he shouted with an eager Cry.

Just as I was, without my Cloaths I fled;   35
(Upon the other Bank my Cloaths were laid)
The more did he with raging Passion burn,
Naked he thought me fitter for his Turn.
As the Dove trembling from the Faulcon flies,
As his fleet Wings th' approaching Falcon plies: 40
So hasten'd I, so he pursu'd his Prize.
Thro' the *Menalian* Groves I sped my Flight,
And gain'd with weary Steps *Cyllene*'s Height.
Nor swifter he, but of superior Force
To lengthen out the long, laborious Course.   45
Yet over shaggy Hills with Brakes o'erspread,
And craggy Rocks and desart Wilds I fled.
Before my Feet I saw a monstrous Shade,
Unless my Fear that frightful Phantom made.
Howe'er his sounding Steps and puffing Breath,   50
That fann'd my Tresses, frighted me to Death.
Spent with the Labour of the Flight, (I said)
I'm caught! *Diana!* oh! thy Huntress aid.
Help in Distress the Nymph that us'd to bear
Thy Bow, thy Quiver, and thy pointed Spear.   55

The Goddess heard my Pray'r, and deign'd to shroud
My panting Body in a pitchy Cloud.

Here tho' I vanish'd from *Alpheus*' sight,
Yet still impatient to pursue the Flight,
Twice he surveys the Cloud with searching Eyes,   60
And *Arethusa! Arethusa!* cries.

To me what Strength! what Life did then remain?
No more, than to the Lamb, that hears with Pain
The howling Wolf around th' Enclosure rove,
Yet from its helpless Mother dares not move.   65
Nor went he on, but kept the Cloud and Place;
For he my Footsteps cou'd no further trace.
O'er all my Limbs an oozing Sweat appears,
My weeping Eyes pour out a Flow of Tears.
Big azure Drops my dewy Hairs distil,   70
From every Pore descends a trickling Rill.
My whole dissolving Body liquid grows,
And where I mov'd my Foot a Current flows.
Nay, sooner than I now the Change relate,
I'm all afloat. Yet conscious of my Fate,   75
The River-God dissolv'd his Form Divine,
And reassum'd his Streams to mix with mine.
Diana cleft the Ground. Through winding Caves
Long time I stray'd unmix'd with Briny Waves.
At length, to kind *Ortygia*'s Shore convey'd,   80
In silver Streams I rear'd my watry Head.

Before proceeding with our examination of the poem, a word should be said about Pope's extraordinarily retentive memory, and—what appears to be connected with it—the charge of plagiarism brought against him from time to time during his life, and after. In his youth he was much concerned about this accusation, and alluded to it occasionally in his letters. In 1706, for instance, he sought Walsh's opinion[1] on the question—'how far the liberty of *borrowing* may extend?' Six years later he was still perturbed enough to write in jesting complaint to Caryll[2] about these calumnious 'whispers'— which he was fated never to be quite rid of. Not long before his death, and apparently during the same conversation about his early work[3] as was quoted above, he told Spence he had 'a vast memory' in those days; and, after talking about his boyish translations of Ovid and Statius, went on to say:

[1] *Letters*, 4to, 1737, pp. 31 f.   [2] *Ibid.*, p. 90.   [3] Spence, pp. 276–80.

My first taking to imitating was not out of vanity, but humility: I saw how defective my own things were; and endeavoured to mend my manner, by copying good strokes from others.

It is worth remembering that this practice has been the self-imposed training of many writers, early and late, of which the best-known modern testimony is that of R. L. Stevenson,[1] who similarly acknowledged having 'played the sedulous ape' to 'many masters'; but, being wiser perhaps than Pope, refused to submit his results to the test of publication.

This practice accounts in great measure for the not infrequent appearance in Pope's verse of phrases from the older poets. As might be expected, they are at the same time more numerous, and retain more of their original identity, in the earlier, than in the later, work; being especially abundant in the translations, where the parallels are sometimes so long and so close as almost to suggest an actual transcription from his exemplar. In certain instances, subconscious memory probably played its unpredictable part; but there can be no doubt that in the main these so-called plagiarisms were meant, *not* as appropriations, but as recognizable quotations. In other words, they were purposely introduced to enrich the quality of the verse by nuances of association, echo, and suggestion, which should dimly hover like poetical harmonics above the cadence of the metrical line. They are thus only another illustration of the various methods by which poets seek to capture in their verses more than the actual words. Indeed, this motive is corroborated by an observation in a *Guardian* essay, most probably written by Pope himself,[2] which was published barely ten months after 'Lintot's Miscellany'. The passage occurs in a discussion on 'Borrowing from the Ancients', which having declared:

Now Nature being still the same, it is impossible for any Modern Writer to paint her otherwise than the Ancients have done.

then goes on to assert in effect that judicious borrowing is commendable rather than blameworthy, because it means that—

Over and above a just Painting of Nature, a learned Reader will find a new Beauty superadded in a happy Imitation of some famous Ancient, as it revives in his Mind the Pleasure he took in his

---

[1] *Memories and Portraits*, Chap. IV.

[2] *The Guardian*, No. 12, March 15, 1713. For attribution to Pope, see Pope's *Prose*, I, pp. lxi ff.; and 88 ff. The idea of 'stratification' and 'vertical variety' in Pope's verse was first published by G. Tillotson in his treatise, *On the Poetry of Pope*, pp. 141–59, where it is admirably demonstrated at length.

first reading such an Author. Such copyings as these give that kind of double Delight which we perceive when we look upon the Children of a beautiful Couple . . . observing the Resemblance transmitted from Parents to their Offspring.

With those passages should be placed this from the 'Introduction' to Pope's *Works*, 1717:

> All that is left to us is to recommend our productions by the imitation of the Ancients . . . For to say truth, whatever is very good sense must have been common sense in all times . . . Therefore they who say our thoughts are not our own because they resemble the Ancients, may as well say our faces are not our own, because they are like our Fathers.

Other passages could be cited to the same effect; but enough has been said to show Pope's views and thus explain the presence of borrowed phrases in his poems: though it should perhaps be added, that, in Pope's use of the expression, 'the Ancients', he also included those early translations of the classics in English verse, in which he first became acquainted with them as a child.

Spence also recorded, as part of the conversation above mentioned, that Pope, when speaking of the translations which best pleased his young mind, said that Ogilby's translation of Homer 'led me on to Sandy's Ovid, which I liked extremely.' It is not surprising, therefore, to find that his two acknowledged translations from the *Metamorphoses* contain very definite echoes of Sandys. Half a dozen or more approximations could be quoted from each poem, but the following will suffice to prove the point. First from *Vertumnus and Pomona*:

> A goad now in his hardned hands he bears,
> And newly seems to have un-yok'd his Steers.
>
> SANDYS.

> Oft in his harden'd Hand a Goad he bears,
> Like one who late unyok'd the sweating Steers.
>
> POPE.

And from *The Fable of Dryope* (first published in *The Works*, 1717):

> A Lake there is, which shelving borders bound,
> Much like a shoar; with fragrant Myrtles crown'd.
>
> SANDYS.

> A Lake there was, with shelving banks around,
> Whose verdant summit fragrant myrtles crown'd.
>
> POPE.

But not only were phrases from the older poets treasured up in Pope's 'vast memory', to be borrowed, consciously or unconsciously, on occasion; he seems to have remembered as clearly his own 'good strokes' in his earlier poems, and borrowed them without explanation or restraint.[1] Many of these echoes are the result of a deliberate re-working of old material, but not all; for it may be supposed, that, out of the innumerable verses he produced, he could not always be sure whether, or where, such and such a phrase that sprang to his mind so appositely, had been previously printed. But whatever the cause the fact of repetition is indisputable, and of the utmost importance for the identification of his unsigned poems.

Former editors of Pope's works have recognized that in the episode of Lodona in *Windsor Forest* he has transmuted the Arethusa fable as told in the *Metamorphoses*, and incidentally adapted two passages from Sandys. But our new-found poem, if Pope's, was apparently written before *Windsor Forest*, for he dated these early translations about 1702. And, on that assumption, *The Story of Arethusa* is immediately per-ceived to fill an intermediate stage between *Windsor Forest* and Sandys's translation, being at the same time nearer to both of them than they are to each other. In other words, Pope seems, when writing the Lodona episode, to have recalled and re-used the Arethusa poem rather than Sandys's Ovid. This becomes clear if typical passages are read in their chronological order, remembering always that the Lodona story does not profess to follow Ovid, but is supposed to be Pope's creation. First, of the maiden's flight from the pursuing god:

> As trembling Doves the eager Hawks eschew;
> As eager Hawks the trembling Doves pursew;
> I fled, He followed.
>
> SANDYS.

> As the Dove trembling from the Faulcon flies,
> As his fleet Wings th' approaching Falcon plies;
> So hasten'd I, so he pursu'd his Prize.
>
> *Arethusa*, 39–41

> Not half so swift the trembling Doves can fly,
> When the fierce Eagle cleaves the liquid Sky;
> Not half so swiftly the fierce Eagle moves,
> When thro' the Clouds he drives the trembling Doves;

---

[1] This idiosyncrasy of Pope's is demonstrated in *Pope's Own Miscellany*, pp. xxxvii–xl; and in Pope's *Prose*, I, Introduction *passim*.

> As from the God with fearful Speed she flew,
> As did the God with equal Speed pursue.
>
> *Windsor Forest*, 185–90

Pope subsequently revised the last couplet of the *Windsor Forest* quotation, diverging still more widely from Sandys:

> As from the god she flew with furious pace,
> Or as the god, more furious urg'd the chace.

It will be convenient here to note that he returned again and again to this image:

> Not half so swift the sailing Falcon flies,
> That drives a Turtle thro' the liquid Skies.
>
> *Iliad*, xv, 266–7

> So fast, and with such Fears the Trojan flew;
> So close, so constant, the bold Greeks pursue.
>
> *Iliad*, x, 431–2

Another incident from the end of the chase may be similarly compared:

> How-ere his sounding steps, and thick-drawn breath
> That fann'd my hair, afrighted me to death.
>
> SANDYS.

> Howe'er his sounding Steps and puffing Breath,
> That fann'd my Tresses, frighted me to Death.
>
> *Arethusa*, 50–1

> Now close behind his sounding Steps she hears; . . .
> And now his shorter Breath with sultry Air
> Pants on her Neck, and fans her parting Hair.
>
> *Windsor Forest*, 192, 195–6

Again, in passing, we should note a later parallel in Pope's description of the chariot-race in the funeral games at the close of the *Iliad* (xxiii, 457, 459):

> Close on Eumelus' Back they puff the Wind . . .
> Full on his Neck he feels the sultry Breeze.

Regarding for the moment only the first two quotations in each set, it is apparent that exactly the same use of Sandys's translation has been made by the author of *Arethusa* as by the author of *Vertumnus and Pomona* (which accompanies *Arethusa* in our miscellany) and *Dryope*. And again some half-dozen other parallels could have been quoted to

the same effect. But over and above the similar debt to the older translation, these groups of quotations reveal affinities between Pope and
the anonymous poet which can hardly be explained by their separate
recourse to Sandys, and which seem to point to their being one and
the same person. Abundant corroboration of their identity is found in
the numerous parallel passages existing in *Arethusa* and Pope's
acknowledged work, of which the more striking are as follows
(*Arethusa* being quoted first in each case):

(a)

The Goddess heard my Pray'r, and deign'd to shroud
My panting Body in a pitchy Cloud.

(56–7)

The Queen of Love her favour'd Champion shrouds
(For Gods can all things) in a Veil of Clouds.
Rais'd from the Field the panting Youth . . .

Iliad, iii, 467–9

But present to his Aid, Apollo shrouds
The favour'd Hero in a Veil of Clouds.

Iliad, xx, 513–14

Pope has at least three other couplets on this model; one of them, in
Statius his Thebais, actually appeared in our miscellany with *Arethusa*.

(b)

And tho' no Toys, no Dress I made my Care . . .
Our Female Arts I scorn'd, preventing Praise.

(11, 13)

She scorn'd the Praise of Beauty, and the Care.

Windsor Forest, 177

No Arts essay'd, but not to be admir'd.

On Mrs Corbet, 4

(c)

. . . thought it ev'n a Crime to please.

(14)

. . . whose Crime it was to please.

Iliad, iii, 234

(d)

To lengthen out the long, laborious Course.

(45)

With oars to cut the long laborious way.

> *Odyssey*, v, 181

Spent as thou art with long laborious Fight.

> *Iliad*, vi, 327

Thence took the long, laborious march.

> *Iliad*, xi, 296

(*e*)

The Streams their Murmurs hush'd . . .

(3)

. . . the Streams their Murmurs shall forbear.

> *Pastoral*, iv, 57

(*f*)

So deep, and yet so clear . . .

(19)

. . . so loud, and yet so clear

> *Temple of Fame*, 374

(*g*)

Big azure Drops my dewy Hairs distil

(70)

. . . big Drops of Sweat distill

> *Iliad*, xvii, 835

(*h*)

From every Pore descends a trickling Rill.

(71)

The humid Sweat from ev'ry Pore descends.

> *Iliad*, xxiii, 830

(*i*)

The pendent Banks with hoary Willows crown'd.

(21)

The fruitful Banks with verdant Laurels crown'd.

> *January and May*, 458

It is hardly worth while, perhaps, to make a full list of the shorter phrases in *Arethusa*, any one of which may have been used by any other poet of the period, but *all* of which, in fact, find their exact parallels in Pope's works—phrases such as 'superior force', 'searching eyes', 'pathless woods', 'craggy rocks', 'silver streams', 'winding caves', 'briny waves', and the rest. Nevertheless, their testimony, while of the slightest if each is regarded alone, has a cumulative effect of some weight. A little more unusual, however, is 'th' Achaian Train' of the seventh line, which appears again in *The Iliad* (xv, 262). Lastly, the vocabulary of *Arethusa*, though for the most part not very distinctive, is everywhere consonant with Pope's usage.

Thus all the verifiable facts and all the probabilities point more or less directly to Pope as the author of the poem; and, as there is no evidence of any kind to suggest even the possibility of its being by another hand, it would seem that *The Story of Arethusa* must henceforward be accepted in the canon of Pope's poems—among the recent discoveries of 'many others done by the Author in his Youth'.

CHAPTER III

'TO A YOUNG LADY.'

ONE of the less puzzling aspects of Pope's character was his foible of stressing and, on occasion, of exaggerating the undeniable precocity of much of his juvenile verse; for although it has unfortunately been responsible for not a few critical and biographical errors, it was a very human trait and therefore understandable. But when, as in the case of the first of Pope's two early epistles *To a Young Lady*, this idiosyncrasy was aggravated by a touch of wilful mystification on his part, not to mention his habitual carelessness about dates, the student may well feel baffled in attempting to relate these poems to the poet's life. Who was the 'Young Lady'? and when were the poems written?—are the natural questions of the reader, questions which (except for the approximate date of the second piece) have received many answers in the past, most of them contradictory and none convincing. And yet these two poems have always been well known—the second of them indeed being regarded by many people as the most delightful thing Pope ever wrote. A fresh examination of all the relevant facts available is therefore proposed in the present chapter in yet one more attempt to answer these everrecurring questions.

Amongst the poems which Pope included under his own name in his first miscellany[1] in 1712, appeared the following epistle:

To a Young LADY,
With the Works of *Voiture*

IN these gay thoughts the Loves and Graces shine,
And all the writer lives in ev'ry line;
His easy art may happy nature seem,
Trifles themselves are elegant in him.
Sure to charm all was his peculiar fate,
Who without flatt'ry pleas'd the fair, and great;
Still with esteem no less convers'd than read;
With wit well-natur'd, and with books well-bred;
His heart, his mistress and his friend did share;

---

[1] *Miscellaneous Poems and Translations*, 1712, see previous chapter.

His time, the Muse, the witty, and the fair.
Thus wisely careless, innocently gay,
Cheerful, he play'd the trifle, life, away,
Till death scarce felt his gentle breath supprest,
As smiling infants sport themselves to rest:
Ev'n rival wits did *Voiture*'s fate deplore,
And the gay mourn'd who never mourn'd before;
The truest hearts for *Voiture* heav'd with sighs,
Voiture was wept by all the brightest eyes:
The Smiles and Loves had dy'd in *Voiture*'s death,
But that for ever in his lines they breath.

    Let the strict life of graver mortals be
A long, exact, and serious comedy,
In ev'ry scene some moral let it teach,
And, if it can, at once both please and preach:
Let mine, like *Voiture*'s, a gay farce appear,
And more diverting still than regular,
Have humour, wit, a native ease and grace;
No matter for the rules of time and place:
Criticks in wit, or life, are hard to please,
Few write to those, and none can live to these,

    Too much your Sex is by their forms confin'd,
Severe to all, but most to womankind;
Custom, grown blind with age, must be your guide;
Your pleasure is a vice, but not your pride;
By nature yielding, stubborn but for fame;
Made slaves by honour, and made fools by shame.
Marriage may all those petty tyrants chase,
But sets up one, a greater, in their place;
Well might you wish for change, by those accurst,
But the last tyrant ever proves the worst.
Still in constraint your suff'ring sex remains,
Or bound in formal, or in real chains;
Whole years neglected for some months ador'd,
The fawning servant turns a haughty lord;
Ah quit not the free innocence of life,
For the dull glory of a virtuous wife!
Nor let false shows, or empty titles please;
Aim not at joy, but rest content with ease.

    The Gods, to curse *Pamela* with her pray'rs,
Gave the gilt coach and dappled *Flanders* mares,

The shining robes, rich jewels, beds of state,
And, to compleat her bliss, a fool for mate.
She glares in balls, front-boxes, and the ring,
A vain, unquiet, glitt'ring, wretched thing!
Pride, pomp, and state but reach her outward part,
She sighs, and is no Dutchess at her heart.

But, Madam, if the fates withstand, and you
Are destin'd *Hymen*'s willing victim too,
Trust not too much your now resistless charms,
Those, age or sickness, soon or late, disarms;
Good humour only teaches charms to last,
Still makes new conquests, and maintains the past:
Love, rais'd on beauty, will like that decay,
Our hearts may bear its slender chain a day,
As flow'ry bands in wantonness are worn;
A morning's pleasure, and at evening torn:
This binds in ties more easy, yet more strong,
The willing heart, and only holds it long.

Thus * *Voiture*'s early care still shone the same,
And *Monthausier* was only chang'd in name;
By this, ev'n now they live, ev'n now they charm,
Their wit still sparkling, and their flames still warm.

Now crown'd with myrtle, on th' *Elysian* coast,
Amidst those lovers, joys his gentle ghost:
Pleas'd, while with smiles his happy lines you view,
And finds a fairer Ramboüillet in you.
The brightest eyes of *France* inspir'd his Muse;
The brightest eyes of *Britain* now peruse,
And dead as living, 'tis our author's pride,
Still to charm those who charm the world beside.

* *Mademoiselle* Paulet.

When, five years later, this poem was included in the first collected
edition of Pope's *Works*, 1717, it was directly associated with another
epistle immediately following it, entitled, *To the same, On her leaving the
Town after the Coronation*. As all the biographies of Pope relate, the poet
very early made the acquaintance of two sisters, Teresa and Martha
Blount, grand-daughters of an elderly neighbour, Anthony Englefield, the younger of whom, Martha, was destined to become Pope's
dearest and life-long friend. It was thus perhaps only natural that one
or other of these ladies should have been identified with the 'Young

Lady' of the two poems, even though Pope himself allowed her to retain her official anonymity for the next twenty years or more. For it was not until the 1735 edition of *The Works* that he changed the title of the first epistle to *To Miss Blount, With the Works of Voiture*, while leaving the title of the second piece unaltered, *To the same*, . . . But besides naming the 'Young Lady', Pope also added to the title of the first epistle the words, 'Written at 17 years old' (which would mean in 1705)—a statement which was repeated in 1736, but *not* in the later editions from 1739 onwards to Warburton's edition of 1751, whether because it was a mistake or because it pointed too uncompromisingly to Miss Blount's age, does not appear. What, however, does appear is that this long-delayed statement of date of composition is not compatible with the person addressed, whether 'Miss Blount' referred to Martha or Teresa.

In 1749, on being questioned by Pope's friend, Joseph Spence,[1] Martha Blount made several attempts to recall and date the beginning of her long friendship with the poet. The event having happened so many years before, and Martha being then on the verge of sixty, it is perhaps understandable that the actual date eluded her. Her replies were (i) 'My grandfather Englefield . . . was a great lover of poetry and poets. He was acquainted with Mr. Pope, and admired him highly. It was at his house that I first used to see Mr. Pope.' (Pope's acquaintance with Anthony Englefield has not been traced earlier than 1706, when Martha, who was born in 1690, was seventeen years old.) (ii) 'It was after his Essay on Criticism was published?' 'O yes, sir, —I was then a very little girl, my uncle used to say much of him, but I did not attend to it at that time.' (Martha was two years younger than Pope; the *Essay on Criticism* was published on May 15, 1711, when she was twenty-one and Pope twenty-three.) (iii) 'My first acquaintance with him was after he had begun the Iliad.'[2] (Pope told Spence 'I began translating the Iliad in my twenty-fifth year'[3]; that is, before May 21, 1712; the 'Proposals' for the work were published in the following year. Thus Martha's last statement would mean that she first met Pope after he had not only written but published the epistle *To a Young Lady*; and after the date of his earliest extant letter to her.[4]) There is also Pope's account of the beginning of their friendship in the confessedly 'witty' letter he wrote to Teresa from Bath in September 1714,[5] in the course of which he remarks: 'Even from my infancy I

[1] Spence, p. 356. [2] *Ibid.*, p. 357 n. [3] *Ibid.*, p. 177.
[4] Letter dated 'May yᵉ 25. 1712' (Mapledurham, 1).
[5] *Works*, v (Cooper), 1737, p. 125.

have been in love with one after the other of you, week by week', and
then proceeds by playful computation to show that he had met
Teresa some thirteen weeks earlier than Martha in the year 1707—
which, despite the extravagant tone of the letter, might be true, but
would still place the acquaintance two years later than the temporarily ascribed date (1705) of the poem. The only other comment
Pope seems to have made about the date was the note added to the
Epistle to Jervas in the 1739 edition of *The Works*, thus: 'This Epistle,
and the two following [*i.e.* the two epistles to 'Miss Blount'], were
written some years before the rest [*i.e.* the epistles to Addison, Craggs,
Oxford, and Arbuthnot, and the Ethic Epistles], and originally
printed in 1717.' But, unfortunately, as neither the *Epistle to Jervas*,
nor any of 'the rest' was begun earlier than the winter of 1713–14, the
note is no help in determining the date of the 'Blount-Voiture'
epistle, while that of the 'Blount-Coronation' epistle has—as we shall
see—never been in question.

Once again Pope's foible, already alluded to, of ante-dating his
early work appears to have manifested itself with regard to the first of
the two epistles *To a Young Lady*; for if we put on one side (as Pope
later did) his temporary date of 1705, what little evidence has survived suggests rather that the piece was written some four or five
years later. For instance, in a letter to Henry Cromwell (one of the
youthful poet's elderly friends) Pope seems to anticipate some of its
lines, rather than to be making a prose translation of them, when, on
August 29, 1709, he wrote:

> Tho' Life for the most part, like an old Play, be still the same, yet
> now & then a New Scene may make it more entertaining. As for
> myself, [I would] not have my life a very Regular Play, let it be a
> good merry Farce, a G—ds name, and a figg for the Critical
> Unities.[1]

In the *Epistle to a Young Lady, With the Works of Voiture*, the thought is
versified thus:

> Let the strict life of graver mortals be
> A long, exact, and serious comedy,
> In ev'ry scene some moral let it teach,
> And, if it can, at once both please and preach:
> Let mine, like *Voiture*'s, a gay farce appear,
> And more diverting still than regular . . .
>
> (ll. 21–6)

[1] Rawl. letters 90, f. 15.

Again, more than a year later, on December 5, 1710, to be precise, Cromwell actually discusses, and quotes from, the poem—not as one would criticize an old poem by a friend, but a new production warm from his brain and still under consideration. 'Your poem', he writes, 'shews you to be, what you say of Voiture—*with books well-bred.*' Then, after some flattery, he proceeds: 'But hold, I shall lose . . . your opinion of my sincerity; yet I must say, 'tis as faultless as the fair to whom 'tis address'd, be she never so perfect.'[1]

It should also be noted that this letter of Cromwell's throws some light on the other problem—the identity of the 'Young Lady' addressed in these two poems; for it is practically certain, that, as Pope's friend, he had by this time been made acquainted with the Blount sisters, exactly as he had become a friend of their grandfather Englefield, their uncle Caryll, and others of Pope's circle in the Windsor Forest neighbourhood. That being so, it would seem significant that when writing to Pope about the new poem, he shows not the slightest knowledge of—or even the faintest interest in—the identity of 'the fair to whom it is addressed'. And that would appear to rule out the possibility of either of the Blount girls being the 'Young Lady' apostrophized—the 'Young Lady' who, according to some of Pope's later editors,[2] was Teresa, and according to his more recent biographers was Martha,[3] while one or two other students of the poet have regarded her identity as 'an open question'.[4]

But the most important evidence of all seems to have been persistently overlooked, namely, the letter which accompanied what was actually, but accidentally, a present from Pope to Martha Blount of this very *Epistle* only five days after it was published. On May 25, 1712, Pope began a letter to Martha with these words: 'Madam, At last I do myself the honour to send you the Rape of the Locke', and then went on to explain the delay of its publication, and to deprecate the fact that she and Teresa 'must needs have been surfeited already with this Triffle'. He then proceeds to mention 'the rest of this Booke' (which contains fifty-one pieces in all), some parts of which might make her 'Blush for it'; he next pays her a compliment on her blushing, and ends the letter with a final touch of gallantry.[5]

It was therefore extremely interesting to discover, as the present writer did, this self-same presentation copy of Pope's first miscellany

---

[1] *Works*, v (Roberts), 1737, p. 106.
[2] Ward (Globe Ed.), p. 451; and Boynton (Complete Poetical Works), p. 80.
[3] Sitwell, p. 88, and Sherburn, p. 98.
[4] EC, III, p. 223.   [5] Mapledurham, 1.

in the library at Mapledurham amongst the books that once belonged
to the Blount sisters. The volume is inscribed in Pope's hand with
Martha's name, his own initials, and a couplet hitherto unknown and
now printed for the first time—

Martha Blount; A: P:

Each pretty Carecter with pleasing Smart
Deepens the dear Idea in my heart.

(In passing, it is worth noting that Pope first wrote, 'Deepens your
dear Idea . . .' then crossed out 'your' and wrote 'the' above the line;
and also that by 'Each . . . Carecter' he meant Carect or Character,
that is, each letter in her name—possibly in conjunction with his own
initials.)

But the important fact about this presentation, for our immediate
inquiry, is that the book that contains *The Rape of the Locke* (which was
the only—or perhaps one should say the chief—reason for giving it to
Martha) happens also to contain amongst the fifty other poems, the
epistle *To a Young Lady, With the Works of Voiture*. And it is this fact
which makes it incredible, that, if the epistle had been addressed to
either of the sisters, Pope should not have at least mentioned it, or her,
on such an occasion, either in letter or inscription—for, after all, it
was his first full-dress poetical compliment to a young lady, and (presumably) would have been the young lady's first public tribute from a
rising young poet.

In view of the existence at Mapledurham of this presentation copy
of Pope's first miscellany, and of many other books given by him to the
Blount sisters,[1] it is certainly not without interest to find that amongst
them there is no trace of the copy of 'the Works of Voiture' which
originally must have accompanied Pope's epistle, and which might
reasonably have been expected to survive, had either sister been the
'Young Lady' concerned. Their only 'Voiture' apparently was a copy
published three years later, namely, *The Works of the celebrated Mon-
sieur Voiture*, 2 vols. 1715, which belonged to Martha, and which,
incidentally, contains a reprint of Pope's epistle, *To a Young Lady*, in
its preliminary pages. No stress, of course, can be laid on the absence
of an earlier edition, but, for what it is worth, it tends to confirm the
foregoing argument.

The cumulative effect of all the available evidence, new and old,
makes it virtually certain that the first of the two epistles *To a Young*

---

[1] Others are mentioned on pp. 166-7.

e

Lady was originally addressed neither to Martha nor to Teresa, but in all probability to a young man's quite impossible she who could not object when her beauty, learning, and virtue were publicly appropriated to 'Miss Blount' twenty-five years later. Pope, however, did not explicitly indicate which Miss Blount was at that late date addressed in the epistle; but after the wilful Teresa had provoked the quarrel with Pope which led to their estrangement in the early seventeen-twenties,[1] there was for him and his circle only one Miss Blount, Martha; and there can be no doubt that from 1735 onwards the poem was ostensibly addressed to her. But if this unfortunate though intelligible wish of Pope's publicly to honour his dearest of friends in this way, has confused his readers for two centuries, his omitting to alter the title of the second epistle at the same time (and presumably for the same reason) so far from saving further confusion, has doubled it.

As has been seen, the first epistle, *To a Young Lady*, *With the Works of Voiture*, was published in 1712, having been most probably completed about 1710 (though that is not to deny that a first draft of the poem may have been sketched out as early as 1705, for Pope's acquaintance with the Blount sisters is no longer a prerequisite for its inspiration). The second epistle, *To the same*, about which a word must now be said, was obviously written very shortly after the coronation of George I on October 20, 1714, to which the rest of its title refers.

To the same,

On her leaving the Town after the Coronation.

AS some fond virgin, whom her mother's care
    Drags from the town to wholsom country air,
Just when she learns to roll a melting eye,
And hear a spark, yet think no danger nigh;
From the dear man unwilling she must sever,
Yet takes one kiss before she parts for ever.
Thus from the world fair *Zephalinda* flew,
Saw others happy, and with sighs withdrew;
Not that their pleasures caus'd her discontent,
She sigh'd not that They stay'd, but that She went.

    She went, to plain-work and to purling brooks,
Old-fashion'd halls, dull aunts, and croaking rooks,
She went from Op'ra, park, assembly, play,

[1] See *post*, p. 171.

To morning walks, and pray'rs three hours a day;
To part her time 'twixt reading and Bohea,
To muse, and spill her solitary Tea,
Or o'er cold coffee trifle with the spoon,
Count the slow clock, and dine exact at noon;
Divert her eyes with pictures in the fire,
Hum half a tune, tell stories to the squire;
Up to her godly garret after sev'n,
There starve and pray, for that's the way to heav'n.
  Some Squire, perhaps, you take delight to rack;
Whose game is Whisk, whose treat a toast in sack,
Who visits with a gun, presents you birds,
Then gives a smacking buss, and cries,—No words!
Or with his hound comes hollowing from the stable,
Makes love with nods, and knees beneath a table;
Whose laughs are hearty, tho' his jests are coarse,
And loves you best of all things—but his horse.
  In some fair evening, on your elbow laid,
You dream of triumphs in the rural shade;
In pensive thought recall the fancy'd scene,
See Coronations rise on ev'ry green,
Before you pass th' imaginary sights
Of Lords, and Earls, and Dukes, and garter'd Knights;
While the spread Fan o'ershades your closing eyes;
Then give one flirt, and all the vision flies.
Thus vanish sceptres, coronets, and balls,
And leave you in lone woods, or empty walls.
  So when your slave, at some dear, idle time,
(Not plagu'd with headachs, or the want of rhime)
Stands in the streets, abstracted from the crew,
And while he seems to study, thinks of you:
Just when his fancy points your sprightly eyes,
Or sees the blush of *Parthenissa* rise,
G[a]y pats my shoulder, and you vanish quite;
Streets, chairs, and coxcombs, rush upon my sight;
Vext to be still in town, I knit my brow,
Look sow'r, and hum a song—as you may now.

This poem was first published in *The Works* of 1717, where it immediately followed the epistle above mentioned; and as it has always retained this title and relative position in the many successive editions of *The Works* in Pope's lifetime, any change of the person addressed in the first must affect the second. Consequently, many readers and some editors have been misled into thinking that this second epistle was also addressed to Martha Blount—which is exactly what Pope, late in life, wanted to be thought, or he would not have left its title unaltered.

Nevertheless the poem was originally addressed to Teresa, as the early manuscripts show. Ruffhead, for example, when speaking of this poem in his *Life*,[1] plainly states that he 'has now in his hand the original copy of these verses, from whence it appears that our author made some alterations . . . The seventh line in the original stood thus:

> So fair *Teresa* gave the town a view.'

Carruthers also has a note on this same line: 'In the original:

> Thus from the world the fair *Teresa* flew.'

The text as Pope gave it to the world reads:

> Thus from the world fair *Zephalinda* flew.

Now, in a 'fantastic' correspondence which was carried on for some time about the year 1713 between the Blount sisters and a certain H. Moor (or Moore) of Fawley Court, Berks.,[2] Teresa was called and signed herself 'Zephalinda', and Martha 'Parthenissa', while Moor took the name of 'Alexis'. Pope, knowing the girls so well, knew of this correspondence, and in this epistle uses those names for both. Hence, in the forty-sixth line Martha was first alluded to thus:

> Or sees the blush of *Parthenissa* rise.

which, says Carruthers, is likewise the reading of the original manuscript. Martha was also known by this name beyond the Windsor Forest circle; Lord Chesterfield, for example, refers to her as Parthenissa twenty years afterwards in a letter to Lady Suffolk.[3] Pope, however, altered the name to 'fair Parthenia' in later editions.

But the crowning confirmation that this epistle was first addressed to Teresa, is found in a letter Pope wrote to Martha late in 1714 or early in 1715, in which, after playfully praising her good humour at the expense of her looks, he goes on to say, 'That Face must needs be irresistible which was adorned with Smiles even when it could not see the Coronation.'[4] Therefore, as the whole point of the poem lies in the

[1] Ruffhead, pp. 404–5.
[2] See J. T. Hillhouse, *Modern Language Notes*, 1925, pp. 88–91.
[3] *Suffolk*, ii, p. 114. Letter dated Nov. 2, 1734.
[4] Mapledurham, 32.

effect the coronation had on the 'Young Lady' who saw it, the poem cannot have been written to Martha who did not see it. There can be no doubt whatever that the epistle was originally addressed to Teresa in 1714; and consequently, no doubt that the phrase in the title, *To the same*, whether it seemed to refer to the visionary 'Young Lady' of 1712, or the 'Miss [Martha] Blount' of 1735, was in both cases—the poet not being on oath or compelled to reveal more than he wishes to —nothing more nor less than a convenient fiction.

CHAPTER IV

THE 'HADRIAN' POEMS

THERE has been much confusion in the past about the two short poems which Pope based on Hadrian's famous 'last words', namely the translation, *Adriani Morientis ad Animam*, and the adaptation, *Christiani Morientis ad Animam*. This has been due in part to their curiously delayed appearance in print, but chiefly to Pope's 'literary' methods of editing his early correspondence for publication, described on a previous page.[1] By these methods, portions of letters written to his old friend Caryll in 1712 and 1713—letters which were subsequently reclaimed by Pope—were found, on publication twenty years later, to be addressed to Steele and Addison under different dates. Fortunately, however, before the letters were returned to Pope, some one in the Caryll family carefully transcribed them; and it is these 'Caryll transcripts', now in the British Museum, which contain the earliest extant version of the 'Hadrian' poems, as well as the original and indisputable date of the letter containing them. Nevertheless, while the Caryll transcripts have been of extreme value to those students of the poet who desired first and foremost reliable facts and dates concerning his life and works, there have also been others who seem to have made use of them chiefly to accuse Pope of 'manufacturing a fictitious correspondence'[2] and all kinds of reprehensible practices. These charges have already in no small measure been exploded or explained away, thus reducing a nightmare mountain of complicated wickedness to little more than a molehill of peccadillo.

Since the middle of the last century, when C. W. Dilke's discovery of the Caryll transcripts first made them generally known to students, there have been so many varying suggestions put forward about these two poems that it is now impossible to give an account of all the various hypotheses, and approve, or correct, or refute them, in gross or in detail, without taking up a wholly disproportionate amount of space. The present writer (himself not guiltless of advancing fresh evidence) has therefore cut the knot, and retells the whole story as directly as possible, according to the information now available, without attempting to say who first noted this particular point or was responsible for that particular proof or fallacy.

[1] See *ante*, p. 15.　　　　[2] EC, VI, p. 187 n.

The story of the Hadrian poems begins with *The Spectator* of November 10, 1712, which prints a letter from Pope (with a few words of introduction by Steele, of no importance for our purpose), as follows:

MR. SPECTATOR,

I WAS the other Day in Company with five or six Men of some Learning; where chancing to mention the famous Verses which the Emperor *Adrian* spoke on his Death-bed, they were all agreed that 'twas a Piece of Gayety unworthy that Prince in those Circumstances. I could not but dissent from this Opinion: Methinks it was by no Means a gay, but a very serious Soliloquy to his Soul at the Point of his Departure; in which Sense I naturally took the Verses at my first reading them when I was very young, and before I knew what Interpretation the World generally put upon them.

> *Animula vagula, blandula,*
> *Hospes Comesque corporis,*
> *Quæ nunc abibis in loca?*
> *Pallidula, rigida, nudula,*
> *Nec (ut soles) dabis Joca!*

Alas, my Soul! thou pleasing Companion of this Body, thou fleeting Thing that art now deserting it! whither art thou flying? to what unknown Region? Thou art all trembling, fearful, and pensive. Now what is become of thy former Wit and Humour? thou shalt jest and be gay no more! I confess I cannot apprehend where lies the Trifling in all this; 'tis the most natural and obvious Reflection imaginable to a dying Man; and if we consider the Emperor was a Heathen, that Doubt concerning the future Fate of his Soul will seem so far from being the Effect of want of Thought, that 'twas scarce reasonable he should think otherwise; not to mention that here is a plain Confession included of his Belief in its Immortality. The diminutive Epithets of *Vagula, Blandula,* and the rest, appear not to me as Expressions of Levity, but rather of Endearment and Concern; such as we find in *Catullus,* and the Authors of *Hendeca-syllabi* after him, where they are used to express the utmost Love and Tenderness for their Mistresses—If you think me right in my Notion of the last Words of *Adrian,* be pleased to insert this in the *Spectator;* if not, to suppress it.

                                        I am, &c.

The next step was a letter from Pope to Caryll (apparently in answer to one from him no longer extant, commenting on Hadrian's verses above), which is not dated but almost certainly was written in

the latter half of November. A paragraph in this letter, after acknowledging Caryll's opinion of the Latin verses, continued the discussion
of what they mean in much the same vein as the *Spectator* letter, but
added nothing of immediate interest to us.[1] (The real interest, as we
shall see,[2] comes later with the printing of this paragraph in 1735.)

Then on June 12, 1713, we arrive at another indisputable stage,
with Pope concluding a long letter to Caryll by transcribing three
anonymous poems having to do with 'the verses of Adrian'; at the end
of which he adds the request: 'I desire your Opinion of these verses, &
which are best written. They are of three different hands.'[3] The first
of the three pieces is Prior's now well-known translation, beginning,
'Poor, little, pretty, fluttering thing . . .' (with which we have no
further concern); the second and third pieces ran as follows:

Adriani Morientis ad Animam

Ah fleetting Spirit! wandring Fire,
　　That long hast warm'd my tender Breast,
Must thou no more this Frame inspire?
　　No more a pleasing, chearfull Guest?

Whither, ah whither are thou flying!
　　To what dark, undiscover'd Shore?
Thou seem'st all trembling, shiv'ring, dying,
　　And Wit and Humour are no more.

Xani Morientis ad Animam.

Vital Spark of Heavenly Flame!
Dost thou quit this mortal Frame?
Trembling, hoping, lingring, flying;
Oh the Pain, the bliss of Dying;
Cease, fond Nature, cease thy Strife,
Lett me languish into Life.

My Swimming Eyes are Sick of light,
The less'ning world forsakes my Sight,
A damp creeps cold o'er ev'ry part;
Nor moves my Pulse, nor heaves my heart;
The hov'ring Soul is on the wing;
Where, mighty Death! oh where's thy Sting?

---

[1] Add. 28618, f. 16 v.　　　[2] See *post*, p. 64.　　　[3] Add. 28618, f. 17.

I hear around Soft Musick play;
And Angells beckon me away!
Calm as forgiven Hermites rest,
I'll Sleep, or Infants at the breast,
Till the Trumpett rends the ground;
Then wake with pleasure at the Sound.

Considering that *Adriani Morientis* was repeatedly printed and implicitly acknowledged by Pope from 1735 onwards, and *Christiani Morientis* from 1736 onwards, the sentence with which Pope concluded the letter—'They are of three different hands'—was apparently no more than an experimental deception, and cannot be taken seriously. It was, in fact, meant for Caryll's eye alone; for although Pope revised and printed two paragraphs from that same letter (as part of an undated letter to Addison), this final sentence was never published in Pope's lifetime. It was in all probability no more than a young poet's private and temporary expedient to obtain an unbiased opinion—the hardest thing in the world to get from a friend. Eleven days later he confessed to Caryll that he had written the *Christiani Morientis*.

Nothing more is known of the poems for seventeen years. They had neither been printed, nor had they been circulating in manuscript, to judge from the fact that no contemporary transcripts, except the Carylls', have been recorded. They appeared in print for the first time, together and anonymously, in the second volume of D. Lewis's collection, entitled, *Miscellaneous Poems, By Several Hands*, which was published on May 5, 1730.[1] And as at least three other anonymous poems of Pope's are also first printed there, and as in an unpublished letter[2] to the Rev. Samuel Wesley, dated April 24, 1730, Pope invites Wesley and Lewis to stay with him at Twickenham for 'two or three days', it can be taken for certain that Lewis published these poems with Pope's full knowledge and consent, and, presumably, from manuscripts supplied by him. Collation of the original texts in the 'Caryll transcript' of 1712 with the 1730 texts shows the poems to have received only slight revision: in the first piece quoted above, 'shiv'ring' is changed to 'fainting' (line 7); and in the second, 'Till the Trumpet' is changed to 'Till the last Trumpet' (line 17), and in the last line 'Pleasure' becomes 'Transport'. The texts are otherwise verbally identical. These two anonymous pieces seem not to have attracted any

[1] See *The London Evening-Post* of May 2, 1730.
[2] In the Harley MSS. at Welbeck Abbey.

attention in 1730; and it was not until five or six years later that they first became associated with Pope's name.

So far the tale is straightforward; for it is not until the publication of Pope's letters from 1735 onwards—in different editions of which the two poems are included—that textual and bibliographical problems arise. As, therefore, the general opinion of Pope scholars seems now to be that he was *in some measure* involved in all the editions of his letters above mentioned, both the so-called 'surreptitious and incorrect editions' as well as the 'authorized editions',[1] it is assumed that the inclusion, or not, of either poem in any edition was not unconnected with Pope's wishes at the time, however much, or for whatever reason, those wishes might vary from edition to edition. But for our present purpose, the exact degree of his responsibility does not greatly matter.

In 1735, then, Pope reprinted—or caused to be reprinted—in various early editions of his correspondence, his letter to *The Spectator* of November 10, 1712, given above. And the fact that it had been revised for reprinting to the extent of at least nine verbal corrections, not counting the change of address from 'Mr. Spectator' to Steele himself, or the addition of the date, 'November 7, 1712'; and further (and still more to our purpose), that now for the first time the letter ends with the *Adriani Morientis* poem, in a text which follows that in the original letter to Caryll, then unpublished, and not the printed 1730 text—it would seem practically certain that all these alterations are due to the hand of Pope. It is also obvious that the position of the poem was meant to suggest that it was a part of the original letter, and, therefore, by the same hand.

Also in 1735, a paragraph from Pope's letter to Caryll written in the latter half of November, as mentioned above,[2] was printed as a second letter to Steele further discussing the Hadrian lines. It has been much rewritten in parts and is now dated 'November 29, 1712'. The probable explanation of this change from Caryll to Steele, as the person addressed, has already been discussed on a previous page.[3]

Early in the following year, the second poem—now called an ode and entitled, *The Dying Christian to his Soul*—was included amongst the early poems in the octave edition of *The Works of Alexander Pope, Esq; Vol. I.*, 1736. But, except for the first stanza, which has been only slightly corrected, the ode is practically a new poem, the text of which now runs as follows:

[1] See *ante*, p. 17.   [2] See *ante*, p. 62.   [3] See *ante*, p. 16.

The Dying Christian to his Soul.

ODE

I

Vital spark of heavenly flame!
Quit, oh quit this mortal frame!
Trembling, hoping, lingering, flying,
Oh the pain, the bliss of dying!
Cease, fond Nature, cease thy strife,
And let me languish into life!

II

Hark! they whisper; angels say,
'Sister Spirit, come away!'
What is this absorbs me quite?
Steals my senses, shuts my sight,
Drowns my spirits, draws my breath?
Tell me, my Soul, can this be death?

III

The world recedes; it disappears!
Heaven opens on my eyes! my ears
    With sounds seraphic ring:
Lend, lend your wings! I mount! I fly!
O Grave! where is thy victory?
O Death! where is thy sting?

But the problem only begins to get really involved with the publication of Pope's correspondence, in folio and quarto, on May 19,
1737, entitled, *Letters of Mr. Alexander Pope, And Several of his Friends.*
For this, at last, was the much heralded, handsome, authoritative
edition for which the earlier 'surreptitious' editions are supposed to
have acted as a whet; and from this official collection the two Hadrian
poems were excluded. Then, about a month later, they reappear in
another volume, namely, *The Works of Alexander Pope, Esq; Vol. VI.
Containing the Remainder of His Letters.* (Roberts) 1737, the first poem
being appended to the 'Spectator' letter as before, and the second,
The Dying Christian, following two fresh introductory letters, which
then appeared in print for the first time, thus:

Letter VIII

From Mr. Steele.   December 4, 1712.

This is to desire of you that you would please to make an Ode as of a chearful dying spirit, that is to say, the Emperor Adrian's *Animula vagula* put into two or three stanzas for musick. If you comply with this, and send me word so, you will very particularly oblige your, &c.

Letter IX

I do not send you word I will do, but have already done the thing you desire of me. You have it (as Cowley calls it) just warm from the brain. It came to me the first moment I waked this morning: Yet you'll see it was not so absolutely inspiration, but that I had in my head not only the verses of Adrian, but the fine fragment of Sapho. &c.

After which follows immediately the poem, *The Dying Christian to his Soul*, in the extensively revised text given above. Much play has been made in the past about the absurdity, or even disingenuousness, of the sentence in Pope's letter, where, speaking of *The Dying Christian*, he says to Steele: 'You have it . . . just warm from the brain.' Because the version he ostensibly sent with the letter in 1712 is, beyond any dispute, the much revised text which, presumably, was not in existence even so long afterwards as 1730, when, as we have seen, Lewis was given the original 'Caryll' text to publish. But those censurers must have forgotten that such statements were no more than the general practice—Pope's, as well as other people's—of dating a poem from its first sketch or version. Thus, all that this letter to Steele (whether genuine or not) implied, is that the poem was written in such and such a manner in 1712 (the date of Steele's letter); and the fact that a later version was printed with the original letter has nothing whatever to do with that point.

Towards the close of that same year, the two poems are found once more in another edition, the title-page of which reads: *The Works of Alexander Pope, Esq; Vol. V. Containing An Authentic Edition of his Letters. The Second Edition.* (Cooper) 1737, in which the *Adriani Morientis* poem has a remarkable footnote (not in the first edition) saying, 'The Author seems to have but a mean opinion of these verses, having suppressed them in his Edition.' This note appeared again in 1742; and it is difficult to conceive what reason Pope had for writing it, or permitting its insertion in these editions of *The Works*, unless (as is probable) it was to keep up the pretence of their being unauthorized publications. But 'mean opinion' or not, it is interesting to note that while Pope found it necessary to revise *The Dying Christian* almost out of recognition, the *Adriani Morientis* was allowed to remain practically untouched since 1712. There were other reprintings of the poems within Pope's lifetime in various volumes or editions of *The Works*, for the first poem appears again in 1742, and the second in 1740, 1742, and 1743. And they were both incorporated in the canon by Warburton in 1751: the first piece being found in the letters in Vol. VII, while the second is printed twice (an extremely rare occurrence) in the same edition; once as an *Ode* in Vol. I, and once in the letters in Vol. VII.

There is little more to add. Pope's authorship of the two pieces has sometimes been questioned, both because he did not include them in his 'authorized' *Letters* of 1737, and because of his statement to Caryll in 1712, that the three poems he had sent him were 'by three different hands'. As regards the first objection, it would of course be valid only if Pope had included in his official *Works* every poem he had written—which is so far from being the case that he probably did not include even half their total number. The second objection would possibly seem to have a little more weight; but a reasonable explanation of Pope's statement has already been suggested; besides which, it should be remembered that on a few other occasions Pope was not inclined to tell his staid old friend (who not seldom tended to be a little inquisitive as well as interested) *all* the truth about *all* his works, and not only concealed what he was doing at the moment of writing, but perhaps half a dozen times deliberately misled him about his authorship.

But seeing that the first poem, *Adriani Morientis*, in addition to its actually containing phrases from Pope's prose translation in *The Spectator*, was several times included amongst his works in his lifetime, and, therefore, to that extent implicitly acknowledged by him; and that the second piece, *The Dying Christian*, besides appearing in his letters during his life, was also included in his poetical works at the same time; and, moreover, both in its original and its much revised versions was connected with him, and with no other one person, over a period of some twenty-five years; and, lastly, that both pieces were accepted as Pope's by Warburton, his literary executor and editor—there can be no reasonable doubt about his authorship.

CHAPTER V

MR ALEXANDER POPE: PAINTER

I. POPE AND THE ARTS

ONE of the happiest periods of Pope's life was the 'year and a half' which he spent learning to paint in the studio of his friend, Charles Jervas, the fashionable portrait painter. Glimpses of the enthusiasm with which he applied himself to the craft are to be found in a number of his letters, particularly those to Caryll —an enthusiasm which has sometimes been regarded with an amused tolerance by his biographers, who have not always grasped the full significance of this study in his life and work.

Many things concurred to make the period delightful and memorable. To begin with, he was young—only twenty-four when the scheme was initiated; he had already achieved a considerable and gratifying measure of success as a poet, with his *Pastorals*, the *Essay on Criticism*, and the contributions to the Miscellanies, and with *Windsor Forest* on the eve of publication; he was free—as he never yet had been for so lengthy a spell—from family life and its inevitable protections and restrictions (no matter how affectionately applied, or assented to); he was living in London, and, what is more, at the 'St James's end of the Town', meeting the wits and the scholars at the coffee-houses, and, in Jervas's studio, people of rank and fashion who resorted thither for their portraits; and, dating also from this period was the momentous decision to translate the *Iliad*, and with it all the mingled excitement and apprehension attendant on the launching of that great project. But more than all these things that went to make the period an undying memory was this new experience—the freedom of the studio and the licence and liberty to dabble in paint all day long and every day, and so appease that craving for colour which—as is shown later—seems to have been one of the primary needs of his adolescent years.

His anonymous biographer in 1744 relates of Pope, when only a small boy at Deane's school, that:

> At the Hours of Recreation, whilst the Rest of his School-fellows were diverting themselves at such Games and Sports, as was usual with Boys of their Age, Mr. *Pope* used to amuse himself

with Drawing, and such like improving and rational Accomplish-
ments.[1]

And Pope himself, in a letter 'to a lady' written while still in his teens,
tells with much playful gallantry how he has been copying Kneller's
portrait of her 'these three days' with, apparently, little success.[2] Six
years later, when he was twenty-two, he presented a Madonna he had
drawn to Mrs Caryll (who said that 'St Luke himself never drew such
a Madonna')[3]; and, in another letter to Caryll the following year,
after saying that *Windsor Forest* has just been sent to the press, and
explaining how busy he is, goes on to speak of himself as 'a Lover of
painting, the pursuit of which is another of my Employs'.[4] It was at
this point—some time in March, 1713—that Caryll encouraged him
to take up the study of art seriously, for in his next surviving letter
(April 30), Pope writes:

I've been almost every day employ'd in following your advice in
learning to Paint, in which I am most particularly oblig'd to M^r
Gervase, who gives me dayly instructions & examples.[5]

And on June 12, writing again to his old friend, he says:

If you come, you'll find me in ye close pursuit of ye advice you
gave me three months since, painting at Mr Gervase's in Cleveland
Court, by St James's. I generall[y] imploy the mornings this way,
& the evenings in ye Conversation of such as I think can most
improve my mind...[6]

The same news was sent to Addison about the same time, if we may
believe the published correspondence (and, in passing, there seems to
be no reason why Pope should not have done what many worthy
people do: written much the same letter of news to different friends on
occasion).[7] Pope's next piece of news, describing his attempts at por-
traiture, seems similarly to have been more or less duplicated in
letters to Caryll and to Gay. As the Caryll text has survived untouched
and unamended, we may be certain that it represents Pope's thoughts
at the time; for which reason it is quoted below in preference to the
better-known letter to Gay:

I beg leave here to give you some notices of my self, who am so

---

[1] *Life of Alexander Pope, Esq;* (Printed for Weaver Bickerton), 1744, pp. 13 f.
[2] Letter first printed without date, *Correspondence*, i, 1735 (i), p. 76; dated
'March 1, 1705', in *Works*, v (Roberts), 1737.
[3] Add. 28618, f. 92 v.   [4] *Ibid.*, f. 38.   [5] *Ibid.*, f. 14 v.
[6] *Ibid.*, f. 16 v.   [7] See *post*, pp. 330 f.

intierely immerst in the designing Art, (the only sort of designing I shall ever be capable of) that I have not heard a Ryme of my own gingle this long time. My Eyes have so far got the better of my Ears, that I have at pres^t no Notion of any Harmony, besides that of Colors . . . They tell us, when St Luke painted, an Angel came & finish'd the work; and it will be thought here after, that when I painted, the devil put the last hand to my pieces, they are so begrimed & smutted. 'Tis however some mercy that I see my faults; for I have been so out of conceit with my former performances, that I have thrown away three Dr Swifts, two Duchesses of Montague, one Virgin Mary, the Queen of England, besides half a score Earls & a Knight of the Garter . . . I find my hand most successful in drawing of Freinds, . . . insomuch that my Masterpieces have been one of Dr Swift, & one Mr Betterton. [1]

At this point we might remind ourselves that Pope's ludicrous or irresponsible treatment of any subject does not necessarily mean that he thought little or lightly of it. Rather the contrary, in fact. To take one example: if Pope was ever serious about anything, he was—as every one knows—serious about his poetry; yet jesting references to it abound in his correspondence. During the first half of his life especially his flippancy about serious things appears to have been donned almost always to shield his supersensitiveness in such matters. Hence, when he says:

By Mr. J[erva]s's help . . . I begin to discover Beauties that were till now imperceptible to me. Every Corner of an Eye, or Turn of a Nose or Ear . . . have charms to distract me. [2]

he is only describing the unforgettable experience of every student of art during his first days in a studio. And when he goes on to embroider the theme, or (as it may seem to some) to fantasticate on it, and confesses himself 'in some danger even from the Ugly and Disagreeable, since they may have their retired beauties, in one Trait or other about 'em', [3] his extravagant jest is nothing but the sober truism of the

---

[1] Add. 28618, ff. 19 v.–20 r. Letter dated, '31 Aug. 1713'. To make the record complete: in the letter to Gay (August 23, 1713), he says he has thrown away 'three Dr. Swifts . . . two Lady Bridgewaters, a Duchess of Montague, besides half a dozen earls, and one knight of the garter.' He then concludes: 'I have crucified Christ over again in effigy, and made a madonna as old as her mother St. Anne.' Moreover, Spence asserted: 'I have seen, of Mr. Pope's drawing, a grave old Chaucer, from Occleve; a Betterton; a Lucius Verus, large profile; two Turkish heads; a Janizary from the life; Antinous; and St. John praying.' (Spence, p. 336.)

[2] *Correspondence*, I, 1735 (i), p. 188.   [3] *Ibid.*

art student. Thus, so far from showing himself careless of—or indifferent to—his new pursuit, these letters only prove how deeply he has been moved by the revelation of beauty which follows on a sincere study of it.

Later letters of that year contain references to the continued pursuit of art. He refers to Jervas as 'my master' in September; and he is 'still at Mr. Jervas's' in October. How and when the study terminated is not known, whether gradually or suddenly, whether in the early winter or the following spring. Spence, about 1728, reports Pope saying that he 'learned to draw of Jervas for a year and a half'.[1] But on February 25, 1714, Pope wrote to Caryll about the Homer translation recently contracted for, saying:

> I shall now be very much taken up in this worke which will keep me a Poet (in Spite of something I lately thought a Resolution to ye contrary) for some years longer.[2]

Cannot one hear a faint note of regret hovering over the parenthesis, a half-conscious realization that he was about to lay down his brushes for a long time, perhaps the last time; that this twelve—or eighteen—months' interlude was closing; and that to engage in a task that would take up five or six years of his life, was indeed to bid farewell to his youth and those dear dreams of pictorial as well as poetical fame? Years after, he movingly recalled the apprehension he felt on taking up this new task:

> What terrible moments does one feel, after one has engaged for a large work!—In the beginning of my translating the *Iliad*, I wished any body would hang me, a hundred times.—It sat so heavily on my mind at first . . .[3]

It is not surprising, therefore, that, in retrospect as well as at the time, this sojourn 'at Mr. Jervas's', this escape into a new world of colour, light, and form, seems to have taken on a golden glow ('Long summer suns rolld unperceivd away') quite unlike anything else in his experience, except perhaps the fervour of his early teens when poetry beckoned to him with a like enchantment. Nor is it remarkable that he should have repaid his debt to Jervas with the friendliest of epistles, which was not the less sincere for comprising what—two centuries later—may seem some extravagance of statement.

An early version of this poem, probably the first sketch 'warm from the brain', has accidentally but happily been preserved amongst the 'Homer Manuscripts', simply because some lines of Pope's translation

[1] Spence, p. 23.   [2] Add. 28618, ff. 22 v.–23 r.   [3] Spence, p. 218.

f

chanced later to be written on the back of it. As this autograph text differs greatly from the 'finished' piece, being more intimate in tone and seemingly still redolent of the studio tang of turpentine and varnish; and as, hitherto, a number of passages have never been correctly transcribed and some half-dozen lines never even deciphered, it has been chosen, rather than the 'official' tribute (to be found in all Pope's *Works*), as best illustrating his attitude to this all-too-brief apprenticeship to art.

To Mr. *JERVAS*

With *Fresnoy's* Art of Painting, Translated by Mr. *Dryden*.

This small well-polishd Gem (ye work of years)
In Drydens diction still more bright appears
Yet here how faint each Image seems to shine
Matchd wth thy Souls rich unexhausted Mine
Whence endless Streams of fair Ideas flow
Rise on ye Sketch, or on ye Canvass glow
Where Beauty, waking all her Forms, supplies
An Angels Sweetness or a Berkleys Eyes.

Nature to thee has all her Graces shown
And gave thee words to make those Graces known
If Raphael writ or if Leandro wrought
The Verse is perishd or the Piece forgot.
Evn Fresnoy painted wth unfruitful pains
The Artist lost, ye Critic yet remains
Of Jervas only future Times shall tell
None practisd better, none explaind so well
Thou only sawst w^t others coud not know;
Or if they saw it, only thou canst show

Like friendly Colors our kind arts unite
Each from ye mixture gathering sweets & light
Their birth, their features wth resemblance strike
As Twins they vary and as Twins are like.
Smit wth ye Love of Sister Arts we came
& met congenial, mingling flame wth flame
How oft in pleasing Labors of ye day
Long summer suns rolld unperceivd away
At night we met each finding like a Friend
Something to blame & something to comend
How oft in fancy long amusement sought
& form the distant Journeys in our thought

Smit wth ye Love of Arts methinks we go
Together tread th'Eternall Alpine Snow
Now catch ye word in some vast Ruins Shade
Now sleep where Tullys worthy head was layd
Each Ruin Fancy Times decays supplies
& sees Imaginary Romes arise
Notions awake & Images renew
From Art to Art ye pleasing Track pursue
Thou oer thy Raphaels monument should mourn
I wait inspiring dreams at Maros urn
Here arts rich Reliques for our Sorrows call
A mouldred marble or a faded wall
There . . .
      . . . well studyd busts attract ye eye.[1]

There can be no question that Pope was profoundly affected both by his study of art under Jervas, and the freedom of the studio; for such lines could not have been written by one who (as has been said) regarded the whole thing as 'a passing amusement'. Nevertheless, when tangible results of his practice of painting are sought for, little is found but disappointment.

Of all those portraits he so gaily enumerated in his letters, a prolonged search has located only one—the Betterton 'masterpiece', which, on the authority of Warburton, Pope's friend and first editor, was stated in 1769 to be in the possession of another friend of Pope, Lord Mansfield.[2] In spite of wide-spread and persistent rumours of its destruction by fire, the picture has remained in the family ever since— a treasured possession.[3] That Pope did occasionally paint from the life, we have Spence's testimony.[4] But, seeing that Kneller had painted Betterton in his lifetime; and that Pope's 'masterpiece' was not painted till 1713, three years after the actor's death; and noting furthermore, that when Pope's and Kneller's portraits of Betterton

[1] This text reproduces as nearly as possible Pope's latest corrections in this particular MS. (Add. 4807, f. 128 v.). It therefore omits a few fragments of lines here and there which he forgot to scratch out after re-writing them. The MS. has no title, which is here supplied from the printed text.

[2] Ruffhead, p. 477.

[3] Owing to unforeseen difficulties it has been found impracticable to include a reproduction of the picture in these pages; but the Earl of Mansfield has assured the present writer that 'the portrait is excellent.'

[4] Spence, p. 336.

were hung near each other in an exhibition in 1867, their resemblance (except for the colour of the wig) was such, that Kneller's was declared to be the original of Pope's,[1] —there can be little doubt that Pope's 'masterpiece' was, to some extent at least, a copy: as indeed one supposes most of these studio exercises to have been.

A late newspaper suggestion, put forward in 1785 without evidence, that the copy might be Jervas's work, has recently been re-suggested on no stronger grounds than that the painting might be too good for Pope.[2] The repetition, however, appears to have been based, not on any first-hand knowledge of his paintings, but on a remark made by Sir Joshua Reynolds about another of Pope's works of art. This was the famous fan 'of the Author's Design, in which was painted the Story of Cephalus and Procris.' Pope's well-known lines, 'On a Fan', were first published in *The Spectator* of November 4, 1712; poem and fan having presumably been presented to Martha Blount some little time earlier. The fan itself has not been seen since it fell into Sir Joshua's hands; but he was probably right—if a little downright—in saying that it was 'such as might be expected from one who painted for his amusement alone; like the performance of a child'[3]; for the simple but unheeded truth is that the fan was painted and presented months before Pope began to take lessons from Jervas. Sir Joshua's criticism, therefore, has no bearing on the Betterton portrait which was painted after months of professional tuition.

Few other pictures by Pope are on record. There is the large oil-painting 'representing the Prodigal Son', the scene of which was engraved, signed 'A. POPE inv', and used as a frontispiece to some editions of *An Essay on Man* from 1745 onwards. Carruthers found the painting[4] in the Stoneham family, where it remained till 1935, when it changed hands and afterwards left the country. Also there was 'a head of Vandyck, drawn by Pope, in black and red chalk, finely executed', last heard of 'at Home Lacy' in 1794.[5] Mention too might be made of the pen-and-wash drawing of 'A View in Pope's garden at Twickenham', in the British Museum, where, after being attributed to Pope for nearly a century, it is now thought by some experts to be the work of his friend, Kent.

Apart from a number of sketch plans of buildings and gardens, and some careful working drawings of wall monuments and similar semi-

---

[1] Whitley, pp. 42 f.   [2] *Ibid.*, p. 43.

[3] *Life and Times of . . . Reynolds*, C. R. Leslie and T. Taylor, i, 1865, p. 25.

[4] See Carruthers, pp. 90, 462 f., where the picture (approx. 4 ft × 3 ft) is described, but miscalled a water-colour.   [5] *Gent. Mag.*, April 1794, pp. 315 f.

architectural designs, found on the backs of some of the Homer MSS. in the British Museum, and elsewhere, the only example of Pope's line drawings known to the present writer is an early pen-and-ink sketch, hitherto unrecorded, of a seated figure in classical drapery. This he discovered in the Bodleian Library amongst a collection of the Pope-Cromwell papers which came into Curll's possession presumably in 1726.[1] The sketch is quite small, measuring about $3\frac{1}{4}$ by $2\frac{2}{3}$ inches; and beneath it Curll has written: 'This Figure is the Delineation of Mr. Pope's Penmanship. E. Curll.' It is practically certain that the drawing dates from the years covered by the accompanying letters, (1708–1711); consequently it belongs to the pre-Jervas period, its interest, as the earliest figure-drawing of Pope's to have survived, being biographical rather than aesthetic.

Was Pope realist enough, one wonders, to have foreseen the future awaiting his various works of art? It is more than probable. At least, as we know now from the manuscript version of the *Epistle to Jervas* above, he had visualized the problem objectively:

> If Raphael writ, or if Leandro wrought,
> The Verse is perishd, or the Piece forgot.

Nevertheless, however much or little skill went to the making of his paintings and drawings, and however completely 'forgot' or 'perishd' is now their all but general fate, his practice of art profoundly influenced his life and remains to this day abundantly perceptible in his work. As early as 1710 he could write to Cromwell:

> To express myself like a Painter, their *Colouring* entertains the sight, but the *Lines* and *Life* of the Picture are not to be inspected too narrowly.[2]

Again, in 1712, he explains to Caryll that his letters are 'Sketches of my Friendship', though they

> give as faint imperfect Images of itt, as the little Landskipps we comonly see in black and white doe of a beautyfull Country. . .deprived of the Life and Lustre of Nature.[3]

Yet already he knew enough about art to realize that a drawing is not necessarily improved by the addition of colour:

> . . . The slightest Sketch, if justly trac'd,
> Is by ill *Colouring* but the more disgrac'd.[4]

[1] Rawl. letters 90, f. 50 v.   [2] *Correspondence*, i, 1735 (ii), p. 303.
[3] Add. 28618, f. 11.   [4] *Essay on Criticism*, 1711.

In the same poem he also shows himself very much aware of the painter's bugbear, fugitive colours, and mourns the loss of beauty which their use entails:

> The *treach'rous Colours* in few Years decay,
> And all the bright Creation fades away![1]

And he returns to the same idea in two early variants in the *Epistle to Jervas* above, both in the line:

> Thou oer thy Raphaels fading Fresco mourn

and again later, where 'our sorrows' are called for by—

> A mouldred marble or a faded wall,

the two lines being merged in the final reading:

> A fading Fresco here demands a sigh.

The love of colour implicit in such lines as these, and there are many like them, was an essential part of Pope's character, which, fundamental though it was, has been overlooked hitherto by students of his work. It is also further proof that his study of painting under Jervas was not a passing fancy that began with their acquaintance. Indeed, as is shown in the following section, 'Pope's Palette', his love of colour ante-dated not only his first printed poems in 1709, but even the writing of them in 1704 or earlier, and without doubt goes back to childhood. It has been suggested as a possibility[2] that his early interest in art derived from the influence of his god-mother, the widow of Samuel Cooper the painter, some of whose pictures hung in the boy's home at Binfield and became his property by delayed bequest in 1710. But as Mrs Cooper died when he was only six, her influence must have been chiefly posthumous and limited to her responsibility for the presence of Cooper's pictures in the house.

But however Pope's interest in art was acquired or evolved, it would inevitably follow, with a youth of his inquiring mind and observant eye, that his aesthetic perception developed with the years of adolescence, and from delight in colour went on to the appreciation of architecture—not uncritically, but with a growing sense of proportion. This is apparent as early as 1711, when he could write:

> Thus when we view some well-proportion'd Dome,
> (The *World*'s just Wonder, and ev'n *thine*, O *Rome*!)
> No single Parts unequally surprize;
> All comes *united* to th'admiring Eyes;

[1] *Essay on Criticism*, 1711; later editions read '. . . colours the fair art betray'.
[2] Sherburn, p. 102.

> No monstrous Height, or Breadth, or Length appear;
> The *Whole* at once is *Bold*, and *Regular*.[1]

All these artistic interests, even his antiquarianism and his land-scape-gardening, were alike disciplined and fostered by the training of hand and eye to which he submitted himself under Jervas. Day by day his vision was schooled to a quicker recognition of the subtleties of form and a still finer appreciation of, and delight in, the harmony and contrast of colours; of the latter of which he spoke in the above epistle, first in these words:

> Like friendly Colors our kind arts unite
> Each from ye mixture gathering sweets & light

then, with greater stress on the fact of the interdependence of colours, which is a painter's knowledge:

> Like friendly colours found our arts unite,
> And each from each contract new strength and light.[2]

And at the same time, day by day his hand was slowly learning the technique of the craft:

> . . . I must paint it.
> Come then, the colours and the ground prepare!
> Dip in the Rainbow, trick her off in Air. . .[3]

Although in Pope's day any one might think that 'preparing' the colours was a preliminary to painting, only one who had stretched his own canvas and primed it would have thought of adding 'and the ground prepare'. Such references to the secrets of the studio abound in his work, often being introduced by way of simile, as in the follow-ing:

> Wine awakens and refreshes the lurking passions of the mind, as varnish does the colours that are sunk in a picture, and brings them out in all their natural glowings.[4]

Pope, however, spoke even more frequently as the artist than as the craftsman. Such verses, as 'Free as thy stroke and faultless as thy line'; and 'The lines tho' touch'd but faintly are drawn right'; and 'To draw the naked is your true delight'; and 'The lights and shades whose well-accorded strife', are typical of the many short passages known to lovers of his works.[5] Indeed, his vocabulary is permeated with the

---

[1] *Essay on Criticism*, 1711, ll. 247–52.   [2] *Epistle to Jervas*, in *Works*, 1717.
[3] *Of the Characters of Women*, 1737.   [4] Mapledurham, 32.
[5] For longer passages, see especially, *Epistle to Jervas*, ll. 35–44, 63–70; *Epistle to Burlington*, ll. 145–8; *Characters of Women*, ll. 151–6, 181–98; *Essay on Criticism*, ll. 293–6, 484–93; *Essay on Man*, ii, ll. 207–10.

phraseology of the studio, and he is at ease and familiar with the technical meaning of such words as draft, sketch, design, compose, copy, trace, outline, and drawing; models, figure, drapery, and posture; hue, tint, tincture, tone, colour, glaze, dye, and stain; and also understood something of the various graphic arts, fresco, landscape, portrait, charcoal, crayons, enamel, tapestry, black-and-white, and engraving. His interest in sculpture is similarly obvious from the number of times he referred to it, and made occasion to use such words as statue, bust, effigy, carving, bold relief, marble, bronze, mould, and cast. But whether his appreciation of it preceded his antiquarianism and his study of 'medals', or followed them, is not known.

He had likewise much to say about architecture and landscape gardening. The *Epistle to Burlington* almost amounts to a disquisition on those 'sister arts', not omitting numerous examples of how *not* to do it; his golden rule being:

> To build, to plant, whatever you intend,
> To rear the Column, or the Arch to bend,
> To swell the Terras, or to sink the Grot;
> In all, let *Nature* never be forgot.[1]

His noble friends were not backward in consulting Pope on these matters,[2] and, as his biographers have pointed out, several of the magnificent English gardens of the eighteenth century owed much to his suggestions and plans. He also followed his own advice, as far as he was able, in and about his river-side villa and his five-acre garden where 'there were not ten sticks in the ground' when he went there to live. But while it is well known that he transformed the garden (not to mention the grotto) into one of the minor wonders of the age, his enthusiasm for additions and alterations to the house has for the most part escaped record. One considerable change, however, can be traced in his correspondence with Lord Burlington, hitherto unpublished, in which he tells of the addition of a portico to the house. For example, on September 19, 1732, he writes:

My Portico is in hand, . . . but I will not proceed till I have y^r Lordship's sanction of it. The Basement, if continued no further on ye sides than the Pillars, w^d be too thin & want a flight of steps to spread it: which w^d spoil a Design I have, to make that Basem^t include a Cold Bath & a fall of water. Your opinion of this, as it stands, with relation to its connection to ye rest of the Front, will greatly oblige me.[3]

---

[1] Lines 31–4.   [2] Butt, p. 183 n.   [3] Devonshire MSS., 1st Ser. 143, 16.

On 'Novr. 6th' it is:

> I am very impatient to be building my Portico, but Mr Kent admonishes me to defer ye Brickwork & Plaistering till Spring, wch I grieve to comply with. [1]

Then there is an undated letter which may be given entire:

> My Lord
>
> The Zeal of my Portico has eaten me up, so that I cannot be from home to day; I sent yesterday & missed of you. I cannot proceed in my Stucco-ing, till I see your Ldship & have yr directions abt ye Upper Cornish of my house, & ye Moldings & members of ye Entablature. I therefore beg you to throw away one hour upon me at Twitn'am as soon as is not inconvenient. I need not say how impudent your Kindness has long made me, you see I think it extends to ye Smallest Triffles. I am with truth
>
> My Lord
>
> Yr ever obligd Servant
>
> Thursday.   A. Pope. [2]

One other letter, [3] also undated, probably alludes to the portico, the chief news about it being—'We now stand still for Materials'—a very trying experience for one whose 'zeal' is eating him up. But although the completion of the work is not recorded in the correspondence, the portico in all its glory can be seen in one or two of the early engravings of 'Pope's Villa'. Unfortunately, most of the pictures that have survived were made later than 1760, when, it seems, a pediment was added to Pope's portico by an irreverent hand, and the 'Front' suffered further 'improvements'. These were likewise followed by yet others before the turn of the century, when the whole building was razed to the ground. It might be added as a pendant (though prelude would be the better word) to all this 'building and planting' of Pope's, that the same correspondence reveals him actively interested in architecture much earlier. Before he went to Twickenham in 1718, he had been making plans to build a house at Chiswick 'in that piece of ground behind Burlington House'; and in one of the letters he promises Burlington 'to build on ye same Plan & Front with Ld Warwick's, so as not to clash with any regular design.' [4]

This care for architectural good manners also goes to show that Pope's 'taste', and his feeling for art, were genuine expressions of his character, besides largely explaining why his opinions were respected

---

[1] Devonshire MSS., 1st Ser. 143, 18.   [2] *Ibid.*, 143, 22.
[3] *Ibid.*, 143, 24.   [4] *Ibid.*, 143, 2.

and sought in a society in which the poseur and the dabbler flourished. But although he had inside knowledge of these various arts, there is no doubt that, of them all, the one that lay nearest to his heart, next to poetry, was painting. His life may have been influenced to a greater or lesser degree by contact with the other arts, but painting, as will be shown, influenced his work as well.

In the long story of English literature there have been, besides Pope, few poets of any distinction who can be said to have had a technical knowledge of painting as well as poetry, and to have practised the two arts for a longer or shorter period. The best-known of these painter-poets, or poet-painters, omitting the living, are Dyer, Blake, and Rossetti, none of whom equalled Pope's use of colour in the general run of their verse,[1] though having him for example, who himself had none.

One last word must be added here on the relation of Pope's work to the 'cult of the picturesque' which subsequently became so popular. Seeing that Pope was seriously working at painting and poetry earlier even than Dyer (whose first poem, *Grongar Hill*, was published in 1726), it is no surprise to find him one step ahead of his contemporaries in the recognition and application of the 'picturesque' in poetry and painting. The word itself was a new-comer in England in Pope's day; for although it had apparently been introduced by Steele in *The Tender Husband* in 1705, it was Pope himself who was the first to use the word with any frequency; and to judge from the way he and Steele used it, its original meaning was—as it is to-day—'like a picture', or 'fit to be the subject of a picture'. For example, as early as 1712, writing to Caryll, Pope said:

> Mr Philips has two Lines wch seem to me what the French call very *Picturesque* ...
>
> > All hid in snow, in bright Confusion lye,
> > And with one dazling Waste fatigue the Eye.[2]

And again, in a conversation on the Thames some years later, Spence reports him saying:

---

[1] This statement is based on the number of colour-words used in representative poems as follows. Dyer: *Grongar Hill* (158 ll.), and *A Country Walk* (156 ll.) together average one colour-word to every 11 lines; *The Ruins of Rome* (545 ll.) one to every 18 lines; and *The Fleece* (2,705 ll.) one to every 17 lines. Blake: *Songs of Innocence* (393 ll.) and *Songs of Experience* (492 ll.) together average one colour-word to every 19 lines; and *Thel* (129 ll.) one to every 18 lines. Rossetti: *The House of Life*, Sonnets 1–50 (700 ll.) average one colour-word to every 30 lines; and *The Blessed Damozel* (144 ll.) one to every 20 lines. For Pope's use, see next section *passim*.

[2] Add. 28618, f. 13.

That Idea of the Picturesque, from the swan just gilded with the sun amidst the shade of a tree over the water.[1]

And in between those two utterances Pope had used the word two or three times in print in exactly the same sense. By the middle of the century, however, 'picturesque' had taken on a special connotation which for many years more or less displaced its former general meaning. During this interregnum, as has been shown in a comparatively recent work,[2] the word conjured up for most people a vast but vague picture which can be best described by Walpole's rapturous enumeration of Nature's charms—

Precipices, mountains, torrents, wolves, rumblings, Salvator Rosa . . . glorious desolate prospects . . . hanging woods . . . rocks . . . cascades . . . an old footbridge . . . a leaning cross, a cottage . . . the ruin of a hermitage—[3]

or by a composition of as many of these items as can be crowded together on page or canvas in a romantic Gothic gloom. In other words, 'picturesque' still meant 'like a picture', or 'fit to be the subject of a picture', only *now* the picture must have been painted by Claude, or Poussin, or—preferably—Salvator Rosa, or at least look like it. The cult of the picturesque was the cult of Italian landscape painting, and *vice versa*—a cult which is generally considered to have originated with the poet Gray, and to have virtually dominated English taste in art and letters in the latter half of the century. Pope himself, however, had little enough to do with this vogue. A few lines in *The Temple of Fame* are said to 'come close to Claude',[4] but they are preceded and followed by a dozen other pictures in the same poem, which reveal no trace whatever of Italian influence; (though it may be noted in passing, that, subsequently, his landscape gardening was not quite free of it). Rather will it be shown that Pope was the first of the great English landscapists in verse to compose his picture within the frame and paint it in the colours of nature. Neither to Dyer, nor to Thomson does that priority belong, as has been asserted[5]; for Pope had finished his series of masterpieces before ever they began, in 1726, to follow in his steps, and to adopt in some measure both his technique and his language.

---

[1] Spence, p. 11.   [2] Manwaring, Chap. VII.

[3] Letter to Richard West, Sept. 28–30, 1739. Walpole, I, pp. 36–8.

[4] Manwaring, p. 97.

[5] 'Dyer and Thomson were the first of the great landscape designers in poetry, in their century.' Manwaring, p. 96.

II. POPE'S PALETTE

Whether or not Pope was the first of the painter-poets to attempt to combine something of the two arts in the same work, he was, apparently, the first of our poets to explore the possibilities of colour composition in poetry, and the first whose verse might often be called a gallery of pictures in colour. But although his study of painting under Jervas undoubtedly aided and abetted this practice, it did not begin it. Pope's innate love of colour had led him to make an increasing use of colour-epithets in his poems from his early teens onwards, with the result that his first published pieces, while remarkable for other things, are still more important by reason of these experiments.

In all but the earliest juvenile verses, Pope shows himself growingly dissatisfied with plain description and the indirect suggestion of colour. In effect, he chooses very early to say, 'The sky is blue', rather than, 'The sky is cloudless'—a method of approach to colour charged with much more significance than the distinction between positive and negative statement. But this is not only a difference in speaking, it is a difference in presentation. By the one method, the named colour is flashed on the inward eye of the reader instantaneously; by the other the suggested colour can only reach the mind's eye (if it gets there at all) in a roundabout way by means of deductive reasoning, which may go wrong either because of insufficient data (for example, was the sky cloudless at noon or at sunset?), or because of different personal associations (for example, the much-used epithet 'flame-coloured' means for different people different colours, yellow, orange, red or even purple, according to individual experience).

These two methods of conjuring up colour effects in poetry correspond in some measure to the two main schools of colourists (often mutually intolerant) and of colour-lovers. These may for convenience be called the 'full-colour school' and the 'grey-colour school'. The former delights in brilliant colours of all kinds, with the primaries and secondaries in vivid juxtaposition; and is perhaps represented at its best in England by the Pre-Raphaelites, and at its worst by a child's painting book—'lumps of raw colour' would be its definition by some of the opposite camp. The latter, on the contrary, abjures the more strident notes of the primaries and secondaries, and sees salvation chiefly in infinities of gradation and subtleties of suggestion amongst the tertiaries, the best known exponent of this school being, perhaps, Corot; and its greatest danger a tendency towards monochrome, with (as its enemies say) its puritanical sacrifice of colour. It is not a little

startling, therefore, to discover that Pope had a most unusual capacity of combining the principles of the two schools; not of course in
the same 'picture', for that is impossible, but in different pictures
which sometimes may occur in the same work. For, as regards colour
perception, he was very far from being like the generality of mankind
—or even of poets.

Now there is much evidence to show that many—probably most—
people are not normally conscious of colour as colour, in this workaday
world of ours. That, however, is not to suggest that most of us cannot
distinguish between, say, ripe and unripe fruit, or the 'stop' and 'go'
of the traffic signal-lights; but that most people's awareness of—and
reactions to—colour are in general limited to its utilitarian significance. Nevertheless, on every side, wherever we go, year in and year
out, colour surrounds us completely, multitudinous in tint and tone,
but with each of its hues existing only by virtue of its neighbours, as
they by it, in mutual dependence on harmony or contrast for the
perceptible difference between them; yet, with it all, shifting and
changing with every movement in eternal flux and renewal, never to
be shut out from morning to night except by closed eyes—nor even
then while secret kaleidoscopic patterns glow and fade and glow
again behind our eyelids. But although colour is present everywhere
about us, it is for the most part unregarded except when some unusual
display of magnificence or crudity, in sunset or shop-window, shocks
us into momentary applause or protest, after which we comfortably
forget again. It is arguable, therefore, if by some biological sport all
mankind suddenly became blind to colour, whether the conscious
loss of that faculty would, after a very short period of adaptation, be
regarded as a major catastrophe except by painters and other
specialists in colour.

It would thus seem to follow that the simple naming of an object in a
poem would not induce the inward eye of the reader consciously to
see and recognize its colour, any more than does the actual object
when seen with his bodily eyes. Exception, however, might possibly be
made of the names of two or three flowers which by virtue of their
colour and long familiarity may occasionally be regarded as colour-
words, but only in those instances—comparatively few in number—
when the poet himself unmistakably uses them with a particular
colour suggestion as his principal motive. The poet's intention must
always, of course, be the criterion. Two examples will suffice. Wordsworth's oft-quoted line, 'A violet by a mossy stone',[1] is not, as might

[1] *She dwelt among the untrodden ways*, l. 5.

appear at first sight, a suggestion of colour, because when it is re-placed in its context we see it to be a statement of natural fact, in which a violet is used as a simile or image of the utter loneliness of a country maiden, of her shyness, of her beauty—of anything rather than her colour. The words composing the line, therefore, are no more a statement of colour than would be a black and white drawing of the same subject. Again, in Goldsmith's well-known line, 'The primrose peeps beneath the thorn',[1] the flower is likewise found to be a simili-tude of the modesty, sweetness, and innocence, but surely not the yellowness, of another maid.

The exact contrary of these two illustrations is to be seen in one of the earliest of Pope's poems,[2] in the line, 'Here on green Banks the blushing Violets glow', which is unquestionably an attempt at some-thing more than a statement of fact. It is a picture of colour, which recognizes the physical phenomenon—usually disregarded or un-known—that by the law of complementary colours, the green of the surrounding grass causes the eye to call up its complement, red, by way of equipoise, thus giving the violets a warm purple tint that makes them seem to blush or glow—altogether a piece of precise colour observation astonishing in a young poet at that time.[3]

The conclusion to be drawn from the whole argument is, that if colour suggestion in poetry is to have communicable meaning and effect, the colours must be specifically named or unambiguously in-dicated; and that so far as the poet fails to evoke in the reader a mental vision of his colour, or the reader sees colours not intended by the poet, just so far is his poem at fault—whatever its other merits may be. It all depends of course on what he set out to do. It appears to follow, therefore, that as a poet's colour-words and colour-phrases are the chief—if not the only—means of inducing the reader to react to the colour suggestion of the poem, then the only practicable method of ascertaining the extent to which any particular poet relies on colour to create his effects and express his ideas is to count and tabulate the colour-words he uses. Only thus is it possible to arrive at such illum-

---

[1] *The Deserted Village*, l. 330.   [2] *Spring. The First Pastoral* (1709 text).

[3] Some readers at this point may recall Milton's allusion to 'the glowing violet'; forgetting perhaps that the phrase appears in a 'catalogue' of spring flowers where most of the names are accompanied by some descriptive epithet or other, amongst which black ('jet') and 'white' are the only colours mentioned. As the list is ten lines long and contains eleven flowers, it is obvious that Milton's chief aim was not to suggest colour, whether in harmony or contrast; whereas, in Pope's line, colour was just as obviously his main concern.

Use of Colour-Words from Shakespeare to Pope

DATE	AUTHOR	TITLE OF WORK	LENGTH	AVERAGE USE OF COLOUR-WORDS
1600	Shakespeare	A Midsummer Night's Dream	2,174 lines	1 to every 47 lines
1611	,,	The Tempest	2,058 ,,	1 ,, ,, 114 ,,
1601	Donne	Progress of the Soul	520 ,,	1 ,, ,, 58 ,,
1616	Jonson	To Penshurst	101 ,,	1 ,, ,, 25 ,,
1632	Milton	L'Allegro and Il Penseroso	328 ,,	1 ,, ,, 21 ,,
1651	,,	Paradise Lost, Bk. IV (Description of Eden)	1,010 ,,	1 ,, ,, 40 ,,
1641	Suckling	Ballad on a Wedding	132 ,,	1 ,, ,, 44 ,,
1642	Denham	Cooper's Hill	354 ,,	1 ,, ,, 44 ,,
1646	Crashaw	Hymn to St Teresa	182 ,,	1 ,, ,, 30 ,,
1648	Herrick	A Country Life	144 ,,	1 ,, ,, 48 ,,
1651	Marvell	Appleton House	776 ,,	1 ,, ,, 45 ,,
1656	Cowley	Davideis, Book I	934 ,,	1 ,, ,, 47 ,,
1662	Dryden	Astraea Redux	323 ,,	1 ,, ,, 27 ,,
1697	,,	Virgil's Aeneid, Book IV	1,009 ,,	1 ,, ,, 35 ,,
1700	Hughes	The Court of Neptune	381 ,,	1 ,, ,, 22 ,,
1705	Addison	The Campaign	476 ,,	1 ,, ,, 64 ,,
1708–9	Philips	Pastorals, I–VI	699 ,,	1 ,, ,, 32 ,,
1710	Swift	Description of a City Shower	63 ,,	1 ,, ,, 63 ,,
1713	Tickell	On the Prospect of Peace	465 ,,	1 ,, ,, 59 ,,
1713	Pope	Windsor Forest	434 ,,	1 ,, ,, 7 ,,

inating but wholly unsuspected facts, as that, for example, more than three-quarters of Shakespeare's *Sonnets* contain no colour-word at all[1]; and that Gray's *Elegy*, the most characteristically English poem in our literature, does not name a single colour in all its thirty-two stanzas— if the verb 'to blush' and the epithet 'hoary' (in the sense of age, not colour) may be excepted.

While such statistics cannot pretend to solve all the problems that are raised by the use of colour in poetry, they do at least indicate how little the poets from Shakespeare to Pope's contemporaries had direct recourse to it. A glance at the foregoing table will show the varying infrequency of definite colour-words in well-known poems of the seventeenth century[2] which have been chosen as representative of their authors, and also as being mainly descriptive in character, and comparable in subject and scope, as far as possible, with certain poems by Pope now to be considered.

The first work of Pope's to be published consisted of the three con-tributions he made to the sixth volume of Tonson's *Poetical Miscel-lanies*, 1709, namely, his *Pastorals*, his modernization of Chaucer's *Merchant's Tale*, entitled *January and May*, and his translation of *The Episode of Sarpedon . . . from . . . Homer's Iliads*. From subsequent state-ments made by him, it is clear that the first two were originally written about 1704, and *Sarpedon* about 1707–8. Our present inquiry commences with the *Pastorals*, for it is here, in the four poems under that title, that Pope's unusual love of colour was first revealed. Oddly enough, examples of both the conventional and exceptional use of colour appear in the same miscellany, which opens with Ambrose Philips's six *Pastorals* (four of which had appeared the previous year), and closes with Pope's; for while Philips's use of colour-words is not noticeable in any way, being more or less normal for the period, Pope's *Pastorals* at the other end of the volume show him using colour more than three times as often as the older poet, his colour-words averaging one to every ten lines—a frequency not previously remarked in English poems of similar length.[3]

[1] Out of a total of 154 sonnets, 117 have no colour-words.

[2] The limits of this survey excluded Shakespeare's *Venus and Adonis* (1593), which, with its 1,194 lines averaging one colour-word in every 20 lines, is much richer in colour than the rest of his works. Nevertheless, it only just betters Milton's best, and falls far short of Pope's practice as shown in *Windsor Forest*.

[3] See preceding table. It is obvious, of course, that a short lyric of any century might chance to include several colour-words in a very few lines if addressed, say, to the poet's mistress, all rosy cheeks, golden hair, blue eyes, red lips, and white teeth; but in such cases this localized group of conventional epithets could have little or no relation to the normal colour vision of the author.

Pope's early delight in colour is also deducible from the other two pieces, although they are both translations of poems not particularly suggestive of colour. Thus in the piece from Chaucer, Pope adds six more colour-words to those he found in the original; while in the 'Sarpedon' episode, which in the Greek contains only six colour-words all told, no fewer than sixteen appear in Pope's translation.

But it was in *Windsor Forest* (1713) that Pope's predilection for colour was first allowed to have its way. Since writing the *Pastorals*, he had, as we have seen, been making some efforts to paint. Now, on the completion of *Windsor Forest*, he resolves to take up his residence with Jervas and study the art seriously as a pupil. The preceding December he had written to Caryll about his last touches to the poem:

> I am endeavouring to raise up round about me a painted Scene of Woods, and Forests in Verdure and Beauty, Trees springing, fields flow'ring, Nature laughing . . .[1]

And, considering Pope's attitude of mind at that particular juncture, one feels it was more than a matter of common form that he used the word 'painted' for 'described'. It has often been remarked that Pope in later life grew (or pretended to have grown) a little scornful of poems (his own as well as other people's) in which 'pure Description held the place of Sense'. But even from the first, in *January and May*, he was inclined to scoff at the 'long Descriptions', in French romances and elsewhere, which tired the reader. It is, therefore, not altogether too fanciful, perhaps, to see in the letter to Caryll, quoted above, an intentional distinction, born of his unparalleled use of colour-epithets, between the usual 'description' of other poets and his own 'painted Scene'.

However that may be, it would seem that Pope's conscious references to colour in *Windsor Forest* are carried to a pitch never before attained by any poet, in which the direct colour-words average as many as one to every seven lines—not counting numerous phrases in which this or that colour is suggested though not actually mentioned. With such a continuous naming and placing of hue and tint, Pope's colour-words may reasonably be said to take on something of the function of a painter's pigments. But that is not all. Whenever the earlier poets had occasion to use a colour-word it was as an epithet that merely specified one of the qualities of the object mentioned. It never, or only rarely, had anything to do with other colour-words occurring in the same poem, except in such obvious couples as the 'red and white' of a

[1] Add. 28618, f. 13. Letter dated Dec. 21, 1712.

g

woman's face. Normally, before Pope's experiments, colour-words in a poem were separate and distinct.

Now, in *Windsor Forest*, in addition to its unprecedentedly rich colour content, Pope is definitely beginning to see colours in relation to each other, and deliberately to group or compose them, like a painter, within the frame of his picture. Thus, in the poem, after sketching two or three little landscapes in black and white, he suddenly dips his brushes in colour—

> Here in full Light the russet Plains extend;
> There wrapt in Clouds the blueish Hills ascend:
> Ev'n the wild Heath displays her Purple Dyes,[1] . . .

These three consecutive lines present something new in poetry—at least in English poetry. Pope's acknowledged prototype, *Cooper's Hill*, has nothing comparable, neither has Milton's 'Eden'. Here for the first time (as far as the present writer can ascertain) a natural landscape has been composed and painted in words that flood it with light and colour. The passage itself may not be great poetry, but it marks a great moment in the history of poetry—a successful attempt to extend the poet's vision and domain and thus to create new poetic values. Nevertheless, although the lines display his characteristic skill in versification, they also reveal that he has still something to learn about the handling of colour in poetry. The former is seen, for example, in the cunning antithetical play of the couplet, in which practically every word in the first line finds its contrast in the second (Here—There; in full light—wrapt in clouds; hills—plains; extend—ascend; and with even the colours, russet—blueish, in almost complete opposition); while the latter is shown in his colour-words, which are not only all adjectives, but uniformly placed in the same position before their respective nouns—with the result that, as Jervas might have said, there is no variety in the brush-work.

But although, as we shall see, Pope was to do better, technically speaking, in later poems, this little landscape must be praised for the new revelation of beauty it brought into the world. It reminds one of the work of the early water-colourists in its quiet range of tint and tone, its broad simple washes, and its feeling for atmosphere, not to mention its aerial perspective which suggests distance by colour alone and not by stated miles. 'See, (Pope seems to cry) how the wide sunburnt fields here in the foreground stretch away yonder, and yonder how the rugged moorland glows with the bloom of the heather; while

[1] *Windsor Forest*, ll. 23–5.

there, look! on the far-off horizon, are the hills, barely seen—not blue, with all those clouds about, nor yet insubstantial enough for pale blue; more grey than blue, really, but a colder grey than the surrounding clouds—blueish, to be precise.' Only a painter, potential or actual, would have patience enough to analyse—or would bother himself enough to render—such niceties.

That is not to say, of course, that nature, or natural scenery, had never been written about before. It had, a thousand times and in a variety of ways. It had been personified:

> But looke, the Morne in Russet mantle clad,
> Walks o're the dew of yon high Easterne Hill. [1]

or (as on Cromwell's death) dramatized:

> . . . His last Breath shakes our Isle,
> And Trees uncut fall for his Fun'ral Pile: . . .
> Nature her self took Notice of his Death,
> And, sighing, swell'd the Sea with such a Breath
> That to remotest Shores her Billows roll'd. [2]

or moralized:

> View from hence the glittering Pile above . . .
> Environ'd round with *Natures* shames, and Ills,
> Black Heaths, wild Rocks, bleak Craggs, and naked Hills. [3]

or made proud:

> It was an hill plaste in an open plaine,
> That round about was bordered with a wood
> Of matchlesse hight, that seem'd th'earth to disdaine. [4]

or described in contemporary literary terms:

> *Windsor* her gentle Bosome doth present;
> Where no stupendious Cliffe, no threatning heights
> Accesse deny, no horrid Steepe affrights. [5]

or catalogued piecemeal, leaving nothing out:

> Landskips of rising Mountains, shaggy Woods,
> Green Vallies, smiling Meadows, silver Floods,
> And Plains with lowing Herds enrich'd around,
> The Hills with Flocks, the Flocks with . . . [6]

or treated in a dozen other modes. But never before had English land-

---

[1] *Hamlet*, I, i, 176–7.   [2] Waller: *Upon the late Storm.*
[3] Cotton: *Wonders of the Peak*, 1681, p. 76.   [4] Spenser: *Faerie Queen*, VI, x, 6.
[5] Denham: *Cooper's Hill*, 1642, p. 4.   [6] Hughes: *Court of Neptune*, 1700, p. 4.

scape been seen, and composed, and depicted, so clearly because so
naturally, as in *Windsor Forest*, in which Pope began to show his
capabilities as a colourist. For the remarkable thing about this picture
is that it was neither a happy fluke nor a *tour de force*. The poem
abounds in such felicities; and not only with broad landscapes
broadly painted, but also with more than one 'still life', arranged and
coloured with the precision and rapture of an old Dutch master:

> The bright-ey'd Perch with Fins of *Tyrian* Dye,
> The silver Eel, in shining Volumes roll'd,
> The yellow Carp, in Scales bedrop'd with Gold,
> Swift Trouts, diversify'd with Crimson Stains . . .[1]

Purple—silver—yellow—gold—crimson; what a glorious dazzle of
colour! Pope also, like many a painter since his day, found interest on
several occasions in viewing his landscape upside-down, as in this
poem; and it is noticeable to any one who has painted a river scene
composed wholly, or mostly, of reflections in the water, that the poet
was amused enough to work out the details of his picture in vertical
reverse, and observant enough to perceive that the prevailing colours
(however much their innumerable tints merged or trembled) were
blue and green. Thus he tells how, gazing at the reflections—

> . . . the musing Shepherd spies
> The headlong Mountains and the downward Skies,
> The watry Landskip of the pendant Woods,
> And absent Trees that tremble in the Floods;
> In the clear azure Gleam the Flocks are seen,
> And floating Forests paint the Waves with Green.[2]

But there is one particular picture which has often been praised—
though chiefly for its pathos—on which Pope expended his highest
skill as a poet-painter, touching and retouching it with colour until its
final beauty cries out for ever against the pitiful destruction it depicts.

> See! from the Brake the whirring Pheasant springs,
> And mounts exulting on triumphant Wings;
> Short is his Joy! he feels the fiery Wound,
> Flutters in Blood, and panting beats the Ground.
> Ah! what avail his glossie, varying Dyes,
> His Purple Crest, and Scarlet-circled Eyes,
> The vivid Green his shining Plumes unfold,
> His painted Wings, and Breast that flames with Gold?[3]

---

[1] *Windsor Forest*, ll. 142–5.   [2] *Ibid.*, ll. 211–16.   [3] *Ibid.*, ll. 111–18.

It was when he had arrived at this stage of colour perception, that the young poet seems to have realized his eye had outstripped his technical capacity as a painter. Thus it came about that, with *Windsor Forest* committed to the printers, he resolved to take up painting seriously; and, urged thereto by Caryll, set himself to the arduous yet exciting training of the hand, under Jervas's instruction. But colour does not, after all, exist apart from the object coloured, and the object must have shape, and shape must have light and shade; consequently he soon found his quest broadening to include also some study of form and chiaroscuro.

Thus, as the months passed in the studio, drawing and painting by day and endlessly talking by night, Pope grew wise on many of the aspects and relationships of art. In the last of the essays he wrote that year for Steele's *Guardian*, 'On Gardens',[1] he made great fun of the current vogue for topiary work (the subsequent disuse of which, incidentally, is generally placed to his credit). In the course of this paper he alluded to the gardens of Alcinous, and translated Homer's description of them into English verse. It is not without significance that the essay was written after several months' application to painting; for every colour mentioned in the following excerpt was deliberately placed there by Pope to enhance the picture; none of them being present in the Greek, or even so much as suggested.

> Four Acres was th'allotted Space of Ground,
> Fenc'd with a green Enclosure all around.
> Tall thriving Trees confest the fruitful Mold;
> The red'ning Apple ripens here to Gold,
> Here the blue Figg with luscious Juice o'erflows,
> With deeper Red the full Pomegranate glows,
> The Branch here bends beneath the weighty Pear,
> And verdant Olives flourish round the Year.

The whole passage of thirty-four lines is interesting both as having been written and published so long before the *Odyssey* translation (where it was included in 1725 without change),[2] and as being one of the most richly coloured of all Pope's poems, the incidence of the colour-words rising as high as one to every four lines.

As already mentioned, it was some time towards the end of Pope's sojourn with Jervas that he made one of the most important decisions of his life, and, on March 23, 1714, entered into a contract with Lintot to translate the whole of the *Iliad*. The work was put in hand at once,

[1] *The Guardian*, Sept. 29, 1713; see Pope's *Prose*, I, p. 143.
[2] In Book VII, ll. 142–75.

if with some reluctance. It is therefore not very strange that after his beloved painting had been turned out of doors, we should find it creeping back again through the window, and, with the paint still tacky on yesterday's canvas, reasserting itself with even greater cunning in the numerous descriptive passages of Pope's translation. Thus from the very beginning of the task, and notwithstanding all his reverence for the classics and worship of Homer, it became possible for Pope to take a high hand with his author's text, and (one of the greatest of crimes known to modern scholarship!) attempt to better it.

It seems to have been generally agreed that, although Homer excels in descriptions of the various effects of light and darkness, colour-suggestion is not one of the more striking features of his verse. Indeed, some scholars in the past have not hesitated to assert that his epics are lacking in that particular quality; and others have actually called him colour-blind. It is certain, at least, that much of what at first sight appears to be colour in the *Iliad* is due to the endless repetitions of a set of conventional epithets or attributes, which, however striking originally, have by long and constant use become so worn and familiar as to have lost all colour value; such, for example, as 'the black ships', 'the rosy-fingered Dawn', 'the silver-footed Queen', 'the gray-eyed Goddess', and so on. Hence, one of the problems confronting Pope from the first was how to make these and similar repetitions tolerable to the more sophisticated ear of a later age. This he sought to accomplish in several ways: amongst them by changing the epithets for others which may or may not have a similar colour connotation; or, more simply, by omitting them altogether. On the other hand, he will sometimes alter a colour for reasons not always apparent; thus the original epithet 'golden' will become 'yellow' or vice versa; and 'black grapes' be changed to 'purple grapes'.

More interesting for our present inquiry are the numerous arbitrary additions of colour to his translation, which the painter-poet seems to have thought necessary to render the old Greek story attractive to his contemporaries. A typical example from the 'Gardens of Alcinous' has already been quoted; another instance occurs on one of the occasions when Zeus summoned the gods to council, in the description of which every colour-word used (verdant—rosy—azure —silver) has been inserted by Pope:

> Not one was absent; not a Rural Pow'r
> That haunts the verdant Gloom, or rosy Bow'r;
> Each fair-hair'd Dryad of the shady Wood,
> Each azure Sister of the silver Flood. [1]

[1] *Iliad*, xx, ll. 11–14.

Others may be found in 'The Catalogue of the Ships', where he gratuitously adds notes of colour to towns or districts mentioned in certain groups: '*Thisbè*, fam'd for silver Doves, . . . *Platæa* green, . . . And *Arnè* rich, with purple Harvests'.[1] So frequently do these colour-epithets appear here and elsewhere, that they almost seem to have been added to the page for the sheer pleasure of seeing them there, like the illuminations of a mediaeval manuscript.

At other times Pope will raise some quite ordinary simile or metaphor to the plane of imaginative presentation by an added stroke of interpretative colour. Such, for instance, as Homer's description of the assembled armies: 'In the very likeness of the leaves of the forest or the sands of the sea are they marching along the plain to fight against the city'[2]; which Pope concentrates into a vivid picture with the colour-word 'blacken', thus:

> Thick as Autumnal Leaves, or driving Sand,
> The moving Squadrons blacken all the Strand.[3]

And again, but more rawly and forcefully as befits the height of battle, when, according to Homer: 'Woful Discord was glad at the sight, for she alone of the gods was with them in the war'[4]; which Pope pictures thus:

> Discord alone, of all th'immortal Train,
> Swells the red Horrors of this direful Plain.[5]

It is perhaps also worth remarking of these contributions of Pope's, that—for one reader at least—after encountering several groups of them in the text, they begin to take on a curious extra-literary character; and instead of remaining a chance series of colour-notes, on being thus struck arpeggio-wise in consecutive lines, they assume a collective individuality like a chord of music. For example, there is one evening scene in which Homer has no more colour than is found in the words: 'the river . . . darkness was come down over the earth . . . the old man . . .'[6] Pope starts to paint the scene thus:

> Now Twilight veil'd the glaring Face of Day,
> And clad the dusky Fields in sober Gray;

and in the next couplet carries on the crepuscular harmony by calling the old man 'hoary', and making the river reflect the last gleam of light with the epithet 'silver'—altogether a lovely minor chord:

---

[1] *Iliad*, II, ll. 601–6.
[3] *Iliad*, II, ll. 970–1.
[5] *Iliad*, XI, ll. 101–2.
[2] Lang, Leaf and Myers, p. 41.
[4] Lang, Leaf and Myers, p. 183.
[6] Lang, Leaf and Myers, p. 440.

'twilight—dusky—grey—hoary—silver'.[1] And there are other evenings and mornings with other 'chords'. There is, too, the once famous night-piece, or moonlight sonata, in the key of blue, in which azure is no sooner sounded than the key is changed with a burst of stars to that of gold, from which the colour-music modulates slowly through yellow and silver back to blue again. The actual words are:

> As when the Moon, refulgent Lamp of Night!
> O'er Heav'n's clear Azure sheds her sacred Light, . . .
> Around her Throne the vivid Planets roll,
> And Stars unnumber'd gild the glowing Pole,
> O'er the dark Trees a yellower Verdure shed,
> And tip with Silver ev'ry Mountain's Head: . . .
> The conscious Swains, rejoicing in the Sight,
> Eye the blue Vault, and bless the useful Light.[2]

Similarly, Homer's achromatic description of one group of nereids evoked from Pope the harmony: crystal—sea-green—silver—blue[3]; while another bevy called up: verdant—pearly—black—amber—ivory.[4] Many other 'chords' could be cited, in which, as in all the foregoing, every note of colour, named or suggested, derives from Pope and not from Homer; and yet others in which Homer has struck the key note and Pope has supplied the rest of the harmony. Lastly, with the 'chords' should also be classed the much more numerous, but less striking, 'double-notes' of colour, which appear on nearly every other page of the Homer translations, and for the most part are due to Pope, such as the coupled 'green' and 'silver' in the lines:

> And shaded with a green surrounding grove,
> Where silver alders, in high arches twined, . . .[5]

His favourite double-note was purple and gold; a half-dozen others, as examples, being: green and yellow, snowy and rosy, blue and purple, amber and gold, grey and auburn, gold and black.

The last two volumes of Pope's *Iliad* were published on May 12, 1720[6]; and so much was it in accord with the taste of the period, that, in spite of a few dissidents, the completed work was received with the greatest acclaim. Panegyrics and compliments abounded; but though most of them make poor reading two centuries after the event, there is, amongst the anonymous epigrams on the occasion then circulating in print, at least one worth recalling for the wit of its tribute:

---

[1] *Iliad*, xxiv, ll. 427–8.
[2] *Ibid.*, viii, ll. 687–8, 691–4, 697–8.
[3] *Ibid.*, xviii, ll. 43–50.
[4] *Ibid.*, xviii, ll. 58–67.
[5] *Odyssey*, xvii, ll. 239–40.
[6] *The Post-Boy*, May 10–12, 1720.

To Mr. POPE on his Translation of HOMER

So much, dear *Pope*, thy *English Illiad* charms,
Where Pity melts us, or where Passion warms,
That after-Ages shall with Wonder seek
Who 'twas translated *Homer* into *Greek*. [1]

In all this chorus of praise, however, no one seems to have remarked Pope's colouring of Homer's descriptions; possibly because this idiosyncrasy of his had already become unconsciously familiar, for every one read Pope while comparatively few read Greek. By that time, he had of course published other things besides *Windsor Forest* and *The Iliad*. There was the expanded version of *The Rape of the Lock*, for instance, and *The Temple of Fame*, both of which contain a high rate of colour-words (the former, one to every fourteen lines; the latter, one to thirteen). Was ever a landscape more wonderfully painted in the key of white than in these eight lines of the latter poem?—

So *Zembla*'s Rocks (the beauteous Work of Frost)
Rise white in Air, and glitter o'er the Coast;
Pale Suns, unfelt, at distance roll away,
And on th' impassive Ice the Lightnings play;
Eternal Snows the growing Mass supply,
Till the bright Mountains prop th' incumbent Sky:
As *Atlas* fix'd, each hoary Pile appears,
The gather'd Winter of a thousand Years. [2]

And there were other pieces, some of which first appeared in the collected *Works* of 1717, amongst them being such famous things as *Eloisa to Abelard*, in which there was a deliberate exclusion of bright colour in favour of 'black Melancholy' whose 'gloomy presence saddens all the scene'. On the completion of *The Iliad*, Pope's attention was next engaged by his edition of Shakespeare, and—more to our present purpose—the *Odyssey* translation, which together filled his days for the five following years. But as *The Odyssey* has already been considered in the discussion of his treatment of Homer, nothing remains to add except that the 'books' for which Pope was wholly responsible, were painted with the same brush as *The Iliad*, though perhaps not quite so exuberantly.

Pope's unprecedented use of colour in poetry has likewise escaped notice in the only two articles on the subject known to the present writer—though not known to him until this volume was actually set

[1] *The Grove*, 1721, p. 265.   [2] *Temple of Fame*, 1715, p. 11.

up in type. The first of them[1] contains what purports to be a kind of 'token census' of colour-words in literature, from primitive man down to the end of the nineteenth century, as counted in half a dozen ancient, anonymous writings from four different sources, and in selections from the works of twenty-one authors, mostly poets, from Homer to D'Annunzio—a survey that might have inspired more confidence had not the most important colourist of all been overlooked. Briefly, the main conclusion there reached is that there are 'three things' which colour in literature describes or symbolizes: 'nature, man, imagination'. Thus the predominance in a poet's works of blues and greens, 'the colours of vegetation, the sky, and the sea', means that he is a poet of nature; if the reds occur most frequently his chief interest is in man and woman, 'for these are the colours of blood and love'; if the colours most used are the blacks, whites, and yellows, the first two being 'rare in the world' and the last 'the colour of golden impossibilities', then the poet is 'singing with, as it were, closed eyes, intent on his own inner vision'. As might have been expected from so restricted a census, this hypothesis is too great a simplification of the problem, for besides over-weighting the imaginative and philosophic group, it leaves unanswered many awkward questions. The second paper[2] seeks to demonstrate by similar statistics—and to explain— Spenser's 'waning use of colour and light' in the last three books of *The Faerie Queen*; but the discussion includes statements[3] needing much modification in the light of the foregoing pages. However, as both these earlier investigations were practically limited to listing and counting the colour-words used in certain works rather than to noting what the writers did with them, they are of little help to us, whose present purpose is the recognition, analysis, and demonstration of Pope's methods of combining words of tint and tone and hue so as

[1] By Havelock Ellis, entitled, *The Colour-Sense in Literature*, in the *Contemporary Review*, May 1896.

[2] 'Some Observations on the Changing Style of the *Faerie Queen*', by J. V. Fletcher, in *Studies in Philology*, XXXI, April 1934, pp. 152–9.

[3] For example, Mr Fletcher says that no poet before Keats equalled Spenser's colour vocabulary; whereas even accepting his catholic list comprising 47 words chosen 'for color sensation rather than for color names', Pope is shown in the accompanying table to have used upwards of 70 words with a specific colour meaning. Similarly the highest frequency he claims for Spenser is found in *The Faerie Queen*, Book I, which averages one colour-word to every 25 lines—a frequency which, on a much stricter counting, is bettered by a number of poets before Keats, such as Milton and Hughes (see table, p. 85), Dyer and Blake (see note, p. 80), and Gray, Coleridge, and Wordsworth (see note, p. 100), not to mention Pope.

POPE'S PALETTE

Colour-Words used in his Works

REDS	PURPLES	BLUES	GREENS	YELLOWS	BROWNS	BLACKS	WHITES
Red, etc.	Purple, etc.	Blue, etc.	Sea-green	Yellow, etc.	Brown, etc.	Black, etc.	White, etc.
Vermilion	Tyrian Dye	Blueish	Green	Saffron	Imbrown'd	Sable, etc.	Snowy
Scarlet	Amaranthine	Cerulean	Vivid Green	Amber	Nut-brown	Jet, etc.	Milky, etc.
Cochineal	Violet	Azure	Emerald	Gold, etc.	Russet	Ebon	Chalky
Ruddy, etc.		Sapphire	Beryl	Gild, etc.	Dun	Ink	Foamy
Sanguine			Verdant	Brass, etc.	Brindled	Charcoal	Lily
Blood, etc.					Bronze	Sooty	Silver, etc.
Rust, etc.					Buff	Pitchy	Argent
Ruby					Tawny		Crystal
Rubric					Auburn	GREYS	Ivory
Rosy, etc.					Sunburnt	Grey	Pearly
Roseate					Swarthy	Hoary, etc.	Marble
Blush, etc.					Copper	Lead	
Crimson						Steely	
						Livid	

NOTE: 'etc.' stands for derivatives or inflexions of the word, used by Pope.
Thus 'White, etc.' includes: whiten, whitens, whitening, whited, whiter, and whiteness.

to compose, and present to the inward eye, a poem-picture in colour.

Of what colours, then, did Pope's palette consist?—a question less difficult to ask than to answer. At the outset, it is obvious that a number of his words mean colour at one time, and some other quality at another: he has, for example, 'golden bowl', 'golden hair', and 'golden year'. In such cases, when the names of metals or jewels, or of substances like blood or snow, are used, the word is counted only when the actual colour was intended as its first meaning. 'Black' and 'white' and their synonyms are included as colour-words; as are all words used to specify or indicate a particular colour or a modification of it, but in each instance the colour itself must be unmistakable. Hence, such a phrase as 'the painted vessel' or 'the coloured rainbow', which suggests colour but not a specific colour, is not counted as a colour-word.

The colour-words actually used by Pope are listed on the previous page in eight groups—reds, purples, blues, greens, yellows, browns, blacks (with greys), and whites—to which a note might be added that the words in each group should only rarely be regarded as synonyms for each other. As already shown, Pope had a nice sense of colour, and was normally precise in its nomenclature; though it must be admitted that occasionally he lapsed into using the conventional poetic epithets for blood, which may be 'red', 'crimson', 'purple', 'black', 'sable', or, when shed on the earth, 'blushing'. Unfortunately, the only concordance to Pope's works, E. Abbott's, by omitting all his translated verse, leaves out considerably more than half of his poetry, which seriously diminishes its usefulness. From an independent examination of all his verse, however, it is now possible to record, in addition to Pope's colour vocabulary, that the twelve direct colour-words most often used by him, beginning with the most frequent, are as follows: black, silver, golden, purple, white, green, sable, gold, red, blue, azure, rosy. But, to make an end of statistics,[1] although that is the order in which the specific colour-words were most often used by Pope, it is not the order of his favourite colours. These can only be ascertained when the colour-words are ranged according to their colour-group and not as

[1] As these figures and others in this chapter represent for the most part a single counting, they are claimed only as indicatively correct. The edition used for these statistics was Pope's *Complete Poetical Works*, edited by H. W. Boynton, U.S.A., 1903, omitting however, 'The Bassett Table', but adding 'Sober Advice from Horace' (see Butt, p. 71). The counting also included the poems attributed to Pope in the present volume, and in the forthcoming 'Miscellaneous Poems' of Pope, by N. Ault, which will form Vol. VI of the 'Twickenham Edition'.

particular tints. Consequently, in the list which follows, 'white' includes 'silver', 'snowy', etc.; 'red' takes all the 'blood' reds, as well as the others; 'yellow', itself a small class (not more than twenty-one all told), comprises the numerous 'golds' and 'gilts'; 'black' combines with 'sable'; 'green' with 'verdant', and so forth; each colour being accompanied by a figure indicating the number of times it appears in his poetry. Pope's preferences in colour, then, run as follows: white (251), red (246), yellow (225), black (180), green (108), blue (85), purple (85), grey (32), brown (25).

Now it is a truism of literary history, that with most poets the lyric note in their work becomes less and less vocal as they approach middle-age; its place being taken by graver tones, which may or may not be as felicitous, but are certainly different. It is also a truism that Pope rarely practised the lyric mode after early adolescence. One wonders therefore whether his colour-consciousness was not a 'compensation' on the aesthetic plane for his relative lack of lyric expression, and all this happy splashing and clashing of bright colour a transmutation of the lyric urge, seeing that it, too, became less and less insistent from about his thirty-eighth year onwards. However that may be, it appears that, approximately coincident with Swift's visit to England, in 1726, after a lapse of twelve years, and closely following the resumption of the old intimacy between them, Pope may be said to have been reborn as an original poet. Thenceforward a profound change becomes apparent in the subjects of his verse; and with social satire and moral philosophy filling his mind and requiring of colour nothing but a few sombre tints ('Sense' now taking the place of 'pure Description'), the poet to all intents and purposes shut up his old paint-box.

Although Pope had shown the way, and in spite of the 'cult of the picturesque', the eighteenth-century poets—apart from Dyer and Blake[1]—seem to have used colour-words only a little more freely than their predecessors—if a general familiarity with their work, and a particular examination of a representative half-dozen world-famous poems,[2] can afford any real indication.

[1] See *ante*, p. 80.

[2] Specifically—Thomson's *Winter*, 1727–46 (1,069 ll.), which averages one colour-word to every 38 lines; Johnson's *London*, 1738 (263 ll.), one to every 38 lines; Gray's *Prospect of Eton College*, 1742 (100 ll.), one to every 20 lines; Goldsmith's *The Deserted Village*, 1770 (430 ll.), one to every 47 lines; Coleridge's *The Ancient Mariner*, 1798 (658 ll.), one to every 15 lines; and Wordsworth's *Lines written above Tintern Abbey*, 1798 (160 ll.), one colour-word to every 26 lines.

Pope himself, with his change of message from 1726 onwards, and, consequently, his different requirements of verse as its vehicle, was too true an artist not to know when colour was wanted, and when it would be 'such a sin to paint'. This can be most easily demonstrated by a momentary return to statistics, which reveal in the later poems what appears to be an almost complete reversal of his former attitude to colour. In brief, the first edition of *The Dunciad*, 1728, has one colour-word to every thirty lines of text; the *Moral Essays*, which began to be published in 1731, an average of one to every fifty-five; the *Satires*, beginning in 1733, one to every fifty lines; and the *Essay on Man*, 1733-4, which contains only seventeen colour-words in all its thirteen hundred lines, averages as few as one to every seventy-six lines—easily the least 'coloured' of Pope's longer poems.

Nevertheless, in spite of the growing influence of the moral philosopher in him, there is every reason for thinking that Pope retained his feeling for colour throughout the latter half of his life, though he expressed it differently. Thus, as the years passed, helped by his early training of hand and eye, and the intense interest in the arts that developed with it, he became—even amongst connoisseurs—the acknowledged arbiter of 'Taste', in architecture and landscape-gardening no less than in art and literature; for Pope always had possessed that 'something previous ev'n to Taste', which, he said, was so needful—'Good Sense'.

Other evidence exists to show that his love of colour survived the years. Thus, only a few months before his death, when at work on the closing book of that terrible masterpiece, *The Dunciad*, we can watch him pause a moment now and then to comfort his heart with the loveliness of colour, with 'purple . . . wines' and 'lilly-silver'd vales', with 'ebon wand' and 'emerald', and, in the gathering gloom of despair, see him cast a last glance at the 'gilded clouds' and 'varying rainbows' ere they too are blotted out, and all things end in 'universal darkness'—the negation not only of light but of colour also.

CHAPTER VI

POPE AND ADDISON

I. HOSTILITIES

Quod Te Roma legit, Rumpitur Invidia!

If meaner Gildon draws his venal Quill,
I wish the Man a Dinner, And stand still:
If Dennis rails and raves in furious Pet,
I'll answer Dennis when he's out of Debt.
'Tis Hunger and not Malice makes them Print;   5
And who'd wage War with Bedlam or the Mint?
But were there One whom better Stars conspire
To form a Bard, and raise his Genius higher;
Blest with each Talent, and each Art to please,
And Born to Write, Converse and live at Ease;   10
Should such a One, too fond to Reign Alone,
Bear like the Turk, no Brother on the Throne:
View him with Jealous, yet with Scornful Eyes,
And Hate for Arts, which caus'd himself to Rise;
Damn with faint Praise, Assent with Civil Leer,   15
And without Sneering, teach the Rest to Sneer;
Willing to wound, but yet afraid to Strike,
Just hint a Fault, and Hesitate Dislike;
Alike reserv'd to Censure, or Commend,
A timerous Foe, and a suspicious Friend;   20
Fearing e'en Fools; by Flatterers besieg'd,
And so obliging, that he ne'er oblig'd:
Who when two wits on Rival Themes contest
Approves of Both, yet likes the worst the best;
Like Cato, gives his little Senate Laws,   25
And sits attentive to his own Applause;
While Wits and Templars every Sentence raise,
And Wonder with a Foolish face of Praise:
Who but must Grieve, if such a One there Be,
Who would not Weep, if Addison were He?   30
(Welbeck: Harley Papers)

Great must have been the provocation, one would have thought, or scarcely human the malignity, that prompted the writing of these searing lines of Pope's. But for two hundred years little attention was paid to any possible provocation, with the result that a legend of Pope's treachery to his friends, as exemplified chiefly by these verses, was handed down from generation to generation of readers. It has likewise been too frequently forgotten that Pope spoke just as publicly with quite another voice in his *Epistle to Mr. Addison, Occasioned by his Dialogues on Medals*, where, after describing the antics of mere anti-quarians, he proceeds thus:

> . . . Theirs is the Vanity, the Learning thine:
> Touch'd by thy hand, again *Rome*'s glories shine;
> Her Gods, and god-like Heroes rise to view,
> And all her faded garlands bloom a-new.
> Nor blush, these studies thy regard engage;
> These pleas'd the Fathers of poetic rage;
> The verse and sculpture bore an equal part,
> And Art reflected images to Art.
>   Oh when shall *Britain*, conscious of her claim,
> Stand emulous of *Greek* and *Roman* fame?
> In living medals see her wars enroll'd,
> And vanquish'd realms supply recording gold?
> Here, rising bold, the Patriot's honest face;
> There Warriors frowning in historic brass?
> Then future ages with delight shall see
> How *Plato*'s, *Bacon*'s, *Newton*'s looks agree;
> Or in fair series laurell'd Bards be shown,
> A *Virgil* there, and here an *Addison*.

With the publication of these two pieces, Pope himself would seem to have raised, and challenged, the question: Which is the more blame-worthy, to have written both—or to have inspired both? This ques-tion, as hinted above, has generally been answered in one way. But although present opinion, deriving in great measure from the two recent biographies of the poet previously mentioned,[1] leans towards another answer, the problem is still far from being settled. One more endeavour to trace the history of what are generally known as the 'Atticus' lines, and their relation to the *Epistle to Addison*, may therefore be attempted; especially as the familiar facts are to be re-examined in the light of much new evidence.

---

[1] Namely by Edith Sitwell, 1930; and G. Sherburn, 1934.

As early as 1709, Pope published a translation of parts of the twelfth and sixteenth books of the *Iliad*.[1] But this translation had been handed about in manuscript still earlier, and had been seen by—amongst others—his old friend, Sir William Trumbull, who wrote enthusiastically on April 9, 1708, urging him, but without success, to translate the whole work. Some five years later, during which time he had turned four other fragments of Homer (three of them from the *Odyssey*) into English verse, Addison succeeded where Trumbull had failed. This generally neglected truth about the beginnings of Pope's great undertaking was explicitly and unmistakably told, once and for all, in its 'Preface' in 1715, without a breath of correction or denial from any one concerned. The statement runs:

> Mr. *Addison* was the first whose Advice determin'd me to undertake this Task, who was pleas'd to write to me upon that Occasion in such Terms as I cannot repeat without Vanity.

Pope also later printed two letters—whose authenticity has not been disproved—written by Addison soon after the project had been decided upon, showing the older man's warm interest in it and conveying his good wishes for its success.[2] As these are dated respectively October 26 and November 2, 1713, and as Bishop Kennett noted in his diary about this time (Dr Johnson dates the entry, November 2) that Swift was busily enlisting subscribers for 'Mr. Pope (a papist) who had begun a translation of Homer into English verse . . . [which] the author shall not begin to print till I have a thousand guineas for him'[3]; it is also certain that the long and arduous undertaking was well started before the close of 1713. News of the project spread; and before long a kind of opposition party of Whig complexion began slowly to take shape. Within a fortnight of the signing of the agreement between Pope and Bernard Lintot, the bookseller, on March 23, 1714, the first attack in print on Pope and the *Iliad* project appeared in an anonymous 'play' entitled, *A New Rehearsal, or Bays the Younger*. This was a slashing criticism, cast in dialogue form, of the works of Rowe and Pope, by Charles Gildon, a minor author, dramatist, and compiler of miscellanies, who, besides damning *The Rape of the Lock*, then recently published, made an apparently unprovoked attack on its author, in which his claim to a knowledge of Greek and ability to translate Homer were unmercifully ridiculed. Gildon's attack was published on April 6, 1714,[4] and was followed within four days by

[1] *Poetical Miscellanies: The Sixth Part*, 1709, pp. 301–23.
[2] Letters, 4to, 1737, pp. 99 f.   [3] Ball, II, pp. 414–15.
[4] According to *The Evening Post*.

h

another, this time an anonymous epigram much advertised in the newspapers by its title, *Advice to Mr. Pope, On his intended Translation of Homer's Iliads*[1]; and in this Pope is taunted with making more money out of the *Iliad* than ever Homer did, with the very successful subscription of the translation then going forward: 'First take the gold—then charm the list'ning Ear.' Next month saw the republication of his *Proposals for a Translation of Homer's Ilias*, this time accompanied by 'a List of those who have already Subscrib'd'[2]; and on June 8, 1714, Gay writes to Swift that 'Book I' is already completed.[3] On August 10, advertisements[4] of 'the 5th Edition' of Oldmixon's miscellany again prominently name the *Advice to Mr. Pope on his intended Translation of Homer* among the principal attractions of the book.

These attacks, however, were but affairs of outposts, preliminaries to the main battle which seems to have begun when the newspapers joined in at the end of the year. On December 10, 1714, for example, Philip Horneck published in *The High-German Doctor* a long bantering account of a fictitious interview with Lintot, in which, after the bookseller carefully explains the delay in publishing *The Iliad* ('We have been Nine Months Debating about the first Word of the Book, whether we should express Μηνιν by the English Word *Rage*, or *Wrath*'), the dialogue proceeds to ridicule the whole undertaking, its subscribers as well as its publisher, its poet's religion as well as his lack of classical scholarship. It may have been this attack which induced Pope to announce on December 25,[5] and during the next two weeks, that the translation of the first four books of the *Iliad*, which was to have been published 'by the Beginning of May next . . . shall be deliver'd two Months sooner than the Time promis'd'. And it is this announcement, doubtless, that explains why so many of Pope's enemies chose to concentrate their activities on this particular month of March, 1715; for besides the well-known major attacks by the pseudonymous 'Mr. Preston'[6] (March 5), by Burnet and Duckett[7] (March 7), and by the unknown Author of *A Complete Key to . . . The What D'ye Call It* (April 2 or earlier), there were Burnet's further

---

[1] Published in *Poems and Translations. By Several Hands*. (Ed. J. Oldmixon), 1714. The piece was in fact written by John Hughes, but it is probable that Pope did not know who wrote it until many years later.

[2] Advertised in *The Evening Post*, from April 3 to April 10, 1714.

[3] Ball, ii, p. 145.　　　[4] In *The Post Boy*.　　　[5] In *The Evening Post*.

[6] In an imitation of Pope's recently published 'Temple of Fame', called *Aesop at the Bear Garden*, 1715.

[7] In *Homerides . . . By Sir Iliad Doggrell*, 1715.

attack in *The Grumbler* (March 10, or 17)[1] and another instalment
from Horneck's pen[2] (March 15). Indeed, these last two gentlemen
were peculiarly persistent, and returned to the attack from time to
time, Horneck[3] once again on April 23 and Burnet[4] on May 6, not to
mention some slighter things; in addition to which there should also
be noted a reissue of Gildon's *New Rehearsal*, probably on May 14 (as
will be shown later), and a 'Second Edition' of *Homerides* on May 30.
Then on June 4,[5] Pope having postponed publication in March to
circumvent his enemies, the first volume of *The Iliad*, containing the
first four 'Books', at last appeared to a waiting world.

Unfortunately that is not the whole story. Four days later a rival
translation, entitled *The first book of Homer's Iliad*, was published with
Addison's approbation and praise.

How much of this persecution of Pope was due to Addison's instigation and active participation will probably never be known. Several of
his friends have testified to the fact that he did not like the young poet.
For instance, Burnet wrote to his friend Duckett the following year
(June 1, 1716): 'I have [often] seen Addison caressing Pope, whom at
the same Time he hates worse than Belzeebub and by whom he has
been more than once lampooned.'[6] Also it was no secret that most of
Pope's enemies at this time were Addison's friends or partisans—
fellow-frequenters of that haunt of the Whigs, Button's coffee-house.
Indeed there is indubitable proof that Addison was implicated to
some extent both in the general attempt to discredit Pope and his
great translation (the very work which, as already shown, he himself
had persuaded Pope to undertake), and also in the rival publication
put forward in Tickell's name. For, as regards the first, besides much
masterly use of a pre-Nelsonian blind eye to the manifest activities of
his friends, there are Burnet's letters[7] still surviving to prove that
Addison had a hand in the revision of *Homerides* for the press; and, as
regards the second, there is his own admission to Pope, that he had had
Tickell's translation in his hands to 'look over'.[8] It should also be
noted that Thomas Tickell, who was then probably Addison's most

---

[1] According to subsequent references; but these two numbers have not yet been
located.

[2] In *The High-German Doctor*. [3] *Ibid.*

[4] In *The Grumbler*. [5] See *The Evening Post*.

[6] In Add. 36772. Printed by D. Nichol Smith in *Letters of Thomas Burnet to George
Duckett, 1712–1722* (Roxburghe Club), p. 99. No such lampoon is known to Pope
scholars, except the 'Atticus' lines, then unprinted.

[7] *Ibid.*, p. 81. [8] Spence, p. 147.

intimate friend, and, later, his literary executor, was thought by many of Pope's contemporaries—not all of them his friends—to be little more than Addison's stalking-horse in this affair; and from Pope's remarks it is apparent that he too inclined to the same opinion from time to time. And he was so far justified, that, whether the idea of a competitive translation originated with Addison, as some said,[1] or with a suggestion of the rival bookseller, Tonson, as others opine,[2] Addison was, to all intents and purposes, its literary sponsor. Nevertheless, it was Tickell who signed the agreement with Tonson (the publisher of several of his earlier works) to translate the whole *Iliad*; for the document has recently been discovered[3] bearing his signature, and the date, May 31, 1714, which is two months later than the date of Pope's agreement with Lintot. It is likewise certain that Pope's translation was well on its way before that of his rival, which is said to have been written at Oxford in the summer of 1714.[4] And then, when Tickell's 'Book I' was finished, instead of proceeding as usual to publication without reference to Pope's undertaking, as might have been expected of an innocent poem, the interested parties seem to have held it for months ready for immediate issue, as though playing a grim kind of cat and mouse game with Pope's volume.

The attacks on Pope did not entirely cease with the publication of the rival translations, even though Tickell had announced that he would not proceed with his version. Addison—with the Buttonian crowd as chorus—appears to have been more outspoken than ever in his praise of Tickell's translation and his preference of it to Pope's, and he sent copies of it to his friends signifying his approval.[5] Lintot, commenting on 'Mr Tickles Book' in a letter to Pope,[6] dated June 10, 1715, reports that 'the malice & juggle at Buttons' is, next to politics, the talk of the town.' And on July 8, 1715, Gay wrote to Pope, who was then in the country hard at work on the next volume of *The Iliad*:

> I have just set down Sir *Samuel Garth* at the Opera. He bid me tell you, that every body is pleas'd with your Translation, but a few at *Button*'s; and that Sir *Richard Steele* told him, that Mr. *Addison* said *Tickel*'s translation was the best that ever was in any language . . . I am inform'd that at *Button*'s your character is made very free with as to morals, &c. and Mr. *A[ddison]* says, that your translation and

---

[1] See excerpt from *Mist's Weekly Journal* below, p. 111.
[2] See *Thomas Tickell and the Eighteenth Century Poets*, R. E. Tickell, p. 36.
[3] *Ibid.*, p. 39.   [4] *Ibid.*, p. 42.
[5] See Burnet, p. 92.   [6] Add. 4807, f. 96 v.

Tickel's are both very well done, but that the latter has more of *Homer*.[1]

Such, then, is a summary of the state of affairs to which Pope alludes in the famous satire on Addison above quoted. But in addition to all these specific and verifiable actions and reactions, there are the less demonstrable but not less real effects of the mutual misunderstanding which persistently dogged the association of the two men, and which can only be explained by the fundamental incompatibility of their temperaments. The grave reserve, conscious 'correctness', and slightly patronizing manner of the older man and the brilliance, irritability, and high-spirited indiscretions of the younger—almost every characteristic facet of either personality must have been an all too frequent cause of offence to the other. What if the beginning of all the trouble between them—the incident which settled their attitude to each other for ever—had no more importance than a boyish quip at a pretence of modesty by a grown man of the world?

Addison's poem, *A Letter from Italy*, was addressed to Lord Halifax in 1701; but it was not published till 1704, in Tonson's *Poetical Miscellanies: The Fifth Part*, where it was given pride of place as the opening poem, and where, about the same time or a little later, it was seen by young Pope. The boy, who was then only 'sixteen or seventeen years of age', and still unknown to Addison, was himself busy on a translation (as he called it) of Chaucer's *Merchant's Tale*, entitled *January and May*; and, on reading Addison's poem, was apparently struck by the difference between the slightly grandiose air of the poet, especially in the lengthy descriptive passages, and the verbal humility of his closing lines. For although admittedly 'fired with the name' of Nassau the poet rather ingloriously ends:

> I bridle in my struggling Muse with Pain,
> That longs to launch into a bolder strain.[2]
>   But I've already troubled you too long,
> Nor dare attempt a more advent'rous Song.
> My humble Verse demands a softer Theme,
> A painted Meadow or a purling Stream,

---

[1] *Correspondence*, I, 1735 (ii), p. 102.

[2] Not to interrupt the argument, the reader might like to be reminded in a footnote of Dr. Johnson's remarks on this couplet of Addison's:—'To *bridle* a *goddess* is no very delicate idea; but why must she be *bridled*? because she *longs to launch*; an act which was never hindered by a *bridle*: and whither will she *launch*? into a *nobler strain*. She is in the first line a *horse*, in the second a *boat*, and the care of the poet is to keep his *horse* or his *boat* from *singing*'. Johnson, II, p. 406.

> Unfit for Heroes; whom Immortal Lays,
> And lines like *Virgil*'s, or like yours shou'd praise.

And the boy, who, it appears, was then writing about (but not 'describing') January's 'spacious garden', demurely slips in a couplet, the real significance of which seems hitherto to have been overlooked, because he later [1] changed the epithet in his allusion to Addison, from 'the *boldest* Bard' to 'the *gentlest* Bard', with the consequence that his little jest at the *diminuendo* from Addison's 'bolder Strain' to his 'softer Theme' disappeared. What Pope originally wrote about January's garden, and what Addison originally read, was—

> . . . this charming Place—
> A Place to tire the rambling Wits of *France*
> In long Descriptions, and exceed *Romance*;
> Enough to shame the boldest Bard that sings
> Of painted Meadows, and of purling Springs.

Pope's *January and May* was published (with the *Pastorals* and an *Episode* from the *Iliad*, together making his first appearance in print) in *Poetical Miscellanies: The Sixth Part*, 1709, some three weeks before he was twenty-one. Was it, one wonders, this little sparkle of youthful high spirits which the lofty-minded Addison remembered, when, two and a half years later, he sat down to review *An Essay on Criticism* in *The Spectator* for December 20, 1711? For Addison's article, which is supposed to have first made them acquainted, was afterwards remembered by the young poet not so much for the praise that concluded it (which could not but please him), as for the snub with which it began. The review opens with these words: 'There is nothing which more denotes a great Mind, than the Abhorrence of Envy and Detraction'; and, after expatiating on that theme at some length, continues as follows:

> In our own Country a Man seldom sets up for a Poet, without attacking the Reputation of all his Brothers in the Art . . . But how much more noble is the Fame that is built on Candour and Ingenuity, according to those beautiful Lines of Sir *John* Denham, in his Poem on *Fletcher*'s Works!

> > But whither am I stray'd? I need not raise
> > Trophies to thee from other Mens Dispraise:
> > Nor is thy Fame on lesser Ruins built,
> > Nor needs thy juster Title the foul Guilt
> > Of Eastern Kings, who, to secure their Reign,
> > Must have their Brothers, Sons, and Kindred slain.

---

[1] In *The Works*, 1717.

I am sorry to find that an Author, who is very justly esteemed among the best Judges, has admitted some Stroaks of this Nature into a very fine Poem. . .

The title of the poem is thereupon untactfully misquoted as *The Art of Criticism*. Pope, as it happened, did not see this number of *The Spectator* until December 29; and thinking his friend Steele was the author, he wrote to him the next day[1] and thanked him for his praise of the poem, and also for his 'candour and frankness' in pointing out 'the error I have been guilty of in speaking too freely of my brother moderns'. Pope then went on to say that if a second edition should be called for, he would 'strike out all such strokes which you shall be so kind as to point out to me'. (It is noticeable that he does not admit knowledge of the 'errors'.) Steele replied on January 20, 1712, that the paper was written, not by himself, but 'by one wth whome I will make you acquainted'[2];—that is, by Addison; and in that way, it seems, Pope and Addison at last met. The acquaintance, however, did not really prosper; and it soon becomes apparent that the criticism, which the touchy young poet was ready (when convinced) to accept from a friend who obviously wished him well, he was not prepared to take from a stranger whose attitude to him was so markedly different from Steele's, and who—Pope soon came to believe—had a personal reason for his censure. Thus it was that, before the year was out, Pope had written some indignant lines directly rebutting Addison's charge, and even made them the 'curtain' of his next major work, *The Temple of Fame*. This reply to Addison seems also to have escaped comment hitherto, probably because—although the poem had been written and sent to Steele, some time before November 12, 1712[3]—its publication was for various reasons delayed until February 1, 1715,[4] so that *The Rape of the Lock*, *Windsor Forest*, and the *Ode for Musick* had appeared in the meantime and obscured the connection. No more than ten lines of the close of *The Temple of Fame* can be given here, in which it will be noticed that while they are a general repudiation of Addison's strictures, in the third couplet in particular Pope makes an effective use of the third line of the six his critic had reprovingly quoted from Denham.

> Nor Fame I slight, nor for her Favours call;
> She comes unlook'd for, if she comes at all:
> But if the Purchase costs so dear a Price,
> As soothing Folly, or exalting Vice . . .

[1] EC, VI, p. 388.   [2] Add. 4807, f. 159 v.
[3] *Correspondence* I, 1735 (ii), p. 33.   [4] Griffith, I, i, p. 39.

> Or if no Basis bear my rising Name,
> But the fall'n Ruins of Another's Fame:
> Then teach me, Heaven! to scorn the guilty Bays;
> Drive from my Breast that wretched Lust of Praise;
> Unblemish'd let me live, or die unknown,
> Oh grant an honest Fame, or grant me none!

Only a denial of the charge as yet, while the man who made it is allowed to go scot free. Counter-attack did not come till later, when to injury (not very serious, perhaps, except for its after effects on a sensitive young poet) Addison had added something very like treachery in his relations with Pope about the *Iliad*, and had, moreover, given Pope greater cause to suspect *him* of jealousy, than could ever have been found in the *Essay on Criticism* to suspect Pope. Then it was, and only then, that Pope was exasperated enough to retort Addison's censure upon Addison himself in the satire with which this chapter opens, where, to add to its sting, he subtly paraphrased the root idea of the verses Addison had quoted at him, in a couplet of franker statement, presently to be noted. Furthermore, their mutual misunderstanding (if misunderstanding by this time has not become too mild a term) had led Pope to suspect that sinister motives lay behind Addison's attempt to dissuade him from making any alterations in the first version of *The Rape of the Lock*—alterations which, when once carried out, made the poem the supreme masterpiece of its kind. Neither can Addison be said—nor can Pope have thought him—to have behaved quite straightforwardly in the matter of Pope's championship of *Cato*[1] against Dennis's criticisms; and there were other things of the kind, of which space forbids mention. And it is against this background of strained relations, mutual friction, and sense of injury, that the ancient story of Pope's alleged treachery must once again be discussed.

It has always been recognized that the gravamen of the charge rests in the main on the date of the undated satire. Was it written and shown to Addison in his lifetime, as man to man and poet to poet? or was it an attack on a dead friend no longer able to defend himself?

Now one of the most obvious truths about Pope's literary habits is that, for various reasons—æsthetic, political, personal, or what not—he frequently delayed the publication of his pieces, oftentimes for many years, so that with the majority of them the date of printing is no guide at all to the date of composition. That fact is indisputable.

---

[1] In writing and publishing *The Narrative of Dr. Robert Norris*, 1713; see Pope's *Prose*, I, pp. xxviii ff.

Nevertheless, as Addison died on June 17, 1719, and as neither the satire nor the epistle was published during his life, Pope's enemies (amongst whom may strangely be numbered some of his editors) have often asserted that the satire, if not the epistle also, was written after its subject's death. No material evidence supports their contention. All they could point to were the supposed dates of publication, and a late anonymous attack on Pope (one of the first repercussions of *The Dunciad*) in *Mist's Weekly Journal* of June 8, 1728. In the course of this amazing and lengthy diatribe, which purports to sketch Pope's literary life and works, and accuses him of various misdemeanours while so doing, the author, who signs himself 'W. A.', makes the absurd statement that Pope's rise 'from an humble Obscurity', his fame, friends, and social success, not omitting his acquaintance with 'the whole Body of our Nobility', were all owing to Addison who had 'strongly supported' him from the first. The writer then goes on to relate how Addison, not approving of Pope's translation of the *Iliad*, 'employ'd a younger Muse[1] in an Undertaking of this Kind, which he supervis'd himself,' and which 'the World allow'd' was in consequence every way better than Pope's. He says also, that, notwithstanding Pope's natural chagrin at this 'Judgment of Mankind', he hid his real feelings, and sought to retain Addison's friendship. The narrative naïvely continues thus:

> He therefore continued his Assiduity to his generous Benefactor, making . . . Poems to his Fame, as a certain *Dissertation upon Medals* can testify. . . . But no sooner was his Body lifeless, . . . but the Author, whose Works are now in Question, reviving his Resentments at the Expence of all Gratitude and Decency, libelled the Memory of his departed Friend, traduced him in a sharp Invective, and what was still more heinous, he made the Scandal publick.

That, in effect, is the tale which continued for so long to hold the general ear, and those its foundations. And after it had been judicially confirmed in 1778 by the learned Blackstone—who summarized the case on the facts as then known, and adjudicated in favour of Addison[2] —the legend became gospel. Unfortunately, Pope's own account of the genesis of the satire—as recorded by Spence—had, until recently, contained two or three apparently irreconcilable statements, and so failed to command belief. Now, however, thanks partly to the dis-

[1] Meaning Thomas Tickell, though he was actually two years older than Pope, having been born in 1686; Pope in 1688.

[2] *Biographia Britannica*, I, 2nd Edn, 1778, pp. 56-8.

covery of Spence's original punctuation,[1] and partly to some other new evidence, those impossibilities are reduced to mere difficulties.

The opening words of Pope's account, as printed in the *Anecdotes*, ran: 'Gildon wrote a thing about Wycherley, in which he had abused . . .' Now, with those first six words corrected according to the manuscript,[2] the relevant passage reads:

> Gildon wrote a thing (about Wycherley?) in which he had abused both me and my relations very grossly. Lord Warwick[3] himself told me, one day, . . . that Addison had encouraged Gildon to publish those scandals, and had given him ten guineas after they were published. The next day, while I was heated with what I had heard, I wrote a letter to Mr. Addison, to let him know, that I was not unacquainted with this behaviour of his; that if I was to speak severely of him in return for it, . . . it should be something in the following manner. I then subjoined the first sketch of what has since been called my satire on Addison. He used me very civilly ever after; and never did me any injustice, that I know of, from that time to his death, which was about three years after.[4]

Happily, Pope's account can be substantiated by the independent testimony of several of his contemporaries (inimical as well as friendly) at least as regards the existence of the poem before Addison's death. Pope's friend, Lord Oxford, wrote in his copy of the *Epistle to Arbuthnot*, 1734, now in the Bodleian, a note to line 209, saying: 'The Assertion of some anonymous authors that Mr. P. writ this Character after the Gentlemans death, was utterly untrue; it having been sent him several years before, and then shown to Mr Secretary Craggs, & y⁰ present Earl of Burlington . . .' Similarly, a bitter enemy, Lady Mary Wortley Montagu (for it was long after the famous quarrel), speaking to Spence of these lines, said emphatically, 'Yes, that satire *was* written in Addison's life time'.[5] And, on another occasion, Dr. Trapp, who apparently was no more than an acquaintance of Pope's, though a close friend of Tickell's at Oxford, informed Spence, with much surprise that there should be any doubt about it, that 'many people, and he himself for one, had seen it in Addison's life-time.'[6] To these witnesses should be added the corroborative testimony of Bishop Warburton,[7] and—if it is not the same voice—Pope's bio-

---

[1] See 'Pope, Addison, and the "Atticus" Lines', by A. E. Case, in *Modern Philology*, November 1935, pp. 187 ff.

[2] Egerton, 1960.   [3] Addison's prospective step-son.   [4] Spence, pp. 148–9.
[5] *Ibid.*, p. 237.   [6] *Ibid.*, p. 149.   [7] Warburton, IV, pp. 26 ff.

grapher, Ruffhead[1]; besides which there is also Pope's letter to Craggs of July 15, 1715,[2] not yet proved apocryphal, which contains a prose counterpart—echo or anticipation—of portions of the poem. Lastly, but not least important, is the inference to be drawn from Addison's warning to Lady Mary (either on her return to England not long before his death, or in the two or three months before her departure on August 1, 1716), when, speaking of Pope, he said: 'Leave him as soon as you can, he will certainly play you some devilish trick else: he has an appetite to satire'.[3] As no sustained piece of satire by Pope had then been published—except the early lines, *To the Author of Successio*, in 1712, and, perhaps one should add, the anonymous prose *Narrative of Dr. Robert Norris*, in 1713—his 'appetite to satire' could not have been very evident at that time; and Addison seems to have spoken too feelingly not to have spoken from personal experience. Not even Addison, who (as shown above) had condoned —and, in one instance, revised—his friends' attacks on Pope, could have pumped up such vicarious indignation, either about a boy's ridicule of Settle in the former piece, written when Pope was only fourteen years old; or about the genuine fun with which Pope overwhelmed Dennis and his criticisms of Addison's own play, *Cato*, in the latter.

With all this evidence available—if not all made use of—to rebut the charge of treachery against Pope, and establish both the early date and Addison's knowledge of the satire, too much importance has recently been attached to a page in Pope's autograph among the Homer MSS., containing some half-dozen sketches of couplets.[4] For this page, long known to students, and printed as early as 1776,[5] is not 'the "Atticus" portrait in early embryo', as has been stated,[6] any more than it is the origin of the *Epilogue to the Satires, Dialogue II*, which likewise enshrines one of the couplets; or the first sketch of an *Epigram* on Moore-Smythe (then about thirteen years old!), which makes use of another; or a projected revision of the *Essay on Criticism*, because yet another couplet is a re-writing of two lines in that poem. The truth is, the page is nothing but a number of attempts at more or less disconnected couplets, all of them on the subject of wit, and all except one mentioning it. Thus while at least three of the couplets were used in other poems of Pope's, only one was, after some remodelling, inserted in the satire. This couplet, as Pope first sketched it here, ran as follows:

[1] Ruffhead, pp. 192 ff.
[2] *Letters*, 4to, 1737, pp. 117 f.
[3] Spence, p. 237.
[4] Add. 4807, f. 118 v.
[5] *Additions*, I, p. 56.
[6] Sherburn, p. 146.

> But our Great Turks in wit must reign alone
> & ill can bear a Brother on yᵉ Throne.

But the idea in this version of the couplet—sole point of contact with the 'Atticus' portrait though it is—had at that time already acquired something of a history in Pope's hands, so that 'embryo' seems hardly the *mot juste* for it; for, as we have seen,[1] it had been etched on Pope's memory by Addison's acid use of Denham's lines to censure him in 1711. It also reappears in Pope's translation from Statius (which, though dated 1703, was not published until May 20, 1712), where, speaking of the two brothers who shared a throne by alternate occupation, he tells how they were each consumed with envy of the other,

> And impotent Desire to reign alone,
> That scorns the dull reversion of a throne.   (ll. 180–1)

Moreover, the same idea yet once again reappears in his translation of the first book of the *Iliad* (completed on or before June 8, 1714)[2] in the line:

> What King can bear a rival in his sway?   (l. 383)

So that, even if the statement, 'the writing on this leaf must date about July 1715',[3] had been proved to be true—which it probably is—its alleged 'significance with regard to the origin of the portrait'[4] would still be of no importance; because all that would have been established thereby, would be, not that Pope began to write the character of Atticus at that date, but only that he was continuing earlier attempts to shape the same idea into a more telling couplet than that which Addison had quoted against him, apparently for future use against some unspecified person.

Similarly, difficulties are raised by the most recent attempts to identify the particular attack by Gildon, to which Pope referred in his conversation with Spence, and is supposed to refer in the much-discussed epithet 'venal' of the first line of the satire: 'If meaner Gildon draws his venal Quill'. This attack has been thought to be that delivered in Gildon's anonymous *Memoirs of . . . Wycherley*, 1718,[5] and much ingenuity was exercised to reconcile it with Pope's statement—but in vain. A later suggestion,[6] however, is that the abuse, which Addison paid Gildon to print, was the anonymous libel, entitled, *A True Character of Mr Pope and his Writings*, 1716—a suggestion that raises more problems than it solves. For not only did Pope at different

---

[1] See *ante*, pp. 108–9.   [2] See *ante*, p. 104.   [3] Sherburn, p. 146.
[4] G. Sherburn in *Philological Quarterly*, xxi, ii, pp. 215 f.
[5] Sherburn, pp. 147 f.   [6] Case, pp. 191 ff.

times think that different people wrote it (for example, he gives it to
Dennis in an autograph note in his own copy of *A True Character*, now
in the British Museum[1]; to Gildon in one place in *The Dunciad*,[2] and to
Dennis and Gildon jointly in another[3]); but Professor Sherburn and
Professor Case favour each a different candidate for its authorship,
and—as Pope himself asked—'Who shall decide when Doctors dis-
agree?' The date of the pamphlet, *A True Character*, also raises insuper-
able obstacles; because, as it was published on May 31, 1716,[4] it
would follow that Pope's warning letter to Addison, and the 'subjoined' poem also, must have been written and sent *after* that date.
But so late a date for the letter squares neither with Pope's statement
nor the known facts. Addison had already begun to make amends to
Pope by praising his *Iliad* in *The Freeholder* as early as May 7, 1716; and
this change of face and policy had become a matter of gossip amongst
his 'little Senate' before the end of May; for on June 1, Burnet wrote
to tell his country friend, Duckett, that Addison and his 'gang' had
'dropt their resentment' against Pope.[5] It is incredible that Addison,
arbiter of morals and pattern of propriety for so long, should have
extended a conciliatory hand to Pope on May 7, and then later in the
self-same month paid Gildon (if the pamphlet is his) to publish that
furious abuse of him; and quite as unlikely that Pope should have
written complaining of Addison's hostile attitude to his *Iliad* weeks
after the older man had at last begun publicly to write in its praise.[6]

The truth is that no printed attack yet suggested agrees with Pope's
account and the known facts, not to mention other evidence (for the
most part overlooked hitherto) which seems to point to yet another
publication. On April 6, 1714, as already mentioned, Charles Gildon
published an anonymous 'play' called *A New Rehearsal, or Bays the
Younger*, which contains what seems to have been a quite gratuitous
attack on Pope and his friend Rowe, the playwright, and which, in
consequence, is probably the original cause of Pope's subsequent resentment against its author. Amongst other things, Pope is grossly
caricatured in the play as 'Sawny Dapper', an absurd little poet who
is held up to ridicule for his pretentious claim to a knowledge of Greek

---

[1] B. M., 1421, g. 6 (5), p. 16. See also below, p. 118.

[2] In 'Testimonies of Authors', Sutherland, p. 25.

[3] *Ibid.*, p. 42.   [4] According to *The Flying Post*.   [5] Burnet, p. 99.

[6] Since this paragraph was written, Mr Sherburn has changed his mind, and,
without citing any evidence to solve the above-mentioned difficulties attaching to
Mr Case's conjecture, now thinks *A True Character* is 'still a good suggestion'.
Philological Quarterly, XXI, ii, p. 215.

and an ability to translate Homer. Pope is also—by the mouth of that caricature—made to confess that he himself had actually written Wycherley's panegyric, *To my Friend, Mr. Pope, on his Pastorals*.[1] Here is offence enough, one might suppose, for any reprisals; and, incidentally, here is also a probable explanation of the curious way in which Wycherley's name (mentioned also elsewhere in the play) has been caught up into the Pope-Gildon-Addison imbroglio in Spence's report of Pope's conversation.

A New Rehearsal not only fills the part as regards subject-matter and author, but its appropriate date of publication and its mention of Wycherley together remove the sole obstacle which some have found to the acceptance of Pope's account of the 'Atticus' lines. Only in one small detail does its identification with Gildon's 'thing' seem to fall a little short of Pope's description, and that is, that it does not contain any very obvious abuse of Pope's relations. There is, however, one small scrap of dialogue (on pages 40–41) which looks like a covert sneer at the social status of the Pope family, insomuch that it touches on the way 'Sawny Dapper' has managed to 'raise himself' by his poetry above his earlier circumstances. But even if that cannot be counted 'gross abuse' the discrepancy could easily be explained by the simple fact that Gildon made two or three attacks on Pope within three or four years, in at least one of which he had abused the elder Mr Pope. It is very probable, therefore, that when describing these events to Spence, after an interval of some twenty busy years, Pope simply forgot for the moment, either which particular 'thing' of Gildon's had ridiculed his father, or the date of its publication. All the other evidence available, together with the absence of any probable —or even possible—alternative publication by Gildon before or during 1715, suggests that this was the abuse of which Pope complained.

But with all the *New Rehearsal*'s provocation of Pope, it is questionable whether, in 1715, Gildon would have achieved dishonourable mention in this immortal rebuke of Addison, if he had only been content to be the first of the pamphleteers to damn Pope's great translation before it was written; but the offending pamphlet was reissued with a new title-page,[2] once, if not twice, during that critical summer

---

[1] *Poetical Miscellanies: The Sixth Part*, 1709, p. 253.

[2] *Remarks on Mr. Rowe's Tragedy of the Lady Jane Gray*. The *Remarks*, amounting to no more than a dozen pages which are prefixed to this reissue of *A New Rehearsal*, was published on May 14, 1715, according to *The Post Boy*; and a 'Second Edition' was announced as 'just publish'd' in *The Weekly Packet*, July 2, 1715.

of 1715. How could all the persecution of the preceding twelve months
not be recalled to Pope's mind when he heard the gossip of the youthful Lord Warwick (not the staidest or most reliable of young men
about town)? And if the gossip was true only so far as it mirrored
Addison's antipathy to Pope, and if money had ever been known to
pass from Addison, the leader of the Whig literary party, to Gildon, an
occasional writer for the Whig party, for services rendered (no matter
the service)—it is conceivable that Pope, at such a juncture, 'heated',
as he says, 'with what I had heard', genuinely accepted the whole
miserable story at its face value, in spite of what to-day seems its in-
herent improbability, and acted accordingly. Such a natural course of
events could explain Pope's statement—if explanation were needed;
and that such a course of events was also probable may be seen in a
begging letter in the British Museum,[1] which was sent to Addison by
Gildon but written by an amanuensis because of his increasing blind-
ness. This document reveals Gildon actually appealing to Addison's
'native generosity' for what seems to have been occasional, if not
habitual, 'Releif, which Justice requires to my Sufferins,' but whether
it was solicited from his private purse or party funds is uncertain. For
although this letter was not written until four years later—actually,
February 12, 1719—it does at least indicate the way in which some
previous 'Releif' or payment might have coincided more or less with
the publication of *A New Rehearsal*, or some other pamphlet attacking
Pope, and might all unmaliciously have been thus misrepresented by
young Warwick's gossip.

Yet another indication of Gildon's venality in this affair is supplied
by Pope's notorious lampoon on Curll, the piratical publisher, *A Full
and True Account of a . . . Revenge by Poison, On the Body of Mr. Edmund
Curll*, in which Gildon is asserted to have received extra payment
expressly to abuse Pope in this very pamphlet, *A New Rehearsal*.[2]
Pope's lampoon was published at the end of March, 1716, not improbably about the time that he dispatched the warning letter, with
the 'subjoined' satire, to Addison. If, therefore, in March 1716 Pope
could state in prose that Gildon's pen had been purchasable two years
previously, it follows that the much discussed phrase, 'his venal pen',
could have appeared in a poetical allusion to the same incident,
written, so it seems, only a little earlier than the prose, namely, in 'the
first sketch on my satire on Addison'. As a matter of fact, it actually
does appear in the Welbeck transcript given above, which is apparently the earliest surviving version of the satire.

[1] Egerton, 1971, ff. 33–4.   [2] Pope's *Prose*, I, p. 263.

But although in Pope's account of the satire Gildon alone is singled out for blame (apart, that is, from Addison), in the satire itself John Dennis, the critic, stands pilloried beside him, and consequently demands a word at this place. The story of the famous quarrel between Pope and the old critic has been recently retold more than once[1]; and there is now no doubt that Pope's rapier was ever ready to answer Dennis's bludgeon, though thrust and blow cannot to-day be always related to each other with certainty. Thus Pope's lamentable thrust at his old enemy's poverty may be nothing more than a part-payment of old scores—a return for blows of a much greater brutality. But, seeing that the occasion of the satire was primarily the translation of *The Iliad* and Addison's dubious activities in connection with it, and that Gildon's crime was connected with the same sorry business, it is reasonable to suppose that Dennis—the only other person named in the early versions—had likewise sinned in some way against Pope's great translation. No attack by Dennis on that work, however, has been found earlier than the *True Character of Mr. Pope*, above mentioned, in which he almost certainly had a hand, and in which, after making some derogatory remarks about Pope's *Iliad*, he (or another) promises to publish proofs of them at some future date. To this statement, Pope, in his copy of *A True Character*, has added a marginal note in his own hand, recognizing Dennis's authorship in these words: 'As he did ye next y^r in his Remarks on Homer'. It is, therefore, a not unlikely conjecture that Dennis, who seems to have regarded each major poetical work of Pope's as a personal affront,[2] and who was as big a bully in speech as in print, had given vent to some typical Dennisian 'remark' about *The Iliad* by word of mouth ('If Dennis raves and rails in furious Pet'); and that Pope heard of it in due course, and straightway popped him into the imperishable amber of his verse alongside Gildon, harmlessly there to rail and rave for ever.

It is, however, just possible, perhaps, that the allusion to Dennis was added to 'the first sketch' at some date after May 31, 1716; that is, after the publication of *A True Character*. The suggestion is quite warrantable; for if there is one thing beyond question, it is that Pope touched and retouched his portrait of Addison from time to time in

[1] Sherburn, Chap. IV; and Pope's *Prose*, I, pp. xi–xxxiii. See also 'The End of Dennis', *post*, pp. 286 ff.

[2] Dennis wrote: *Reflections Critical and Satyrical upon . . . An Essay upon Criticism; Remarks upon Mr. Pope's Rape of the Lock; Two Letters concerning Windsor Forest, and the Temple of Fame;* and *Remarks upon Mr. Pope's Translation of Homer.*

tireless revision. Consequently, any alterations or additions could have been indistinguishably incorporated in the poem at any stage between 'the first sketch' of 1715 and the first printed text of 1722. Indeed, the four contemporary manuscript texts known to the writer differ not only from each other but from the printed texts also. For instance, it seems certain[1] that the version at the head of this chapter —the Harleian transcript at Welbeck Abbey[2]—preserves what is probably the oldest surviving text, if not actually 'the first sketch' sent to Addison; while, on the other hand, the Longleat manuscript, which is in Pope's autograph, just as certainly represents his latest revision of the poem in its original short form of thirty lines. But revision by no means ceased with publication, and the subsequent developments of the Addison portrait must be noted in passing. After at least four appearances in print between 1722 and 1726, each differing from the others, the poem was suddenly expanded (by additions not materially affecting the Addison portrait) to sixty-eight lines in 'The Last Volume' of the Swift-Pope *Miscellanies*, 1727[-8], where it was printed and acknowledged—though only indirectly—by Pope for the first time. The poem again received considerable modifications and interpolations when it came to be inserted in the *Epistle to Arbuthnot* in 1734, in which place 'Atticus' was first substituted for 'Addison' (or 'A——n') in the last line of the previous texts. Later still, the 'Miscellanies' version was further corrected on its appearance in the 1742 edition, and was thus the last text to pass through Pope's hands.

II. ARMISTICE

Turning now to the more pleasing aspect of the Pope-Addison relationship, the first remarkable fact to be noted is that Pope's encomium of Addison, quoted above,[3] has been far too frequently excluded from previous discussions of the problem, to the consequent distortion, if not actual misrepresentation, of the truth. And even when admitted, the uncertainty about the occasion and date of the epistle itself has made possible, if not encouraged, the most extra-

---

[1] As will be shown in the forthcoming volume of Pope's *Miscellaneous Poems* ('The Twickenham Edition', Vol. VI).

[2] Recorded and printed for the first time in an article by the present writer in the R.E.S., XVII, October 1941 (pp. 428–51), in which much of this chapter appeared.

[3] See *ante*, p. 102.

i

ordinary statements about them, from those of *Mist*'s Mr 'W. A.' down to, and conspicuously including, the remarks of Elwin and Courthope.[1] Thus, as the troubled year, 1715, is one of the dates ascribed to the epistle, and as it would appear highly improbable that the satire and the eulogy derive from the same period, like two sides of the same medal, it is obvious that the 'Atticus' aspect of the problem cannot be settled without first reaching some reasonable solution of the difficulties presented by the epistle.

This, at the outset, is made easier by the discovery of an early text hitherto unrecorded and unknown. Addison's *Works*, in which this epistle has been thought to have first appeared in print, was published on October 2, 1721.[2] But it now seems certain that the poem had been previously published in an edition (probably pirated) of Pope's *Works*, 'Printed by T. J. for the Company', and dated 1720. A copy of this little-known book is now to be found both in the Bodleian and the British Museum, and in both copies the *Epistle* occupies the last two leaves; and as these leaves have consecutive pagination and signatures with the rest of the book, and display the same printer's ornament there can be no question that they belong to, and were issued with, these copies. Mr R. H. Griffith, however, lists a copy[3] lacking these leaves; which would seem to suggest that there were two issues of the book in the same year, one with and one without the *Epistle to Addison*.

Pope himself made different statements at different times about the date of the epistle:

(i) In the 'Appendix' of all the editions and issues of the 'Variorum' *Dunciad* in 1729, Pope included a page of which the heading and first few lines run thus:

'A LIST OF ALL OUR AUTHOR'S GENUINE WORKS.

The Works of Mr. Alexander Pope . . . 1717. This Edition contains whatsoever is his, except these few following, which have been written since that time.

Inscription to Dr. Parnel's Poems; To the . . . Earl of Oxford . . .
Verses on Mr. Addison's Treatise of Medals, first printed after his death in Mr. Tickel's Edition of his Works.
Epitaphs: On the . . .'

(ii) Six years later, in various editions of his *Works* in 1735, Pope added a note to the *Epistle to Addison*, stating: 'This was written in

---

[1] EC, III, p. 201.

[2] The date was announced in *The Post Boy*, September 26–28, 1721.

[3] Griffith, I, i, p. 95.

1715, at which time Mr. Addison intended to publish his Book of Medals. It was some time before he was Secretary of State.'

(iii) To the foregoing note, Pope, in 1739, and in later editions, appended the further statement: '. . . but not printed till Mr. Tickel's Edition of his works in 1720, at which time the Verses on Mr. Craggs which conclude this Epistle were added'.

(iv) The editions of *The Works* which first saw the expanded note (No. iii, above), saw also a new note appended to the *Epistle to Jervas*, which reads: 'This Epistle, and the two following [to Miss Blount], were written some years before the rest [i.e. before the Epistles to Addison, Craggs, Oxford, and Arbuthnot, and the Ethic Epistles], and originally printed in 1717.' Thus, as the *Epistle to Jervas* could not possibly have been written before 1713, and almost certainly not until the close of the year, 'some years' should mean that the *Epistle to Addison* must be later than 1715.

As with other poems of Pope's which present the same problem of variously ascribed dates, the solution would seem to be found in his methods of composition, which allowed longer or shorter periods of time to elapse, not only between the first draft and the corrected version, but also—as he frequently pointed out—between the writing of different parts of the same poem (such as *Windsor Forest*, *The Rape of the Lock*, *The Dunciad*, and the *Epistle to Arbuthnot*—to name only the best-known examples). It is probable, therefore, that Pope was not intentionally untruthful or misleading in his varying statements about this poem, simply because when he made them he was thinking chiefly of one or other of the separate parts, of which it seems to have been composed.

Thus the first half of the *Epistle to Addison*,[1] which is not even in epistolary form since it is not addressed to any one, and which has no mention of, or allusion to, Addison, might well have been first sketched out as an impersonal poem on classical antiquities with special reference to coins and medals, as early as the stated year, 1715. Indeed, its beginnings not improbably date a little earlier, for the following reasons. First, it was during 1713 and 1714—that is, contemporaneously with the commencement of the work on his translation of Homer—that Pope's interests took so decided a bent towards antiquarianism. This is clearly demonstrated by the *Epistle to Jervas*, written towards the end of 1713, and *Martinus Scriblerus*, discussed, projected, and to some extent drafted at the meetings of the 'Scriblerus Club' in the first half of 1714; both of which have much in common in

---

[1] That is, lines 1–44, omitting the passage (ll. 5–10) first added in 1726.

subject and phrase with the *Epistle to Addison*, and especially the section under discussion. Secondly, while it is difficult—in the light of the foregoing pages—to imagine any friendly intercourse between Pope and Addison for some months before and after the publication of the first volume of *The Iliad* (or, in other words, at any time during the troubled year 1715), their previous relations, though never very cordial, are known to have been amicable enough for ordinary social intercourse; and they used to meet freely and frequently in the popular coffee-houses and elsewhere. In the summer of 1713 Addison took over temporary control of *The Guardian* while Steele was away electioneering[1]; Pope was contributing to the paper at that time and must have seen the 'Essay' on Medals which Addison wrote and included in the issue of July 1. It may, therefore, have been this essay which quickened, if indeed it did not awaken, Pope's interest in these relics of the antique world; and with this subject occupying both their minds in 1713–14, that would appear to be the most likely time for Addison to have shown Pope the manuscript of his *Dialogue on Medals*, which had been begun as far back as 1702, and which Pope unquestionably saw before it was printed in 1721. Again, it would seem to be about this time that Addison spoke to Pope of publishing his *Dialogues*, though the actual publication may have been planned for 1715, as Pope states. What looks like a hint at this project of Addison's (hitherto discounted as another of Pope's misstatements), has recently been found in a book entitled, *The Knowledge of Medals . . . Written by a Nobleman of France. Made English by an Eminent Hand. The Second Edition. To which is added, An Essay concerning The Error in Distributing Modern Medals. By Joseph Addison, Esq.*, 1715, where a reprint of Addison's 'Guardian' essay, which occupies its last pages, ends with the following note:

> An Eminent Writer assures us, that Mr. Addison has not a little applied himself to the Study of Medals; the Mystical Meaning of whose Reverses he has explain'd in a Work well worthy to be made Publick, and which it is hoped he will soon oblige the World with.

This book, *The Knowledge of Medals*, which was originally published in 1697, republished on February 22, 1714,[2] and again, with Addison's essay included for the first time, on August 6, 1715,[3] is further evidence that an interest in classical antiquities was growing more general as the new century progressed. It is not, therefore, surprising

---

[1] Pope's *Prose*, I, pp. xx, xxvii. [2] According to *The Evening Post*.
[3] According to *The Post Boy*.

to find that this section of the *Epistle to Addison* does not entirely derive either from that author's *Dialogues* or his *Essay* on Medals; as is shown by the fact that Pope includes much detail not found in either. (For instance, in lines 26–30, of the six or more verifiable coins alluded to by Pope, only the first one, bearing the inscription 'Judæa Capta' is mentioned by Addison.)

The next section of the *Epistle* (lines 45–62) is that in which Addison is addressed and perhaps excessively praised—lines, therefore, which could not possibly have been written by Pope, either during the time when Addison was disparaging his translation of the *Iliad* and promoting that of his rival, Tickell, or until sufficient time afterwards had elapsed for the resultant soreness in Pope's mind to have healed: for even in the winter of 1716–17, he was still feeling resentful enough to allude to the Addison-Tickell conspiracy in *Sandys's Ghost*. Hence, agreeably to the poet's assertion in *The Dunciad*, 1729, this encomiastic section of the epistle (not to mention the conclusion) was in all probability not written until after the publication of *The Works of Mr. Alexander Pope* on June 3, 1717[1]; another reason being, that, had the epistle been so near completion earlier, it was too important a poem to have escaped inclusion in that magnificent volume. At the other extreme, as these lines were obviously written before Addison's death, they cannot be later than June 1719.

The final section of the poem (lines 63–72) is devoted to somebody else entirely—Mr 'Secretary' Craggs. This seemingly strange conclusion of an epistle to Addison appears hitherto to have been generally accepted by readers in the belief that Pope was somehow commemorating the deaths of two friends in the same poem. But even that unsatisfactory explanation is no longer tenable; because, since the discovery of the above-mentioned early text, it is certain that at least Craggs was not dead when these lines were first printed; and, seeing that Pope addresses Addison, in line 63, not as one evoking a recently disembodied spirit, but as one man to another—'Then shall thy Craggs (and let me call him mine)'—it is quite as certain that Addison also was alive when it was written. The 'intrusion' of Craggs into this epistle can at last be explained by the facts that Addison was not only alive when these lines were penned, but was actively planning a collected edition of his *Works* with Tickell's assistance; and that he had not only arranged for it by June 4, 1719, but had actually written its 'Dedication', in which he 'publicly bequeathes' his 'writings' to his and Pope's mutual friend, Craggs. Unquestionably, Pope must have

---

[1] Announced in *The Daily Courant*.

learnt this from one or other of them; whereupon he composed this conclusion to be added to the epistle (already in existence and possibly intended to accompany the *Dialogues*) in the knowledge that that treatise, as part of Addison's *Works*, would now first appear in print under Craggs's ægis. (The accident that, in 1727, Pope found it possible, by a small alteration introducing the word 'wept', to convert the last six lines into an epitaph on Craggs, has, of course, nothing to do with the date of the original lines.)

The last stage in the composition of the *Epistle to Addison* was not reached until 1726, when a further six lines were added near the beginning (lines 5–10); and these are the only lines it is safe to say Addison never saw. It thus appears at last possible that Pope's various statements about the date of the epistle can be clarified to this extent: that although, when applied to the poem as a whole, they are obviously contradictory, they are, to a great extent and all unexpectedly, correct when applied to its various parts. Thus, the first part was written not later than 1715 (statement No. ii, above); the second part was written between 1717 and 1719 (No. i); the third part was literally added in 1720 to the epistle already written (No. iii); and, lastly, the poem as a whole was in fact first printed in 1720 as claimed, though 'Mr. Tickel's Edition' was not published until 1721 (No. iii).

When all the foregoing facts concerning Pope's two poems, the satire and the epistle, are considered, it will be seen that his account to Spence of the early history of the satire, could have been, and probably was, on the whole and in intention, true—bating, perhaps, some natural lapses of memory about events then nearly twenty years old.[1] Certainly nothing has been found seriously to contradict it; and certainly it is nearer to the truth than is the tradition of his treacherous and unprovoked attack on Addison, which obtained for some two hundred years. That the satire was Pope's reaction to Addison's dubious attitude and activities in the long-drawn-out 'Battle of the *Iliad*' cannot now seriously be contested on the known evidence, or that it was sketched out at some time between June 1715 and May 1716; that is, *after* the publication of the rival Addison-sponsored translation and *before* Addison's initial attempt to propitiate Pope in *The Freeholder*. Between those two dates the order of events is unfortunately sparsely documented; but it would appear that after Pope's accumulated resentment had found relief in a satirical sketch of Addison's character, he put it on one side for a time, and nothing more happened, until he heard 'one day' from Lord Warwick that Addison

[1] The account occurs in the section dated 1734–36.

had in effect hired Gildon to attack him. Whether the report was true, and whether the 'thing' in which the attack was made can now be identified, have strictly no bearing on the argument. The important point about Warwick's gossip is that Pope believed it, and, incensed beyond measure, promptly sent Addison the first sketch of the satire with an accompanying letter warning him of what 'he could an he would'. But whatever the particular course of events may have been between June 1715 and the following May, the evidence is indisputable that Addison, for some unrevealed reason that greatly puzzled his friends at Button's, suddenly changed his attitude towards Pope—the first effects of which are seen in his public praise of Pope's translation on May 17, 1716, and, not less significantly, in Burnet's surprise at his *volte-face*. Thereafter, until he died 'about three years after,' Addison used Pope 'very civilly'—according to Pope's own statement to Spence.

But what Pope failed to mention in his account is that, for his part, he met Addison's attempts at conciliation more than half way, and not only withheld the satire from immediate publication, but, when the last soreness had passed away, at some date between June 1717 and June 1719, wrote in lavish praise of his quondam enemy, in a 'full-dress' epistle to him, which he allowed to be published in 1720.

Later still, three and a half years after Addison's death, Pope's satirical lines on him crept anonymously into print in *The St James's Journal* for December 15, 1722, and apparently aroused no attention or comment whatever. In the *Journal* the satire was introduced in the postscript of a letter about other matters, in these words: 'P.S. The following Lines have been in good Reputation here, and are now submitted to Publick Censure.' The letter itself is dated 'Button's, 12 Decemb. 1722' and is signed 'Dorimant'. On this evidence alone it has been suggested that 'Dorimant' is one of Pope's pseudonyms; this signature, however, was a popular one at the time and for long afterwards; it is found in the newspapers from 1722 to 1730, appended to numerous letters and articles with which there is not the least evidence or reason to suppose that Pope had any connection. It is not known who was responsible for that first publication of the satire; but for some months previously the poem was being handed about in manuscript, to judge from Bishop Atterbury's letter to Pope (February 26, 1722)[1] asking for a copy of it; and from the fact that the transcript found among Lord Oxford's papers at Welbeck—which, as previously

[1] *Letters*, 4to, 1737, p. 220.

stated, differs from the printed version—is endorsed in the Earl's autograph '1722'. This private circulation clearly shows that the poem could have been sent to the *Journal* without its author's knowledge or consent; it likewise explains how Curll—who was certainly responsible for the next three reprints of it, and who was the first to reveal its author's name—could have obtained his copy, which also differs not a little from both the Welbeck manuscript and the first printed text.

Lastly may be mentioned the fact that Pope never publicly acknowledged or printed the satire until the longer text was authoritatively published by him in 'The Last Volume' of his and Swift's *Miscellanies*, as mentioned above; in the Preface of which he owned it for the first time (though only by implication) in a sort of semi-apology to Addison, thus:

> In regard to two Persons only, we wish our Raillery, though ever so tender, or Resentment, though ever so just, had not been indulged. We speak of Sir *John Vanbrugh* . . . , and of Mr. *Addison*, whose Name deserves all Respect from every Lover of Learning.

There remains Pope's last reference to Addison, which also should be noted in this connection, both because of its importance as the utterance of his latter years, and because it unalterably sets the balance of generosity heavily in his favour. It is found in the *Epistle to Augustus*, 1737, where, after speaking of the poets of 'Charles's days', he proceeds to contrast with them those of his own time, beginning with Addison:

> And in our [days] (excuse some Courtly stains)
> No whiter page than Addison remains.
> He, from the taste obscene reclaims our Youth,
> And sets the Passions on the side of Truth;
> Forms the soft bosom with the gentlest art,
> And pours each human Virtue in the heart.

From all of which it will perhaps appear, that—apart from the later poems, the Satires, Moral Essays, and so forth—where the *genre* not only permits but postulates a freedom of reference—it is not always necessary either to condemn Pope's irritability when on occasion he seems to attack some one with rhyme but without reason, or to allude to the inferiority complex of a cripple psychology to explain or excuse it. In such cases, as the following chapters abundantly prove, research has generally revealed that what may appear an unjustifiable attack was really of the nature of reprisal or punishment for injuries received, or believed to have been received. And though this settling of old scores in the lusty Old Testament manner may not be the loftiest morality conceivable, it is at least a step in the right direction. For so, Pope may begin to lose some of that diabolic malignity with which popular legend still reproaches him, and at the end of two centuries of misrepresentation come to be recognized as tolerably human after all.

CHAPTER VII

POPE AND ROWE

I. FIRST CONTACTS

AMONGST the friendships of Pope's youth, that of Nicholas Rowe, the dramatist, claims more than passing comment, not only because they were happy in each other's affection until Rowe's too early death at forty-five, but because their relations led to literary undertakings between them, which have posed more than one problem for students of the period in general, and Pope scholars in particular. How they first became acquainted is not known; but not improbably they met at the house of Pope's neighbour in the Forest, the old secretary of state, Sir William Trumbull; or possibly in a coffee-house which, on his visits to London, the young poet used to frequent in company with his elderly friends (survivors of the Dryden regime) such as Cromwell, Walsh or Wycherley. But that they were acquainted as early as 1707, is shown in a rhymed letter Pope wrote to Cromwell in July of that year,[1] in which he has a joking allusion to Rowe's strong political principles and his enthusiasm for the Union with Scotland then being concluded. Within twelve months, however, when Pope was just twenty and Rowe thirty-four, there occurred all the makings of a literary quarrel between them, which was only avoided by their mutual good sense and forbearance.

On June 1, 1708, John Ozell published his translation of Boileau's *Lutrin*, in which he reflected upon Wycherley (to use Pope's phrase) in the description of the mock battle in Canto V, where the combatants arm themselves for the fray with 'ammunition books'—

> One with vindictive Hand light *Durfey* shakes;
> Another *Wycherly* more weighty, takes;
> A Third tore *Westly* from the Dusty Wood . . .
> A fourth Up-heaves a leaden *Basnage* high—

The offensiveness of the allusion derives from the fact that Wycherley's *Miscellany Poems*, which had been rather impressively published four years earlier in an unusually large folio (a copy in the Bodleian measures 14 by 9 inches and contains nearly 500 pages), had been something of a failure, in spite of his fame as a playwright. To make

[1] *Miscellanea*, I, pp. 79 ff.

matters worse, Rowe, in an appreciative introduction to Ozell's
Lutrin, spoke of the translator's 'mustering up a Set of English
Authors of equal Degree and like kind of Dulness with those mention'd
by M. Boileau'; and went on to say that he found 'the Satyr upon our
own Countrymen . . . very just and entertaining'. This was too much
for young Pope, who was at that time actually engaged in selecting,
correcting, and revising Wycherley's poems, published and unpublished, at the old dramatist's urgently repeated request. Faced with a
dilemma, for both men were his friends, the youthful poet was
chivalrously impelled to champion the older man and older friend;
and he wrote and sent him an epigram on the subject, to which
Wycherley replied on November 13, 1708—'I thank you for the
Friendship as well as the Wit of your Epigram, which I cou'd praise
more were it less to my own Praise.'[1]

Subsequently Pope's autograph of the Epigram (now in the Bodleian)[2] fell into Curll's hands, who entitled it 'The Translator', and
printed it as Pope's in *Miscellanea*, Vol. I, 1727, and thus supplied the
version hitherto found in the poet's *Works*. But Pope revised it later
and himself included it in that extremely rare book, *The Posthumous
Works of William Wycherley, Esq.*, Vol. II, 1729, from which it is now
reprinted for the first time:

EPIGRAM

Occasion'd by
Ozell's Translation of *Boileau*'s *Lutrin*

Printed for *E. Sanger*, and recommended by Mr. *Rowe*, in which
Mr. *Wycherley*'s POEMS printed in 1704, were reflected on.

> *OZELL*, at *Sanger*'s Call, invok'd his Muse, ⎫
> For who to sing for *Sanger* could refuse? ⎬
> His Numbers such, as *Sanger*'s self might use. ⎭
> Reviving *Perault*,[3] murd'ring *Boileau*, he
> Slander'd the Ancients first, then *Wycherley*;
> Not that it much that Author's Anger rais'd,
> For those were slander'd most whom *Ozell* prais'd:
> Nor had the toothless Satyr caus'd complaining,
> Had not sage *Rowe* pronounc'd it *Entertaining*.[4]

---

[1] EC, v, p. 395.   [2] Rawl. letters 90.

[3] 'He had before translated Perault's Characters, &c.' [Pope, 1729.]

[4] Rowe's own word of commendation, see above.

How great, how just,[1] the Judgment of that Writer!
Who the *Plain-dealer*[2] damns, and prints the *Biter*.[3]

That the epigram was never acknowledged by Pope is probably to be
explained by its censure of Rowe, with whom Pope became increasingly friendly as the years passed. It was not even printed until long
after Rowe's death, and only then without Pope's consent. One might
also note that the tenacity of Pope's dislikes (or of his affection—it
depends on the point of view) is seen in the fact that, more than
twenty years after Ozell's offence, he was still resentful enough of it to
include this epigram anonymously in his volume of Wycherley's
Posthumous Works, and also to allude in another footnote elsewhere in
the book to Ozell's poor translation, and state once again that 'it reflected upon Mr. Wycherley by name.' A further reason for concealment may have been that Pope and Rowe were meeting in 1708–9 in
connection with the younger poet's contributions to *Poetical Miscellanies: The Sixth Part, 1709,* for the editing of which Rowe is said to have
been more or less responsible[4]; though from the letters of Tonson[5] and
Wycherley[6] it would seem that Pope transacted most of this business
with Tonson direct.

In the years that followed, while the friendship of Pope and Wycherley underwent some temporary eclipse owing to Pope's too enthus-
iastic corrections of those unfortunate poems, that of Pope and Rowe
flourished apace, until by 1713 it had grown into something like
intimacy with the exchange of visits to each other's homes. For
instance, Rowe writing to Pope on August 20, 1713, thanks him for
his letter, and then proceeds:

> To do something, then, that is perfectly kind, Come and Eat a
> Bit of mutton with me to morrow at Stockwell. Bring whom you
> will along with you . . . & you Don't know how much you will
> oblige your most affectionate and faithfull humble servant.[7]

[1] Rowe's own words of commendation, see above.

[2] Wycherley wrote this play, and was himself so called occasionally.

[3] 'An unequal Piece of Mr. Rowe's, which met with very ill Success.' [Pope,
1729.]

[4] See pamphlet entitled, *Books Printed for E. Curll,* 1735, which on p. 14 has the
following item:

V. The Original Genuine-Edition of Miscellany Poems and Translations. Begun
by Mr. *Dryden* in the Year 1684, and continued by Mr. *Rowe* to 1709, concluding
with Mr. *Pope*'s Pastorals. In six Volumes. Price a Guinea.

[5] Add. 4807, f. 172 v.   [6] *Works*, IV, i (Cooper), 1742, pp. 28 f.

[7] Add. 4807, f. 81 v.

Exactly a month later, on September 20, Pope, writing to Caryll, says:

I am just returned from the Country, whither Mr Rowe did me the favour to accompany me and to pass a Week at Binfield; I need not tell you how much a Man of his Turn could not but entertain me . . . there is a Vivacity and Gayety of Disposition almost peculiar to that Gentleman, which renders it impossible to part from him without that Uneasyness and Chagrin which generally Succeeds all great pleasures. [1]

Nevertheless their customary places of meeting, when Pope was in town, would still be the coffee-houses, Button's, or Will's, or some other. And it was probably at one of them a few months earlier, when Addison's *Cato* [2] had achieved its phenomenal success and 'the Pro-logue-Writer . . . was clapp'd into a stanch Whig sore against his will', [3] that Pope and Rowe had met and witnessed together, not with-out amusement, all the partisan excitement about the play, and seen the Grub-street panegyrics upon it passing gravely from hand to hand and from group to admiring group. Sooner or later, on that occasion or another, one of the most egregious of these poetical tributes, the 'Epigram on a Lady who wept at Cato', fell into their hands, and so provoked them to mockery that they promptly set about burlesquing it in Latin and English verse. In some such manner, it seems, the two friends came to concoct the two versions of that semi-famous but infrequently printed epigram—'On a Lady who shed her Water at seeing the Tragedy of *Cato*.' Whether we call it school-boy humour or Rabelaisian humour, it is as old as the human race, and an only too natural reaction to pomposity, super-human gravity, or dispropor-tioned enthusiasm. (In parenthesis, Pope—it should be remembered —like Swift and others of his circle, was the product of his age; an age when sanitary science had a long way to go before it became the invis-ible servant of the body it is to-day, and when humour was one of the ways of discounting some of the more objectionable concomitants of physical existence.) This improper but most popular of epigrams seems to have escaped the printers for some months, probably because transcripts were not available; but early in the following year it appeared anonymously in print for the first time, in the fifth number of a periodical miscellany called *The Poetical Entertainer*, dated 1713 but not published until February 14, 1714. [4]

[1] Add. 28618, f. 35.
[3] Add. 28618, f. 14 v.
[2] Produced, April 14, 1713.
[4] See *The Post Boy* of that date.

ON A LADY WHO P—ST
at the TRAGEDY of *CATO*;
Occasion'd by an
EPIGRAM on a LADY who wept at it.

While maudlin Whigs deplor'd their *Cato*'s Fate,
Still with dry Eyes the Tory *Celia* sate,
But while her Pride forbids her Tears to flow,
The gushing Waters find a Vent below:
Tho' secret, yet with copious Grief she mourns,
Like twenty River-Gods with all their Urns.
Let others screw their Hypocritick Face,
She shews her Grief in a sincerer Place;
There Nature reigns, and Passion void of Art,
For that Road leads directly to the Heart.

On March 18, one of Addison's circle, Tom Burnet, writing to his
friend Duckett in the country, reported: 'That Copy of Verses of a
Lady bepissing her self at Cato, was written by Pope & Rowe both in
Ridicule of those that cryed at Cato.'[1] Three or four months later the
piece was included by Curll, probably without leave, in the third
edition of Rowe's *Poems*, 1714 (amongst whose works it has since been
usually printed), only to appear again later and anonymously in
several poetical collections. It was included by Pope himself in his and
Swift's *Miscellanies. The Last Volume.* 1727, like the rest of the pieces
without attribution; and its presence there may have some significance, seeing that nothing by Rowe is known to have been included,
and that it was marked under Pope's direction,[2] as 'not by Swift' in
the 1742 edition. But that is not all, because, as Pope edited the *Miscellanies*, it must have been he who altered the title (not unnoticed by
The Daily Journal of April 3, 1728, which accused him and Swift of
plagiarism from Rowe), and, more significant still, had at the same
time revised seven of the epigram's ten lines; for none of these corrections has ever figured in the text in Rowe's works, either before
or after his death. Moreover, in the two copies of this volume of *Miscellanies* at Welbeck, which Lord Oxford gave to his wife and daughter,
the epigram has been marked by the ladies, 'By Mr. Pope,' apparently
on the authority of Oxford who himself was a great friend of Pope—as
indeed were the ladies.[3] Later still, but still within Pope's lifetime,
Joe Miller's Jests of 1742 (and later editions) gave the epigram to

[1] Add. 36772, f. 86.   [2] See *post*, p. 254.   [3] See *post*, p. 231.

Pope; but the majority of printed and manuscript copies of it before his death are anonymous. On its first printing, and frequently afterwards, the English version of the epigram was accompanied by a Latin 'imitation', but that throws no light on the problem of authorship except to suggest the possibility that Pope wrote one version and Rowe the other. And it should also be remembered that the English version was first attributed to Rowe by the piratical bookseller, Curll, without authority; and that, as Rowe failed to collect and publish his works before he died in 1718, no authority attaches to the inclusion in his works of this epigram, either by Curll or the other editors who followed him in text as in time. Taking all things into consideration, then, it is virtually certain that Pope was in some way connected with the epigram; and that the balance of probabilities favours his authorship of the English lines, which were 'Thus turn'd into Latin' very likely at the same sitting, by Rowe, who undoubtedly was the better classical scholar of the two, being, as Dr Johnson said, 'master of . . . the classical authors both Greek and Latin.'

II. THE REJECTED EPILOGUE

One of the minor mysteries of Pope scholarship surrounds the story of his second theatrical piece, the Epilogue to Rowe's *Jane Shore*. The first piece that he had been asked to write, the Prologue to Addison's *Cato*, shared in that play's tremendous success as well as contributed to it. Indeed, the Prologue actually appeared in print (together with Garth's Epilogue) earlier than the play itself, in *The Guardian* of April 18, 1713; and then afterwards, on April 27, in its proper place in the printed play-book. Three days later still, Pope had the gratification of being able to report to his old friend Caryll: 'the Prologue & Epilogue are cry'd about the streetts by the Common Hawkers'; and although no copy of this broadside seems to have survived, there is no reason whatever to doubt the statement.

How different the fate of the Epilogue of the following year for *Jane Shore*! Here is a poem written at Rowe's request (a much dearer friend than Addison) and expressly designed for a particular speaker, the actress, Mrs Oldfield; yet it was never spoken at the theatre by the one nor included in the printed play by the other! Nevertheless, although it had thus failed of performance and was left unpublished for more than three years, Pope thought it good enough for inclusion in the imposing edition of *The Works*, 1717; and yet, including it, labelled it

in effect a failure—an epilogue that had never achieved a voice—
Epilogue to Jane Shore. Design'd for Mrs. Oldfield. Such apparent contradictions, left unresolved for two centuries, call for some attempt at
explanation.

Jane Shore was acted on February 2, 1714, at which time, as we have
seen, Pope and Rowe were fast friends. It is evident, therefore, that the
rejection or neglect of the Epilogue was not due to any questionable
action on Rowe's part; for with such a sensitive creature as Pope that
would have affected their subsequent relations beyond all concealment. With Rowe ruled out, there remains only Mrs Oldfield of the
named parties in the affair. And the question arises, why did Pope
name her at all in this quite unusual fashion when he printed the
Epilogue so long after the occasion? For his statement, that it was
'design'd' for her, certainly was not due to his humility which needed
the recommendation of her name; nor could it add anything to the
significance of the lines—unless, indeed, it added much too much.

Leaving that point for the moment, many people in the past have
remarked that Pope's dislike of Mrs Oldfield is apparent in the two or
three passages in which he alluded to her after her death in 1730. To
cite one example:

> 'Odious! in woollen! 'twould a Saint provoke,'
> (Were the last words that poor Narcissa spoke)
> 'No, let a charming Chintz, and Brussels lace
> Wrap my cold limbs, and shade my lifeless face:
> One would not, sure, be frightful when one's dead—
> And—Betty—give this Cheek a little Red.'[1]

That is the whole of the reference; but although the lady is nowhere
named, a footnote to the passage said that 'Several attribute this in
particular to a very celebrated Actress, who, in detestation of the
thought of being buried in woollen [according to a law then still in
force], gave these her last orders with her dying breath'. Nevertheless,
as Narcissa, the heroine of Cibber's *Love's Last Shift*, was one of Mrs
Oldfield's most popular rôles, there could have been little doubt in the
public mind about the allusion.

The actress was a friend of Cibber, and consequently Pope's aver-
sion to her is usually explained as a by-product of the great Pope-
Cibber feud, just as the feud in turn is supposed to have sprung from
performances of that unlucky farce, *Three Hours after Marriage*, 1717,
the joint production of Gay, Pope, and Arbuthnot, in which both

[1] *Moral Essay*, I, ll. 246–51.

Cibber and Anne Oldfield had acting parts. Pope's quarrel with Cibber occupies a later chapter[1] and must not detain us here. But the theory that the poet's dissatisfaction with the actress began in 1717 can no longer be held in face of evidence of previous discord to be found in his lampoon on the Curll-emetic incident[2] early in 1716, where he seems quite gratuitously to drag in her name when speaking (in the voice of Curll) of the 'Life' of Mainwaring, her one-time protector and the father of one of her children.

Now, it is becoming increasingly apparent of late, that, contrary to general belief, Pope rarely if ever attacked any one unprovoked; careful examination of the facts usually discovers that he struck only in retaliation for some slight or injury received, real or imaginary. That is not to deny, of course, that the provocation may at times have occurred only on a fairly high plane—that of philosophy, for instance, or aesthetics—quite out of sight of many worthy people then and now; or that, on other occasions, a time-lapse may have intervened between cause and effect, so that the original offence may seem to have been overlooked by Pope and forgotten by others for months or even years, when, suddenly, out of the blue the bolt descends, and the seeming victim squeals—often with a chorus of chance spectators—that he has done nothing to deserve it.

Returning to the *Epilogue to Jane Shore*, it is not improbable that for some reason unknown the famous actress refused (possibly at the eleventh hour, a favourite moment with temperamental actresses) to speak the lines Pope had written for her, and that Rowe, or the manager of the theatre, could not afford to offend her, and so was compelled to obtain and substitute the anonymous epilogue printed in the play. This would not have been an exceptional occurrence apparently; for after the first night of *Three Hours after Marriage*, she is said to have refused for a short time to act again in it[3]; and, as we know from Spence,[4] she had previously objected to a passage in Addison's *Cato*—and had carried her objection. A similar objection on her part to Pope's Epilogue would explain all the difficulties—all except one, or rather two related problems: why did he retain her name in the title when she had had nothing to do with the piece? and why retain it in that particular form of words?

It is possible that Pope thought so well of the poem as to be con-

---

[1] See Chapter **xx**.
[2] *A Full and True Account*; see Pope's *Prose*, I, p. 264.
[3] So, at least, runs the story in Breval's *Confederates*, 1717.
[4] Spence, p. 151.

k

vinced that every one would think her a fool to have refused to speak such excellent and telling lines, so that by this twist the *implied* heading 'Not spoken by Mrs. Oldfield' becomes (since Pope was not the man to advertise his failures) an equivocal recommendation of the rejected Epilogue. But Pope's motives were not always—probably not often—single, and the foregoing explanation still leaves unexplained his use of those ambiguous words, 'Design'd for Mrs. Oldfield'.

The present writer has recently examined a large number of plays of the first thirty years of the eighteenth century to verify his memory of the conventional phrases commonly used as headings of prologues and epilogues. Though every playbook of the period has not been seen, the two hundred and more representative plays examined have shown that the most frequent form of words is the simple 'Prologue to [Title]' with or without the addition 'Spoken by Mr. [Blank],' and with, in some cases, the name of the writer of the verses. On the contrary, the word 'Designed' was very rarely used, and almost without exception only in connection with the *title* of the play, thus: 'Prologue, Designed for the Pastoral Tragedy of Dione'. Pope himself has a 'Prologue, Design'd for Mr. Durfy's last Play'; and Gay, once only, has a conflation of the two forms, as follows: 'The Epilogue, Design'd to be spoken by . . ' But Pope's brief phrase has not, as yet, been encountered anywhere else; and, if not unique, is of the extremest rarity. Thus the question still remains: why did he use it? and what does it mean?

The only hypothesis which covers all the known facts is that Pope deliberately invented (or adopted) this equivocal phrase so that one of its meanings should show his displeasure at Mrs Oldfield's refusal to speak the Epilogue; that it is in effect a veiled 'attack' on her, at least so far as the *woman* is identified with the *character* who is speaking the lines, and is thus made to designate herself 'a sister sinner' (which, it seems, she technically was). In other words, the Epilogue was 'design'd for'—that is, 'design'd to fit'—Mrs Oldfield. And one wonders if the poem as Pope printed it in 1717, *after* the further bother over *Three Hours after Marriage*, was the poem she had refused to speak three years earlier, or whether Pope's 'corrections', which almost invariably preceded publication, increased or diminished its objectionableness in her eyes. And if their quarrel went back further still, and if Pope's private letter of April 30, 1713, to his grave old friend, Caryll, wherein he transcribes an epigram, *On Cato*, of which Mrs Oldfield is the butt, shows that his dislike was even then alive—that would not affect the foregoing hypothesis, except that her rejection of the Epilogue would have been an aggravation, instead of the initiation, of his grievance.

The epigram, *On Cato*, which is presumably Pope's, but which no one has yet ventured to print (possibly because there seemed no reason for it), refers to the inordinate applause, semi-political in origin, which greeted and accompanied the performances of *Cato* already discussed. Towards the end of that letter to Caryll, which describes all the excitement about the play, Pope goes on to say:

> But of all the world none have been in so peculiar a manner enamour'd with Cato, as a young Gentleman of Oxford, who makes it the sole guide of all his Actions . . . he dates every thing from ye first or third night &c of Cato: he goes out of Town every day it is not play'd, & fell in love with Mrs Oldfield for no other reason than because she act'd Cato's Daughter! This has occasioned the following Epigram, which was dispers'd about ye Coffee houses in holy week, & is much approv'd of by our Witts.

On *CATO*

> You ask why Damon does the College seek?
> Tis because Cato's not Rehearsd this week;
> How long at Oxford then will Damon stay?
> Damon returns not till they Cato play:
> Oldfield wants Damon—when will he be at her?
> Oh, not till Oldfield shall be Cato's Daughter:
> Why then if I can guess what may insue,
> When Cato's clapp'd, Damon will be so too. [1]

There can be little doubt about the authorship of this epigram. It is introduced in the letter in the same equivocal way that Pope on occasion employed; it is one more witness to his dislike of Mrs Oldfield; it incorporates the dubious pun on the word 'clap' for which he seems to have had a curious partiality, it being also found in, amongst other places, a letter to Teresa Blount in 1718, with 'thunder-clap' instead of 'applause' as one of its meanings. [2] Then there is the still more significant fact that the epigram is found only in this letter of Pope's, and nowhere else either in print or manuscript; and lastly, it was emphatically *not* Pope's practice to brighten his correspondence with the witty verses of other men, though not infrequently with his own.

[1] Add. 28618, ff. 14 v., 15.   [2] See *post*, p. 333.

If, then, Pope's original grievance against the actress, Mrs Old-field, dates back to his first experience of writing for the theatre, and cannot be traced beyond, it looks as though his dislike of her must have begun—as long-continued quarrels often do—with some trivial mis-understanding, too small for contemporary gossip to notice, in the very first stages of their acquaintance. This could have happened during a rehearsal of *Cato*, which Pope seems to have attended, pos-sibly in his office of 'prologue-writer'; for he told Spence, that once, when she had objected to a passage in the play, he himself had suggested the alteration which Addison carried out.[1] And doubtless on such occasions other opportunities occurred for misunderstandings and cross-purposes capable of starting a mutual life-long antipathy, which would not be lessened by subsequent causes of friction, such as her refusal to speak Pope's *Epilogue to Jane Shore*.

III. THE LOST PROLOGUE

Pope's known contributions to English dramatic literature are neither so numerous nor so extensive but that additions to them—could any of his lost pieces of the kind be recovered—would be sure of a welcome. In the 'Homer Manuscripts' in the British Museum, Pope's trans-lation of lines 288–317 of the sixth book of the *Iliad* is written on the back of a letter in Rowe's autograph, which reads:

> Dear Sr
>
> If you will favour me with your Prologue by this bearer I will Return it to morrow & allways Reckon it among the Obligations you have been so kind as to lay upon,
>
> Yr most faithfull humble Servant
>
> N. ROWE.[2]

The only comment which this letter has evoked from students of the period hitherto seems to be the footnote to it in the Elwin and Court-hope edition of Pope's correspondence; and that baldly states: 'No Prologue written by Pope for Rowe is now in existence, though there is an Epilogue by the former to *Jane Shore*.'[3]

Rowe's letter is unfortunately not dated; but Pope, writing to Jervas about the end of June 1715, happened to report what progress he was making with the second volume of *The Iliad*; from which it

---

[1] Spence, p. 151.   [2] Add. 4807, f. 83 v.   [3] EC, x, p. 110.

appears that Books V–VII ('except a small part of the latter end of the 6th') were written during the first half of 1715. Seeing that Book VI contains 679 lines, Pope's statement shows that the lines 288–317 on the back of Rowe's letter were well within the completed portion of the translation when he wrote; and further, that in all probability the letter itself—and consequently the Prologue also—was written some time during that period (*i.e.* January to June 1715), especially as the other letters thus made use of in Book VI belong to the same time, with one exception dated 1713. Now the only play in which Rowe is known to have been particularly interested during those months was his own *Tragedy of the Lady Jane Gray*, which was produced at Drury Lane on April 20, 1715, and published by Lintot ten days later (April 30). The printed play is properly equipped with a Prologue and Epilogue each in its own place, written possibly by Rowe himself, but certainly not by Pope if internal evidence has any meaning at all. But the significant thing about this publication, in the light of Rowe's letter to Pope, is that, immediately following the Epilogue and occupying the whole of the last page of the book, it includes a supernumerary Prologue (which does not seem to have been reprinted, except by the present writer,[1] since the eighteenth century), as follows:

A PROLOGUE to LADY *JANE GRAY*
Sent by an Unknown Hand

WHEN waking Terrors rouze the guilty Breast,
    And fatal Visions break the Murd'rer's Rest;
When Vengeance does Ambition's Fate decree,
And Tyrants bleed, to set whole Nations free;
Tho the Muse saddens each distressed Scene,
Unmov'd is ev'ry Breast, and ev'ry Face serene;
The mournful Lines no tender Heart subdue,
Compassion is to suff'ring Goodness due.
The Poet your Attention begs once more,
T'atone for Characters here drawn before: 10
No Royal Mistress sighs through ev'ry Page,
And breathes her dying Sorrows on the Stage:
No lovely Fair by soft Persuasion won,
Lays down the Load of Life, when Honour's gone.

[1] In an article on these lines, entitled 'Pope's Lost Prologue' in *The Times Literary Supplement* for September 19, 1936.

Nobly to bear the Changes of our State,
To stand unmov'd against the Storms of Fate,
A brave Contempt of Life, and Grandeur lost;
Such glorious Toils a Female Name can boast.
Our Author draws not Beauty's heavenly Smile,
T'invite our Wishes, and our Hearts beguile.   20
No soft Enchantments languish in her Eye,
No Blossoms fade, nor sick'ning Roses die:
A nobler Passion ev'ry Breast must move,
Than youthful Raptures, or the Joys of Love.
A Mind unchang'd, superiour to a Crown,
Bravely defies the angry Tyrant's Frown;
The same, if Fortune sinks, or mounts on high,
Or if the World's extended Ruins lie:
With gen'rous Scorn she lays the Scepter down,
Great Souls shine brightest, by Misfortunes shown: 30
With patient Courage she sustains the Blow,
And triumphs o'er Variety of Woe.
Through ev'ry Scene the sad Distress is new;
How well feign'd Life does represent the true!
Unhappy Age! who views the bloody Stain,
But must with Tears record *Maria*'s Reign?
When Zeal by Doctrine flatter'd lawless Will,
Instructed by Religion's Voice to kill.
  Ye *British* Fair! lament in silent Woe,
Let ev'ry Eye with tender Pity flow: 40
The lovely Form through falling Drops will seem
Like flow'ry Shadows on the silver Stream.
Thus Beauty, Heaven's sweet Ornament, shall prove
Enrich'd by Virtue, as ador'd by Love.
Forget your Charms, fond Woman's dear Delight,
The Fops will languish here another Night.
No Conquest from dissembling Smiles we fear,
She only kills, who wounds us with a Tear.   48

Before discussing the poem in detail, and the facts which suggest that it is the Prologue mentioned in Rowe's letter, it should be remarked that the concealment of its author's name is no evidence against Pope's authorship. Apart from his predilection for anonymous publication, discussed in an earlier chapter,[1] reasons were not

[1] See *ante*, pp. 4 f.

wanting at that time amply to account for the ascription of a prologue by Pope to an 'Unknown Hand'. Gay's 'Tragi-Comi-Pastoral
Farce', *The What d'ye call it*, was produced on February 23, 1715, and
published on March 19; and though Pope's name appeared nowhere
officially in connection with it, he was generally credited with a share
(and by his enemies, a major share) in its authorship. The play had a
very mixed reception; and he and Gay were together attacked in
newspaper and pamphlet for any one of a dozen reasons—because it
burlesqued Addison's *Cato*, or ridiculed Ambrose Philips, or was
extravagant or stupid, indecent or dull—the truth being that it provided Pope's enemies with one more opportunity for disparagement,
and in addition was essentially a manoeuvre in the larger attack on his
Iliad previously described.[1] Such hostility alone, whatever the reason
for it, would probably have been enough to make Pope pause before
putting his name to anything for the stage at that moment. Nevertheless, another possible deterrent may be found in Horneck's ridicule,
barely four months earlier, of the only theatrical piece to which Pope
had set his name, the *Prologue to Cato* (1713). In his paper, *The High-
German Doctor*, for December 7–10, 1714, Horneck had jeered at the
'Old *Roman* Spirit' in which Pope had written that Prologue, and
which had concealed its 'Modern *Roman* Bigottry' to such effect that
even Addison had at first been taken in by it. With so much to dis-
courage him from subscribing his name to another Prologue, added
to his life-long practice of mystification (this same month he published *A Key to the Lock* pseudonymously),[2] it is clear that no argument against Pope's authorship of the poem can be drawn from its
anonymity.

Little more need be said about the friendship of Pope and Rowe at
this time. As we have seen, the two men were, and long had been, on
an intimate footing such as would explain a much greater 'obligation'
than this on either side. And when it is remembered that Pope wrote a
Prologue for Addison in 1713, and is generally credited with another
for Durfey's 'last play' (probably the benefit performance given him
on June 15 of the same year), and that he followed these with an
Epilogue for Rowe in 1714, and a Prologue for Gay in 1717, his well-
known refusal subsequently to write either prologue or epilogue for
the plays of other, but less intimate, friends (*e.g.* for Hughes in 1719,
Fenton in 1722, and Hill in 1731),[3] cannot be objected against the

---

[1] See *ante*, p. 104.

[2] *A Key to the Lock* was published about April 25, 1715 (see Pope's *Prose*, i,
pp. lxxiii f.)
[3] For details, see *post*, p. 209.

probability that Pope wrote these verses for Rowe in 1715. And the recent discovery of evidence that he subsequently wrote two other anonymous pieces of the kind for Gay[1] (not to mention the prologues for Thomson in 1730, and Dennis in 1733, often attributed to him) still further suggests that such refusal was discriminative rather than absolute.

The case for the identification of Pope with the 'Unknown Hand' rests on more than the absence of evidence against it, on more even than Rowe's testimony to the existence of a Prologue written by Pope presumably for him in 1715, and his inclusion of a superfluous and mysterious Prologue in his play in 1715. In these circumstances it is difficult to believe it was entirely a coincidence that rumour was connecting Pope's name with *Lady Jane Gray* the year before it was acted. Gildon, in his *New Rehearsal*, 1714, went so far as to say that 'the Popish Poet' was 'Writing a Play of the Lady *Jane Grey*'.[2] But although— as Pope dryly explained later in *The Dunciad*—'it afterwards proved to be Mr. Row's', it is noticeable that not only does that denial *not* apply to the Prologue, but also that Pope, by italicizing Gildon's words thus: 'he was writing a *play* of the Lady Jane Grey',[3] seems to be implicitly acknowledging some other connection with Rowe's tragedy— which could well be his hand in this Prologue.

The argument for Pope's authorship, however, is most firmly based on the internal evidence of the poem itself in conjunction with these things. To the perceptive ear, the cadences of its lines are as reminiscent of Pope's earlier verse as the witty sparkle of its concluding couplet is of *The Rape of the Lock*. More easily demonstrable, though not perhaps more convincing, are those passages in which phrases from his acknowledged work are strangely echoed—or still more strangely anticipated. Pope's life-long habit of repeating himself more or less closely in expression and idea in different works, sometimes after a lapse of years, has already been illustrated on a previous page.[4] The habit, whether conscious or not, is indisputable; and to it is owing in great measure the long deferred recognition of his authorship of a number of anonymous pieces, both in this volume and elsewhere. And once again, this prologue is found to contain parallels to his known poems in such number and of such individuality that they cannot reasonably be explained except as the work of the same hand (thus markedly contrasting with the proper prologue to the play, which bears not the slightest trace of Pope).

---

[1] See *post*, Chapters XIII and XIX.   [2] *A New Rehearsal*, p. 48.
[3] *The Dunciad*, 1743, 'Testimonies of Authors', p. lxiii.   [4] See *ante*, pp. 44 ff.

Only the more important parallels can be quoted here, the first passage in each example being taken from the prologue under discussion.

(*a*)   Tho the Muse saddens each distressed Scene.
                                        (5)
          Her gloomy presence saddens all the scene.
                                        Eloisa to Abelard, 167.

It is noteworthy that the Oxford English Dictionary (hereafter O.E.D.) cites this line from *Eloisa to Abelard* as the first appearance in English literature of the word 'saddens' with this particular shade of meaning. Whether Pope originated the usage or not, it was employed by him, and apparently by him alone, several times between 1715 and 1717; for example, 'And a still Horror saddens all the Deeps' (*Iliad*, VII, 74); and 'Blank Horror sadden'd each celestial Face' (*Iliad*, XV, 109).

(*b*)   No Blossoms fade, nor sick'ning Roses die.
                                        (22)
          The sick'ning stars fade . . .
                                        Dunciad A, IV, 636.

The O.E.D., quoting this phrase from *The Dunciad*, gives Pope the credit for the first use of 'sickening' in this figurative sense (and, curiously enough, in the literal sense also, for which *The Odyssey* is cited).

(*c*)   To stand unmov'd against the Storms of Fate.
                                        (16)
          A brave Man struggling in the Storms of Fate.
                                        Prologue to Cato, 21.

This was a particularly favourite image of Pope's; he uses it at least six other times in more or less similar phraseology, four of which occur within a year or two of 1715.

(*d*)   No soft Enchantments languish in her Eye.
                                        (21)
          See the last sparkle languish in my eye!
                                        Eloisa to Abelard, 332.
          Fade from thy Cheek, and languish in thy Eye.
                                        Iliad, III, 516.

All three were published within little more than two years of each other, the first and third actually within five weeks.

(f)   Lays down the Load of Life . . .

(14)

. . . you groan beneath the Load of Life.

Iliad, VI, 584.

These two passages were written at approximately the same time. Among the shorter phrases that might be quoted are one or two curious doubles like 'flatter'd lawless Will' (l. 37) and 'flatter lawless Sway' (*Temple of Fame*, 517), which appeared in print within three months of each other, and are extremely difficult to account for unless Pope wrote them both. Then, too, there are several parallels in line construction, having in addition much the same colour and feeling, like the following passages which were published within five weeks of each other:

(g)   Like flow'ry Shadows on the silver Stream.

(42)

His silver Current thro' the flow'ry Meads.

Iliad, II, 623.

The first of which has also in idea an exact double in one of Pope's early poems:

The gliding Shadows o'er the polish'd Glass.

January and May, 237.

Other parallels could be quoted; points of similarity (in versification, construction, treatment, and vocabulary) between Pope's *Prologue to Cato* and this *Prologue to Lady Jane Gray* could be demonstrated; and Pope's knowledge of Rowe's play *before* it was produced could be proved from the letter he and Gay wrote jointly to Caryll in the early part of April 1715—did space but allow. It may, however, be noted in conclusion that, of the parallels in Pope's acknowledged works, some appeared before the Prologue was printed, and some afterwards; so that if Pope was not the author of it, he must have borrowed the one group from the Prologue writer, and the Prologue writer the other group from Pope—which is perhaps possible. But if so, what is to be said of those parallels, of which there are several (drawn from the first volume of *The Iliad*), where both the original passage and its echo must have been standing in type, unpublished, at the same time? From the foregoing it would appear that the only hypothesis capable of covering all the available facts is that the 'Unknown Hand'—which presumably wrote the Prologue as well as sent it—was the hand of Alexander Pope.

IV. TWO EPITAPHS

Between the writing of Pope's *Prologue to Lady Jane Gray* in 1715 and
Rowe's premature death in 1718, the friendship of the two poets suffered no diminution, rather increased in cordiality, if anything. Rowe
was made Poet Laureate in the year first mentioned (an office for
which Pope had no desire and little regard), but the change in Rowe's
status brought no change in their relations. It needed the subsequent
elevation of such men as Eusden and Cibber[1]—Rowe's successors in
office—to move Pope to satiric comment on the laureateship.

During these last three or four years of Rowe's life, Pope made a
number of allusions to him in occasional poems and pamphlets, as well
as in his correspondence. A letter already quoted tells how Pope
delighted in his friend's high spirits, his vivacity and gaiety, so much
so that even after having him as a guest in the house for a week, Pope
could not part with him without uneasiness and a sense of disappointment and loss. Right to the end of Pope's life he would recall with unfailing pleasure the care-free happy times they had spent together.
And once when Spence remarked to Pope that he had 'thought Rowe
had been too grave to write such things' as nonsensical epigrams,
Pope's reply was—'He! why he would laugh all day long! he would do
nothing else but laugh'.[2] It is therefore a characteristic glimpse we
catch of him in Pope's sparkling *Farewell to London In the Year 1715*:

> To drink and droll be *Rowe* allow'd
> Till the third watchman toll . . .

He is mentioned, too, in playful or friendly manner elsewhere in that
poem, and also in *Umbra* (1715), in *Sandys's Ghost* (1716), and, the
same year, in the first lampoon on Curll, in which Pope makes the
piratical bookseller say that he had paid Gildon double to attack Pope
and Rowe together in the *New Rehearsal*.[3] Then in 1717, the two
friends reversed the relative positions they had occupied with respect
to Tonson's miscellany in 1709; for this time it was Pope who compiled
and edited anonymously a new miscellany, entitled, *Poems on Several
Occasions*,[4] Rowe being a contributor only. His name stands fifth on the
title-page amongst the 'Eminent Hands' represented in the collection,
and it is interesting to note that the first of his three poems is called,
Verses made to a Simile of Mr. Pope's. Lastly, late in 1717, or early in
1718, Pope wrote and addressed to his friend a pamphlet attacking

---

[1] See *post*, pp. 315 ff.   [2] Spence, p. 284.   [3] See Pope's *Prose*, I, p. 263.
[4] Reprinted as *Pope's Own Miscellany*, ed. N. Ault.

Cibber, entitled, *A Clue to the Non Juror . . . In a Letter to N. Rowe, Esq*[1]; the opening and closing paragraphs of which showed their old friendly relations still flourishing.

William Ayre, who need not always be mistrusted, wrote of the familiar intercourse between the two friends very pleasantly.

> Mr. *Rowe* . . . was in the Number of Mr. *Pope*'s select Friends. When-ever Mr. *Pope* gave any of his Verses into his Hands, and receiv'd them from him again, he us'd to say they were like Gold three times tried in the Fire; for their Esteem of each other (each being Counsellor to each) was reciprocal. Mr. *Rowe* held Mr. *Pope* in the highest Esteem, Mr. *Pope* had a very great Regard both for the Person and Writings of Mr. *Rowe*, and oftentimes pass'd whole Days in his Company.[2]

Small wonder if, after Rowe's death on December 6, 1718, Pope was—in Ayre's words—'very strongly affected'.[3] He would in any case have long felt it as a personal loss, but Parnell's death had occurred only a few weeks earlier, and Garth's death only a few weeks later. Small wonder, too, if his thoughts turned for sympathy to friends who had been their friends, seeking in memories of happier days some anodyne for grief. Writing to Jervas the painter, who was making a long stay in Ireland about this time, he says:

> I can't express how I long to renew our old intercourse and con-versation, our morning conferences in bed in the same room, our evening walks in the park, our amusing voyages on the water, our philosophical suppers, our lectures, our dissertations, our gravities, our reveries, our fooleries, or what not?—This awakens the memory of some of those who have made a part in all these. Poor Parnelle, Garth, Rowe! You justly reprove me for not speaking of the death of the last! Parnelle was too much in my mind . . . Yet I have not neglected my devoirs to Mr. Rowe; I am writing this very day his Epitaph for Westminster-Abby.[4]

Now, as many people know, there is an epitaph on Rowe still extant in the Abbey, which has been the cause of much perplexity and no little dispute in the past, it being frequently asserted that this epitaph is not the one Pope told Jervas he was writing 'for Westminster-Abby',

[1] See Pope's *Prose*, I, pp. 303–14.   [2] *Memoirs*, I, p. 209.

[3] *Ibid.*, p. 211.

[4] *Letters*, 4to, 1737, pp. 190 f. This letter is either wrongly dated or a combination of two or more, written at different times (see *ante*, p. 14): it is headed 'Decemb. 12, 1718'; but Garth did not die until the following month.

which he included later in *The Works*, 1735, under the title—*Intended for Mr. Rowe. In Westminster Abbey*. Not the one! But, it might well be asked, at what stage in the development, or correction and revision, of a poem can that poem be said no longer to exist but to have become another poem? Is it a matter of degree or of opinion? It is at least demonstrable in the present case that no less than four lines of the eight in the first printed version (1720) remain in much the same form in the final Abbey version of ten lines (omitting the pendant).

Furthermore, this last version has recently been said by a number of people not only to be in effect a different poem, but also to have been written by a different person[1]; add to that, a report of a veiled reference to it (years before it was written!) found in one of Pope's late Satires, and other similarly conflicting identifications, annotations, and judgements, and it would seem to be high time that another attempt was made to arrive at the truth of the matter.

Amongst the papers of Pope's friend, the Earl of Oxford, in the British Museum, is a manuscript[2] containing an epitaph of eight lines as follows:

> Verses designed for Mr Rowes Monument by Mr Pope,
> at the request of Mr Rowes Widow.

> To Rowes dear Reliques be this Marble just
> Laid Sacred here, by Dryden's awful Dust,
> And let it guide the Worlds enquiring Eies
> To find that Speechless Stone where Dryden lies.
> Peace to thy gentle Shade, & Endless Rest!
> Blest in thy Genius! in thy Love too blest!
> One grateful Woman to thy Fame supplies
> What a whole thankless Land to His denies.

This version (which seems never to have been printed before) also exists amongst Lord Oxford's papers at Welbeck and at Longleat; the copy at Welbeck having been transcribed by Adrian Drift (the editor of Prior) almost certainly in 1719. There can be little doubt that this is the earliest version yet discovered. However, Pope was not satisfied with it for long. Perhaps the first few words, the natural expression of immediate grief, were afterwards felt to be too revealing for one who did not usually air his private sorrows in public. Whatever the reason, he revised it the following year, and printed the epitaph for the first

[1] *e.g.* Sherburn, p. 271.   [2] Harl. 7316, f. 90.

time in the third edition of his first miscellany, *Miscellaneous Poems and Translations*, 1720. His corrections, however, were in the main limited to the first four lines, which now run thus:

Epitaph Design'd for Mr. ROWE in *Westminster-Abbey.*
By Mr. Pope
To the Memory of Nicholas Rowe *Esq*;
his Wife erected this Monument.

Thy reliques, ROWE, to this fair Shrine we trust,
And sacred, place by DRYDEN's awful dust;
Beneath a rude and nameless stone he lies
To which thy Tomb shall guide inquiring eyes.
Peace to . . .

[The rest as above, except that the rhyming words of the final couplet were changed to 'supply'd' and 'deny'd'.]

Once in print, the epitaph became quite popular and was frequently reprinted in Pope's lifetime. But although it appeared at least twenty times elsewhere, it failed to appear in the place for which it was 'design'd'—on Rowe's monument in the Abbey. The explanation, though not generally known, is simple. There was no monument there to inscribe the epitaph on: the truth being that, for some reason unnoted, Rowe's tomb was left without the proposed memorial until shortly before Pope himself died. It is not a little ironical that Mrs Rowe's monument to her husband, which, as Pope envisaged it, would point to the place where Dryden lay nameless, failed to materialize for nearly a quarter of a century, while Dryden's monument with a 'plain inscription' had been erected by the Duke of Buckingham not long after, and as a result of, the publication of Rowe's epitaph in the 1720 miscellany. Fifteen years later the same version was first included in *The Works*, Vol. II, with two trifling corrections in the final couplet, where 'supplies' and 'denies' return to their old places. And there, in the official section entitled 'Epitaphs' (with the final change of 'shrine' to 'urn' in the first line), it has ever since been retained, first by the poet himself and afterwards by all his principal editors, down to the present day. When, however, the monument to Rowe was at last erected in the Abbey, the epitaph on it was found to differ so greatly from the familiar version in *The Works*, that Pope's hand in it was not recognized at the time, and is still often disputed or completely ignored. Can the question be settled at this late date?

It has, not infrequently, been mentioned as something extraordinary, if not actually shameful, that Mrs Rowe—who, on her husband's death in 1718, had been left with an infant daughter, Charlotte—should have married again, even though she had allowed a decent interval of five or six years to elapse before doing so. Her second spouse was a Colonel Alexander Deanes, but nothing seems to be known of their married life from 1724 onwards. On October 7, 1739, however, she suffered a second bereavement, her daughter Charlotte (now Mrs Fane) dying 'in ye 22^d year of her Age'. Three years later the following entry was made in the Chapter Book of Westminster Abbey, as one of 'The Acts of a Chapter held on friday', October 29, 1742:

> Ordered   That leave be given to put up a Monument in the South-Cross of the Abbey—between Shakespears and Mr Gays, for Mr Rowe the Poet, on the payment of Twenty Guineas.[1]

The work must have proceeded slowly, for it was not until June 25, 1743, that the weekly paper, *Common Sense*, printed a new epitaph on Rowe, of ten lines plus a four-line pendant, and announced it thus:

> The following is the Inscription on the Monument lately set up in *Westminster-Abby*, in Memory of the late Mr. Rowe, the famous Poet, viz. . . .

As, however, the published epitaph[2] contains several unauthorized typographical variants, the text here printed is taken from the actual inscription on the stone.

> Thy Reliques, *Rowe*! to this sad Shrine we trust,
> And near thy *Shakespear* place thy honour'd Bust,
> Oh next him skill'd to draw the tender Tear,
> For never Heart felt Passion more sincere:
> To nobler Sentiment to fire the Brave,
> For never *Briton* more disdain'd a Slave!
> Peace to thy gentle Shade, and endless Rest,
> Blest in thy Genius, in thy Love too blest,
> And blest, that timely from Our Scene remov'd
> Thy Soul enjoys that Liberty it lov'd.

[*Underneath, divided from the above by a space, inscribed in smaller lettering, and set back a little, are the following lines*]

[1] Chapter Book 9, 1738–49.
[2] The epitaph also appeared the same day in *The Universal Spectator*, and shortly after in *The London Magazine*.

To these,[1] so mourn'd in Death, so lov'd in Life!
The childless Parent & the widow'd Wife
With Tears inscribes this monumental Stone,
That holds their Ashes & expects her own.

To take first the case against Pope's authorship of this version of the epitaph. It has sometimes been asserted that because Pope neither 'signed' these lines, nor acknowledged them by including them in his *Works*, he was not responsible for them. The supporters of this view apparently forgot that anonymity was no new trick or feature of his publications, many of which—including a number of major works from *An Essay on Criticism* to *An Essay on Man*, from *The Rape of the Lock* to *The Dunciad*—were first published without his name. New editions of an author's works cannot be produced at a moment's notice simply to incorporate an expanded revision of a short poem already included in it; while, as regards Pope's *Works*, the truth is that no new poem found its way into them between the date of the inscription in the Abbey and his death. No one seems to have remarked how brief and constrained a period that was for Pope; for though it is not recorded exactly when the monument was completed and the epitaph cut, reports show it could have been very little earlier than the end of June 1743—and before June came round again, Pope himself was dead. With only those few months remaining to him of unremitting illness and ever-increasing physical feebleness, it is obvious that arguments against his authorship of the epitaph cannot reasonably be based on things omitted or left undone, even if it had not been his habit to leave poems nameless, or not collected, often for many years, as these pages repeatedly testify.

But another argument against Pope's authorship of the expanded epitaph has recently been advanced with more show of authority.[2] This, however, depends entirely on a remark made to Malone by Lord Hailes[3] who told him (without producing any evidence) that a certain couplet about widows in the *Epilogue to the Satires, II,* 1738, referred to Mrs Rowe. The particular lines run thus:

[1] The two parts of the epitaph are inscribed, without heading or title, on the main pedestal of the monument; and, if read alone, the first words of the pendant, 'To these', are not clear. They refer to an inscription on the pedestal of the bust of Rowe some three or four feet above them, which reads as follows:

To the Memory of/NICHOLAS ROWE Esq./*who died in* 1718 *Aged* 45./*And of* Charlotte *his only Daughter*/*The Wife of* Henry Fane *Esq.*/*who, Inheriting*/*her Fathers Spirit,*/*and Amiable in her own*/*Innocence & Beauty,*/*died in y*e 22d *year of her Age,*/1739.

[2] See R.E.S., VII, 1931, pp. 76–9. A. Jackson's *Pope's Epitaphs on Rowe.*

[3] Malone, p. 253.

> But random Praise— . . .
> Each Widow asks it for the Best of Men,
> For him she weeps, and him she weds agen.
>
> (ll. 106, 108–9)

The argument based on this identification asserts that, as the couplet was printed in 1738, and Rowe's daughter did not die until 1739, Pope must have written the epitaph mentioning her *after* the couplet, which is absurd; therefore he did not write the epitaph! The correct reply to that is—if Pope did not write the epitaph, it must follow that the couplet did not allude to Mrs Rowe, therefore the whole thing cancels out. But a much greater objection attaches to the argument. Pope himself said in a letter already quoted,[1] that he was 'writing this very day' (December 12, 1718) an epitaph on his dead friend, not only without the faintest breath of a grumble that Mrs Rowe's 'request' was at all extraordinary (always supposing the MS. title, given above, was not a polite fiction on which to hang the final couplet—the climax of the epitaph), but actually calling it 'my devoirs to Mr. Rowe', as though he was writing it on his own initiative. But, however that may have been, it is unlikely in the extreme that twenty years later this allusion to an unnamed 'Widow' refers back to that occasion when (as has been shown above) he himself was so deeply moved. Thus— still on the assumption that Pope's couplet did allude to Mrs Rowe— the questions arise: when, or on what occasion, was Mrs Rowe's request made? and for whom did she ask it?

Now the change in the position of Rowe's monument, from the spot 'by Dryden's awful Dust' (in the earlier version) to a place 'between Shakespears and Mr. Gays' (according to the order in the Chapter Book), means that the expanded epitaph, which shows cognizance of the change, could not possibly have been written before October 29, 1742, when the necessary permission was granted and recorded. Consequently, that entry is of itself sufficient to acquit the 'Widow' couplet of any sneer at Mrs Rowe. For it now seems certain that she could not have 'asked' Pope for anything before October 1742, and after that date had 'asked'—*not* for more praise of her long-deceased husband, in the twentieth year of her married life with his successor—but only for the necessary correction of the lines in the epitaph which allude to the position of the monument; possibly at the same time expressing a natural wish that Charlotte might also be referred to in it. Neither of which requests could conceivably have been made before the coup-

[1] See *ante*, p. 146.

l

let in the Satire was written. The conclusion of the whole discussion is, that, as Mrs Rowe was not the widow Pope had in mind, the argument hitherto based on that assumption (namely, that the expanded epitaph was not written by Pope but by some one else) falls to the ground. Lastly, as a *coup de grâce*, is the extreme unlikelihood of a poet of Pope's character and standing allowing any one else to revise and expand a poem, which was still figuring in the latest edition of *The Works* published that same year, 1743, for use as a public inscription in the Abbey, where no less than five other epitaphs of his on famous men witnessed also to his own fame as a memorialist.

Nevertheless, as it is impossible to prove a negative, and as the discovery of the real criminal is the best method of acquitting an innocent suspect—so Mrs Rowe would be best vindicated by a correct identification of the 'widow'. If, therefore, Pope's satirical couplet was anything more than a witty generalization, a far better subject than Lord Hailes's unfortunate guess is the lady suggested by Horace Walpole[1] (a nearer contemporary of Pope than was Hailes). This was Mrs Nugent, who was thrice married, and at whose request Pope wrote an epitaph on her second husband, John Knight,[2] as the poet's letters show.

In this instance, all the dates are compatible with the identification. The lady was a sister of Pope's friend, Secretary Craggs; and she married first, in 1712, John Newsham, who died in 1724; her next marriage, in 1727, being to John Knight, who died in 1733. Three years later she asked Pope to write an epitaph on Knight, which he did, and it was sent to her on May 17, 1736.[3] In less than a year afterwards she married once again (on March 23, 1737), her third husband being Robert Nugent; and it was this marriage that evoked Pope's acid couplet on epitaph-begging widows, which was published in July 1738. Such an indisputable sequence of events must finally and completely overthrow the case for the unknown authorship of the 1743 epitaph, as based on Mrs Rowe being the 'widow' of Pope's couplet.

The case for Pope's authorship of the longer, as well as the shorter, version of the epitaph on Rowe is founded on evidence gathered from several widely varying sources. In the first place, the lack of Pope's actual acknowledgement of the piece is in no little measure counterbalanced by the testimony of Warburton, his friend and first editor, to whom he bequeathed much of his literary property. Whatever may be thought of Warburton as editor, he was extremely conservative in his compilation of the Pope canon; and if he overlooked, or rejected,

---

[1] Fraser, p. 86.   [2] See *post*, pp. 333 f.   [3] EC, IX, pp. 455 f.

many poems we have reason to believe Pope's, he at least never included in all his nine volumes a single poem with which Pope has since been proved to have had nothing to do; although some doubt exists about the *extent* of Pope's responsibility (whether collaboration, correction, or revision) as regards two of the included pieces. Warburton's acceptance of the longer version as Pope's, though tardy, was none the less whole-hearted or convincing; for after omitting to insert it in the earliest editions, he included it first in 1758 under 'Variations' and then in the 1760 edition of *The Works* with the following emphatic note: 'He altered it much for the better, as it now stands on the monument erected to Rowe and his daughter'. And Warburton, because of his close association with Pope from 1739 to 1744, and his subsequent access to the dead poet's papers, should have known the facts. There must also be taken into account the earlier testimony (made within eighteen months of the inscription of the poem on the monument) by William Ayre, who reprinted the new version in full in his *Memoirs*,[1] with the statement 'wrote by Mr. Pope'.

More conclusive still, for any one familiar with Pope's poetical idiosyncrasies, is the internal evidence of the expanded epitaph, which corroborates Warburton's statement. For example, in the first line, 'shrine' has been restored from the earlier texts; for the last three editions of *The Works*, including the current one, 1743, read 'urn'. It is more difficult to believe that a mere expander, who was altering Pope's words and adding new lines, would bother to look up and restore a former variant of the epitaph, than that Pope, with the huge monument at last in place, should revert to his earlier reading as being now the more appropriate. Again, the new fourth line—'For never Heart felt Passion more sincere'—repeats Pope's opinion of Rowe previously expressed in 1737 in one of his *Imitations of Horace*, where, discussing the chief merits of former poets, he wrote, 'But, for the Passions, Southern sure and Rowe'.[2] Once again, amongst the new additions is the couplet that really concludes the epitaph on Rowe (the rest is mere appendix):

> And blest, that timely from Our Scene remov'd
> Thy Soul enjoys that Liberty it lov'd.

This too finds its parallel in an early epitaph of Pope's which similarly closes with the couplet:

> Such this man was; who now from earth remov'd,
> At length enjoys that liberty he lov'd.

[1] Published January 1745 (*Gent. Mag.*).   [2] Hor. Ep. II, i, l. 86.

And if an explanation of this strange repetition were needed, it might perhaps be found in the fact that the early epitaph in which it appeared was not an actual tombstone inscription, but originally a literary tribute to an anonymous person, which itself was partly borrowed from a still earlier epitaph, then unprinted, on John Lord Caryll, and which was not given Trumbull's name until the 1735 edition of *The Works*. Scores of more or less similar doubles have been cited in these pages and elsewhere, as proof that Pope had a foible for such repetition. And the repetition under discussion might be nothing more than another example of that practice, followed in this case as in so many others, by his subsequent neglect of the poem.

On the other hand, there is in many respects an exact parallel to Pope's apparent neglect of the epitaph on Rowe and his daughter, and its exclusion from the 1743 edition of *The Works* (always supposing it was completed in time). This is to be found in his unswerving refusal during the last years of his life to include the epitaph on Bishop Atterbury and his daughter in *The Works* of 1735 and every edition thereafter; so that, like the Rowe epitaph, it was left to Warburton to include it in the canon. The curious story of the Atterbury epitaph, showing to what lengths Pope would go to efface the embarrassing results of an oversight, is told on another page.[1] It is sufficient here to say that the earlier suppression strongly suggests that on this occasion Pope temporarily forgot how closely the couplet, with which he concluded the main part of the Rowe epitaph, echoed the concluding couplet of the Trumbull epitaph, until the inscription had been irrevocably cut on the Abbey monument. But although it was then too late to alter it, he would realize that, luckily, it need not be 'signed' (most sepulchral verses were not), nor need it be talked about. Also he could forget to substitute it for the old epitaph on Rowe (which is numbered 'IV') in the official section of *The Works* headed 'Epitaphs', where it would have stood *next but one* to the Trumbull epitaph (numbered 'II').[2] It did not matter so much in the Abbey— the other epitaph was not there, and people do not go about with books of verse in their pockets—and they forget! And Pope, apparently, was content to leave it like that.

A last word may be added. The epitaph in the earlier version totalled eight lines in all; in the later version the lines relative to Rowe are ten in number, six of which (as we have seen) are Pope's lines more or less corrected, while a seventh states his personal view of Rowe's

[1] See *post*, pp. 281 ff.

[2] For the order of the 'Epitaphs' in the 1735 vol., see *post*, p. 284 n.

work as a vehicle or portrayal of passion. Many of Pope's pieces have been corrected or expanded as much as this, and their authenticity never questioned. It seems not yet to be generally realized that Pope could rarely keep his pen from 'correcting' his own verses even after they were printed; indeed, this propensity was so overmastering at times as to cause him to treat his friend's verses like his own. An extreme instance of the one is Martha Blount's 'Birthday Poem' which over a period of many years was corrected almost out of recognition,[1] while an amusing example of the other is the younger Richardson's[2] story, which tells how once when Lady Mary W. Montagu was showing Pope some of her verses and his hand was itching to correct them, he was suddenly stopped by her crying out—'No, Pope, no touching!' It would thus appear that when Pope came to make the necessary topographical alteration in his old friend's old epitaph, waking memories and a desire to speak more of Rowe and less of Dryden combined with his passion for revision to compel him to 'touch' it here and there and elsewhere, until at last the lines took on their final shape which, for nearly two hundred years, has been known to visitors to the Abbey's world-famous 'Poets' Corner'—but apparently to be known there no more.

In the autumn of 1936, following the discovery of early mural paintings on the south wall of the south transept, the monuments of two of Pope's dearest friends, Nicholas Rowe and John Gay, were transferred aloft to the unfrequented gallery of the triforium, where not only is the general public denied the right to see them, except by special permission, but Pope's epitaphs themselves are made sheer nonsense. It seems a pity, when life-size statues and memorials of lesser poets are still suffered to overcrowd the 'Corner'; and (remembering the solemn contracts[3] recorded in the Chapter Books) something more than a pity, that these two monuments should have been allowed without protest to be thus—

> *Untimely* from our Scene remov'd.

---

[1] See *post*, pp. 195 ff. [2] Spence, p. 233 n.
[3] The agreement about Rowe's monument is given above (p. 149); an agreement to the same effect concerning Gay's monument was made on October 31, 1733.

CHAPTER VIII

THE FIRST PSALM

T HE story of Pope's unfortunate 'burlesque on the first Psalm'[1] is inextricably mixed up with his famous quarrel with the piratical bookseller, Edmund Curll. The original edition of the poem, a single sheet which has survived in only one copy, was announced in *The Flying-Post*, June 28–30, 1716 (amongst other papers), thus:

> This Day is publish'd, A *Roman Catholick* Version of the First Psalm; for the Use of a Young *Lady*. By Mr. POPE. Printed for R. Burleigh in Amen Corner, pr. 2*d*.

But both in this advertisement and in the imprint on the sheet itself, Mrs Burleigh's name was nothing more than a screen for Curll[2] (he had others), and this publication under her name was one of his shrewdest strokes against the poet. For not only did it profoundly shock the public who condemned poem and poet alike with no uncertain voice, but it provided his enemies in the years to come with a taunt that never lost its sting. Reprobation was immediate as well as lasting, and less than a fortnight later found voice in such protests as that in *The Flying-Post*, July 12–14, 1716:

> Mr. Pope having writ a prophane Ballad by way of Burlesque, on the first Psalm in Metre, as it is Sung in the Churches, it may be of Service to put a stop to a farther Design, which it seems he has to Burlesque the Penitential Psalms, if you insert his Blasphemous Ballad with the following Eccho, which justly exposes it. Certainly every Man who has the least Regard to the Sacred Text, as the Rule of his Faith and Manners, must resent such an unparallel'd Piece of Impiety.

> A VERSION OF THE FIRST PSALM,
> for the Use of a Popish Lady.

> By Mr. *POPE*

> The Maid is Blest that will not hear
> Of Masquerading Tricks,
> Nor lends to Wanton Songs an Ear,
> Nor Sighs for Coach and Six.

[1] The substance of this chapter was first printed in R.E.S., October 1942 (pp. 441–7), where it was entitled 'New Light on Pope'.   [2] Straus, pp. 63 f.

To Please her shall her Husband strive
  With all his Main and Might,
And in her Love shall Exercise
  Himself both Day and Night.

She shall bring forth most Pleasant Fruit,
  He Flourish still and Stand,
Ev'n so all Things shall prosper well,
  That this Maid takes in Hand.

No wicked Whores shall have such Luck
  Who follow their own Wills,
But Purg'd shall be to Skin and Bone,
  With *Mercury* and *Pills*.

For why? the Pure and Cleanly Maids
  Shall All, good Husbands gain:
But filthy and uncleanly Jades
  Shall Rot in *Drury-Lane*.

The poem in the newspaper is immediately followed by the 'Eccho', of which, since it has never been reprinted, a few stanzas may be given:

The Eccho to *Pope*'s Drury-Lane Ballad.

The busy World can not agree,
  Tho' sure, methinks, it should,
Whether the Pope or Devil be,
  The better Friend of God . . . [2 stzs. omitted]

We have a *Pope*, than both more vile,
  Who dares God's Word Blaspheme,
By lewd, prophane, uncleanly Style,
  In Terms, I dare not Name.

The Royal David's Harp he takes,
  To play his Wanton Song,
And screws and strains its Strings, so makes
  His smutty Notes sound strong.

No Atheist, Deist, Devil yet,
  Thus rudely touch'd that Lyre;
To prostitute thus Holy Writ,
  As do's this POPISH Squire . . . [3 stzs. omitted]

> May High-Church Fury seize the Wretch,
>   And stop his filthy Tune,
> Lest Heaven it self its Arm out stretch,
>   And stop his Vitals soon.

There is not much to be said for it; but an 'Eccho' can hardly be expected to improve on the original voice. Nevertheless, other people joined in; and Pope shrank before the storm his 'Drury-Lane Ballad' had provoked, and began to take steps to evade it. He wrote to Swift[1] —'I have begun to take a pique at the Psalms of David, if the wicked may be credited, who have printed a scandalous one in my name.' He even felt compelled to make what purported to be a public repudiation of the poem, in an ill-starred advertisement in *The Post-Man* of July 28–31, 1716, as follows:

> Whereas there have been publish'd in my Name, certain scandalous Libels, which I hope no Persons of Candor would have thought me capable of, I am sorry to find myself obliged to declare, that no Genuine Pieces of mine have been printed by any but Mr. Tonson and Mr. Lintot. And in particular, as to that which is entituled, A Version of the first Psalm; I hereby promise a Reward of three Guineas to any one who shall discover the Person or Persons concerned in the Publication of the said Libel, of which I am wholly ignorant.   A. Pope.

And he repeated this sorry quibble three days later in *The Evening Post*. With this advertisement Pope became fair game for those of his enemies who knew the facts of the case. 'Mrs. Burleigh' advertised in turn that she was ready to show the MS. of the poem in the poet's own handwriting to any one who would call at her shop.[2] Pope remained silent. But the gibe was too good to be dropped, and nearly twenty years later Curll was still baiting him with it: 'Did you not offer a Reward of Three Guineas, by an Advertisement in the *Post-Man*, to know the Publisher of your Version of the *First-Psalm*? And when you were informed, did you ever pay the Premium?'[3] But if Pope made no further public move, on August 7, that is within four days of the second advertisement, he was writing to Teresa Blount: 'If you have seen a late Advertisement, you will know that I have not told a Lye

---

[1] The letter has been dated June 20, 1716, probably incorrectly. There is much reason for thinking Pope wrote it about July 29, 1716, which is the date of a letter he sent to Parnell in Ireland *at the same time* as this to Swift (EC, VII, p. 461). Swift's reply is dated August 30, 1716.

[2] Straus, p. 64.   [3] *Correspondence*, II, 1735, p. xii.

(wch we both abhominate) but equivocated pretty genteely. You may be confident twas not done without leave from my spiritual director'.[1] After all this publicity, Pope could hardly have owned the poem, even supposing he ever wanted to; but his equivocation would seem to corroborate the general opinion of his authorship almost as satisfactorily as would his signature. There is, however, in addition, Blackmore's indignant protest against the burlesque,[2] which leaves us in no doubt about the identity of its 'godless author'—at least in Blackmore's mind. Lastly, those few of Pope's editors and biographers who have mentioned the burlesque at all, have, while accepting his authorship, uniformly declined to print it, and, at the same time, have repeated the old reprobations. Thus one, for example, calls it, 'an impious and indecent parody of the first Psalm'; another, 'this tavern piece of truly impious buffoonery'; and a third, 'an indecent and blasphemous parody'.

The foregoing, then, constitutes the indictment (though never so fully documented before) which has for two centuries and more charged Pope with blasphemy. Nevertheless, when all is said and done, the case against him will be found to have been based on a misconception, and he himself shown to be something less than the 'devil' he has been portrayed. The simple truth is that Pope scholars have all along overlooked the fundamental fact that he was *not* burlesquing Holy Scripture in this unpleasant parody, but only ridiculing what was, poetically, a burlesque of it—a key to which interpretation of the facts is not entirely lacking in the first newspaper attack on him quoted above, in the words 'in Metre'.

Pope's care for the art of poetry and his overwhelming scorn of poor craftsmanship—being as they are, the obverse and reverse of the major passion of his life[3]—cannot in questions of this kind be simply taken for granted, and as simply forgotten, for they lie at the very core of the episode. Consequently, Pope's life-long ridicule of 'bad poets' must once again be recalled, because he used so frequently to cite Sternhold and Hopkins, the sixteenth-century versifiers of the Psalms, amongst the most incompetent of them all. And if one wonders for a moment why he was so obsessed with those two dim Elizabethan figures in particular, wonder passes with the remembrance that in Pope's day their metrical versions of the Psalms were still extremely popular among a large proportion of the Protestant communities: indeed, no fewer than twenty-six different editions of them, issued

[1] Mapledurham, 56.   [2] See *Essays*, Vol. II, 1717, p. 270.
[3] See *ante*, pp. 6, 22.

between 1700 and 1716, may be seen in the Bodleian alone. Now, it is generally agreed that Pope was the author of the ballad called *The Monster of Ragusa*[1] which was written about this time (1716) though not published until the following year. Thus it happened that when, later, he was preparing a new edition of his first miscellany where he was again reprinting that ballad, he wrote to Swift a long letter (dated October 15, 1725) towards the end of which, after scoffing at Hopkins and Sternhold, he jokingly alluded to himself as 'a modern imitator of theirs', and quoted a stanza from *The Monster of Ragusa* to prove it. In 1716, therefore, when *The Whole Book of the Psalms Collected into English Metre, By Thomas Sternhold, John Hopkins, And Others*, was reprinted and published yet twice again, it is not impossible that it was one of these re-issues which provoked Pope in a moment of high spirits to out-Sternhold Sternhold himself; for a comparison of the Elizabethan's metrical version of the First Psalm with Pope's burlesque proves beyond a shadow of doubt that Pope did not write in parody of the Psalm itself, but wholly and solely in mockery of Sternhold's pedestrian verses, the 1716 text of which is as follows:

PSALM I.
T[homas]. S[ternhold].

The man is blest that hath not lent
    to wicked men his ear:
Nor led his life as sinners do
    nor sat in scorners chair.

But in the law of God the Lord
    doth set his whole delight:
And in the same doth exercise
    himself both day and night.

He shall be like a tree that is
    planted the Rivers nigh:
Which in due season bringeth forth
    its fruit abundantly.

Whose leaf shall never fade nor fall
    but flourishing shall stand:
Even so all things shall prosper well
    that this man takes in hand.

[1] See *Pope's Own Miscellany* (pp. xlvi ff., and 92–5), for text and evidence of authorship.

As for ungodly men, with them
  it shall be nothing so:
But as the chaff which by the wind
  is driven to and fro.

Therefore the wicked man shall not
  in judgment stand upright:
Nor in assembly of the just
  shall sinners come in sight.

For why? the way of godly men
  unto the Lord is known:
Whereas the way of wicked men
  shall quite be overthrown.

Pope's skit, which was obviously never meant for publication, was in all likelihood written in company in one of the coffee-houses, Button's, Will's, or another, frequented by him and his friends when in town—where, in fact, he was residing during the first half of 1716. That would explain how his busy persistent enemy, Curll, could have both obtained a copy of it, and—unknown to Pope—published it like a street ballad in Pope's name and to his defamation. But that was not the worst. On the original ballad-sheet, below the word 'Finis', Curll inserted the libellous statement: '*N.B.* Speedily will be Publish'd, *The* SEVEN *Penitential Psalms.* Collected into English Metre. By Mr. POPE'; and had the further malignity to publish the whole thing under a title ('A *Roman Catholick* Version . . .') which was an offence to, and injury of, all Pope's co-religionists as well. For at this time—it may be remembered—following on the rebellion of 1715, anti-Catholic feeling was running high, and members of that Church were suffering under a minor but very real persecution, of civil restrictions and political disabilities. And even if Pope in his young-manhood (he was then about twenty-eight) was not the most devout of Catholics, there can be no doubt whatever that he was a thoughtful and, in many ways, a religious man. It is now known, for instance, that the world-famous *Universal Prayer,* though not published until 1738, was written only a few months earlier than this burlesque.

For all these reasons, Pope's horror when confronted with this outrageous piratical publication of Curll's can well be imagined. And though, largely as a result of the bookseller's action, he had reason to complain (as he did in a letter to Swift written during the general outcry): 'I suffer for my religion in almost every weekly paper', he tried to put a brave face on it and make fun of the accusation of authorship.

He was nevertheless so shocked by the clamour against himself, that even to Swift he dared not, or did not, confess his work. And as the newspapers also began to repeat Curll's lie that he had 'a farther Design to Burlesque the Penitential Psalms', the growing public indignation seems to have driven him to consult his spiritual director, who, lest worse should befall where no intentional sin had been committed, advised, or agreed to, the public advertisements of that unfortunate equivocation—doubly unfortunate, insomuch that Pope's allusion to it in his letter to Teresa Blount, above quoted, has done perhaps more even than the burlesque itself to alienate modern readers;—trebly unfortunate, because, as it occurs in an otherwise playfully gallant letter, its forthrightness of statement (addressed as it is to a dear friend and fellow Catholic) has generally been mistaken for a cynicism which was far from Pope's thought at that moment, as is proved by the words that immediately followed: 'My next News is a triffle . . .'

In conclusion, it may be remarked that while to many Protestants brought up in the use of the metrical version of the Psalms in public or private worship, that version would have assumed the authority and sanctity of Holy Writ, to one of Pope's religion—not to mention his poetical genius—Sternhold and Hopkins' versification could be no more sacrosanct that any other of the numerous paraphrases in verse of the Scriptures, which were then all the fashion in the miscellanies and periodicals; and he could therefore make fun of its feeble verse with no consciousness of impiety. A travesty of this argument which acquits Pope of blasphemy was put forward by Dennis, to prove his authorship of the 'Blasphemous Ballad'. He asserted that as no 'rhyming persons who have been brought up *Protestants*' could possibly have written the burlesque, it must therefore have been the work of 'a *Popish rhymester* . . . brought up with a contempt for those sacred writings', and ended triumphantly with—'Now show me another *Popish rhymester* but he'.[1] On any view of the facts the main fault lay with Curll. And one remembers that Swift wrote to Pope on this very occasion: 'I think the frolics of merry hours, even when we are guilty, should not be left at the mercy of our best friends, until Curll and his resemblers are hanged'. But still more to the point, perhaps, was Curll's own rejoinder (in his account[2] of a conversation with Pope about this time), when to Pope's assertion 'Satires should not be Printed', he answered: 'They should not be wrote, for if they were, they would be Printed'.

---

[1] See Sutherland, *Dunciad* A, ii, 256 n.   [2] *The Curliad*, 1729, p. 21.

CHAPTER IX

VERSES SENT TO MRS. T. B.

I N the year 1721 there appeared yet another poetical miscellany in London, with an unusually picturesque title and an imposing display of contributors' names, but with no mention at all of its editor. The title-page reads:

> The Grove; or, A Collection of Original Poems, Translations, &c. By W. Walsh, Esq; Dr. J. Donne. Mr. Dryden. Mr. Hall of Hereford. The Lady E— M— Mr. Butler, Author of Hudibras. Mr. Stepney. Sir John Suckling. Dr. Kenrick. And other Eminent Hands . . . London: Printed for W. Mears, at the Lamb without Temple-Bar. 1721.

Why the 'other Eminent Hands' were not also named, was not—for once—because they were not 'Eminent', but for quite another reason, as explained in the nameless editor's rather querulous complaint in the Preface:

> There are several Gentlemen's Names of Note, who furnish'd other Parts in this Collection, (and whose Character might give a check to any Over-freedom in Censure) that might be added, but that I am not at Liberty to insert them.

According to the list of names set out in the preliminary pages, Pope was one of the original subscribers, taking as many as four copies in 'Royal Paper'—an unusual number for Pope, which indicates an unusual interest in the miscellany. Ostensibly he had no connection whatever with it; and although it contains two anonymous pieces (a panegyric and a four-line epigram) addressed to him on his translation of the *Iliad* completed the previous year, one would suppose that was hardly enough—at least as late as 1721—to explain a desire for four copies! On the other hand, if his name had been one of those the editor was 'not at Liberty to insert', such an interest would become understandable, as the copies might be wanted for presentation. It could even be—seeing that Pope's actions rarely sprang from single impulses—that the purchase of redundant copies was in part prompted by a good-natured wish to help this or that person concerned in the book's success. The book, however, was something of a failure—to judge from the fact that eleven years later the still unsold copies were numerous enough to be given a new title and a new pasted-in title-page, and reissued by the same bookseller as a new book, *A Miscellany of Original Poems, Translations &c. . . .* 1732, whose chief interest for us is the appearance in it of Lewis Theobald's name as (what would now be called) its compiler and editor.

The long and bitter quarrel between Pope and Theobald, which culminated in the elevation of the latter to the throne of the Dunces in 1728, lies beyond our immediate purview; and too little is known of their relations before the publication of *The Grove* in 1721, for forthright statement about its beginnings. It can, however, be stated that Theobald began hostilities as early as 1715, if, as Pope thought and maintained years later, he was in part responsible for *A Complete Key to . . . The What D'ye Call it*,[1] which attacked the farce that Pope had helped Gay to produce. But it is also true that Theobald wrote in praise of Pope's *Iliad* in *The Censor* of January 5, 1717—though that of course could have happened without personal feeling in the matter, or even personal acquaintance. No time, however, need be wasted over the so-called 'collaboration' of Pope and Theobald in translating a part of Ovid's *Metamorphoses* for Sewell's edition (dated 1717, but published late in 1716),[2] which has been cited as evidence of their friendship. This collaboration simply disappears on examination, it being obvious that the artful publishers, of whom Curll was one, have merely reprinted—though presumably with permission—Pope's *Vertumnus and Pomona*[3] (1712) in 'Book XIV', together with some of Theobald's translations, and labelled the compound 'by Mr. Pope and Mr. Theobald'. Remains this new item of evidence: Pope's subscription in 1721 for four copies of *The Grove* (of which he may, or may not, have known Theobald was the concealed editor), and this, as has already been shown, might mean various things. Altogether, then, while it is obvious that on the available evidence no conclusion can be reached about their mutual relationship at the time *The Grove* was first published, it is just as obvious that for some reason or other Pope was interested in the publication of the collection—a collection containing a short, unsponsored epigram addressed to the Duke of

---

[1] 'It was written by one *Griffin* a player, assisted by *Lewis Theobald*'; *Correspondence*, I, 1735 (ii), p. 91. Also '. . . by Griffin a Player, supervis'd by Mr. Th—'; *Works*, II, 1735, Appendix to *The Dunciad*, p. 183.

[2] *Ovid's Metamorphoses. In Fifteen Books. A New Translation. By Several Hands.* 2 vols. 1717. The dedication is signed 'G. Sewell'.

[3] First printed in *Miscellaneous Poems and Translations*, 1712; see *ante*, p. 31.

Argyle, which there is reason to think is Pope's,[1] and, next to it, the following anonymous poem.

VERSES
Sent to Mrs. *T. B.* with his
WORKS.
By an AUTHOR.

This Book, which, like its Author, You
By the bare Outside only knew,
(Whatever was in either Good,
Not look'd in, or, not understood)
Comes, as the Writer did too long,
To be about you, right or wrong;
Neglected on your Chair to lie,
Nor raise a Thought, nor draw an Eye;
In peevish Fits to have you say,
See there! you're always in my Way!
Or, if your Slave you think to bless,
I like this Colour, I profess!
That Red is charming all will hold,
I ever lov'd it—next to Gold.

Can Book, or Man, more Praise obtain?
What more could *G—ge* or *S—te* gain?

Sillier than *G—ld—n* cou'dst thou be,
Nay, did all *J—c—b* breath in thee,
She keeps thee, Book! I'll lay my Head,
What? throw away a *Fool in Red*:
No, trust the Sex's sacred Rule;
The gaudy Dress will save the Fool.

Attention was first called to this poem by W. T. Brooke in *Notes and Queries* for June 1881, who suggested that the 'Author' might be Pope; 'Mrs. T.B.', Teresa Blount; and the 'Works', the 1717 volume of *The Works of Mr. Alexander Pope*—a copy of which, inscribed to Teresa, had been said by Carruthers to be in existence at Mapledurham. Those were the main points of a letter which, except for a non-committal note by E. Solly in the same paper six months later, seems to have been

[1] See *post*, p. 173.

completely disregarded ever since. The attribution, nevertheless, is not improbable even on the scanty evidence there adduced; and it becomes more and more convincing on further examination.

The poem itself seems never to have been reprinted in its entirety except in 1881; there is therefore only one text to be considered, though a contemporary transcript of a few lines (of which more later) preserves a variant reading of much interest. Written in the same kind of half-whimsical, half-teasing strain that Pope so often employed in poems addressed to his more intimate friends, these anonymous *Verses* bear many of the authentic marks which long familiarity with his un-official poems leads one to expect—verifiable occasion, unmistakable personalities, and characteristic allusions, as well as affinities of style and manner, and even—though so short a piece—textual parallels.

First, then, the occasion. The 'Author' tells in these *Verses* of the presentation of his 'Works', bound in red covers, to a lady, 'Mrs. T.B.', who knows books only by their outsides; he then goes on to inform the book that it will receive the same treatment as he has received from her for so long, and be neglected or misunderstood, or both; and that although she has no use for either of them, yet she will not dismiss them, but keep them about her for show. That in effect is the anonymous author's story, and, in spite of some playful exaggeration, it follows with remarkable closeness a similar incident in Pope's life. He, too, on publication of his *Works*, 1717, presented a copy to his dear friend, Teresa Blount (of whom some account has already been given[1]) in whose early home at Mapledurham the actual volume happily still finds place amongst the books once belonging to the two sisters. The present writer has recently had the pleasure of examining the Pope-Blount treasures preserved there, not least of which is this presentation volume of Pope's. This is a copy of the handsome quarto edition in its original binding, which in this instance was obviously a special 'dress' for a special occasion; for the book is bound *not* in the normal brown calf of the period, but in red morocco.

The inscription, which reads as follows: 'Teresa Maria Blount[2] giuen by the Author', has been said to be in Pope's autograph; but several reasons make it practically certain it was written by Teresa. In the first place, the hand, while only remotely like Pope's, closely resembles her own signature in several other books. Secondly, she has similarly written her name in full in other inscriptions, and at the same time used the letter 'u' for 'v' in 'given'; whereas Pope is not known, on

---

[1] See *ante*, pp. 51 f.
[2] Not 'Teresa Martha Blount', as stated in EC, ix, p. 272.

the one hand, ever to have written her second name, Maria, in any of his presentation volumes or letters, or, on the other, to have used the spelling 'giuen'. And, lastly, it is not in character that Pope—who appreciated the beauty of the printed page and could himself write an elegant 'print-hand'—should ever have thus ruthlessly spoilt the half-title-page of so fine a volume by carelessly scrawling the inscription partly above and partly on each side of the printed words. (In passing, it may be noted that another hand has intruded a date, either 1717 or 1727, the third figure being uncertain owing to subsequent alteration.)

For purposes of address and reference, Teresa was normally 'Mrs. Teresa Blount' for Pope and his friends, as witness his autograph inscription in the first volume of his *Iliad*, 1715—'To Mrs. Teresa Blount, from her most faithful humble Servt A. Pope'. Thus as there is no poem in the canon addressed to her by name for comparison; and as there is one addressed to Martha Blount in these words: 'To Mrs. M.B. sent on her Birth-Day', it is only reasonable to assume that if Pope had addressed this poem publicly to Teresa, the title would probably read (as this one does)—'Verses Sent to Mrs. T.B. with his Works. By an Author'.

As with the 'Works', so with the lady to whom the volume was sent. Pope, perhaps more than others, had a way of 'loading every rift' of his jokes with truth; and 'Mrs. T.B.', as she is described in the poem, is the very double of Mistress Teresa Blount, as revealed in Pope's letters and her own. For example, Teresa, like 'T.B.' had an acute distaste for reading: 'You, who read nothing', Pope once wrote to her in 1714,[1] when comparing Martha's interest in books with her lack of it (as he did on more than one occasion). Like 'T.B.', Teresa loved outside show: 'Let her put on new Gowns to be the Gaze of Fools', said Pope in a letter to Martha about Teresa (c. 1716).[2] And Teresa, as much as 'T.B.', was lacking in sentiment and sympathy, and was always too concerned about money; in 1718,[3] he wrote to her: 'Since you prefer three hundred pound to two true Lovers', which is only one of several of his jesting indictments of her usual preoccupation and heartlessness.

More significant still is the revelation that the 'Author' and Pope had likewise much in common—for in addition to the similarity of their unfortunate relations with ladies who themselves were spiritual twins, they each had a strange partiality for books with red leather bindings (which, incidentally, Pope mentions on several occasions).[4]

---

[1] Mapledurham, 26.   [2] *Ibid.*, 33.   [3] *Ibid.*, 57.
[4] See, for example, Warton, VIII, p. 371 and *Dunciad* B, I, l. 138.

m

And still more curious is their separate and personal dislike of the same two people, Gildon and Jacob, and also, as we shall see later, their individual ridicule of James Baker.

Pope's reasons for hating Gildon have been discussed at some length in previous pages[1]; that they were abundantly justified, humanly speaking, is beyond doubt. Some readers may therefore ask if it is like Pope, having these genuine grievances against Gildon, to attack him with a comparatively mild epithet like 'sillier'. When, however, one realizes that the egregious Gildon had recently elected himself as the critic and arbiter of English poetry with the publication of his *The Complete Art of Poetry*, 2 vols., 1718; and *The Laws of Poetry . . . Explain'd and Illustrated*, 1721, it is understandable that Pope—supreme exemplar of the 'correct', past master of versification, and flawless stylist—would be, more than any one else, likely to be amused enough, or irked enough, to forget for the moment past injuries, and with the nicest judgement select this particular word to fit Gildon in his latest impersonation.

As for Giles Jacob (legal hack-writer and compiler turned poet), he too had given Pope reason enough for dislike by 1721. As early as 1717, he had published a poem (his first) whose title and theme were a kind of prurient burlesque 'In Two Books' of the original version in two cantos of *The Rape of the Lock*, which he irritatingly entitled *The Rape of the Smock*, giving it also Pope's sub-title *An Heroi-Comical Poem*. It is a poor thing seeming all the poorer by its self-invited comparison with a masterpiece, which it can only dully imitate in such obvious ways as naming its heroine's lap-dog, 'Shock'. But that is not the whole of Jacob's offence. He used the Preface to the book to attack the comedy *Three Hours after Marriage* (the joint production of Gay, Pope, and Arbuthnot) for obscenity; calling it 'that stupid Farce' and 'the smuttiest Performance', possibly to excuse his own lubricities. This charge he repeated in *The Poetical Register*, 1719–20; and, moreover, went out of his way to give Gay unjustly inadequate notices in those volumes. Pope, who was even readier to resent attacks on his friends than on himself, grew so angry at this invidious treatment of Gay, that ten years later he was still incensed enough to complain that Jacob had 'very grossly, and unprovok'd, abused in that book the Author's Friend, Mr. Gay'.[2]

Two other personal allusions remain to be noticed, but they are far from clear, and the suggestions that follow are put forward with some diffidence. At first sight 'G—ge or S—te' would appear to mean

---

[1] See *ante*, pp. 103, 112 ff.   [2] *Dunciad* A, iii, l. 149 n.

'George or Senate'; but as neither King nor parliament seems to have earned, or received, any special meed of praise between 1717 and 1721, there would not be much point in the allusion. W. T. Brooke thought the letters might stand for 'Gage' and 'Southcote'. Gage, it may be remembered, had a sister, the unfortunate Mrs Weston, who was known tó, and championed by, Pope in his youth. The man himself, Count Gage, was a strange and romantic figure of European notoriety in the first half of the century; he at one time amassed incredible wealth, which many people would think a praiseworthy achievement. In marked contrast, Thomas Southcote, a Roman Catholic priest and Pope's friend, was a really commendable man: it was he who was instrumental in saving Pope's life in his youth, for which he won the poet's gratitude and praise, and, twenty or more years later, an abbacy on his recommendation.

There remains for comment one other allusion, also having a Pope connection. It first occurs in a contemporary transcript of the last six lines of the poem, the address to the 'Book'. The manuscript itself once belonged to Pope's friend, Lord Oxford, and is now in the British Museum.[1] The lines, which are anonymous and written in an unknown hand, are headed: 'Wrote in Mr Gay's Works, Presented to a Lady the Book finely Bound. To the Book'. Excerpted in this way these half-dozen lines could of course be applied by any one to any gorgeously bound volume written by any author; and this separate appearance of them may mean no more than that. Nevertheless, in addition to giving Gildon's name in full, the transcript contains one major and two minor variant readings, the first alone being of any interest, insomuch that it substitutes the name 'James Baker' for 'all J—c—b'; and, as the present writer has shown elsewhere,[2] James Baker was a favourite butt of Pope's at that time. Fifty or more years later, these six lines, with much the same title and practically the same variants, appeared in print in The St. James's Chronicle, October 5–7, 1775, whence they were reprinted the following year, but still with no implication of authorship, in Additions to the Works of Alexander Pope, Esq; 1776, amongst the pieces about Gay.

So, with the evidence in favour of Pope's authorship gathering weight piece by piece, we come at last to the actual text. At first glance this appears to be cast in an unusual metre for Pope. Nevertheless, although in his acknowledged poems he rarely if ever used octosyllabic couplets, except when imitating Swift, in his anonymous occasional pieces they occur with surprising frequency—as may be

---

[1] Harl. 7316, f. 109 v.   [2] Pope's Prose, i, pp. cx–cxiii.

seen in the present work. Possibly he thought that his hand would be less noticeable in this metre than in his famous heroic couplets; or, again, he might have chosen it in a holiday mood as a change, and therefore a relief, from turning 'ten thousand verses' of the other. But, whatever the reason, the use of the shorter line in this poem most certainly does nothing to lessen the probability of his authorship, while the presence, in these same lines, of textual parallels to Pope's known verse actively supports it. For example, he has been credited by the Oxford English Dictionary with the first use of the word 'breathe' to mean 'breathe through, or animate', as in the passage in the *Essay on Man* (1732), where he says that God

> Breathes in our soul, informs our mortal part.[1]

He had, however, made an earlier use of the same meaning in the fifth book of *The Iliad* (1716) in the line:

> And all thy god-like Father breathes in thee.[2]

And now here in the poem, *Verses Sent to Mrs. T.B.*, written in the following year (1717), he seems not only to have used it once more, but has also incorporated it in a very close parallel to the whole line:

> Nay, did all Jacob breathe in thee.[3]

Not less striking, perhaps, is his playful banter of 'Mrs. T.B.' in such lines as—'Or, if your Slave you think to bless' (l. 11), which is in exactly the same key of high-spirited gallantry that pervades Pope's letters to Teresa Blount about this time, as well as the poem he had addressed to her barely three years earlier, one line of which runs—'So when your Slave, at some dear idle time'.[4] And in this connection it is just worth remarking that Pope seems never to have styled himself in verse the 'slave' of any other woman.

Such are the facts, then, concerning *Verses Sent to Mrs. T.B. with his Works*, and although the interpretation of them may err in detail here and there, it is incredible that there were two contemporary authors who not only met with the same unusual experiences but disliked the same people in the same way; who both published their 'Works' not very long before 1721, and presented a copy bound in red, each to his own lady, both of whom had the same initials and similar characters and tastes. Most readers will agree that such a protracted series of involved and diverse coincidences is, humanly speaking, impossible, and, therefore, that 'Mrs. T.B.' was Mrs Teresa Blount, and the 'Author' Pope.

[1] Book i, l. 275.   [2] Book v, l. 163.   [3] Line 18.
[4] *To a Young Lady, On her leaving the Town after the Coronation*, l. 41. See *ante*, p. 56.

If that is conceded, it becomes possible to go a step further. The occurrence in the Harleian transcript of James Baker's name, in place of Jacob's in the first printed text, suggests that there had been some revision of the poem between its original composition in 1717, and its publication in 1721. And because for two or three years before the latter date, Pope is known to have dropped the 'James Baker' theme as a literary joke (which he had begun to use as early as 1715, in the second edition of *A Key to the Lock*)[1]; and as Giles Jacob had not published *The Poetical Register* before 1719–20, it is at least possible that 'James Baker' was the original reading at the time of the presentation, and that Jacob's name was substituted by Pope when, according to his usual practice, he revised the piece prior to publication.

Speculation may perhaps be allowed one step further still. On re-reading *Verses* and comparing it with the only other poem (barring a frivolous couplet or two) Pope wrote to Teresa, 'On her leaving the Town after the Coronation' in 1714, it becomes manifest that the later piece, *Verses*, has something of an astringent quality in its quizzing gallantry, and even, perhaps, a drop or two of acid in Pope's designation of himself as a 'slave', not perceptible in the earlier poem. And one wonders if this sub-acid flavour was present in the original version, and if it was due to the developing tension which actually began to show itself in their letters two or three months later; or whether it was introduced in the poem just before going to press in 1721. Whatever the answer, their changing relations (for which Pope was blameless) had worsened in the meantime; and that may account for the appearance of *Verses Sent to Mrs. T.B.* in print in 1721: it was a reminder to Teresa that Pope was something besides a 'slave' to old affection.

Thus the publication of *The Grove* in all probability marked a definite stage in their growing estrangement. Certainly the book had some significance for Pope, or why four copies? and, almost as certainly it meant something to Teresa, or why did all correspondence between them cease from 1721 onwards? In the light of the foregoing pages it is not without interest to know that amongst the books at Mapledurham which once belonged to Teresa and her sister is a tall copy of *The Grove*, 1721. As it is not one of the ordinary issue it is most probably one of Pope's four. It has no inscription.

---

[1] Pope's *Prose*, i, pp. cxi, and 181.

CHAPTER X

POPE AND ARGYLE

Amongst the men of action and public affairs with whom Pope was friendly over a long period of years was John Campbell, second Duke of Argyle. When or how their acquaintance began is not known; but in December 1716, or early the next month, when writing to Martha Blount[1] Pope happened to mention as a matter of course at the end of the letter: 'I dined yesterday wth Jacky Campbell at the D[uke] of Argyle's'. Thus, as this seems to be the earliest surviving letter of Pope's to mention the Duke, it may be taken that their friendship was already well established by the end of 1716. It is nevertheless curious that so few records exist of the relations between these two strongly contrasted personalities. Here and there in the Pope correspondence brief allusions flash a restricted light on them; but as they are fewer than half a dozen in all, with the first written in 1716 and the last in 1741, vast areas of unrelieved darkness remain. In addition to these, however, a similar number of epigrams and short poems have been found in contemporary publications, addressed to, or referring to, Argyle, which have been, or may be, ascribed to Pope with varying degrees of probability; and it is these occasional pieces that the present chapter now proposes to discuss.

To begin with, as four of these pieces were written between 1716 and 1720, it would be useful to glance at the known references to Pope and Argyle and their recorded meetings during that time. The first has already been noted and its implication is abundantly confirmed by the next extant letter from Pope mentioning the Duke. This is dated August 6, 1717, and was written in high holiday humour to John Caryll,[2] some two months after the publication of *The Works*. Pope was then on one of his 'rambles'; but this time, in view of the reception everywhere accorded to the author of that imposing volume, his ramble might be said almost to have become a Royal Progress as he journeyed from house to house of his great—if not his greatest—friends:

> I have been indispensably obliged to pass some days at almost every house along the Thames... After some attendance on my Ld Burlington, I have been at ye Duke of Shrewsbury's, D: of Argyle's, Lady Rochester's, Ld Percival's... [and so on, half a dozen more names being given].

[1] Mapledurham, 10.   [2] Add. 28618, f. 59 v.

Next is the comment on their friendship found in John Gay's happy congratulatory poem, written, presumably in 1720, 'upon Mr. Pope's having finished his Translation of Homer's *Iliad*', and entitled *Mr. Pope's Welcome from Greece*. In the course of this poem Gay names the numerous friends of the poet who are supposed to gather on the quay to greet his home-coming. One of the stanzas, less frequently printed than the rest, begins:

> See there two Brothers greet thee wth applause
> Both for prevailing Eloquence renown'd,
> Argyll the brave and Islay learn'd in laws
> Than whom no truer friends were ever found.[1]

There can be no doubt therefore about the existence of friendly relations between the two men in 1719, when, towards the end of the year, Southern's last tragedy, *The Spartan Dame*, was produced. This play was dedicated to the Duke of Argyle by the author in extremely laudatory language, which, though typical of the period, was the cause of an anonymous epigram that first appeared in print in a miscellany called *The Grove*, 1721.

Pope's connection with *The Grove* has already been discussed at some length,[2] and mention was then made of this unsponsored epigram which is placed in the miscellany next to the poem entitled, *Verses Sent to Mrs. T.B.*, likewise anonymous but almost certainly written by Pope. Such juxtaposition may mean that the two pieces were associated with each other in the compiler's mind, not improbably because they were known to be by the same hand. In *The Grove*, the epigram, which seems not to have been reprinted since the eighteenth century, runs as follows:

In behalf of Mr. SOUTHERNE.
To the Duke of ARGYLE.

EPIGRAM.

> *ARGYLE* his Praise, when *Southerne* wrote,
> First struck out this, and then that Thought;
> Said *this* was Flatt'ry, *that* a Fault.
> How shall the Bard contrive?
>
> My Lord, consider what you do,
> He'll lose his Pains and Verses too;
> For if these Praises fit not You,
> They'll serve no Man alive.

---

[1] Faber, p. 670.   [2] See *ante*, pp. 163 ff.

After having been printed anonymously in 1721 (re-issued in 1732), and reprinted, again without ascription, in the two editions of *A Collection of Epigrams*, 1727, and 1735, this poem was first attributed to Pope in the year following his death, in *The General Advertiser* for Saturday, October 26, 1745, where it was introduced thus:

> The following Lines were lately found amongst Mr. Pope's Papers in his own Hand-Writing.

That statement may be challenged but cannot be disproved; and it has at least the support of the accompanying text which was certainly *not* taken from the earlier printed version; for it contains two different readings,[1] which, as they are improvements, suggest the usual late revisions of Pope's normal practice. Although several subsequent printings repeat the statement about Pope's autograph, the epigram has wholly escaped editorial notice hitherto.

Pope's friendship with 'honest Tom Southern' was of long standing, going back at least to his youth, the old playwright being one of the few people to whom the young poet showed his *Pastorals* in manuscript as early (he said) as 1704. Indeed Southern seems to have known him earlier still; for he it was who thought the boy's voice so naturally musical that he used to call him 'the little nightingale'.[2] Their friendship lasted throughout Pope's life, who, barely two years before he died, wrote the well-known poem on the old man's eighty-second birthday. He could thus have learnt the amusing inner history of Southern's dedication either from the Duke or the dramatist. And as the epigram is very like Pope's manner, with its deftly turned compliment; and as, in addition, it is consistent with his invariable practice (which was by no means universal), when rhyming, of pronouncing 'fault', 'fau't', it would seem, when everything else is taken into account, that the probabilities are very much in favour of Pope's authorship of it.

.   .   .

The Duke of Argyle was created Duke of Greenwich on April 27, 1719, at which time Pope was busily engaged in bringing to a close his long labours on the translation of the *Iliad*. So preoccupied was he that the year 1719 was, as regards original poems, one of the most barren of his poetical life. Nevertheless, he did look around him occasionally, and, probably in acute reaction to the unintermitting strain of translation, would throw off from time to time—even if he did

---

[1] Line 4, 'the' is corrected to 'your'; line 8, 'serve' to 'fit'.
[2] Lord Orrery's *Remarks*, 1752, p. 225.

not publish or acknowledge—some caustic, witty, or complimentary rhymes on current affairs in which he was personally interested. Such would appear to be the explanation of the epigram discussed above; and such would account for the lines, now to be considered, on Argyle's acquiring this same year yet another title. This is a short anonymous poem which in Pope's life-time and for long afterwards was to be found only in one or other of the last four editions of his first miscellany,[1] that is in *Miscellaneous Poems and Translations*, from the 'Third Edition', 1720 to the 'Sixth Edition', 1732.[2] It is now reprinted probably for the first time for a hundred and fifty years.

To His Grace the Duke of ARGYLE,
upon reading the following short
Preamble to the Patent creating him
Duke of GREENWICH

Cum viri illius, cui novos hisce literis patentibus Titulos decernimus, & egregia in nos Patriamque suam Merita, & illustre Genus, & Majorum res gestæ, Historiarum Monumentis celebratæ, satis inclaruerint, quibus rationibus adducti sumus eum summo inter Proceres honore dignari, nil opus est pluribus recensere.

> Mindless of fate in these low vile abodes,
> TYRANTS have oft usurp'd the style of GODS:
> But that the MORTAL might be thought DIVINE,
> The HERALD strait new-modell'd *all his line*;
> And venal PRIEST with well-dissembled lye,
> *Preambled* to the crowd the *mimick* DEITY.
> Not so great SATURN's son, imperial JOVE
> HE reigns, unquestion'd, in his realms above:
> No title from *descent* HE need infer,
> *His red right arm* proclaims the THUNDERER.
>   This, CAMPBELL, be thy pride, illustrious Peer!
> Alike to shine distinguish'd in your sphere:
> All *merit* but your *own* YOU may disdain,
> And KINGS have been your ANCESTORS in vain.

After Pope's death the poem was not printed again until 1763, when it was included in *The Poetical Calendar*, edited by F. Fawkes and W. Woty, who were the first to attribute it to Pope. Poem and attribution

---

[1] See *ante*, p. 35.
[2] Renamed *Miscellany Poems* from 1726 onwards.

next appeared in *The New Foundling Hospital for Wit*, VI, 1773 (and later editions), and yet again in *Bell's . . . Fugitive Poetry*, VI, 1789. Five years later G. Wakefield, who knew of it only in *The New Foundling Hospital*, came to the conclusion that it was authentic Pope and included it in the first and only volume of his uncompleted edition of Pope's *Works* in 1794; since when it seems to have been completely forgotten until 1922, when R. H. Griffith listed it in his bibliography without comment as a Pope item; in which ascription he has since been followed by G. Sherburn who asserted it to be Pope's work on the sole ground that it was 'published by Pope himself'.[1] However, all things considered, the piece is probably Pope's, and its overwhelmingly classical reference is almost certainly due to its having been written at a time when Pope, as we have seen, was unusually engrossed in the facts and fancies of the Homeric world. But until further evidence is forthcoming, it must remain an attributed piece.

Two other epigrams on Argyle, which Pope was said at the time to have written, appeared on February 21, 1717, in a small book called *The Parson's Daughter. A Tale. For the Use of pretty Girls with small Fortunes . . . To which are added, Epigrams, and the Court Ballad, By Mr. Pope. From correct Copies*—a title so calculatedly ambiguous that no one can say with certainty what is or is not ascribed to Pope. Exactly three weeks previously, *The Court Ballad* had been published alone, with Pope's name attached, unquestionably on Curll's responsibility; and it is practically certain that the same predatory bookseller was behind this publication also. For although the book purports to have been 'Printed for J. Harris', he (or she) appears to have had as little actuality as the later and more famous phantom of that name, if one may judge by the plentiful lack of other books with his (or her) imprint, and by the fact that even the name, 'J. Harris', disappears from subsequent issues or editions of this book, in favour of Curll's more usual screen, [Mrs] R. Burleigh,[2] the nominal publisher of *The Court Ballad* itself. Moreover, Curll advertised *The Parson's Daughter* in his own lists, and, from August 8, 1717, onwards for many years, was actually printing these *Epigrams* in his various miscellanies, in which the attribution to Pope varies from the implication of the above-quoted title-page to the definite statement, 'Pieces by Mr. Pope', in the *Literary Correspondence* of 1735. That the *Epigrams* were intended to form a kind of pendant to *The Court Ballad* by the same hand, is sug-

---

[1] Sherburn, p. 271.   [2] See also *ante*, p. 156.

gested by the fact that in the only manuscript copy[1] of them known to the present writer, as well as on their first appearance in print, the *Epigrams* follow immediately on *The Court Ballad*; and, in fact, in the manuscript are explicitly entitled, *Epigrams into the Bargain*. Further proof of this original association of occasion and authorship is found in the advertisements of the book, which announced them as *Court Epigrams, and the Court Ballad*. The text which follows is that of the first printing, except that the names have been completed within square brackets.

THE COURT BALLAD

To the Tune of, "*To all you Ladies now at Land*," &c.

I

To One Fair Lady out of Court,
    And Two Fair Ladies in,
Who think the TURK and POPE a Sport,
    And Wit and Love no Sin,
Come these soft Lines with nothing Stiff in
To B[ellende]ne, L[epel]le, and G[riffi]n.
        With a fa, la, la.

II

What passes in the Dark Third Row,
    And what behind the Scene,
Couches and crip'led Chairs I know,
    And Garrets hung with Green;
I know the swing of sinful Hack,
Where many Damsels cry alack.
        With a fa, la, la.

III

Then why to Court shou'd I Repair,
    Where's such ado with T[ownshen]d.
To hear each Mortal Stamp and Swear,
    And ev'ry Speech with Zouns end,
To hear 'em Rail at honest S[underlan]d
And rashly Blame the Realm of Blunderland.
        With a fa, la, la.

[1] Lansd. 852, ff. 204 v., 205.

IV

Alas! like S[chut]z I cannot Pun,
  Like C[layto]n Court the *Germans*,
Tell P[ickenbour]g how Slim she's grown,
  Like M[eadow]s Run to Sermons,
To Court, Ambitious Men may Roam,
But I and *Marlbro'* stay at Home.
              With a fa, la, la.

V

In truth by what I can discern,
  Of Courtiers 'twixt you Three,
Some Wit you have and more may learn,
  From Court than *Gay* or *Me*,
Perhaps in time you'll leave High Diet,
And Sup with Us on Mirth and Quiet,
              With a fa, la, la.

VI

At *Leicester-Fields* a House full high,
  With Door all Painted Green,
Where Ribbons Wave upon the Tye,
  (A Milliner I mean)
There may you Meet Us Three to Three,
For *Gay* can well make Two of Me.
              With a fa, la, la.

VII

But shou'd you catch the Prudish Itch,
  And each become a Coward,
Bring sometimes with you Lady R[ic]h,
  And sometimes Mistress H[owar]d.
For Virgins to keep Chaste must go
Abroad with such as are not so.
              With a fa, la, la.

VIII

And thus Fair Maids my Ballad ends,
  God send the King Safe Landing,
And make all Honest Ladies Friends,
  To Armies that are Standing,

> Preserve the Limits of these Nations,
> And take off Ladies' Limitations.
> *With a fa, la, la.*

Now *The Court Ballad* is by way of being famous, and whether it is known by that name, or by Curll's later title for it, 'The Challenge', the piece has been so long and universally taken to be Pope's that everybody now regards it as authentic beyond all question. Nevertheless it is his only by attribution which in the last resort depends on a statement by Curll. Pope himself never acknowledged it by word or deed, and the only two contemporary manuscripts of it on record are anonymous.[1] Warburton, Pope's official editor, who must have known the poem, omits it without comment in his editions of *The Works*; and it was left to Warton to include it in the canon, eighty years after it was written—which he did without citing its source or his reasons. In these respects Warton has been followed by all subsequent editors of Pope, except Elwin and Courthope, who did at least attempt to name the source, albeit in a footnote whose eight and a half lines contain four mis-statements of fact.[2] It thus comes about that scholars have been misled into accepting Pope's authorship of *The Court Ballad* as definitely established; and have proceeded thence, following Breval,[3] to suggest that there was a connection between the *Ballad* and the comedy, *Three Hours after Marriage*,[4] in writing which Gay, Pope, and Arbuthnot had collaborated. The implication is that the *Ballad* was a kind of letter of thanks to the three Maids of Honour (the Misses Griffin, Bellenden, and Lepel), for their having sent Gay a purse of gold in token of the pleasure the comedy had given them. But there is nothing in the poem to give the slightest colour to that suggestion, and the occasion of *The Court Ballad*, and therefore of the *Court Epigrams* as well, must be looked for elsewhere.

First, however, it would be more satisfactory if some evidence could be adduced to support Curll's attribution of the *Ballad* to Pope. Happily we have not to look beyond its third line for confirmation:

> Who think the TURK and POPE a Sport.

For Pope was never loth to pun on his name, and on several occasions repeats this same joke on Turk and Pope, such as, for example:

> Verse prays for Peace, or sings down Pope and Turk.[5]

[1] Lansd. 852, and Stowe 973. [2] EC, IV, p. 478.
[3] The *Confederates*, 1717.
[4] Produced, January 16, 1717. See *ante*, p. 25; and *post*, pp. 298 f.
[5] Hor. Ep. II, i, l. 236.

He had picked up this joke originally from a prayer at the end of the metrical psalms by Hopkins and Sternhold, who (as he said to Swift) [1] 'prayed against me with the Turk'; the allusion, as Croker pointed out long ago, being to the line:

> From Pope and Turk defend us, Lord.

Another pointer to Pope's authorship is to be found in the forty-first line:

> For Gay can well make two of Me.

Because, in addition to its being characteristic of Pope to make fun of his diminutive size like this, the line looks like another of his 'true words spoken in jest', and if taken literally identifies the writer beyond any doubt; there being of course no other contemporary poet only half Gay's bulk. The line, moreover, recalls several other passages where Pope has coupled Gay with himself in exactly this same playfully affectionate manner; for instance, 'but Gay alone . . . may starve with me' (*Farewell to London*). Two other characteristics of Pope find place in *The Court Ballad*; one being a typical specimen of his ridiculous rhymes (mentioned elsewhere in these pages),[2] 'Zouns end' rhyming with 'Townshend'; the other being his pretended inability to pun, which in his letters and unofficial poems he is continually stating in so many words and immediately nullifying, as he does here in the last stanza. The most absurd example of this humour is the single sheet publication, *God's Revenge against Punning*, 1716, of which the present writer has shown reason to believe him the author.[3] All things considered, though it lacks his signature, there can be no reasonable doubt about Pope's authorship of *The Court Ballad*; and that being so, the discussion of *Court Epigrams* must now be resumed.

The first point to be made is that both *Ballad* and *Epigrams* date from approximately the same time. Internal evidence proves the former to have been written between December 12, 1716, and January 18, 1717, and contemporary newspapers show that it was published on January 31 as a folio half-sheet with R. Burleigh's imprint, and entitled, *The Court Ballad. By Mr. Pope*. Three weeks later saw it incorporated in a small book, as described above, where it is accompanied by six short epigrams, likewise ascribed to Pope, entitled, *Epigrams, Occasion'd by An Invitation to Court*. Secondly, it is significant that these little pieces were all, except the last one (which has to do with Argyle only), addressed to, or concerned with, the

---

[1] *Letters*, II, 4to, 1741, p. 39.   [2] See *post*, p. 257.
[3] Pope's *Prose*, I, pp. cx–cxiv.

same three Maids of Honour as were addressed by the *Ballad*; and, furthermore, that the *Epigrams* were admittedly occasioned by an invitation to Court from the three Maids to Pope (and presumably Gay), and that the *Ballad* is mostly taken up with the two poets' reasons for *not* going, and a suggestion for an alternative meeting. It was not an accident that during this same period, December–January, Pope wrote the letter with which this chapter opens—'I dined yesterday wth Jacky Campbell at the D[uke] of Argyle's. Gay dines daily wth ye Maids of honour'; or that 'Jacky' Campbell (later third Duke of Argyle) married Mary Bellenden, one of the three Maids, in 1720; or, yet again, that two of the epigrams (numbers III and VI) are compliments to the Duke. The whole set, which seems not to have been printed since the eighteenth century, runs as follows:

EPIGRAMS,
Occasion'd by
An Invitation to Court.

I

In the Lines that you sent, are the *Muses* and *Graces*;
You've the *Nine* in your *Wit*, and *Three* in your *Faces*.

II

They may talk of the *Goddesses* in *Ida* Vales,
But *you* show your *Wit*, whereas *they* show'd their *Tails*.

III

You *Bellenden, Griffin*, and little *Lepell*,
By G— you all lie like the D—l in Hell;
To say that at Court there's a Dearth of all Wit,
And send what *Argyle*, would he *write*, might have writ.

IV

Adam had fallen twice, if for an apple
The D—l had brought him *Bellenden* and *Lepell*.

V

On Sunday at Six, in the Street that's call'd *Gerrard*,
You may meet the *Two Champions* who are no Lord *Sh[erra]rd*.

VI

They say *A[rgy]ll's* a Wit, for what?
For writing? no,—for writing not.

Lastly, it is not without significance that a poem, which has hitherto existed only in one copy in Pope's handwriting, and is his work beyond all reasonable doubt,[1] uses the stanza and metre of *Epigram*, *III*, with strikingly similar effect. The new poem, moreover, is likewise concerned with Maids of Honour, not to mention the Devil in hell. No more need be quoted here than the first two lines:

> A Tower there is, where six Maidens do dwell;
> This Tow'r it belongs to the Dev'l of Hell, . . .

In fine, so many contacts and coincidences make it difficult to escape the conclusion that if Pope wrote *The Court Ballad* then he also wrote the appended *Epigrams, into the Bargain.*

. . .

Passing over the well-known tale Pope told to Spence in the seventeen-thirties, how he overheard the Duke of Argyle, 'in the next box to us' at the first night of *The Beggar's Opera* (1728), foretell its success when every one else was in great uncertainty about it; Pope's last *acknowledged* poetical allusion to him occurs in that almost passionate declaration of love for those 'worthy' statesmen who had suffered injustice or banishment, or were otherwise distressed. This passage is found in the *Epilogue to the Satires*, *II*, written in 1738, where after mentioning Sommers, Halifax, Shrewsbury, Carleton, Stanhope, Atterbury, Pulteney and Chesterfield, he continues—

> ARGYLE, the State's whole Thunder born to wield,
> And shake alike the Senate and the Field:
> Or WYNDHAM, just to Freedom and the Throne,
> The Master of our Passions, and his own.
> Names, which I long have lov'd, nor lov'd in vain,
> Rank'd with their Friends, not number'd with their Train.

In the following year, however, a short anonymous poem, entitled, *On lying in the Earl of Rochester's Bed at Atterbury*, appeared almost simultaneously in two periodicals, in *The London Magazine* for August, 1739,[2] first, and then, only a few days later (as shown by internal evidence) in *The Scots Magazine* for the same month. These two printings—which agree verbally—were followed by a third in *The Gentleman's Magazine* for September, 1739, where the piece was entitled, *Verses left by Mr. Pope, upon his lying in the same Bed . . .* (The full title is given below); since when the poem has been admitted in the canon without question by practically all Pope's editors. Neverthe-

---

[1] See *post*, p. 276.

[2] *The London Magazine*'s Index at the end of the year ascribed the poem to Pope.

less, it must be noted that the poem was never included in Pope's works either by himself in his life-time, or by Warburton his friend and appointed editor; nor is Pope known ever to have acknowledged his authorship of it directly or indirectly. The only recorded comments on its authenticity are by Wakefield, in 1794, who thought it genuine, and by Elwin and Courthope who asserted 'the style is sufficient evidence' that it is by Pope. But unsupported opinion or assertion is not as impressive as it once was, and obviously more evidence if discoverable would be very welcome. But before continuing the discussion, some readers would probably like to renew their acquaintance with the poem, the text of which—from *The Gentleman's Magazine*—now follows.

VERSES *left by Mr.* POPE, *upon his Lying in the same Bed which* WILMOT, *Earl of* ROCHESTER *us'd at Atterbury, a Seat of the Duke of* ARGYLE'*s, in Oxfordshire, July 9, 1739.*

> With no poetick ardor fir'd,
>   I press the bed where *Wilmot* lay:
> That here he lov'd, or here expir'd,
>   Begets no numbers grave or gay.
>
> But in thy roof, *Argyle*, are bred
>   Such thoughts, as prompt the brave to lie
> Stretch'd out in honour's nobler bed,
>   Beneath a nobler roof, the sky.
>
> Such flames as high in patriots burn,
>   Yet stoop to bless a child or wife:
> And such as wicked kings may mourn,
>   When freedom is more dear than life.

Fortunately Pope's extant correspondence for the year 1739, meagre though it is, is found on examination to corroborate the above title of the poem with evidence bearing on such diverse matters as date, place, and occasion, and even the persons concerned—that is, on everything to do with the poem, except its author's name. From it we learn, that, frail and ailing as the poet was that summer, he nevertheless went on one of his beloved 'rambles' from house to house of his friends. On Wednesday, July 4, 1739, he was at Stowe, the seat of Lord Cobham; and writing that day to Martha Blount, he tells her where next to address her letters to him.

n

Y^r next direction is to Sr Tho[mas] Lyt[telton] at Hagley near Stowerbridge, Worcestershire, where I hope to be on ye Tenth, or sooner if Mr Lyt[telton] come: Mr Grenville was here, & told me he expected him in 2 or 3 days, so I think we may travel on the 8th or 9th . . . I dread that [journey] to Worcester & back, for every one tells me 'tis perpetual Rock, & ye worst of rugged roads; wch really not only hurt me at present, but leave Consequences very uneasy to me. The Duke of Argyle was here yesterday, & assures me what Mr Lyt[telton] talks of as one day's Journey must be Two, or an intolerable Fatigue.[1]

Then on Saturday, July 7, writing again from the same place to Martha, he tells her towards the end of the letter the latest news:

Mr Lyttelton is just arrived, and I set forward on Munday [July 9]. On Tuesday I hope to get to his house . . .[2]

That is, to the house at Hagley; he thus proposed to spend, as Argyle advised, two days on the road. Consequently, in view of the fact that one of the best roads from Stowe to Hagley passes through Atterbury (now Adderbury) where the Duke had a house, formerly the seat of Lord Rochester, it is inconceivable that another poet should also have been on that road and stayed that self-same night of July 9 at the Duke's, while Pope lodged in some near-by but nameless place. It may be taken, therefore, as virtually certain that Argyle not only succeeded in persuading Pope to take two days on the journey, but also to stay the night of the ninth at his house—and Rochester's bed did the rest!

Two other small scraps of evidence support this conclusion. First, the three contemporary transcripts of the poem which have been found all belonged to Pope's friends and are attributed to him; two of them being amongst Lord Oxford's papers at Longleat,[3] and the other amongst the Cowper family papers in the British Museum.[4] And, secondly, the poem is like the other four Argyle epigrams previously considered, in that it similarly pays a compliment to Argyle, but otherwise is couched in the loftier style of his official poetical tribute (above quoted) of the preceding year.

Seeing, therefore, that the poem as given in *The Gentleman's Magazine* shows four corrections of the earlier text as well as a more explanatory and detailed title, it is not impossible that Pope himself,

---

[1] Mapledurham, 8.   [2] *Ibid.*, 23.

[3] Portland, XIII and XVIII.   [4] Add. 28101, f. 86 v.

vexed with the faulty text that had somehow crept into print, sent or caused to be sent a corrected version to the magazine. At least he was back again in London in time, and could have done it: for in a letter dated August 17, 1739,[1] he speaks of 'my return from my rambles', and of having 'dined yesterday with Jervas upon a venison pasty'. Or, had the poet not wanted to appear in the matter, Jervas could have acted for him, as he had done previously on more than one occasion, and conveyed the poem to the office of the magazine with the assurance that it was the work of the famous Mr Pope.

---

[1] R. Warner's *Original Letters*, 1817, p. 58.

CHAPTER XI

'DUKE UPON DUKE'

THIS little-known ballad, like most of the pieces it imitates, was issued anonymously; but that for the moment was its only likeness to them, except its amusing mimicry of their versification. For the first edition (a copy of which is in the Bodleian) ran to no less than six folio pages, on the third of which was a musical setting by a named composer. *The Daily Post* for Monday, August 15, 1720, announced its publication, thus:

> This Day is publish'd, DUKE upon DUKE. An excellent new Play-House Ballad; set to Musick by Mr. Holdecomb; printed on superfine Paper, for A. Moor . . . Price Three-Pence

The ballad immediately became so popular as to be worth pirating within three days, as Moor's later advertisement shows, which concludes by stating:

> N.B. The great Demand there is for this Ballad has tempted some Pyrates to print a Grub-street Copy of it; but Gentlemen will easily distinguish the right Copy by the Musick printed at the Head of it, and by the Goodness of the Paper and Character.[1]

A copy of what appears to be the pirated edition has survived in the Douce collection at the Bodleian, in the form of a broadside (18 by 12¾ in.) with a woodcut illustration. But although the ballad itself has the same thirty-seven stanzas as Moor's edition, the title is quite different—which probably explains why it has escaped notice hitherto:

> An Excellent Old Ballad, called
> Pride will have a Fall,
> As set forth in the True and Delectable History of the deadly Strife between the Dukes of *Guise* and *Lancastere* which fell out in the Reign of *Richard Coeur de Lion*.

There were at least two other editions: an undated single sheet, printed both sides, but with better printing and paper than the broadside, with music but no imprint, probably also pirated, a copy of which is in the British Museum; and another edition (or issue) by Moor, in folio, six pages, dated 1723, which was advertised as—*An*

[1] In *The Post Boy*, Aug. 16–18, 1720.

Account of a late Re-encounter. DUKE upon DUKE[1]; etc. Between 1723 and 1742, the ballad appeared anonymously in some half-dozen song-books; and lastly (as far as the present inquiry is concerned) it was included again without attribution, in the rearranged edition of Swift and Pope's *Miscellanies. The Fourth Volume.* 1742.[2]

The early history of this poem has been related with this particularity, because, of the few students who have known it, the majority have usually supposed it to have been first printed in an even later edition of *Miscellanies* than 1742, while the most recent reference to it known to the present writer does not trace it back earlier than Moor's edition of 1723. It is not surprising, therefore, to find that since its appearance in *Miscellanies*, the ballad has been ascribed 'by assertion', forthright or tentative, to at least four people, namely, Swift, Arbuthnot, Gay, and Pope—singly to Swift, and to various combinations of two or three of them, and once (in 1752) to all four. But seeing that in no instance has the slightest evidence for any attribution been put forward, and that the most recent and scholarly of the editors of Gay[3] and Swift[4] have each refused it a place in his author's works, it would be profitless to examine these arbitrary—and often contradictory—ascriptions in more detail.

Owing to earlier mis-statements of editors, Pope is usually supposed to have had nothing at all to do with the rearranged edition of *Miscellanies*, 1742; but, as is shown in a later chapter,[5] he really played a very active part in preparing it for the press. And it is virtually certain that he was responsible for introducing in 'The Fourth Volume' the curious method of indicating Swift's poems by marking all the others with an asterisk. In this way, *Duke upon Duke* is unmistakably shown to be *not* by Swift.

But more important still is the one definite and authoritative statement about the ballad, which seems to have been disregarded consistently since it was first printed more than a hundred years ago. About the time the ballad was included in *Miscellanies*, Pope himself told Spence that he had been responsible for a good portion of it. Spence's actual words read: 'Good part of the ballad on Lechmere and Guise was written by Mr. Pope'[6]; and he reports that Pope went on to say that he had written other ballads with 'Mr. Pulteney'—

---

[1] *The Whitehall Evening-Post*, April 4–6, 1723; a copy of this issue was described by Messrs Maggs Bros. in their Catalogue 653, No. 1009.

[2] Published July 3, according to *The London Evening Post* of that date.

[3] *Works*, 1926, Ed. G. C. Faber.   [4] *Poems*, 1937, Ed. H. Williams.

[5] See *post*, pp. 254, 258 f.   [6] Spence, p. 285.

thereby implying that whoever his collaborator in this instance may have been, it was not Pulteney. Another pointer in the same direction is the fact that the ballad was revised in more than twenty places before its inclusion in *Miscellanies*; which suggests that it must have been Pope who took this opportunity to correct the poem; because at that date Gay and Arbuthnot had been dead several years, and Swift worse than dead.

Whether Pope's collaborator ever will be known or not, a new and interesting piece of evidence shows that Pope, and Pope alone, was immediately credited with it. Exactly a week after its publication another ballad was announced in *The Daily Post*:[1]

> This Day is publish'd, An Answer to Duke upon Duke, &c. With a Key, set to Musick by the same Hand . . . Printed for A. Moore . . . Price 3d.

For this reply, issued by the same publisher, is addressed to Pope throughout, as the sole author of *Duke upon Duke*. It begins—

> Thou Pope; oh Popery burning hot,
>   for none but Papists would
> Enter into a cursed Plot,
>   'gainst Protestant so good.

A few of the other apostrophes to Pope worth noting, are—

> For this thine *Homer* have I bought,
>   All thy smart Things on *Curle*? . . .
>   (Stz. iii)

> Take heed thou Satan's crooked Rib.
>   For though not tall I'm strait . . .
>   (Stz. v)

> Take heed then little crooked Wight . . .
>   (Stz. viii)

> To thee, O *Pope*, to thee, again . . .
>   (Stz. xxix)

As an 'Answer' it is not a success; as a poem it is a tedious failure. But although its forty-one stanzas (four more than its exemplar) are redeemed by never a spark of wit or life, the piece leaves no doubt about the person it attacks for having written *Duke upon Duke*. Unfortunately, it is not so explicit about the quarrel itself, in which it is

---

[1] For August 22, 1720.

not peculiar; for documentary evidence of the cause of the trouble seems to be entirely lacking, while an examination of the newspapers of the spring and summer of 1720 has failed to light on any report of the original encounter thus burlesqued by Pope. Yet the affair must have given rise to no little gossip at the time, as is proved by the ballad's being pirated so quickly.

It is, however, satisfactory to note that Pope's published correspondence yields one characteristic allusion to the quarrel; and that, in so complete a dearth of comment everywhere else, is perhaps as much as might have been expected. In a letter to his great friend Edward Blount (whose wife was the sister of Sir John Guise, the 'Duke Guise' of the ballad) written at Mrs Blount's old home at Rentcomb in Gloucestershire, on October 3, 1721, he tells how intimidated he is by her pictured ancestors on the walls round him, 'whose faces are all upon me'; and then goes on to say:

> I fear none so much as Sir *Christopher Guise*, who being in his Shirt, seems as ready to combate me, as her own Sir *John* was to demolish Duke *Lancastere*.[1]

Little more is known of Sir John, the third baronet, except that he married twice and died November 16, 1732. But the other protagonist, Nicholas Lechmere, Chancellor of the Duchy of Lancaster (1718–1727), and created first Baron Lechmere in 1721, was notoriously so overbearing in manner, hot-tempered, and violent, as to be a fair target for ridicule.

Historical facts, however, hardly matter, for the ludicrous burlesque as unfolded in the ballad really needs no extraneous confirmation or factual prop to add to the reader's enjoyment—or embarrassment. As for its author (or authors), the piece is full of Pope's irresponsible fun, and bears so many marks of his ballad manner, that whoever may have helped in suggesting or working out the theme to begin with, seems later to have been hardly more than a sleeping partner, for there can be very little doubt whose hand held the pen. At the same time it should be remembered that Pope had only recently (on May 12, 1720) published the two final volumes of his great translation of the *Iliad*, which had been his unremitting task, and bed and board companion, for something like six long years. One cannot wonder, therefore, if, in the franker society of the period, such rhyming could bring him relief from such a strain, that he should have sought relief from time to time in such rhyming.

---

[1] *Correspondence*, I, 1735 (i), p. 172.

It remains now to reprint—almost certainly for the first time—the original text of Pope's ballad, as it was published barely three months after he had brought 'the English *Iliad*'—which Dr Johnson called 'the noblest version of poetry which the world has ever seen'[1]—to a successful conclusion.

DUKE upon DUKE
An Excellent New Play-house Ballad

I. To Lordings Proud I tune my Song,
 Who Feast in Bower or Hall;
 Tho' Dukes they be, yet Dukes shall see
 That Pride will have a fall.

II. Now that this same it is Right Sooth,
 Full plainly doth appear;
 From what befell *JOHN* DUKE OF *GUISE*,
 And *NIC of* LANCASTERE.

III. When *Richard Cœur de Lyon* Reign'd,
 (which means a *Lyon's Heart*)
 Like him his Barons rag'd and roar'd,
 Each play'd a Lyon's part.

IV. A Word and Blow was then enough,
 Such Honour did them Prick,
 If you but turn'd your Cheek, a Cuff,
 And if your A—e, a Kick.

V. Look in their Face, they tweak'd your Nose,
 At every turn fell to 't;
 Come near, they trode upon your Toes;
 They fought from Head to Foot.

VI. Of these the *Duke* of *Lancastere*
 Stood Paramount in Pride;
 He kick'd and cuff'd, and tweak'd and trode
 His Foes and *Friends* beside.

[1] Johnson, IV, p. 47.

VII.   Firm on his Front his Beaver sate,
       So broad it hid his Chin;
    For why, he thought no Man his Mate,
       And fear'd to Tan his Skin.

VIII.   With *Spanish* Wool he dy'd his Cheek,
       With Essence oyl'd his Hair;
    No vixen Civet Cat more Sweet,
       Nor more could Scratch and Tear.

IX.   *Right Tall* he made himself to show,
       Tho' made *full short* by G—d;
    And when *all other* Dukes did *Bow*,
       This Duke did only *Nod*.

X.   Yet Courteous, Blith and Debonaire,
       To *GUISE*'s DUKE was he;
    Never was such a Loving Pair,
       Why did they disagree?

XI.   Oh! thus it was, he lov'd him dear,
       And cast how to requite him;
    And having no Friend left but This,
       He deem'd it meet to *fight him*.

XII.   Forthwith he drench'd his desperate Quill,
       And thus he did Indite,
    This Eve at Whisk OUR SELF *will Play*,
       Sir Duke, *Be here to Night*.

XIII.   *Ah no! ah no!* the Guileless *GUISE*,
       Demurely did reply;
    I cannot Go, nor yet can Stand,
       So sore the Gout have I.

XIV.   The DUKE in Wrath call'd for his Steeds,
       And fiercely drove them on;
    Lord! Lord! how rattled then thy Stones,
       O *Kingly Kensington*!

XV.   All in a Trice on *GUISE* he rush'd,
       Thrust out his Lady Dear;
       He tweak'd his Nose, trod on his Toes,
       And smote him on the Ear.

XVI.   But mark! how midst of Victory,
        Fate shews an *Old Dog-Trick*;
        Up leap'd DUKE *JOHN* and knock'd him down,
        And so down fell DUKE *NIC*.

XVII.   Alass, Oh *NIC*! Oh *NIC*, alass!
         Right did thy Gossip call thee,
         As who should say, *Alass the Day*
            When JOHN of GUISE shall maul thee.

XVIII.   For on thee did he clap his Chair,
          And on that Chair did sit;
          And look'd as if he meant therein
          To do *what was not fit.*

XIX.   Up didst thou look, Oh woful DUKE,
        Thy Mouth yet durst not ope,
        Certes, for fear of finding there
        A T—d instead of Trope.

XX.   "*Lye there thou Caitiff vile, quoth GUISE,*
          "*No* Sheet *is here to save thee,*
       "*The Casement it is shut likewise,*
          "*Beneath my Feet I have thee.*

XXI.   "*If thou hast ought to say, now speak.*
        Then *Lancaster* did cry.
        "Knowest thou not ME, nor yet thy self,
          "Who Thou, and WHO AM I?

XXII.   "Know'st Thou not ME, who God be prais'd,
           "Have bawl'd and quarrell'd more
         "Than all the Line of *Lancaster*
           "That battled heretofore?

XXIII.   "In Senates fam'd for many a Speech,
      "And what some Awe must give Ye,
   "Tho' laid thus low beneath thy Breech,
      "Still of the Council Privy.

XXIV.   "Still of the Dutchy Chancellor,
      "*Durante* Life I have it,
   "And turn (as now thou dost on me)
      "My A—e on those that gave it.

XXV.   But now the Servants they rush'd in;
      And DUKE *NIC* up leap'd He,
   I will not cope against such Odds,
      But *GUISE, I'll fight with thee.*

XXVI.   *To Morrow with Thee will I fight*
      Under the Greenwood Tree;
   No, not to Morrow, but to Night,
      Quoth *GUISE*, I'll fight with thee.

XXVII.   And now the Sun declining low
      Bestreak'd with Blood the Skies,
   When with his Sword at Saddle Bow
      Rode forth the valiant *GUISE*.

XXVIII.   Full gently praunc'd he on the Lawn,
      Oft rowl'd his Eye around,
   And from his Stirrup stretch'd to find
      Who was not to be found.

XXIX.   Long brandish'd he his Blade in Air,
      Long look'd the Field all o're,
   At length he spy'd the merry Men brown,
      And eke the Coach and Four.

XXX.   From out the Boot bold *NICHOLAS*
      Did wave his Hand so white,
   As pointing out the gloomy Glade
      Whereat he meant to fight.

XXXI.   All in that dreadful Hour so calm
                Was *Lancaster* to see,
            As if he meant to take the Air,
                Or only take a Fee.

XXXII.   And so he did, for to *New Court*
                His trowling Wheels they run;
            Not that he shunn'd the doubtful Strife,
                But Business must be done.

XXXIII.   Back in the dark, by *Brompton* Park,
                He turn'd up thro' the *Gore*,
            So slunk to *Campden* House so high,
                All in his Coach and four.

XXXIV.   Mean while the *GUISE* did fret and fume,
                A Sight it was to see,
            Benumm'd beneath the Evening Dew,
                Under the Greenwood Tree.

XXXV.   Then wet and weary home he far'd,
                Sore mutt'ring all the way,
            The Day I meet NIC he shall rue
                The Cudgel of that Day.

XXXVI.   Mean time on every pissing Post
                Paste we this Recreant's Name,
            So that each Pisser-by shall read,
                And piss against the same.

XXXVII.   Now God preserve our GRACIOUS KING,
                And grant his Nobles all
            May learn this Lesson from *Duke Nic*,
                That *Pride will have a Fall*.

                    FINIS

CHAPTER XII

MARTHA BLOUNT'S BIRTHDAY POEM

I T is not always realized what pains Pope was capable of taking to correct and polish, and sometimes even remodel, a poem until he was satisfied it could not be further improved. Perhaps the most remarkable example of the lengths to which he would go when this urge for perfection drove him, is to be found in the long and complicated story—now told in its entirety for the first time—of the famous poem originally written to celebrate the thirty-third birthday of his dearest and best friend, Martha Blount. For this poem was progressively altered for fifteen years following its first presentation, while the lady addressed grew older and older, and different versions in part or whole were made to serve more than one person and more than one occasion.

It is not at all surprising, therefore, to find that the poem has survived in a number of versions and numberless variants. Even the original birthday manuscript in his own hand, which is still treasured amongst the Blount family papers at Mapledurham, Martha's early home, reveals last-minute emendations in two places; and Pope's two autograph copies,[1] transcribed by him two years later, show further changes. Indeed, it would scarcely be an over-statement to say that during the poet's lifetime no two copies of the poem, whether in manuscript or in print (except of course those of the same edition), are exactly alike. In consequence, the contemporary bibliography of the five chief versions of these protean lines is extremely involved; and as it is difficult to follow them without some guide, concise lists of editions, versions, and dates have been drawn up and placed in the Appendix[2] for convenience of reference.

To begin at the beginning, the poem was written at Twickenham in the summer of 1723, at a time when Pope was busily employed on his daily stint of the translation of the *Odyssey*. The original autograph version,[3] which seems never to have been printed hitherto, runs as follows:

[1] Portland, XIII; and Stowe 964.
[2] See Appendix C, pp. 365 f.
[3] Mapledurham, 4.

Written, June ye 15th.
On Your Birth-Day.
1723.

Oh be thou blest with all that Heav'n can send!
Long Health, long Youth, long Pleasure—and a Friend.
Not with those Toys the Woman-World admire,
Riches that vex, and Vanities that tire:
Let Joy, or Ease; let Affluence, or Content; 5
And the glad Conscience of a Life well-spent,
Calm ev'ry Thought, inspirit ev'ry Grace,
Glow in thy Heart, and smile upon thy Face!
Let Day improve on Day; and Year on Year,
Without a Pain, a Trouble, or a Fear! 10
And ah! since Death must that dear Frame destroy,
Die by a sudden Extacy of Joy!
In some soft Dream may thy mild Soul remove,
And be thy latest Gasp a Sigh of Love![1] 14
A: Pope.

When, the following year, Pope and Martha again failed to meet on
her birthday, he wrote her a letter—'only to repeat in prose, what I
told you last year in rhyme; (so sincere is my poetry)'.[2] In the meantime copies of the poem had been made for various people. For instance, Pope himself had transcribed it for another friend, Judith
Cowper (with whom he was at that time exchanging complimentary,
pseudo-sentimental letters), and sent it to her with a polite discourse
on friends and friendship, in which he introduces the poem in these
words: 'I was the other day forming a wish for a lady's happiness, upon
her birth-day.'[3] He then goes on to explain what he had attempted to
do in the poem, and says that he has promised Mrs Howard a copy of
it, which he begs Judith Cowper to transcribe and send to her. In
Pope's letter the poem is entitled simply, *To a Lady, on her Birth-day,*
1723. It is therefore amusing to find amongst the Cowper family
papers in the British Museum a copy of this poem (*not* in Pope's autograph) actually entitled, *On Mrs J–d–th C–p–r's Birth Day—By Mr*
Pope.[4] As Pope once complained to his old friend John Caryll, a

---

[1] Students may like to know that, as originally written, 'Long Health' in l. 2 was
'Long Life'; and l. 12 read, 'Oh be it by an Extacy of Joy!'
[2] *Works*, v (Cooper), 1737, p. 137.   [3] *Letters . . . To A Lady*, p. 29.
[4] Add. 28101, f. 42.

relation of the Blounts, that a simpleton of Martha's sex had pretended the poem was addressed to herself,[1] it would seem at least possible that Judith had gone a step further and had persuaded herself, or
her family, it was so—perhaps having mistaken the very complimentary but careful phrasing of Pope's covering letter to her. With
regard to these early autograph copies and transcripts, it is interesting
to note that Pope is still correcting the poem, for the copy he sent
Judith Cowper[2] shows two new variant readings, and other copies a
year or two later reveal yet further changes.

The first publication of this poem has a special interest. Time was,
when bibliographers were well content to state the year that a work
was first printed; then, growing more nice as more information was
made available, they became increasingly particular about the month,
and even the day, of issue. Now, it would seem—at least with Pope—
that the round of the clock must be watched for the precise hour of
precedence. For when the birthday poem was first published on
November 14, 1724, it appeared simultaneously in two newspapers of
that date, namely, *The British Journal* and *The Whitehall Evening-Post*.
Such an occurrence has been noted by the present writer more than
once; and a later example with no less than four apparently syn-
chronous 'first editions' is described in a subsequent chapter.[3] Although in the eighteenth century it was the custom of the trade to
issue weekly and daily papers earlier in the day than the evening
sheets, priority of publication is not always easy to ascertain. Fortunately, *The British Journal* was a weekly and thus the first of the two
to appear. Indeed, this assumption is borne out by an analysis of the
news in the two papers, which shows that the *Evening-Post* includes
under the heading, 'London, Nov. 14', four important items of late
news (amongst them the election of a new Archbishop of York) which
are not found in the *Journal* of the same date, but in the following
week's issue where they are given in the *Evening-Post*'s own words of
the previous week. Thus the poem was first printed in the weekly
paper where it was prefaced by the following letter:

To the Author of the British Journal.   Nov. 6, 1724.
Sir.   I think my self oblig'd to you for the Entertainment you have
     afforded me by inserting several good Pieces of Poetry in your
     late Journals, and believe your Readers would be pleas'd to find
     them more frequently; for which Reason I have sent you the
     following Copy of Verses.   Yours, &c. G. L.

---

[1] Add. 28618, f. 72 v.   [2] *Letters . . . To A Lady*, p. 31.   [3] See *post*, pp. 334, 335.

The WISH; to a Young Lady on her Birth-Day.
By Mr. Pope.

[Whereupon the poem followed in the early version of fourteen lines.]

This introductory letter was of course omitted by *The Whitehall Evening-Post* when, a few hours later, it exactly copied the text of the poem from the *Journal*. Where 'G. L.' got it from, and who 'G. L.' was, are alike unknown. By the end of 1724, however, manuscript copies of the poem were probably being handed about with or without Pope's leave (he told Caryll in 1729[1] that the circulation in manuscript of a later version of the poem was neither his nor Martha's doing). The 'newspaper text' is found on collation to contain some twenty verbal differences from the original autograph given above, but as most of them appear in no other version, it is possible they were not all authentic. The early version of the poem, no matter what variants it may contain, always consists of fourteen lines, and for convenience may be called the 'A' text (other versions have either more or less); and Pope himself at length set his sanction on a printed text of the 'A' version, when he included it—with two or three new corrections—in the fifth edition of his first miscellany (of which an account has been given earlier),[2] now entitled, *Miscellany Poems*, 1726.

The next stage of the birthday poem is the appearance of a new version in *Miscellanies. The Last Volume* (dated 1727, but not published until March 7, 1728),[3] the third of a series of volumes of occasional pieces of prose and verse, sponsored by Swift and Pope, edited by Pope, and consisting for the most part of their own work. In this version of the poem the conclusion has been radically altered, and six new lines inserted after the fourth line, now making twenty lines in all. These new lines, however, had for the most part actually appeared in print the previous year in *The Rival Modes. A Comedy . . . Written by James Moore Smythe, Esq*; 1727, where, in the second act, *Sagely* soliloquizes after *Amoret*'s exit, as follows:

SAGELY. Gone! may the common Curse of Jilts light on you, that not one of your Follies may end, till it gives birth to a worse. Since

> *'Tis thus that Vanity Coquettes rewards,*
> *A Youth of Frolick, an Old Age of Cards;*
> *Fair to no purpose, Artful to no end,*
> *Young without Lovers, Old without a Friend.*

---

[1] Add. 28618, f. 72 v.   [2] See *ante*, pp. 36–7.

[3] *Not* March 8, as usually stated. See *The London Evening Post* for March 7, 1728.

> *A Fool their Aim, their Prize some worn-out Sot;*
> *Alive ridiculous, when dead, forgot.*
>
> [Exit.

It was probably a surprise to many people to find Martha's birth-day poem being suddenly expanded by these apparently borrowed lines. This stage of development constitutes the 'B' text; and the poem now reads as follows:

To Mrs. M. B. Sent on Her Birth-Day
June 15.

> OH, be thou blest with all that Heav'n can send!
> Long Health, long Youth, long Pleasure, and a Friend:
> Not with those Toys the Female Race admire,
> Riches that *vex*, and Vanities that *tire*;
> Not as the World its pretty Slaves rewards,   5
> A Youth of Frolicks, an Old-Age of Cards;
> Fair to no Purpose, artful to no End,
> Young without Lovers, old without a Friend;
> A Fop their Passion, but their Prize a Sot;
> Alive, ridiculous; and dead, forgot!   10
>
> Let Joy, or Ease, let Affluence, or Content,
> And the gay Conscience of a Life well spent,
> Calm ev'ry Thought, inspirit ev'ry Grace,
> Glow in thy Heart, and smile upon thy Face:
> Let Day improve on Day, and Year on Year,   15
> Without a *Pain*, a *Trouble*, or a *Fear*:
> Till Death unfelt that tender Frame destroy,
> In some soft Dream, or Extasy of Joy,
> Peaceful sleep out the Sabbath of the Tomb,
> And wake to Raptures in a Life to come!   20

The reprinting of these lines (ll. 5-10) in Pope's poem, twelve months after their appearance in Moore-Smythe's play, was followed in less than a fortnight by an attack on Pope in *The Daily Journal* of March 18, 1728, in which he was publicly accused of plagiarism in a pseudonymous letter, which was followed up by one or two others to the same tune but with different pen-names. And it has been fre-quently stated, but without any evidence being adduced, that Pope was the concealed author of at least the first of them, which is signed 'Philo-Mauri', and begins as follows:

Sir,—Upon reading the Third Volume of *Pope's* Miscellanies,

o

I found five Lines which I thought excellent, and happening to praise them afterwards in a mixt Company, a Gentleman present, immediately produced a modern Comedy, publish'd last Year, where were the same Verses, almost to a Tittle. I was a good deal out of Countenance to find that I had been so eloquent in Praise of a Felony, and not a little in Pain lest I myself should be understood to be an Accomplice . . .

The story, as generally told, states that Pope granted Moore-Smythe's request to incorporate those six lines (which he must have seen in an unpublished manuscript) in a play then being written; that Pope withdrew his permission a month before the play was acted or printed; that Moore-Smythe justifiably insisted on retaining the lines in his play as though they were his own; that Pope allowed twelve months to pass in silence, and then incorporated them in Martha's birthday poem—his aim being not (as one might have expected) that of a poet, to improve his verses; nor that of a friend, to give further pleasure to the dear lady addressed; nor even that of a mere man, to assert his right to his own work. Any of these would have been understandable and left him human. No, he is supposed to have acted in this affair like some far-sighted schemer, and printed these six lines in the birthday poem solely because it would enable him to 'write a letter to the newspapers' under a fictitious name, charging himself with plagiarism from Moore-Smythe, in order that he might, after more than another year had passed, be in a position to cite this letter in *The Dunciad, Variorum*[1] (published April 10, 1729) amongst a quite large number of other wrongful attacks made on him in the past, and thus at last reveal that not he, but Moore-Smythe, was the real plagiarist!

It may all be true, of course; but it seems a laborious, dilatory, and ineffective way of accomplishing his wish and smiting his enemy, besides leaving out of the picture the two most important facts of Pope's life (his exquisite aesthetic sense which drove him to a ceaseless pursuit of perfect versification, and his enduring love and care for Martha Blount), and, with their absence, the whole *raison d'être* of the poem.

In Pope's summary account of the matter in *The Dunciad, Variorum*, he named Lord Bolingbroke and Hugh Bethel, as well as 'the Lady to whom the said verses were originally addressed', as reputable witnesses ready to vouch for his statement that the lines in question had been known to themselves and others 'long before the said gentleman composed his play'. That assertion, however, does not claim—as some

---

[1] See Sutherland, pp. 33 f.

have accused Pope of claiming—that the 'new' lines were present in the first draft of the birthday poem (which could easily have been refuted at any time by reference to the earliest texts), but only that, when these half-dozen lines were first written, they were addressed to Martha Blount as part of the poem in which they were to be inserted, and in a manuscript copy of which Moore-Smythe probably first saw them.

In the *Epistle to Arbuthnot*, 1735, Pope has a curious statement that in the past he had been 'so humble, he has . . . rym'd for Moor'; which is generally taken as alluding to the presence of these six lines in Moore-Smythe's play. However that may be, no one at this day is likely to uphold seriously Moore-Smythe's 'right' to the lines. On the other hand, there is little or no evidence to show that he ever denied Pope's title to them, or ever explicitly claimed them as his own. Nevertheless it has been pointed out (whether in extenuation of Moore-Smythe's conduct, or in blame of Pope's, is not quite clear) that the playwright made other characters in the play likewise quote without attribution scraps of verse from other poets, as well as a couplet, similarly unacknowledged, from Pope's *Essay on Criticism*, about which Pope made no complaint. To which the answer is, of course, that unacknowledged quotations from printed sources and from manuscript sources are very different matters; the former normally bears the name of its author for all to see, whereas in the latter case there can be no possible kind of check, for which reason priority of use is usually taken to imply authorship. If, therefore, after Pope had changed his mind (as he had every right to do), Moore-Smythe insisted on retaining those lines in his play without acknowledging their source (as he undoubtedly did), the resentment against him which Pope began to show about this time could very well have sprung from this virtual theft of a fragment of unpublished verse destined by its author for another and quite different service. Thus, with a consequent sense of injury embittering both sides, the open hostilities which ensued were after all a natural, if regrettable, result.

For many years, following what may be called Pope's 'recovery' of the stolen lines in 1728, they continued to appear in the poem in the numerous successive editions of the Swift-Pope *Miscellanies*—until, indeed, some years after Pope's death. And as the poem in other places *at the same time* was undergoing further changes at its author's hands, as we shall see, this persistence of the *Miscellanies* version, or the 'B' text (which presumably was due to the restrictions of copyright law), has caused much confusion, past and present, about the sequence of the different versions which were being published contemporaneously over a period of years—a confusion which a glance at the bibliography[1] of the poem should do much to clarify.

Apart from those automatic reprintings of the 'B' text, the last thing to happen to these six lines was seen on the publication of another poem addressed to Martha Blount, namely, the famous 'second moral essay', entitled, *To a Lady Of the Characters of Women*.[2] For it was to that poem that Pope finally transferred them from the birthday poem; and there, in a setting more in accord with their tone and content, they have ever since remained in a self-contained paragraph, thus—

> See how the World its Veterans rewards!
> A Youth of frolicks, an old Age of Cards,
> Fair to no purpose, artful to no end,
> Young without Lovers, old without a Friend,
> A Fop their Passion, but their Prize a Sot,
> Alive, ridiculous, and dead, forgot!

But all this is little more than half the story of Martha's birthday poem, for alongside this progressive correction of it there was another poem of the same kind by Pope being handed about in manuscript, which under different titles crossed and recrossed the track of Martha's poem with much consequent confusion of editorial texts and notes. What seems to be the earliest verison of it was found by the present writer in two contemporary transcripts amongst the papers of Pope's great friend, the Earl of Oxford, one at Longleat, the other in the British Museum. This may be called the 'C' text; it has ten lines, and runs as follows:

On a Late Birth Day. 1724.

> With added Days, if Life bring nothing new,
> But, like a Sieve, let ev'ry Pleasure thro';
> Some Joy still lost, as each vain Year runs o'er,
> And all we gain, some pensive Notion more!
> Is this a Birth-Day? ah! 'tis sadly clear,
> 'Tis but the Fun'ral of the former Year.
> If there's no Hope, with kind, tho' fainter ray
> To gild the Evening of our future Day;
> If ev'ry Page of Life's long Volume tell
> The same dull Story—Mordaunt! thou did'st well.[3]

---

[1] See *post*, p. 365.   [2] Published February 8, 1735; see *The London Evening Post* of that date.   [3] Portland, xviii, f. 153 (also in Harl. 7316, f. 160).

It will be noticed at once that lines from this poem reappear in the familiar final version of the poem on Martha's birthday; but several things were to happen to it before they arrived there. To begin with, this poem seems not to have been originally 'an epitaph on Mordaunt' as has been asserted without evidence more than once.[1] On the other hand, it is virtually certain that it was written on Pope's own birthday, May 21, 1724. Several scraps of evidence indicate this: first, the suicide of Colonel Mordaunt, nephew of another great friend of Pope, Lord Peterborough, had occurred only a fortnight earlier, on May 7, 1724; secondly, Pope's own statement later, that the lines were a 'reflection' on his own birthday[2] (though he did not mention which); thirdly, the consistent dating of the three known copies of the poem '1724'; and, lastly, the fact that in the spring of 1724, Pope had suffered a severe and protracted bout of illness which left him much depressed, as his few surviving letters of this season show.[3] Nevertheless, the piece as a whole was not published until half a century later, when it appeared in print for the first time in *The St. James's Chronicle* for September 28–30, 1775, with the erroneous title, *To Mrs. Martha Blunt, on her Birth-Day, 1724. By Mr. Pope*. In this, the first line was altered to—'If added Days of Life bring nothing new'; and there are other textual changes which all appeared again the following year in *Additions to the Works of Alexander Pope, Esq.*, Vol. I, 1776. The changed title was wrong, as we know from Pope's birthday letter to Martha in 1724, quoted above,[4] but was probably due to an attempt in 1775 to explain how six lines in the final version of Martha's birthday poem could appear in another birthday poem by Pope in 1724.

The next stage of the 1724 poem (the 'D' text) presents something of a problem. Four years later Pope experienced probably the gloomiest winter of his life. From the late autumn of 1728 onwards, he was kept close to the house by the long illness of his mother who for weeks together lay at death's door. Gay also was very ill at that time, and could not come to Twickenham as usual; and, as it happened, other visitors were very few. Writing to Gay in January 1729, after news of some slight improvement in his health, Pope says:

I have now past five weeks without once going from home, and without any company but for three or four of the days . . . I never pass'd so melancholy a time, and now Mr. Congreve's death touches me nearly: It was twenty years and more that I have

[1] See, for example, R. W. Babcock. M.L.N., XLVIII.
[2] *Letters*, 4to, 1737, p. 252.   [3] See EC, VII, pp. 398, 401; VIII, pp. 76, 196.
[4] See *ante*, p. 196.

known him: Every year carries away something dear with it, till we outlive all tendernesses, and become wretched Individuals again as we begun. Adieu! This is my birth-day, and this is my reflection upon it,

> With added days if Life give nothing new,
> But, like a Sieve, let ev'ry Pleasure thro';
> Some Joy still lost, as each vain year runs o'er,
> And all we gain, some sad Reflection more!
> Is this a Birth-day?——'Tis alas too clear,
> 'Tis but the Fun'ral of the former Year. [1]

Any attempt to explain the closing sentences of this letter—in view of the facts that Congreve died January 19, 1729, and that Pope's birthday (as Gay very well knew) was May 21—must take into account the further fact that, like other people of his period, Pope normally edited his letters before publication. He obviously at times regarded them more as essays than as historical or biographical documents; but as his occasionally ruthless methods of preparing his correspondence for the press have already been discussed,[2] no further comment is needed in this place.

Returning, then, to Pope's melancholy letter to Gay: this was first printed in Curll's surreptitious edition of Pope's *Letters* in 1735 (in the publication of which the poet was more or less concerned),[3] and like many others in the volume, it carries no date; nor was it dated in the authorized edition two years later. But the absence of a date does not make the problem any easier. Elwin and Courthope suggested that the letter might be a conflation of two letters of different dates, which is perhaps possible. But the truth is that Pope, especially in the latter half of his life, was notoriously vague or careless about dates (a foible which has also been considered earlier)[4]; and he may have thought that, after six years, other people too would not be able to remember whether Congreve died in the winter or the spring, and that, in any case, the season was immaterial; what mattered and what (to use his words) 'struck me through' was the death of his friend. For it seems certain that the mood in which he wrote to Gay reflected the mood in which he had penned those pessimistic lines on his birthday in 1724, and, living that moment again, he transcribed them so far as they expressed his present feeling. Somehow and strangely, the spirit of Congreve seems to have been the connecting link between the two

---

[1] *Letters*, 4to, 1737, pp. 251 f. [2] See *ante*, pp. 14–15.
[3] See *ante*, pp. 17–18. [4] See *ante*, pp. 12 f.

occasions. For it could not have been mere accident that on Congreve's death he should remember how one of the playwright's verses[1] had woven itself into that sombre final couplet of his own birthday poem—woven itself so inextricably that he never allowed the couplet to be printed, and carefully omitted it, with the lines leading up to it, when writing (or when printing) that most despondent of letters to Gay.

Pope's short poem on his birthday never got any nearer to being published as a whole in his lifetime than in this letter. Two other lines from it, however, had been printed earlier still, when he incorporated, with characteristic thrift, its penultimate couplet in his *Imitations of Horace*, Book II, Satire I, 1733, where it appeared in this guise:

> Whether old Age, with faint, but chearful Ray,
> Attends to gild the Evening of my Day . . . (ll. 93–94)

Thus when its first six lines in their turn became absorbed in Martha's birthday poem about 1738, and the Congreve-Mordaunt couplet had been suppressed for ever, there was nothing left of Pope's own birthday poem to be printed.

The final revision of Martha's poem was probably made shortly before its appearance in *The Works . . . Vol. II, Part II. Containing . . . Pieces . . . Written since the former Volumes.* 1738—which volume there is reason to believe was not published until May 1, 1739.[2] In its official setting the poem is simply headed, *To Mrs. M. B. on her Birth-day* (now, alas, her forty-eighth). Thus, the particularity of the original title having disappeared years before, the poem no longer greets one specific birthday of Martha's, but any of them. Indeed, so many are the successive versions and variants of the poem from 1723 to 1738, that, if they had been spread out only a little more evenly, she could have been given a slightly different version of the same poem on *every* birthday between!

The authoritative text of the poem, which has thus taken fifteen years in the making, follows and concludes the present chapter. It is the 'E' text, that is the 1738 version which substitutes the birthday 'reflection' for the six 'plagiarized' lines. Many readers will be familiar with it, but will perhaps welcome it here for convenience of reference and comparison:

---

[1] 'Will tell the same dull Story o'er and o'er.'—*Ovid's Art of Love*, Book III, l. 504.
[2] Griffith, I, ii, p. 398.

To Mrs. M. B. *on her Birth-day.*

Oh be thou blest with all that Heav'n can send,
Long Health, long Youth, long Pleasure, and a Friend:
Not with those Toys the female world admire,
Riches that vex, and Vanities that tire.
With added years if Life bring nothing new,   5
But like a Sieve let ev'ry blessing thro',
Some joy still lost, as each vain year runs o'er,
And all we gain, some sad Reflection more;
Is that a Birth-day? 'tis alas! too clear,
'Tis but the Fun'ral of the former year.   10

    Let Joy or Ease, let Affluence or Content,
And the gay Conscience of a life well spent,
Calm ev'ry thought, inspirit ev'ry Grace,
Glow in thy heart, and smile upon thy face.
Let day improve on day, and year on year,   15
Without a Pain, a Trouble, or a Fear;
Till Death unfelt that tender frame destroy,
In some soft Dream, or Extasy of joy;
Peaceful sleep out the Sabbath of the Tomb,
And wake to Raptures in a Life to come.   20

CHAPTER XIII

HELP FOR GAY

I. THE UNNAMED EPILOGUE

THE attribution to Pope of an Epilogue hitherto regarded as Gay's is based on the only reasonable interpretation of an autograph letter from Pope to Jacob Tonson, the bookseller (or publisher, as we should now say), which is preserved in the British Museum, and which runs as follows:

Sir,   Tuesday night.

Mr Gay & myself think it absolutely necessary that you should cancel that Leaf in which ye Epilogue is printed, or if it falls out wrong, cancell both leaves rather than fail; It must necessarily be inserted, after ye Title *EPILOGUE* [*Sent by an unknown Hand.*] Whatever charge this Cancelling will cost, shall be paid. It is yet time, I am very sure, to do it, before ye general publication on Thursday. This must be done to oblige him, &

Y^r most humble Servt

A. Pope.

I must go out before ten & shall be glad to see y^u (upon ye other affair) before nine.

[Addressed:] To Mr. Tonson ov^r ag^st Catharine
Street in ye Strand.[1]

This letter was first printed, without comment or note, by Dr G. Sherburn,[2] in a batch of eleven unpublished letters from Pope to Tonson, discovered some little time ago. Unfortunately it is not dated; but it can nevertheless be ascribed for various reasons, and with virtual certainty, to the years 1721–1725, for the rest of the letters (except one negligible note) have all to do with the preparation and publication of Pope's edition of Shakespeare,[3] in the middle of which correspondence this incongruous but exciting letter appears.

To begin with, it is clear that the letter has to do with the imminent publication of an unnamed play in which three people—Tonson, Gay, and Pope—were in one way or another concerned. And an examination of the records shows that within the decade 1720–1730

[1] Add. 28275, ff. 240, 241 v.   [2] Sherburn, p. 309.
[3] Published in six Vols., March 12, 1725.

the only dramatic publications with which these three people might conceivably be connected are, first, Pope's *Works of Shakespeare*, 1725, and secondly, Gay's tragedy of *The Captives*, 1724. But Pope's *Shakespeare* does not in fact include a new Epilogue in the composition of which Pope and Gay could have been implicated, or indeed, a new Epilogue of any kind; nor was it published 'on Thursday', but on a Friday.[1] Moreover, if the letter referred to Pope's *Shakespeare*, why is Gay intervening so clamorously in the affair? That he assisted Pope from time to time in the editing, everybody knows; but not to the extent of Tonson's being compelled to 'oblige' him, as the letter suggests.

There remains, therefore, *The Captives*, which seems to meet all the necessary conditions, and against which no such objections can be posed. For *The Captives* was 'Printed for J. Tonson', and, although anonymous, was dedicated 'To her Royal Highness the Princess' by 'John Gay', while Pope's interest in it is shown by the urgency of the foregoing letter. At the outset, then, it is extremely probable that the 'Epilogue' of the letter is the Epilogue of *The Captives*. This identification is supported by the fact that the letter, which is dated 'Tuesday night', states that the play is to be published 'on Thursday'; for *The Captives* was actually published 'on Thursday', January 23, 1724, according to *The Whitehall Evening-Post* of that day.

Assuming, then, that the 'Epilogue' is thus correctly identified (and no alternative seems possible), the questions immediately arise: What was Pope doing at all in this affair? Why was he so insistent about the anonymity of the Epilogue? and why only of the Epilogue? Although Gay's name does not appear on the title-page of the play, and is only subscribed to the dedication, the play has always been accepted as his, and his also the Prologue and Epilogue. Why, then, all this fuss and expense about the latter—all this cancelling and inserting—simply to include the words 'Sent by an unknown Hand'? It cannot be that Gay was suddenly grown ashamed of the piece and felt compelled to disclaim it; for it is certainly a much livelier performance than the Prologue for which he was (presumably) willing to accept responsibility. Consequently, when it is remembered how frequently Pope had a hand in Gay's productions; and how (as shown in a previous chapter)[2] nine years earlier he had written a Prologue for Rowe's tragedy, *Lady Jane Gray*, which was likewise headed 'Sent by an Unknown Hand', it is difficult to escape the conclusion that his meticulous and arbitrary

[1] See *The Whitehall Evening-Post*, March 9–11, 1725.
[2] See *ante*, pp. 138 f.

instructions to Tonson about this Epilogue mean that he himself had a personal interest in its anonymity and an authoritative voice in its disposition, such as can best, if not only, be explained by his authorship of the piece, partial or complete.

Examination of the published play-book shows that the Epilogue, as Pope had feared, did 'fall out wrong', and that it actually occupies parts of two leaves, namely, the verso of A5 and the recto of A6 (the Epilogue immediately following the Prologue in front of the play, a not unusual position at that date). Thus, as there is no sign or trace of cancellation, and as the Epilogue has been left in its original position and is not headed 'Sent by an unknown Hand', it is evident that Pope's twelfth-hour directions were for some reason deemed impracticable—perhaps because too many copies had already been bound, or because there was too short a time between 'Tuesday night' (which would mean Wednesday morning at the printers) and 'publication on Thursday', for the work of substitution to be satisfactorily carried out. More probably the latter, for Pope himself seems to have had some misgiving about it, and to be trying to convince himself, as much as Tonson, with his—'It is yet time, I am very sure, to do it . . .'

This excessive concern for some one's anonymity revealed in Pope's letter would itself seem to be only another indication of his responsibility for the Epilogue. For after having written several pieces for the theatre in his younger days, he had, since 1718, been refusing to furnish these dramatic ornaments for the plays of friends and acquaintances alike. He had, for example, excused himself early in 1719 from writing a prologue to Hughes's *Siege of Damascus*,[1] and another, presumably in 1722, to a play by the Duke of Buckingham.[2] Then on September 18, 1722, he wrote to Broome explaining why he had similarly declined to supply a prologue to a tragedy entitled *Mariamne*, by their mutual friend Fenton; in which letter he says:

> He knows . . . my reasons and inability . . . As to my writing one, were it to be engaged for as the greatest of secrets, I have learnt by experience nothing of that kind is ever kept a secret; . . . I would most gladly make the prologue, to-morrow, could it be done without any man's knowing it.[3]

Later still, he refused (September 29, 1731) to write an epilogue for Hill's *Athelwold*, citing 'an invariable Maxim' as his excuse; and then going on to say, 'Every poetical Friend I have, has had my Word, I

[1] Warton, VIII, pp. 283 f.   [2] EC, VIII, p. 58.
[3] *Ibid.*, p. 58.

never would.'[1] None of these people was an intimate friend like his beloved Gay, who, with Swift, was always closest to Pope's heart, and whom he was ready to help or please on any and every occasion. Still more to the point is the fact that, at the date *The Captives* was produced (January 15, 1724), Fenton was actually working with Pope on the translation of the *Odyssey*, and he would in all likelihood have been grievously hurt to know that what Pope would not do for him he had since done for Gay. Pope could not afford to jeopardize the major undertaking in that way; and as he and Gay were old collaborators and known to be such, he thus endeavoured to forestall any guesswork about his authorship by all these directions to Tonson. It is not impossible, however, that Pope had a subsidiary motive in writing this letter, for he, more than most people, rarely acted with a single end in view. Thus, as his early dislike of the actress, Mrs Oldfield (discussed in a previous chapter)[2] did not grow appreciably less with the years, and as she not only had a part in the play but spoke the Epilogue as well, Pope may also have wished by the proposed cancellation to remove her name from the caption of the printed Epilogue, where it had been set up in accordance with the prevalent—though not universal—custom. In this way, with the words 'Epilogue: Spoken by Mrs. Oldfield' changed to 'Epilogue [Sent by an unknown Hand]', he would have avoided the possibility of her name being in any way associated with his work—supposing it to be his.

The poem itself, which has probably never before been printed separately from the play, survives in only one authoritative text, namely the first edition of 1724, where it runs as follows:

EPILOGUE:
Spoken by Mrs. *OLDFIELD*

> Shall authors teaze the town with tragick passion,
> When we've more modern moral things in fashion?
> Let poets quite exhaust the Muse's treasure;
> Sure Masquerades must give more feeling pleasure,
> Where we meet finer sense and better measure;   5
> The marry'd Dame, whose business must be done,
> Puts on the holy vestments of a Nun;
> And brings her unprolifick spouse a son.
> Coquettes, with whom no lover could succeed,
> Here pay off all arrears, and love in—deed: 10

---

[1] *Letters ... to ... Hill*, p. 19.   [2] See *ante*, pp. 134 f.

Ev'n conscious Prudes are so sincere and free,
They ask each man they meet—do you know me?
    Do not our Operas unbend the mind,
Where ev'ry soul's to ecstasie refin'd?
Entranc'd with sound sits each seraphic Toast.   15
All Ladies love the play that moves the most.
Ev'n in this house I've known some tender fair,
Touch'd with meer sense alone, confess a tear.
But the soft voice of an *Italian* weather,
Makes them all languish three whole hours together.   20
And where's the wonder? Plays, like Mass, are sung,
(Religious *Drama*)!—in an unknown tongue.
    Will Poets ne'er consider what they cost us?
What tragedy can take, like Doctor Faustus?
Two stages in this moral show excell,   25
To frighten vicious youth with scenes of hell;
Yet both these *Faustuses* can warn but few.
For what's a Conj'rer's fate to me or—you?
    Yet there are wives who think heav'n worth their care,
But first they kindly send their spouses there.   30
When you my lover's last distress behold,
Does not each husband's thrilling blood run cold?
Some heroes only dye.—Ours finds a wife.
What's harder than captivity for life?
Yet Men, ne'er warn'd, still court their own undoing:
Who, for that circle, would but venture ruin?   36

These lines, comparatively few though they are, do not lack internal
evidence to corroborate the foregoing arguments for Pope's authorship. As with other attributed poems elsewhere in this volume, this
testimony is of different kinds; for in its versification the Epilogue not
only reflects stylistically Pope's other works of this sort, but it also
contains characteristic references to two of his pet aversions, the
Italian Opera and the Masquerades of the period—references which
are reminiscent of other allusions to them in his prose and verse, but
quite unlike Gay's reactions to them so far as is known.

For example, the implication of the whole passage on 'our Operas'
(lines 13-20) is the same as Pope stated more forthrightly in (amongst
other places) the sixth chapter of *Martinus Scriblerus*, as follows:

Does not Ælian tell us how the Lybian Mares were excited to
horsing by Musick? (which ought in truth to be a caution to

modest Women against frequenting Operas; . . . you are brought to
this dilemma, either to give up the virtue of the Ladies, or the power
of your Musick).

Or when, a little further on, he speaks of people being drawn 'in as
close attention as . . . that of an Italian Opera when some favourite
Air is just awaken'd.' Similarly the reproach about 'the soft voice of an
Italian weather' (l. 19) is echoed or hinted in half a dozen passages in
The Works, such as these two from the *Imitations of Horace*—

> For what? to have a Box where Eunuchs sing.[1]

> On each enervate string they taught the Note
> To pant, or tremble thro' an Eunuch's throat.[2]

And it was much the same with the Masquerades which he once
described as 'the true epitome of all absurdities, and of all shows to no
purpose the greatest show to the least purpose'. Quite early, in 1714 in
fact, he had spoken of the dangers of 'midnight Masquerades' to un-
guarded maids[3]; and only two or three years later in a letter to Lady
Mary W. Montagu[4] giving 'the news in London', he tells how 'Masquerades at the Theatre in the Haymarket' have become 'very
frequent'; and goes on to comment on the dubious 'adventures' to be
met with there—adventures which the descriptive passage beginning
with the fourth line of the Epilogue appears faithfully to portray.

Pope and the author of the Epilogue also had similar complaints
to make about *Doctor Faustus*. In 1724, shortly before *The Captives* was
produced, two separate pantomimes on Faustus were being performed: *Harlequin Doctor Faustus* at Drury Lane (produced November
1723), and *The Necromancer; or Harlequin Doctor Faustus* at Lincoln's
Inn Fields (produced December 1723). And Pope's grievance was
that these same old 'miserable Farces' in 1728 were still being 'acted at
the end of the best Tragedies', which were frequently shortened to
make room for them—[5]

> To frighten vicious youth with scenes of hell.   (l. 26)

And he has a footnote in *The Dunciad* (1729) which would also explain
this line of the Epilogue, for in it he tells how the two theatres 'rival'd
each other in showing the Burning of Hell-fire in Dr. Faustus'.[6]

It should also be remarked that the scoffs against marriage in the
last paragraph of the Epilogue sound as though they were written

---

[1] Hor. Ep. i, i, l. 105.   [2] Hor. Ep. ii, i, ll. 153–4.
[3] *Rape of the Lock*, i, l. 72.   [4] Warton, viii, p. 409.
[5] See Sutherland, p. 185, n. 307.   [6] *Ibid.*, p. 185, n. 310.

with the same pen that wrote some of Pope's own interpolations in his modernizations of Chaucer:

> . . . Ours finds a wife.
> What's harder than captivity for life? (ll. 33–34)

is in exactly the same key as a number of couplets in *January and May* (1709) such as—

> . . . they stile a Wife
> The dear-bought Curse and lawful Plague of Life.

And, like a miniature, the whole plot and tone of Pope's *The Wife of Bath her Prologue* (1713) is seen in the single couplet which begins the same paragraph:

> Yet there are wives who think heav'n worth their care,
> But first they kindly send their spouses there. (ll. 29–30)

The Epilogue also repeats the rhetorical trick, previously used by Pope, of suddenly thrusting a question direct at the audience:

> For what's a Conj'rer's fate to me or—you? (l. 28)

which recalls the same sort of challenge in his *Epilogue to Jane Shore* (1714):

> And lov'd his Country—but what's that to you?

Lastly, and perhaps more significant, is the unrecorded appearance of two separate words in the Epilogue, which, or rather the exact meaning of which, the Oxford English Dictionary names Pope as the first to use. Significant, because the early repetition, or the anticipation, of the first recorded use of a word would normally point to its originator, and be something of the same nature as his appended signature, especially with a writer like Pope who never hesitated to reuse his earlier phrases or repeat his invented words (or, rather, meanings) as occasion should arise and as these pages frequently testify. Thus no fewer than three shades of meaning of the epithet 'conscious' are credited to Pope, one of them being 'self-conscious', of which an example is also found in the eleventh line of the Epilogue— 'Ev'n conscious Prudes'. Pope is similarly responsible for the earliest recorded instance of the modern use of 'conjurer' to mean juggler or practiser of legerdemain, which—as well as its older sense of wizard or raiser of spirits—is found in his works; for this reason the twenty-eighth line, 'For what's a Conj'rer's fate to me or—you?' seems doubly to betray his hand.

In view of the foregoing evidence, it will perhaps be generally agreed that Pope must have been at least partly responsible for the

Epilogue, though opinions may differ on the question of degree. Was the piece merely corrected by Pope?—or remodelled?—or entirely written by him? In a case like this it is of course impossible to speak definitely; but the clue to this inner problem would seem to lie in the *urgency* of Pope's letter to Tonson. We know, for instance, that Pope had helped Gay from time to time by 'correcting' his verse in manuscript.

> I shall go into the Country about a month hence, and shall then desire to take along with me your Poem of the *Fan*, to consider it at full leisure.[1]

That was written to Gay in 1713; and Gay's own testimony to Pope's continual help is seen in the letter he wrote to Pope four years later, in which he gratefully speaks of 'the Continuance of your dear Friendship and Assistance, never yet withheld from me'.[2] Indeed, it is doubtful whether any important work of Gay's ever went to press without having been first overlooked by Pope—or without its being said that Pope had had a hand in it. And, as will be shown later, the tradition, if not the actuality, of his recurrent help to Gay persisted till his friend's death, and long afterwards. Nevertheless, Gay's poems went out into the world very properly under Gay's name, and as Pope is not known to have shown any nervousness of being thought their author, the extent of his textual contributions was probably rarely more than an occasional couplet or two. Similarly, if not so frequently or fully, Gay seems to have contributed lines now buried indistinguishably in Pope's work; witness, for example, Spence's report of a scrap of Pope's conversation—'The Alley, in imitation of Spenser, was written by Mr. Pope, with a line or two of Mr. Gay's in it'.[3] Hence, if such was the custom between them, it would seem fairly certain that the Epilogue was not Gay's work merely corrected by Pope—or why did Pope want it labelled differently from the Prologue or the rest of the work? It follows, therefore, (since it is inconceivable that Pope's anxiety was about a third poet's involvement in the Epilogue) that Pope must have had reason to regard himself either as its sole author, or as having done so much to it as to have become virtually so. And then, at the last minute, he seems to have been suddenly beset with misgivings that his hand might be recognized in it and publicly challenged, unless his precious anonymity was made doubly sure by the magic formula which had worked so well nine years previously: 'Sent by an unknown Hand.' Hence the mysterious letter with which this chapter began.

---

[1] Correspondence, I, 1735 (i), p. 194.   [2] Memoirs, II, p. 102.   [3] Spence, p. 23.

II. THE PROLOGUE TO 'ACHILLES'

According to contemporary news-sheets, Gay's posthumous opera, *Achilles*, was produced at the Theatre Royal on February 10, 1733, and was followed five days later by the publication of *The First Satire of the Second Book of Horace, Imitated in a Dialogue between Alexander Pope . . . on the one Part, and his Learned Council on the other*. 1733. There is no apparent connection between the two works; but near the end of the month, and just before the book of the opera was published on March 1, the two works, Gay's opera and Pope's satire, were simultaneously attacked in a pamphlet, dated '26 Feb. 1732–3', and entitled, *Achilles Dissected: Being a Compleat Key Of the Political Characters . . . With Remarks on the Whole. By Mr. Burnet. To which is added, The First Satire of the Second Book of Horace, Imitated in a Dialogue between Mr. Pope and the Ordinary of Newgate*, 1733. The first part of the pamphlet, our immediate concern, is in the form of a letter, addressed to 'Lady P****', and signed 'Atex Burnet'—a name which may or may not be a misprint, as Swift, speaking of the author in two different letters about that time, twice called him in effect 'That beast . . . Alexander Burnet'.[1] Whether 'Atex' or 'Alexander', the author is unknown, and should not be confused with Pope's old enemy, Thomas (ultimately Sir Thomas) Burnet, who is not known to have attacked Pope after 1716,[2] or ever to have signed himself either 'Atex', or 'Alex', or 'Alexander' Burnet.

In the course of the pamphlet, 'Burnet' asserts that the opera, *Achilles*, was left unfinished on Gay's death (on December 4, 1732) and that the poet's friends completed it. He also reprints a long article to the same effect from *The Daily Courant* of February 16, 1733, which roundly abuses Pope, Arbuthnot, Pulteney, and others, for the dullness of their (unspecified) contributions. One piece, however, is definitely mentioned by 'Burnet' in the following words:

> Mr. *Gay* has drawn the Drama of this Balladical Entertainment from Statius . . . This Plan Mr. *Gay* has exactly followed. Mr. Quin speaks the Prologue, which was written by Mr. Pope.[3]

Unquestionably the Prologue reads like Pope, especially the Pope of the earlier theatrical pieces, with echoes of his manner, cadence, humour, and phrase; and unquestionably it would have been like Pope to have supplied anonymously a missing Prologue—and more, at need—for his dead friend's play (which is exactly what he had done

---

[1] Ball, IV, pp. 403, 415.   [2] See pp. 104–5.   [3] *Achilles Dissected*, p. 2.

P

more than once for him while yet alive). Consequently, this attribution of 'Burnet's' cannot be dismissed off-hand, but demands serious consideration of the circumstances which preceded its appearance. Thus it becomes imperative to trace the history of Gay's opera in the only available documents—the published correspondence of Pope and of Swift.

It seems then that Gay began to work on the play as early as May 16, 1732, if Austin Dobson's interpretation of a phrase in a letter to Swift of that date is, as is probable, correct:

> I have also a sort of scheme to raise my finances by doing something for the stage. With this, and some reading, . . . I propose to pass my summer.[1]

This vagueness of reference, as he explained later, was intentional 'because I would not have the clerks of the post-office know everything I am doing'.[2] Next, towards the end of July, Swift hears that he is sanguine that 'the work' will be finished 'this summer'[3]; after which there are only two or three veiled references to the play before November 16, when he reports to Swift his arrival in London,[4] whither he had gone to arrange for its production; from which it is obvious that the play must now have been sufficiently completed to make that course practicable. In this letter Gay goes on to say:

> I have not as yet seen Mr. Pope, but design in a day or two to go to him, though I am in hopes of seeing him here to-day or to-morrow. If my present project succeeds, you may expect a better account of my own fortune a little while after the holidays.

The next letter to be noticed in the Swift correspondence is dated December 5, 1732; and in this Pope writes to the Dean of 'the unexpected death of poor Mr. Gay' in moving detail, of which the following passages are relevant to the discussion in hand:

> An inflammatory feaver hurried him out of this life in three days. He died last night at nine a clock . . . His effects are in the Duke of Queensbury's custody. His sisters, we suppose, will be his heirs . . . as yet it is not known whether or no he left a will.[5]

After which the letter goes on poignantly to speak of his and Swift's mutual loss, and ends on that note of personal grief. From Pope's letter to Caryll of December 14 other particulars may be gathered:

---

[1] Ball, IV, p. 301.
[2] *Ibid.*, p. 340.
[3] *Ibid.*, p. 325.
[4] *Ibid.*, p. 364.
[5] *Letters*, II, 4to, 1741, p. 124.

Poor Gay is gon before . . . he had just put a Play into the House, wᶜʰ the D. of Queensbury will take care off, and turn to the benefit of his Relations . . . He has left some other pieces fit for the Press.[1]

And in a later letter to Swift, Pope reports still further details about Gay's death:

As to his writings, he left no Will, nor spoke a word of them, or any thing else, during his short and præcipitate illness, in which I attended him to his last breath.[2]

The next stage is heard of in Charles Ford's letter to Swift, dated December 23, which ends thus:

I am told poor Gay's play is now in rehearsal, and will please. It was that brought him to town a little before he died. . .[3]

And, in the letter previously quoted, Pope further informed Swift (February 16, 1733):

The Duke has acted more than the part of a brother to him, and it will be strange if the sisters do not leave his papers totally to his disposal, who will do the same that I would with them. He has managed the Comedy (which our poor friend gave to the playhouse the week before his death) to the utmost advantage for his rela- tions.[4]

In other words, it becomes apparent from the foregoing quotations, that since the death of Gay, Pope had the management of his friend's papers virtually in his own hands; for obviously the Duke was only too ready to 'do the same that I would with them'. Indeed, a month or two later Swift blamed Pope, quite unjustly as we now know, for allowing *Achilles* to be performed and the second book of *Fables* pub- lished; forgetting for the moment (if indeed he knew them) Gay's own wishes in the matter, and the arrangements he had personally made just before his death for their realization. It also becomes clear that 'Burnet's' wild statements about the play were after all not quite so wild as at first appeared—at least as regards the opportunity which Pope (and, through Pope, Gay's other friends) had, of correcting his manuscript or filling in what gaps he might have left in it. On the other hand, there appears to be no reason for supposing any major gaps had been left in the play on Gay's death; for had there been so, the playhouse people could hardly have completed it for performance so soon afterwards. Nevertheless, it does not follow that Pope found

[1] Add. 28618, f. 99 v.   [2] *Letters*, ii, 4to, 1741, p. 128.
[3] Ball, iv, p. 371.   [4] *Letters*, ii, 4to, 1741, p. 128.

nothing lacking in the script and no alterations necessary during rehearsals. And seeing that the prologue and epilogue (if any) of a play are normally the last things to be settled about it,[1] and that Gay died the week after performance had been agreed on, 'Burnet's' definite attribution of the Prologue to Pope cannot be lightly dismissed.

The Prologue itself, in the only text printed in Pope's lifetime, namely that of 1733, runs as follows:

PROLOGUE

I wonder not our Author doubts Success,
One in his Circumstance can do no less.
The Dancer on the Rope that tries at all,
In each unpractis'd Caper risques a Fall:
I own I dread his ticklish Situation,   5
Critics detest Poetic Innovation.
Had *Ic'rus* been content with solid Ground,
The giddy vent'rous Youth had ne'er been drown'd.
The *Pegasus* of old had Fire and Force,
But your true Modern is a Carrier's Horse,   10
Drawn by the foremost Bell, afraid to stray,
Bard following Bard jogs on the beaten Way.
Why is this Man so obstinate an Elf?
Will he, alone, not imitate himself?
    His Scene now shews the Heroes of old *Greece*;   15
But how? 'tis monstrous! In a Comic Piece.
To Buskins, Plumes and Helmets what Pretence,
If mighty Chiefs must speak but common Sense?
Shall no bold Diction, no Poetic Rage,
Fome at our Mouths and thunder on the Stage?   20
No— 'tis *Achilles*, as he came from *Chiron*,
Just taught to sing as well as wield cold Iron;
And whatsoever Criticks may suppose,
Our Author holds, that what He spoke was Prose.

Although *Achilles* was performed on February 10, 1733, the publication of the book of the play was delayed until March 1.[2] This would explain how 'Burnet's' attack, *Achilles Dissected*, seems to have managed to get published first, according to several scraps of evi-

---

[1] See, for example, letters on pp. 138, 207.
[2] *The Grub-street Journal*, March 1, 1733.

dence which are to be found in it. For example, (a) 'Burnet' refers to the current rumour that the play was not going to be published at all; (b) he also prints several lines of a song from the production itself, which does not appear in the book as printed; and (c) the last thing in the pamphlet containing *Achilles Dissected*, is dated '26 Feb. 1732-3'. If, therefore, the Prologue was already being ascribed to Pope in the pamphlet *before* the play was published, as seems likely, that ascription might well explain the curious heading given in the book to this piece—and to this piece alone out of the whole play—namely, 'Prologue. Written by Mr. Gay. Spoken by Mr. Quin'. For, unquestionably, as regards authorship, that is a quite abnormal and uncalled-for caption in such books as this, when the author's name is writ large on the title-page of the play, and he himself has written his own prologue. It is thus difficult to explain the phrase, 'Written by Mr. Gay', on the prologue page, except on the hypothesis that it was a last-minute insertion by Pope to circumvent 'Burnet's' unauthorized attribution of the piece to him, and so preserve his threatened anonymity. Usually, if Pope had had nothing to do with any piece he was publicly 'accused' of writing—which frequently happened—he would take no notice. Indeed, to judge from his behaviour on similar occasions (as shown in previous pages),[1] it might almost be said that the more loudly he protested against an ascription the more deeply was he implicated in it.

Pope's authorship (partial or complete) of the Prologue is likewise suggested by internal evidence, what there is of it. For instance, in lines 9-10, the collocation of the words, 'Pegasus—Fire and Force—Horse', recalls a closely related idea using the same group of words in one of Pope's *Imitations of Horace*:

> And never gallop Pegasus to death;
> Lest stiff and stately, void of fire or force,
> You limp, like Blackmore, on a Lord Mayor's horse.[2]

But it is perhaps more suggestive still to find Pope publishing the same phrase, 'Fire and Force', five days after the performance of *Achilles*, in the Satire above mentioned:[3]

> ... with Budgell's Fire and Force,
> Paint Angels trembling round his falling Horse.[4]

Furthermore, one of Pope's favourite similes, likening a poet to an old horse jingling its bells . . . , reappears at length here—

---

[1] See *ante*, p. 158.
[2] Hor. Ep. I, i, ll. 14-16.
[3] See *ante*, p. 215.
[4] Hor. Sat. II, i, ll. 27-8.

> But your true Modern is a Carrier's Horse,
> Drawn by the foremost Bell, afraid to stray,
> Bard following Bard jogs on the beaten Way.
>
> (ll. 10–12)

Some examples of his use of it previously in his letters are—

> I should be sorry & ashamed to go on Gingling to the last Step, like a wagginer's horse in the same Road, to leave my Bells to the next silly Animal.[1]
>
> I realy make no other use of Poetry now, than Horses doe of the Bells that gingle about their Ears . . . only to travell on a little more merrily.[2]
>
> As idle, as if a Beast of Burden should go on jingling his Bells, without bearing any thing valuable.[3]

Last to be mentioned are Gay's fears for his play's success. If in every letter to Swift during the last six months of his life he harps on it —thinks its 'success . . . to be precarious'[4]; is 'prepared for disappointment'[5]; and 'promises himself nothing'[6]—one imagines how he must have talked to Pope, his more intimate friend, whenever they met! And it surely is not fanciful to see in the very first line of the Prologue ('I wonder not our Author doubts Success') Pope's characteristic tolerant-teasing reaction to his friend's resolve not to be hopeful.

To sum up—there are grounds for thinking that the opera, *Achilles*, contrary to 'Burnet's' assertion, was left practically finished on Gay's death; and that it either was intended to have no prologue and epilogue, like *The Beggar's Opera* and *Polly*, or was left with a prologue (there is no epilogue) so incomplete, or otherwise unusable, as to require large additions or much revision before production. Pope, who had always been not merely willing but eager to help his beloved Gay in any crisis of his life or work, naturally did what he thought was requisite properly to equip the play for performance, and apparently wrote, or re-wrote, the Prologue in just the same way that he had, not infrequently, helped his friend in the past. It is not, therefore, at this point a digression to remind ourselves that Pope was always careful of Gay's literary reputation, and always resolutely and consistently denied having contributed anything to his work. Even when, in the preface—or 'Advertisement'—of the farce, *Three Hours after Marriage*, 1717, Gay acknowledged the unspecified 'Assistance I have

---

[1] Add. 28618, f. 32.
[2] *Ibid.*, f. 35.
[3] *Correspondence*, I, 1735 (i), p. 170.
[4] On July 24, 1732. Ball, IV, p. 325.
[5] On August 28. Ball, IV, p. 340.
[6] On November 16. Ball, IV, p. 364.

receiv'd in this Piece from two of my Friends' (*i.e.* Pope and Arbuth-not), Pope never betrayed the position or extent of his contributions; and the play, when it is printed at all, appears in Gay's works; and though all Pope's editors since 1824 have, with one exception, credited him with the Prologue to that farce, he himself was content to leave it unclaimed, exactly as he left yet another contribution to his friend's play, *The Captives*, with which this chapter began. Thus, when Pope's careful and determined anonymity was threatened by 'Burnet', at a moment when sudden bereavement had made his heart especially tender of his dead friend's interests, it is not surprising—at least to those who know something of the real man behind the poet—that he should not only have refused to prefix his name to the *Prologue to Achilles* (however much it would have been justified), but should have attempted in his distress to make all sure by adding to its title the redundant and improbable legend, 'Written by Mr. Gay.'

CHAPTER XIV

POPE AND SWIFT

I. EARLY FRIENDSHIP

THE deep and enduring friendship of Pope and Swift is so well known, and its importance for English literature—not to mention their own lives—so well recognized, that it comes as a surprise to most people to learn how seldom they actually met. Indeed, apart from the probability that they had become acquainted (and there is no evidence for thinking it more than that) before Swift left England for Ireland in June 1713, their personal contacts were limited to three short visits of Swift to England, namely, from September 1713 to August 1714, from March to August 1726, and from April to September 1727—barely twenty-one months in all. The intense but natural excitement with which these visits were anticipated by the two friends is glimpsed here and there in their correspondence; and the perceptible quickening of the tempo of their lives on meeting again after such long periods of separation is revealed in several ways, amongst others in an increased literary activity of various kinds, from plans of future works in prose or verse to the impromptu scribbling of ridiculous poems and epigrams by the two friends conjointly or separately. It is not proposed, however, to tell once again the familiar story of their friendship, but only to examine the relevant incidents and situations which occurred during one or other of Swift's visits, for the light they may throw on certain contemporary poems.

In the winter of 1713–14, Pope and his friends formed themselves into a society to ridicule 'all false tastes in learning', to which they gave the name, the 'Scriblerus Club'. Besides Pope, who seems to have been the originator of the scheme, the regular members were Swift, Gay, Arbuthnot, and Parnell. At their meetings, often held in Arbuthnot's rooms, they discussed and in some measure drafted schemes for books which were to be corporate works. Thus *Martinus Scriblerus* came to be projected, and material began to be collected for the *Art of Sinking* (both of which were left ultimately in Pope's hands to be carried out); a suggestion for *The Works of the Unlearned* was talked over, and *Gulliver's Travels* and even *The Dunciad* owe not a little to the proposals and consequent discussions of the club. Guests were invited to their meetings from time to time, amongst the most frequent being Robert Harley, Earl of Oxford, to whom invitations in rhyme were often sent in the names of the members. Pope apparently was the moving spirit in these 'whimsies', and, to judge from several of the original missives preserved amongst Lord Oxford's papers at Longleat, they were also often written out by him.

The invitation that follows is a typical specimen; it is in Pope's autograph and is subscribed by the various members present at the time of writing; the appended couplet being in still another hand, presumably that of Erasmus Lewis, a particular friend of Swift. Swift himself, as it happened, was absent on this occasion. The rhyme runs as follows:

> Tho the Dean has run from us in manner uncivil;
> The Doctor, and *He that's nam'd next to the Devil,   [*Pope
> With Gay, who Petition'd you once on a time,
> And Parnell, that would, if he had but a Rhyme.
> (That Gay the poor Sec.[1] and that arch Chaplain Parnell,
> As Spiritual one, as the other is Carnal),
> Forgetting their Interest, now humbly sollicit
> You'd at present do nothing but give us a Visit.

<table>
<tr><td></td><td>A. Pope.</td></tr>
<tr><td>That all this true is</td><td>T. Parnell</td></tr>
<tr><td>Witness E. Lewis.</td><td>Jo: Arbuthnot</td></tr>
<tr><td></td><td>I. Gay.</td></tr>
</table>

This document,[2] which seems never to have been printed before, is endorsed in Lord Oxford's hand: 'Verses Saturday Mar. 1714. Answrd immediately'. But he does not say whether he addressed the answer to the club in general or any one in particular, which might have indicated his views on the authorship of the lines. Judging from internal evidence, however, it appears that although one or other of the signatories may have suggested a phrase or rhyme here or there, the care-free air of the whole thing as well as the particular references to Swift, Gay, and Parnell are the expression of that affectionately teasing manner which was peculiar to Pope when utterly at ease amongst the friends he loved most, and which Swift, who understood him as few have done, once fondly called 'Mr. Pope's roguery'. Characteristic of Pope, too, is the joke about himself in the second line, and also the way he has pointed it with the asterisk and the

---

[1] At that time Gay was still secretary to the Duchess of Monmouth.
[2] Portland, XIII.

marginal note. And finally when it is remembered that the lines are in his autograph, there cannot remain much doubt about their author.

Within five months of the meeting of the Scriblerus Club to which this invitation refers, Swift returned to Ireland; and as he and Pope did not meet again till 1726, letters were perforce their only means of communication. Unfortunately very little of this correspondence has come down to us, but what has survived reveals the increasing warmth and intimacy of their friendship as the years passed, until towards the end of 1725, when both were looking forward to their reunion the next year, Swift could write:

> If you do not know me when we meet, you need only keep one of my letters, and compare it with my face, for my face and letters are counterparts of my heart.

And Pope could reply:

> Absence does but hold off a Friend, to make one see him the more truly. I am infinitely more pleased to hear you are coming near us than at any thing you seem to think in my favour.[1]

Swift duly arrived in England in March 1726, and left again for Ireland in August with promises to return next year. He had spent the greater part of his time as Pope's guest at Twickenham ('You had maintained me three months at bed and board'),[2] and had enjoyed his visit so much that, when home again in the deanery, his thoughts would dwell wistfully on all he had left behind. In a revealing sentence in his reply to a letter from Pope that had followed him to Ireland, he wrote: 'In answer, I can only swear that you have taught me to dream . . . now I can every night distinctly see Twickenham and the Grotto . . .'[3] From all reports the visit was a great success; in fact, whether by intention or accident, Swift's chief business in London (which was to arrange for the anonymous publication of *Gulliver's Travels*) looked like being squeezed out of the programme, and was not actually undertaken until the eve of his departure. Other literary projects, however, were discussed and planned by the two friends, including the collection and publication of their miscellaneous and occasional pieces of prose and verse in a series of volumes under Pope's editorship and management. As for the corporate poems which this visit inspired, and of which *Molly Mog* is perhaps the best known, Swift possibly minimized the part he played in them, when, writing to Tickell, on July 7, 1726, he said: 'I have been very little more than a witness of any pleasantries you may have seen from London.'

---

[1] *Letters*, II, 4to, 1741, pp. 39, 42. [2] *Ibid*., p. 63. [3] *Ibid*., p. 62.

Three or four weeks after Swift had reached home, a piece of occasional verse was sent to him from Twickenham, with the assurance that his friends had not forgotten him. Owing to an accident, the poem has been ascribed to the wrong author for more than one hundred and sixty years; and the curious story of its origin, authorship, composition, and publication, which was told for the first time as recently as the bicentenary of Pope's death,[1] is now retold with some additional matter in the pages that follow.

II. 'THE POETICAL SOOP'

In most editions of the poems of John Gay published since 1779, there is included a short piece of thirty lines, usually entitled, *A Receipt to make Soup*. And because it has for so long been found there and nowhere else, Gay's authorship of it has been taken for granted. At the very outset of this discussion, therefore, it should be noted that, prior to 1779, not only had the poem never been attributed to Gay, but it had actually been ascribed to Pope, by some such sub-title as 'Sent by Mr. Pope to Dean Swift', in nine of the ten contemporary manuscripts located and collated by the present writer (the tenth being anonymous). Similarly, all the early printed texts give it to Pope, with two absurd exceptions: one, an abbreviated version in *The Weekly Journal* for September 20, 1727, superscribed 'By a certain Dean'; the other a text published by Curll in 1735, in which the usual ascription is reversed thus: 'Sent by Dean Swift to Mr. Pope'. Although these early texts—nearly a score in number—agree in attributing the piece to Pope almost without exception, they differ widely in the wording of its title, no two being exactly alike. In this respect they fall into two groups, the smaller (which includes the earliest text of all) correctly labelling the poem as a recipe for stewing veal, while the great majority insist on calling it a recipe for making soup—which it certainly is not. Space forbids detailed enumeration of the various titles; but one, from a Harleian manuscript,[2] is quoted as the heading of this section, and others are mentioned in the course of the narrative.

The late ascription to Gay can be definitely traced to Thomas Wilkes's edition of Swift's *Letters*, 1766, in whose second volume the poem appears as a fragment of a letter to Swift, said to be in Gay's

---

[1] In the article, 'Mr. Pope's Poetical Soop', by N. Ault; *Times Literary Supplement*, June 3, 1944.   [2] Harl. 7316, f. 195 v.

handwriting. On that authority, thirteen years later the piece came to be inserted for the first time in Gay's poems,[1] where it has since been unquestioningly retained by most of his editors, and similarly accepted by those of his biographers who mention it at all, its date being some-times given as October 22, 1726. On examination, however, this frag-ment[2] is found to be a single small sheet, undated and unsigned, and, contrary to some statements, neither addressed to Swift nor to any one else. It contains nothing more than the poem, half a dozen foot-notes, and a few introductory words heading the first page, thus:

> As We cannot enjoy any good thing without your partaking of it. Accept of the following receipt for Stewing Veal.

Whereupon the poem is transcribed without further remark or title. At present the sheet is pasted by its left edge between the leaves of a letter from Gay to Swift, dated 'Octr 22. 1726', to which place and date it obviously has no claim, seeing that the containing letter is itself an answer to one from Swift commenting on the poem. But although, according to the British Museum experts, the writing of the fragment is indisputably in Gay's autograph, in this particular case their opinion does nothing to invalidate the original attribution of the poem to Pope—for a very good reason.

When, after an absence of nearly twelve years, Swift again came to England for the summer of 1726, his visit was the cause of much re-joicing among his 'old friends'. So much so, indeed, that Pope, who as we have seen was his host in chief, had reason enough towards the end of his visit to write to Bethel: 'My house is like the house of a Patriarch of old, standing by the high-way side, and receiving all travellers'.[3] The summer passed only too quickly, and the middle of August saw the Dean most reluctantly setting out on his return journey to Ireland. He had not been long gone, when, in the second week of September, Pope met with an accident which might very easily have proved fatal. Three of his closest friends, Gay, Arbuthnot, and Bolingbroke, wrote to Swift separately within a few days of each other, to tell him what had happened. The first news came from Gay, whose letter is dated September 16, 1726. He wrote:

> I saw Mr Pope on Sunday [September 11], who hath lately escap'd a very great danger, but is very much wounded across his right hand. Coming home in the dark about a week ago alone in my Lord Bolingbroke's coach from Dawley, he was overturn'd where a

---

[1] In 'Johnson's Edition', 1779.   [2] Add. 4805, f. 126.   [3] *Letters*, 4to, 1737, p. 270.

bridge had been broken down, near Whitton. . . . he was thrown into the river, with the glasses of the coach up, & was up to the knots of his perriwig in water; The footman broke the glass to draw him out, by which he thinks he receiv'd the cut across his hand. He was afraid he should have lost the use of his little finger & the next to it.[1]

The famous London surgeon, St André, was sent for, and was able to allay the fear that his hand would be permanently crippled. News of the accident spread. Voltaire, for instance, on hearing of it later, wrote to Pope in mingled concern and relief about his 'sad adventure'.[2] In similar mood, Pope's friends had at once rallied round him,[3] and his house, in spite of the regretted absence of Swift, again became the centre of what Gay called 'our Twickenham entertainments'.

One day, in the latter half of September, there was a memorable dish of stewed veal which was much approved of by Pope's guests. The recipe had been obtained from Pulteney's cook, Monseiur Devaux; and transcripts of it still exist at Longleat and elsewhere. It was on this hospitable occasion, apparently, that the company then present at Twickenham combined to write a composite letter to Swift, most probably at the instigation of Pope, who was usually responsible for such projects. Bolingbroke also mentions this epistle, which he calls 'that Cheddar letter', because cheese of that name was made from the milk of several dairies. However that may be, it is certain that Pope, Gay, Bolingbroke, Pulteney, and Mrs Howard, each contributed 'some lines' to it; certain, too, that Pope, because of his maimed hand, could not, and did not, write his part of it; and virtually certain that Gay wrote it out for him. Indeed, when Gay referred again to the accident in a later letter (October 22), he assured Swift both that the wound was far from being a joke, and that he himself had

[1] Add. 4805, f. 120.   [2] Ruffhead, p. 212.

[3] Since this page was set up, a new allusion by Pope to his accident has been found in a recent accession to the Harvard Library (see their *Bulletin*, 1948, p. 122, article by G. Sherburn). It is an inscription in a copy of Pope's *Odyssey* which he presented, after the accident, to Nathaniel Piggot who lived near by, and, apparently, had befriended him that night. The lines, thanks to the Library's permission and Dr Sherburn's kindness, are here reprinted for the first time.

> The Muse this one Verse to learn'd Pigot addresses,
>> In whose Heart, like his Writings, was never found flaw;
> Whom Pope prov'd his Friend in his two chief distresses,
>> Once in danger of Death, once in danger of Law.
>>> Sept. 23. 1726.

been attending 'my distrest friend at Twickenham, & been his Emanuensis, which you know is no idle Charge'.[1]

The only surviving fragment of the composite letter is the part in Gay's handwriting which contains a rhymed version of the recipe of that never-to-be-forgotten dish. Here, then, would seem to be the explanation why a poem, which all contemporary reference gives to Pope, began to be attributed to Gay forty years later. It thus becomes obvious that any argument for Gay's authorship based on the handwriting of this fragment can no longer be accepted without additional proof—which Swift's answer does nothing to supply. Indeed, from first to last the joint missive was rather unfortunate; for Swift, as the correspondence shows, seems to have been not a little muddled by it. For example, he failed to notice that parts of the letter had been contributed and written by his newly acquired friends, Mrs Howard and Pulteney; and he actually misunderstood a line in the poem itself. And if such unusual lapses probably were, as Gay surmised, 'owing to a negligence in perusing the manuscript', the same reason would as adequately account for his apparent failure to distinguish between what Gay wrote as Gay and what as Pope's 'Emanuensis'. So that even if, in Swift's reply (which was written to Gay and Pope), the words 'I am going to try your receipt of the knuckle of veal'[2] were addressed to Gay alone, the confusion in his mind about the various parts of the composite letter must largely nullify whatever evidential value his reply might otherwise have had, simply because he might also have mistaken writer for author. And there is no other evidence on record which so much as hints at Gay's authorship of the 'Receipt'.

As for the poem itself, there is an extremely rare broadside of it, without date and imprint, entitled, *A Receipt To make a Soop. By Mr. Pope to D—n S—t*, which may or may not have preceded the first dated edition. There are, however, grounds for thinking that the piece was first printed in Curll's *Atterburyana*, 1727 (published January 5), where it was oddly appended to Curll's signed Dedication, in the guise of a last-minute addition thus—

---

[1] Add. 4805, f. 125 v. Gay's statement is beyond question. Thus Pope's new quatrain being in his (rather shaky) autograph suggests some easement of pain that, after a fortnight, had allowed a brief use of the pen. Gay acted as Pope's amanuensis at other times: e.g. he wrote to Swift in 1731: 'About a fortnight since I wrote to you from Twickenham, for Mr. Pope and myself, he was then disabled from writing by a severe rheumatic pain in his arm.' (Add. 4806, f. 30.)

[2] Ball, III, p. 350.

'POSTSCRIPT. Just arrived from *Twickenham* (as I am assured)
Mr. *POPE*'s Receipt to make Soup
For the Use of Dean *SWIFT*.

> Take a Knuckle of *Veal*,
> (You may buy it or steal)
> In few Pieces cut it,
> In a Stew-Pan put it . . .'

Curll's text, however, lacks authority, besides being faulty in several
places. The best text still remains the earliest of all, Gav's transcript,
which with its notes runs as follows, after the words—

'RECEIPT FOR STEWING VEAL.'

> Take a knuckle of Veal,
> You may buy it, or steal,
> In a few peices cut it,
> In a Stewing pan put it,
> Salt, pepper and mace
> Must season this knuckle,
> Then what's join'd to a place,[1]
> With other Herbs muckle;
> That which killed King Will,[2]
> And what never stands still,[3]
> Some sprigs of that bed[4]
> Where Children are bred,
> Which much you will mend, if
> Both Spinnage and Endive,
> And Lettuce and Beet,
> With Marygold meet;
> Put no water at all;
> For it maketh things small:
> Which, lest it should happen,
> A close cover clap on;
> Put this pot of Wood's mettle[5]
> In a hot boiling kettle,
> And there let it be,

[1] Vulg. Salary.   [2] Suppos'd Sorrell.
[3] This is by Dr Bentley thought to be Time or Thyme.
[4] Parsley. *Vide* Chamberlaine.
[5] Of this composition see the Works of the Copper farthing Dean.

(Mark the doctrine I teach)
About—let me see,—
Thrice as long as you preach.[1]
So skimming the fat off,
Say Grace, with your hat off
O then, with what rapture
Will it fill Dean & Chapter!

As mentioned above, transcripts of the original recipe of M. Devaux have been preserved amongst Lord Oxford's papers. At Longleat it appears on the same page with a transcript of the poem itself, and, as though to distinguish it from the verse, is headed 'The Prose'. As a comparison is interesting, the recipe now follows:

THE PROSE

Take a Knuckle of Veal, Cut it in 3 or 4
Pieces then put it in a stew-pan, and
add to it the proper seasoning of Pepper, and
Salt, and a clove of Mace or two,
according to your tast. Then take Sallary,
Spinnage, Sorrell, Thyme, Endive, Lettice,
Betes, and Marygolds, of each as you like,
till you fill the pot. Then stop it close
that no Water can possibly get into it.
Then put the Pot into a large kettle
of boyling Water, and let it stew for
four hours at least,—the longer the better.
Then serve it up, meat and all, skimming
the fatt off before you serve it.[2]

Several points, which seem to confirm the early attributions to Pope, remain to be noticed. For instance, all that has survived of the composite letter is the passage which introduces the poem: 'As We cannot enjoy any good thing without your partaking of it. Accept of the following receipt for Stewing Veal,'—a remark that would with greater propriety, as well as probability, have originated with the *host* of the feast, Pope, rather than with one of the guests, even though that guest was Gay. Again, those words are demonstrably much more in the tone of Pope's two devoted—almost passionate—letters to

---

[1] Which we suppose to be near four hours.   [2] Portland, XVII, f. 130 v.

Swift, written in the three weeks between his friend's departure for Ireland and his own misadventure, than of Gay's letters to Swift of September 16 and later, telling, among other things, of Pope's accident, which though perfectly friendly are not nearly so intimate.

Similarly, as regards the actual poem, its spontaneous and almost clownish fun is more in the key of Pope's light verse than of Gay's; for it has, in particular, the kind of nonsensical pun Pope favoured, as well as his jocular phraseology and acrobatic rhymes, not omitting the playful little pokes at one or other of his friends, which are so characteristic[1] of Pope's holiday humour and are here exemplified in the quiz at the length of Swift's sermons. It might also be noted that not more than two or three months later, in another high-spirited, anonymous (but privately acknowledged) poem,[2] Pope practically repeats the third line of the 'Receipt', 'In a few pieces cut it', with its rhyme '... put it', so that it appears again thus: 'But first in pieces cut it ... put it'.

It should be added in conclusion, that of the nine contemporary manuscripts in which the 'Receipt' is ascribed to Pope, the manuscript most directly connected with him is one of three transcripts of the poem which, besides two copies of the prose recipe, have been preserved among the family papers of the Earl of Oxford. Oxford was a great friend of Pope, Swift, and Gay, and treasured many of their poems in manuscript, both autograph and transcript. This particular transcript[3] was one which belonged to his daughter, Lady Margaret, later Duchess of Portland, but perhaps better remembered to-day as Prior's 'noble, lovely, little Peggy.' Its original and untouched title runs: *A Receipt to make a Soop, from Mr. Pope to Dean Swift in Irel^d*; and on the back of it, Pope's young friend, who was only twelve years old when the 'Receipt' was versified, has herself written the words— 'giving me by my Papa.'

III. THE 'GULLIVER' POEMS

Connected with Swift's visits to England in 1726 and 1727 are the four well-known poems about Gulliver, which, though never acknowledged by Pope, have been very frequently credited to him during the last hundred years, but with little or no evidence adduced in support of the ascription. That being so, the recent publication of

---

[1] See *ante*, pp. 24–5.   [2] To be found in the forthcoming 'Twickenham Edn.', Vol. VI.   [3] Portland, XVIII, f. 97.

a fifth 'Gulliver' poem as Pope's by the present writer,[1] provides an opportunity for a review of the whole story.

As previously mentioned, one of the reasons for Swift's visit in 1726 was to arrange for the anonymous publication of *Gulliver's Travels*, the manuscript of which he had brought over with him. But the business was put off until the last week of his stay, when Benjamin Motte, the successor of his old publisher, Tooke, was chosen for the undertaking. Under Pope's supervision, presumably,[2] terms were finally settled on August 13; and two days later Swift set out on his return journey to Ireland.[3] The book was published on October 28,[4] and had an immediate success, Pope and Gay[5] reporting to Swift on November 17 that 'the whole impression sold in a week.'[6] Other 'impressions' followed, and a second edition was being talked of as early as February 1727, on the fourteenth of which month Swift wrote to a friend: 'As to Captain Gulliver . . . I hear it hath made a bookseller almost rich enough to be an alderman'.[7] And in the same month, the earliest extant allusion to the 'Gulliver' poems is recorded in a letter from Pope to Swift, written about February 18, 1727, as follows:

> You receiv'd, I hope, some commendatory verses from a Horse and a Lilliputian, to Gulliver; and an heroic Epistle of Mrs. Gulliver. The Bookseller would fain have printed 'em before the second Edition of the Book, but I would not permit it without your approbation: nor do I much like them. You see how much like a Poet I write . . .[8]

Of Swift's reply nothing has survived; but that he consented—or at least did not object—to their inclusion in his book is patent from their presence in the forefront of the 'Second Edition', published (according to the newspapers of the day) on May 4, 1727. Swift, as it happened, had arrived in London a fortnight or so before, and was staying with Pope at Twickenham about this time. And it was possibly at Pope's instigation, that a common friend, Erasmus Lewis, was dispatched to the publisher, Motte, as an emissary from the still anonymous author of *Gulliver's Travels*, with 'full power to treat' for him, and settle out-

---

[1] A large part of this section was published in *The National Review*, June 1944, by N. Ault, under the title, 'Pope and Gulliver'.

[2] Swift once said he 'never got a farthing' by any of his works except *Gulliver's Travels*, 'and that was by Mr. Pope's prudent management for me.' Ball, v, 180.

[3] Ball, iii, p. 331.   [4] *Ibid.*, p. 356.

[5] Pope had not yet recovered from his accident (see *ante*, p. 227).

[6] *Letters*, ii, 4to, 1741, p. 49.   [7] Ball, iii, p. 378.

[8] *Letters*, ii, 4to, 1741, p. 57.

standing matters connected with its publication—which he did, endorsing the authoritative document for Swift on May 4: 'I am fully satisfied. E. Lewis.'[1]

It is probable, therefore, that Pope and Swift read together the following announcement, which appeared in *The Post-Boy* and other papers that same day:

> This Day is publish'd, the 2d Edition of Travels into several remote Nations of the World. By Lemuel Gulliver . . . In Two Volumes. To which are prefix'd, several Copies of Verses Explanatory and Commendatory, never before printed. Printed for B. Motte. . . The Verses may be had single; price 6d.
>
> *N.B.* These Verses being enter'd in the Company of Stationers Book, according to the Directions of the Act of Parliament for Encouragement of Learning; any Person that prints them, without the Consent of the Proprietor, may expect a severe Prosecution for the same.

And the two friends were probably not unamused at this long-overdue warning to the piratical Curll and his congeners. Two days later, the poems began to be advertised separately: *The St. James's Evening Post*, for May 4–6, announcing—

> This Day was published, Several Copies of Verses on Occasion of Captain Gulliver's Travels. Printed for Ben. Motte. . . Where may be had The Second Edition of Captain Gulliver's Travels, with the Verses prefixt.

On examination, these two publications—the *Verses* alone, and the same prefixed to *Gulliver's Travels*—are found to contain, not three poems, as might have been expected from Pope's letter, but most frequently four, and occasionally five, and all alike anonymous. Moreover, the same four pieces appear in all copies of both issues, and always in the following order:

(i) *To Quinbus Flestrin, the Man-Mountain, A Lilliputian Ode.*

(ii) *The Lamentation of Glumdalclitch. A Pastoral.*

(iii) *To Lemuel Gulliver. The Grateful Address of the Unhappy Houyhnhnms.*

(iv) *Mary Gulliver to Captain Lemuel Gulliver.*

The fifth poem, found in a few copies of both issues, is entitled:

The Words of the King of Brobdingnag.

But, whenever it appears in either issue, this piece invariably consists of a pasted-in insertion of two leaves printed from the same setting of

[1] Ball, III, p. 386.

type (except for an alteration of page numbers and catchword). It is therefore evident, that, subsequent to Pope's letter to Swift, two further additions were made to the 'commendatory verses', namely *The Lamentation of Glumdalclitch*, which was written in time to be set up with the three poems Pope mentioned; and *The Words of the King*, which was not set up in type until some time after both issues of the *Verses* had been printed and published, when it was usually added to the unsold copies by inserting its two leaves, midway in the separate publication, and at the end of the section prefixed to *Gulliver's Travels* (though it occasionally may be found midway in the latter also). And there is not the slightest reason to suppose that these modifications of the scheme submitted to Swift were due to any one except its originator, Pope.

The first four pieces are of course readily available to the reader, having been printed in practically all editions of Pope's works since Roscoe thought them his and first included them in the canon in 1824. On the contrary, the fifth poem, owing to its having been inserted in relatively few copies of the *Verses*, has been consistently missed or overlooked by all Pope's editors to date, with the result that it seems to have been reprinted only once[1] since the eighteenth century. The poem is as follows:

The WORDS of the
KING OF BROBDINGNAG,
As he held Captain GULLIVER *between his*
Finger and Thumb for the Inspection of
the Sages and Learned Men of the Court.

In Miniature see *Nature*'s Power appear;
Which wings the Sun-born Insects of the Air,
Which frames the Harvest-bug, too small for Sight,
And forms the Bones and Muscles of the Mite!
Here view him stretch'd. The Microscope explains,   5
That the Blood, circling, flows in human Veins;
See, in the Tube he pants, and sprawling lies,
Stretches his little Hands, and rolls his Eyes!

Smit with his Countrey's Love, I've heard him prate
Of Laws and Manners in his Pigmy State.   10
By Travel, generous Souls enlarge the Mind,

[1] In the article mentioned above, p. 232 n.

Which home-bred Prepossession had confin'd;
Yet will he boast of many Regions known,
But still, with partial Love, extol his own.
He talks of Senates, and of Courtly Tribes,   15
Admires their Ardour, but forgets their Bribes;
Of hireling Lawyers tells the just Decrees,
Applauds their Eloquence, but sinks their Fees.
Yet who his Countrey's partial Love can blame?
'Tis sure some Virtue to conceal its Shame.   20

The World's the native City of the Wise;
He sees his *Britain* with a Mother's Eyes;
Softens Defects, and heightens all its Charms,
Calls it the Seat of Empire, Arts and Arms!
Fond of his Hillock Isle, his narrow Mind   25
Thinks Worth, Wit, Learning, to that Spot confin'd;
Thus Ants, who for a Grain employ their Cares,
Think all the Business of the Earth is theirs.
Thus Honey-combs seem Palaces to Bees;
And Mites imagine all the World a Cheese.   30

When Pride in such contemptuous Beings lies,
In Beetles, Britons, Bugs, and Butterflies,
Shall we, like Reptiles, glory in Conceit?
Humility's the Virtue of the Great.   34

Although this poem shares the same occasion, subject, publication, and (presumably) author with the other four, there is no direct testimony on record of their common origin. Nevertheless, what evidence there is points in no uncertain manner to Pope as the author of the whole set. To begin at the beginning: there cannot be any reasonable doubt that at least the three poems Pope sent to Swift (Nos. i, iii, and iv, which may be called the 'letter group') were written by himself; because, although he nowhere publicly acknowledged them, his words to Swift—especially in the last two sentences quoted—look like an implicit confession of authorship, and therefore virtual proof. Further corroboration, if needed, is to be found in the fact that, as far as we know, Pope never sent other people's poems about in his letters in just that manner, though often his own; and that each of the three poems is found on examination to contain both matter and phraseology which can be paralleled elsewhere in his works. Next, as regards the *Lamentation* (No. ii), it is perhaps not without significance that

when, shortly after the publication of the *Verses*, Pope decided to
include some of them in the 'Last Volume' of his and Swift's *Miscellanies*, 1727 (then intended to be published in October, 1727, but
eventually postponed to March, 1728), he chose only two of the pieces
sent to Swift (Nos. i and iv), and substituted the *Lamentation* for the
Houyhnhnm poem (No. iii). For Pope's grouping the *Lamentation* with
the *Ode* and the Epistle (which we may call the 'Miscellanies group')
again suggests a common source—a suggestion which grows more
convincing when the *Lamentation* is likewise found to contain a number
of echoes from his other poems.

   Much of this argument also applies to the forgotten fifth poem, *The
Words of the King*, in which Pope's style is manifest even more clearly
than in the known four. Though so short a poem, it contains several of
his distinctive mannerisms, each of which, in other contexts, the present writer has had occasion to comment on elsewhere. For example,
Pope had a strange fondness for the phrase, 'Smit with . . .', which in
his youth he had possibly adopted from Milton who used it once in
Paradise Lost. Thus a line in the poem reads:

>   Smit with his Countrey's Love I've heard him prate   (l. 9)

which has most curious echoes in the first *Dunciad*, in a passage Pope
was writing about the same time:

>   And smit with Love of Poesy and Prate
>   *Dunciad*, ii, 350.

with which may also be cited:

>   Smit with the love of Sister-Arts
>   *Epistle to Jervas*, 13.

Altogether nearly a dozen examples of his use of the phrase could be
quoted at need. Similarly, Pope was peculiar amongst his contemporaries in his almost habitual use of the adverbial 'sure' at the beginning
of a line; it appears thus in his works some fifty times. One example
only need be mentioned:

>   'Tis sure the hardest science to forget
>   *Eloisa to Abelard*, 190

Its parallel use here being:

>   'Tis sure some Virtue to conceal its Shame   (l. 20)

As for the several parallels of idea, the following example is striking
enough to deserve quotation:

>   Thus Ants, who for a Grain employ their Cares,
>   Think all the Business of the Earth is theirs . . .
>   And Mites imagine all the World a Cheese.   (ll. 27-8, 30)

Who knows what plots, what achievements a mite may perform
in his kingdom of a grain of dust?

(Letter to Caryll, Aug. 14, 1713)

Another very characteristic device of Pope's, employed by him frequently in his poems and occasionally in his prose, was the trick of the
incongruous context, which consisted of naming some object of worth
or excellence in a list (more or less alliterative) of trivial, base, or contemptible things. And here in the poem (line 32) is a typical example of it, 'In Beetles, Britons, Bugs, and Butterflies'. This matches a
similar line in *The Rape of the Lock*, 'Men, Monkies, Lap-dogs, Parrots,
perish all'[1]; and there is yet another example in the same poem,
'Puffs, Powders, Patches, Bibles, Billet-doux'.[2] Space allows only one
more parallel to be cited in this place, namely, the rather unusual
locution, 'employ their Cares' (line 27), which was used by Pope with
some frequency; earlier and later examples from his pen being 'our
Cares employ' (*Essay on Criticism*, l. 500), and 'his Cares employ'
(*Epistle to Burlington*, l. 1).

But any attempt to establish Pope's authorship of the fifth Gulliver
poem, in common with the others, must also of course take into
account previous attributions of these poems to other authors. For it
should be remembered that the original four poems were anonymous,
and have been thought to be Pope's only since Roscoe included them
in the canon in 1824 (when he reprinted them from the Dublin
edition of the Gulliver poems, 1727, which does *not* contain *The
Words of the King*). John Gay's name was the first to be publicly
associated with any particular poems amongst them, when, in 1773,
the 'Miscellanies group' (Nos. i, ii, and iv) were included in his works[3]
by Bell, without explanation. But although no evidence was advanced
for giving these, and only these, to Gay, the same three poems had in
fact been privately attributed to him as early as 1731, in notes written
in two copies of the 'Last Volume' of *Miscellanies* which the Earl of
Oxford gave to his wife and daughter that year. Both copies are still
treasured at Welbeck Abbey; the Countess's copy, however, gives
only Nos. i and ii of the Gulliver poems to Gay, leaving No. iv unascribed, while Lady Peggy's copy gives him all three. There is also
amongst the Oxford papers at Welbeck an anonymous transcript of

---

[1] *The Rape of the Lock*, i, l. 138.   [2] *Ibid.*, iv, l. 120.

[3] In 1773, Bell and Etherington added *The Miscellaneous Works of Mr. John Gay*,
Vols. iii and iv, to *Poems on Several Occasions. By Mr. John Gay*, Vols. i and ii, which
had been published by Tonson and others in 1767. The 'Miscellanies group' is in
Vol. iv, pp. 103–16.

No. ii, entitled, 'Glumdalcliths Lamentation a Pastoral', which has been carefully corrected in Oxford's own hand. This copy was evidently taken from an earlier as well as longer version than the one published, which, by the time it had reached the printer's hand from Pope's, had been drastically revised and re-arranged, and shortened by at least twelve lines deleted here and there. Later still, some slight further revision was made when Pope included it with the other two in *Miscellanies*. Now it is worth noting that when, forty-six years later, Bell printed the 'Miscellanies group' as Gay's, he printed with it a new fourth piece, entitled, *The Man-Mountain's Answer to the Lilliputian Verses*. This poem has no connection whatever with Pope, and never has been attributed to him; and as it is only an answer to his 'Lilliputian Verses' (*To Quinbus Flestrin*), and frankly imitates it, it can with all confidence be excluded from the Pope canon, especially as Bell claimed this piece, but *not* the 'Miscellanies group', as Gay's, on 'no less authority' than Aaron Hill.[1] Indeed, Gay's most recent editor includes *The Man-Mountain's Answer* as authentic Gay, at the same time that he denies his author's right to the 'Miscellanies group'[2]; but though he refuses to include them amongst the poet's works, he thinks it is just possible that Gay wrote the *Lamentation*, but not probable, it being 'more in the style of Pope'.

Other people have also been credited with the poems from time to time, the earliest of all the printed attributions being found in Faulkner's edition of Swift's *Works*, III, Dublin, 1735 (that is, the *Gulliver* volume), which included the 'Miscellanies group' with the note:

> The three following Poems were written, as we are informed, by Doctor Arbuthnot, Mr. Pope, and Mr. Gay.

The value of such an assertion depends of course on the person who makes it and the source of his information. And in this case both are suspect. Swift, as is well known, made repeated, explicit, and consistent statements over a period of at least three years, to the effect that he had little or nothing to do with Faulkner's edition. But students of his work have recently shown that Swift exaggerated his indifference to Faulkner's undertaking[3]; and it can be proved by internal evidence that some parts at least of the 'copy', collected from various quarters by Faulkner for his four volumes, were seen and corrected by Swift before publication, and more particularly the

[1] Gay's *Miscellaneous Works*, Vol. IV, Ed. Bell, 1773, p. [240].

[2] See Faber, pp. xxxiv, and 214.

[3] See Williams, I, pp. xxx f.; and D. Nichol Smith's *Letters of Swift to Ford*, pp. xliii f., 162.

'copy' for *Gulliver's Travels*. It is thus possible, perhaps, that Swift did see this note of Faulkner's before it was printed, and, as it did not affect his own work, refused (as he said he would) to 'intermeddle' in the matter, being content to let it stand as one more witness to his aloofness from Faulkner's enterprise. But, as will be shown, it is far more probable that he did not see it; in which case it is Faulkner's note merely repeating the usual gossip about the four authors of the *Miscellanies*, of whom (he seems to have calculated) if Swift is ruled out, as he obviously must be, three are left, Arbuthnot, Pope, and Gay—that is, one poem for each person, or three persons in collaboration for each poem, or indeed any other combination one might fancy!

What are the facts? An examination of Faulkner's 'third volume', 1735, shows that *Gulliver's Travels* ends with a bold *'FINIS'* and a tail-piece on page 391 [*i.e.* Cc 4 *recto*], which would have left the last sheet with nine blank pages, or, if a half-sheet had been used, with the last page blank. But the three poems have been added at the end of the book, filling the last nine pages of signature Cc, and an additional quarter-sheet Dd; that is, they begin on page 392, and end on page 404 with the words 'The End of the Third Volume' and a tail-piece. But this quite noticeable addition to the book is nowhere referred to in the volume, neither in the title-page, nor in the 'Contents' (a long detailed list occupying eight pages), nor is it mentioned elsewhere in the pre-liminary pages of 'Advertisement', 'The Publisher to the Reader', and so forth. Not less significant is the omission of the catchword on the last page of the *Travels*, the only page in the whole volume without one —except of course the pasted-in maps, title-page and last page. Taken together these facts of omission show that, down to the moment when the last page of the *Travels* was set up, there was no intention of in-cluding the poems. Corroboration of this is found in the design of the additional pages, which—quite apart from the dissimilarity of prose and verse—differ from the rest of the volume in character and detail, there being no running-title, for example, and the page-numbers, instead of following the style of the book with simple figures in the out-side top corners, are placed in the middle of the top margins, and enclosed in round brackets.

Another point of interest is the fact that Faulkner's text of the three poems was taken from the *Miscellanies*, and not from the second edi-tion of the *Travels*, or from the *Verses* whether as issued in London, or, shortly afterwards, in Dublin, in the (probably pirated) edition pub-lished by Hyde in 1727. For besides including only the 'Miscellanies group', Faulkner unfailingly reproduces the verbal revisions found in

Miscellanies and nowhere else. This in itself supports the argument that his edition of *Gulliver's Travels* was taken from a corrected copy of Motte's first edition which did not include the poems, and not from the second edition, which did. And these facts together make it probable that Faulkner's choice of three out of five poems was neither exclusive nor significant: he did not refuse the other two poems, but simply did not know of their existence.

In conclusion, it appears that when Faulkner found his last sheet, Cc, was short of matter, he had an 'eleventh hour' idea of using the 'Gulliver' poems from the *Miscellanies*, which he had previously drawn on when collecting Swift's poems for 'Volume II'; and, as the rest of the book had already been printed off[1] (from 'copy' embodying Swift's corrections), he had the three poems set up as a sort of pendant to the work. Then, some explanation of their unannounced appearance in the volume being obviously desirable, he repeated a bit of hearsay by way of a prefatory note, but, uncertain of its correctness, evaded responsibility for it with the usual phrase—'as we are informed'. Remembering, on the one hand, that Swift was a past master of simple, clear, and direct prose; and, on the other, that he could not have helped knowing all there was to know about the 'Gulliver' poems, having seen most if not all of them in manuscript, and having also been in England with Pope when they were first published (when, presumably, he was further consulted about the late inclusion of the fifth poem, *The Words of the King*)—it is extremely improbable that he saw, before it was printed, and yet allowed to pass uncorrected, a set of words as vague and uninformed as the introductory note Faulkner prefixed to his belated appendix of poems.

The other attributions have as little foundation. We need not, for example, linger (except, perhaps, to smile) over Boswell's anecdote[2] of the occasion on which he quoted to Doctor Johnson half a dozen lines from what he called 'Swift's humorous epistle in the character of Mary Gulliver to her husband' (No. iv)—the most extraordinary thing about the story being that it was one of the few occasions on which the Doctor did not correct him! Lastly, the original set of the four 'commendatory verses' continues still to be ascribed to Henry Carey in the new, as in the old, Catalogue of the British Museum (which ascription has unfortunately been followed by a number of

---

[1] The last sheet, Cc, and quarter-sheet, Dd, are ornamented with head-pieces and tail-pieces printed from the *identical* blocks which had previously been used in the printing of the main part of the volume.

[2] *Journal of a Tour to the Hebrides*, 'August 31st'.

other libraries). This mistake was possibly the result of a confusion between the first and most famous poem of the set, the Lilliputian Ode *To Quinbus Flestrin*, and still another imitation of it which was actually written, signed, and published by Carey himself, under the title, *A Lilliputian Ode on their Majesties' Accession*. Such ascriptions as these, uncorroborated by any scrap of evidence and contradicting or disregarding the few certainties about the poems, cannot be taken seriously. A working hypothesis that will cover all the known facts may therefore perhaps be attempted in conclusion.

It appears that Pope, who had not seen *Gulliver's Travels* before its publication on October 28, 1726,[1] was so excited on reading it that he wrote three poems on various characters in it, and sent them to Swift in February, with the suggestion that they should appear in the forefront of the second edition of the book. And when Swift fell in with the idea, Pope, possibly with Gay at his elbow (as had often happened before), proceeded to draft the first sketch of yet another Gulliver poem, *The Lamentation*, a copy of which presently reached Lord Oxford, probably by Gay's instrumentality and not impossibly in his autograph; for in their earlier collaborations Gay often acted as secretary, and only a few months previously, after Pope's accident, had been for a time his amanuensis, as we have seen.[2] In this way Lord Oxford, the friend of both Pope and Gay, could have obtained his copy of the early version of the poem, and himself corrected its errors of transcription. It would also seem to be about this time that Gay wrote his *Answer* to Pope's *Lilliputian Ode*, which Pope apparently did not like well enough to use. Thus, sooner or later, Oxford, or his ladies, knowing or hearing that Gay had been occupied on poems about *Gulliver's Travels*, came to assume that *The Lamentation* and one or both of its companion pieces in *Miscellanies* were his likewise, and marked them in their copies accordingly. The last stage was that shortly after the four 'commendatory verses' had been published both 'single' and 'prefixt', Pope was moved to write the fifth poem, *The Words of the King*, which was at once set up in type, printed by itself on a quarter-sheet, and inserted in the unsold copies of both issues of the *Verses*.

To sum up, the probabilities of Pope's authorship of the first four 'Gulliver' poems (with Gay's possible collaboration in *The Lamentation*) are so overwhelming that, unless and until they are proved to

---

[1] 'Upon my word I never saw it, till printed'—Letter to Caryll, December 1726 (Add. 28618, f. 66 v.) This would not prevent him supervising its publication.

[2] See *ante*, pp. 227–8.

have been written by Gay or another—a remote prospect—they must not only retain their present places in the Pope canon as attributed pieces, but be accompanied henceforward by the fifth 'Gulliver' poem —*The Words of the King of Brobdingnag*.

IV. 'TO LADY MARY WORTLEY'

During Swift's visit to England in 1727, which he had misgivings would be (as it was) his last, Pope was again his chief host. Writing to Caryll in October,[1] he said: 'I had indeed the Company here constantly of Dr Swift, who made my Retirement his own for near four months, & is but just gone for Ireland'. But this visit unfortunately was not as felicitous as that of the previous summer: Pope's aged mother was gravely ill and could not be left, and for the latter part of the time the two friends themselves were far from well. Nevertheless much of their thought and conversation was of literary matters and projects. Swift had come over with several schemes in mind, one of them being the long-pondered Memoir of the first Earl of Oxford for which he hoped to collect material on this visit; and Pope, as usual, was full of half a hundred projects. One of their first tasks must have been to furnish their forthcoming *Miscellanies* with the Preface which is signed and dated: 'Jonath. Swift. Alex. Pope. Twickenham, May 27, 1727'—the first two volumes of the collection, consisting of prose pieces only, being published the following month. There was also Pope's *Dunciad*, on which he was then at work, to be discussed between them, Gay's *Beggar's Opera* to be overlooked and corrected piecemeal[2]; and the third volume of *Miscellanies* (which is called 'The Last Volume', and which contains some of the best-known of the shorter poems of Pope and Swift) to be talked over—all of which three works, appearing in the first five months of 1728, combined to make it a miraculous year in English literature.

But our immediate concern is not with famous satire, enchanting songs, or familiar poems, but with the unnoted results of intimate fireside chat or casual garden stroll, when one or other of the two friends chanced to start some humorous idea, in immediate pursuit of which they join in blithe rivalry, each one's suggestions being improved or capped by the other, until in a climax of laughter the whole absurd or derisory improvisation shatters and vanishes. Not always, perhaps, or not wholly; for the thrifty Pope, conserver of ideas as well

[1] Add. 28618, f. 69.   [2] Spence, p. 159.

as of paper, seems on at least two such occasions to have picked up the pieces, and subsequently refashioned them to please himself or (more probably) another, or to annoy some one else. Something like that—quite natural and unimpressive—would seem to have been the history of the first sketch of the 'heroick epistle', *Bounce to Fop* (discussed and printed on a later page)[1]; and such, the origins of a poem published a few months after Swift's departure, in the 'Last Volume' of *Miscellanies*, entitled, *The Capon's Tale: To a Lady who father'd her Lampoons upon her Acquaintance*.

Although Pope himself never acknowledged *The Capon's Tale*, and although it has never before been attributed to him, the recent identification of a copy of the original version in his autograph,[2] the subtitle of which reads 'To Lady Mary Wortley', is proof presumptive of his authorship, or at least part-authorship. For he so little made a habit of copying out other people's verses in extenso, without their author's name, that no such transcript in his hand-writing has—so far as is known—ever been recorded. Corroborative evidence of this attribution is not far to seek. For instance, the poem seems never to have been printed in Pope's life-time except by his own act and consent, it having been found only in the successive issues of his and Swift's *Miscellanies* (or a Dublin reprint). These volumes were edited by himself, and in the last two he included upwards of a score of anonymous poems that a consensus of opinion for two hundred years has regarded as his work, though he himself never admitted more than nine of them into the more dignified precincts of *The Works*. Furthermore, in the later editions of *Miscellanies*, that is from 1742 onwards, of which the rearrangement was in Pope's hands,[3] *The Capon's Tale* is distinguished with an asterisk to signify it was not by Swift. And finally, in the two copies of 'The Last Volume' of that series, which Lord Oxford, friend of both Pope and Swift, gave to his wife and daughter (and of which mention has previously been made),[4] the poem is marked, presumably on information supplied by his lordship, 'By Mr. Pope', with the addition, in the daughter's copy, of a sub-title: 'A Satyr upon Lady Mary Wortley'.

As Pope's autograph of the poem is practically unknown and seems never to have been printed hitherto, and as the text varies not a little from the version he included in *Miscellanies*, which is more or less accessible to students, the autograph has been chosen for printing in this place.

---

[1] See *post*, pp. 342 ff.
[2] In the Pierpont Morgan Library, New York.
[3] See *post*, p. 254.
[4] See *ante*, p. 132.

The CAPON'S TALE:

To Lady *Mary Wortley*.

There liv'd in Wales a goodly Yeoman,
Whose Wife, a clean pains-taking Woman,
Fed num'rous Poultry in her Pens,
And saw her Cocks well serve her Hens.

   A Hen she had, whose tuneful Clocks
Drew after her a Train of Cocks;
With Eyes so piercing, yet so pleasant,
You would have sworn this Hen a Pheasant:
Lord! what a Brustling up of Feathers
While the plum'd Beau-Monde round her gathers!
Morning from Noon there was no knowing,
There was such flutt'ring, chuckling, crowing;
Each forward Bird will thrust his head in,
And not a Cock but would be treading.

   Yet tender was this Hen so fair,
And hatch'd more Chicks than she could rear.
Our prudent Dame bethought her then
Of some Dry Nurse to serve for Hen.
She made a Capon drunk in fine,
(He eat the Sops, She drank the Wine:)
His Rump well-pluck'd with Nettles stings,
And claps the Brood beneath his Wings.
The feather'd Dupe awakes content,
O'erjoy'd to see what God had sent;
Thinks he's the Hen, clocks, keeps a pother;
A Foolish Foster-Father-Mother.

   Such, Lady Mary, are your Tricks,
To make us Capons own your Chicks.
Hatch on, fair Lady! make dispatch,
Our Tails may smart for what you hatch.
The Simile yet one thing shocks,
We're not two Capons but two Cocks.

In spite of the asterisk in the 1742 *Miscellanies*, Swift has been suggested occasionally in the past as the author of this piece, without any attempt to substantiate the idea or explain why he made this sudden and sole attack on Lady Mary. In direct contrast, the most recent editors of his poetry will have nothing to do with the poem. Nevertheless, in what is apparently the original version, the student is now confronted with an unsuspected conclusion, the last six lines of which unquestionably show that Pope was speaking for another as well as himself: 'We're not two Capons but two Cocks'. And seeing that the poem was shortly afterwards printed in his and Swift's *Miscellanies*, there would seem little doubt about the identity of the other 'Cock'. Thus, although on this occasion, as on others, the poem is in his handwriting, it appears that Swift, who had part in the injury, had likewise part in the retort, if only to the extent of suggestion or emendation; which also seems to show that the offence, like the reprisal, occurred while Swift was staying with Pope at Twickenham, either in 1726 or 1727.

In *The Capon's Tale*, therefore, Pope and Swift accuse Lady Mary Wortley Montagu of having published at least two satirical pieces of her own, either under their names, or in such a manner as suggested they were the authors. It is just possible, of course, that each had had a lampoon attributed to him separately, but their united protest suggests that their names had been similarly joined; and this would seem to be made still more probable by the fact that Lady Mary and Swift never knew or saw each other, much less corresponded or quarrelled; so that if the Dean was dragged into this affair at all—as now seems certain—it would be as Pope's partner. Consequently, as there was no known reason why their names should have been thus coupled before the publication of their joint *Miscellanies* in June 1727 (which in fact created no small stir with its forthright and provocative Preface carrying their twin signatures), it follows, that, if the subscription of their two names to Lady Mary's lampoons was to have any meaning for the public, these lampoons must have appeared after June 1727, and before March 7, 1728, which saw the publication of *The Capon's Tale* in the 'Last Volume' of *Miscellanies*.

In parenthesis, it may be remarked that Pope's moral indignation in the matter—if it existed at all, which is doubtful—seems to have been largely simulated for the sake of the joke against Lady Mary. For this 'trick' of hers was after all nothing more than one of the several ploys or artifices frequently practised in literary warfare. It is thus amusing to find, that, some six years later, Pope himself made use of the same device, when, under provocation, he wrote *An Ode for the New Year. Written by Colley Cibber, Esq; Poet Laureat*—the story of which is told for the first time in a subsequent chapter.[1]

But *The Capon's Tale* raises another problem—what were these lampoons of Lady Mary's that she fathered on Pope and Swift? Several suggestions have been made in the past, most of them deriving from the famous newspaper sensation of the last three months of 1721, which culminated in the trial of Arthur Gray, a footman, for attempted criminal assault, pistol in hand, on Mrs Joanna Baillie Murray in her father's house at night. Lady Mary, who wrote a long poem on this affair, which she entitled, *Epistle From Arthur Grey, the Footman*, has been accused of being also the concealed author of an indecent 'ballad', which was published shortly before the trial of Gray on December 7, with the title, *Virtue in Danger: Or Arthur Gray's last Farewell to the World*. In the three known texts of this piece the authorship is variously ascribed, the first to 'a Gentleman at St. James's', the second to 'a Lady', and the third (in 1776) to 'Lady M. W. Montague'. There is, however, no contemporary evidence to prove either that Lady Mary wrote the ballad herself, or that she ever attributed it to Pope and Swift singly or jointly. Yet from her letters to her sister, Lady Mar, in Paris, it is clear that in 1723 Mrs Murray suspected she had written it; and a later letter, undated but assigned to 1725, shows Mrs Murray's suspicion changed to conviction. Lady Mary wrote:

> A very odd whim has entered the little head of Mrs. Murray; do you know that she won't visit me this winter? I . . . desired to explain with her on the subject, and she answered that she was convinced that I had made the ballad upon her, and was resolved never to speak to me again. I answered (which was true) that I utterly defied her to have any one single proof of my making it, without being able to get any thing from her, but repetitions that she knew it . . . She won't curtesy to me wherever she meets me, which is superlatively silly (if she really knew it), after a suspension of resentment for two years together.[2]

It has been pointed out that Lady Mary did not really deny her authorship of the ballad in this letter; it has also been suggested that she may have told Mrs Murray that it was Pope who wrote it; and yet another theory submits, that, when Pope visited his friend Jervas the painter in London, as he often did, 'a Gentleman at St. James's'

[1] See *post*, pp. 316–22.
[2] *Letters and Works of Lady Mary Wortley Montagu*, ed. Wharncliffe, i, 1893.

could well apply to him. But all these suppositions leave Swift out of the picture entirely, besides failing to agree with what we know of the date of the poem; there is not a shred of evidence to support them. Thus, as a careful inspection of the newspapers of 1726–1728 has thrown no light on the offending lampoons, it is obvious that the full story of *The Capon's Tale* must await further discoveries.

In the meantime it is interesting to note that when Pope later revised the poem for the press, he not only supplied the explanatory sub-title as quoted earlier, but rewrote the last paragraph as follows:

> Such, Lady *Mary*, are your Tricks,
> But since you hatch, pray own your Chicks:
> You should be better skill'd in Nocks,
> Nor like your Capons, serve your Cocks.

Whatever Lady Mary's offence may have been, this retaliatory *Tale* was certainly written after she and Pope had become estranged by their famous—if obscure—quarrel, of which it seems to be the earliest extant public expression. But after the breach between them had become known and their friends had taken sides, and when what may well be described as open warfare was being mercilessly waged by both parties, there emerge definite grounds for thinking, that, despite the continued failure to identify these 'lampoons' of Lady Mary's, the charge brought against her in *The Capon's Tale* was true. The reason is that we see her again resorting to that self-same 'trick' about 1734, when, after the publication of *An Essay on Man*, she wrote the bitter attack on Pope, to be found in all collected editions of her works, and entitled it—*An Epistle From Pope to Lord Bolingbroke*.

CHAPTER XV

POPE'S LAST MISCELLANY

I. 'ENGLAND'S ARCH-POET'

O<small>N</small> October 4, 1732, a little-known anonymous poem, whose title has sometimes been conveniently shortened to *Verses On England's Arch-Poet*, was published attacking Sir Richard Blackmore, physician to William III and (what has more to do with the poem) writer of interminable epics. Though not of the first importance as a poem, the lampoon is interesting as a work newly attributed[1] to the author of *The Dunciad*. The piece was first printed in the so-called 'Third Volume' (chronologically the fourth) of Swift and Pope's *Miscellanies*; and for many years afterwards appeared only in the various editions and rearrangements of them, always without attribution. The 1732 text, with the original footnotes, runs as follows:

VERSES
To be placed under the Picture of
England's Arch-Poet: *Containing
a compleat Catalogue of his Works.*

S<small>EE</small> who ne'er was or will be half read!
  Who first sung ¹*Arthur*, then sung ²*Alfred*,
Prais'd great ³*Eliza* in God's anger,
Till all true *Englishmen* cry'd, hang her!
Made *William*'s Virtues wipe the bare A—
And hang'd up *Marlborough* in ⁴*Arras*:

  Then hiss'd from Earth, grew Heaven'ly quite;
Made ev'ry Reader curse the ⁵*Light*;
Maul'd human *Wit* in one thick ⁶*Satyr*,
Next in three Books, sunk ⁷human *Nature*,
Un-did ⁸*Creation* at a Jerk,
And of ⁹*Redemption* made damn'd Work.

---

[1] In an article in R.E.S., October 1943, 'Pope and "England's Arch-Poet",' by N. Ault, reprinted with additional matter in this chapter.

Then took his Muse at once, and dipt her
Full in the middle of the Scripture.
What Wonders there the Man grown old, did?
Sternhold himself he *out-Sternholded*,
Made [10]*David* seem so mad and freakish,
All thought him just what thought King *Achiz*.

No Mortal read his [11]*Salomon*,
But judg'd *Roboam* his own Son.
Moses[12] he serv'd as *Moses Pharoah*,
And *Deborah*, as She *Sise-rah*:
Made [13]*Jeremy* full sore to cry,
And [14]*Job* himself curse God and die.

What Punishment all this must follow?
Shall *Arthur* use him like King *Tollo*,
Shall *David* as *Uriah* slay him,
Or dext'rous *Deb'rah Sisera*-him?
Or shall *Eliza* lay a Plot,
To treat him like her Sister *Scot*,
Shall *William* dub his better *End**
Or *Marlb'rough* serve him like a Friend?
No, none of these—Heav'n spare his Life!
But send him, honest *Job*, thy *Wife*.

[1] Two Heroick Poems in Folio, twenty Books.
[2] Heroick Poem in twelve Books.   [3] Heroick Poem in Folio, ten Books.
[4] Instructions to *Vanderbank* a Tapestry-Weaver.   [5] Hymn to the Light.
[6] Satyr against *Wit*.   [7] Of the *Nature* of Man.   [8] *Creation*, a Poem in seven Books.
[9] The *Redeemer*, another Heroick Poem in six Books.
[10] Translation of all the *Psalms*.   [11] *Canticles* and *Ecclesiast*.
[12] Paraphrase of the Canticles of *Moses* and *Deborah*, &c.
[13] The *Lamentations*.   [14] The whole book of *Job*, a Poem in Folio.
* Kick him on the Breech, not Knight him on the Shoulder.

The poem remained unclaimed and unascribed until 1773, in which
year it was included, quite arbitrarily and without comment, in Bell's
edition of *The Miscellaneous Works of Mr. John Gay*, Vol. IV, the editor
of which (we have recently been told) 'had no special clue, denied to
other editors, to help him'.[1] Later, most of the imitators of Bell's

[1] Faber, p. xxv.

Poets also followed Bell in giving the *Verses* to Gay, again without evidence; and J. Underhill made the same unsupported attribution in 1893 (reprinted 1905).[1] Next, Gay's latest editor, Mr G. C. Faber, excluded it from the canon in 1926, both because of the lack of any reason for including it, and because it 'is not at all in Gay's manner'.[2] Since then, however, Gay's authorship of the piece has been reasserted by Dr G. Sherburn,[3] who, following Elwin and Courthope's lead,[4] gives the poem to Gay on the evidence of Pope's letter to Jervas in Ireland, dated November 14, 1716, the third paragraph of which runs—

> *Gay* is yours and theirs [Dean Swift and Dr. Parnell's]. His Spirit is awakened very much in the Cause of the Dean, which has broke forth in a courageous Couplet or two upon Sir *Richard Bl[ackmore]*. He has printed it with his name to it, and bravely assigns no other Reason, than that the said Sir *Richard* has abused Dr. *Swift*.[5] I have also suffered in the like Cause, and shall suffer more.[6]

It is this 'couplet or two' attacking Blackmore, which has been taken, or rather mistaken, as an allusion to the *Verses on England's Arch-Poet*— mistaken, because, even in its title the poem claims to give 'a compleat Catalogue' of Blackmore's works, and in the text explicitly names at least three major poems which had not been written or published at the date of Pope's letter, or for several years later. There is no reason to suppose that *Verses* was either published before 1732, or printed 'with Gay's name to it' earlier than 1773. Final proof is reached, of course, with the correct identification of the then recently published poem to which Pope alluded. This is, without doubt, *An Epistle to the Right Honourable the Earl of Burlington. By Mr. Gay*, more easily recognizable perhaps under its sub-title, *A Journey to Exeter*. Here Gay's 'courageous' but elusive 'couplet or two' attacking Blackmore appear in the concluding paragraph, at the point where the travellers, approaching their journey's end, alight at an inn—

> Upon whose Sign this courteous Motto stands:
> *This is the ancient Hand, and eke the Pen;*
> *Here is for Horses Hay, and Meat for Men.*

---

[1] Gay's *Poetical Works*, ed. J. Underhill, 1893 (Muses' Lib.).
[2] Faber, p. xxv.   [3] Sherburn, p. 167.   [4] EC, viii, p. 22 n.
[5] That is, in Blackmore's *Essays*, in which Swift is called, amongst other things, 'this impious Buffoon' (p. 217). This volume was published by Curll on March 8, 1716, according to *The Post Boy* of March 6–8, and other papers of that date.
[6] *Correspondence*, i, 1735 (ii), p. 115.

Upon which Gay breaks his narrative and proceeds to deploy an attack on Blackmore (and, incidentally, on Ambrose Philips too, in lines 135–140) in these words:

> How Rhyme would flourish, did each Son of Fame   127
> Know his own Genius, and direct his Flame!
> Then he, that could not Epic Flights rehearse,
> Might sweetly mourn in Elegiac Verse.   130
> But were his Muse for Elegy unfit,
> Perhaps a Distich might not strain his Wit;
> If Epigram offend, his harmless Lines
> Might in gold Letters swing on Ale-house signs.
> Then *Hobbinol* might propagate his Bays,   135
> And *Tuttle-fields* record his simple Lays;
> Where Rhymes like these might lure the Nurses Eyes,
> While gaping Infants squawl for farthing Pies:
> *Treat here, ye Shepherds blithe, your Damsels sweet,*
> *For Pies and Cheesecakes are for Damsels meet.*   140
> Then *Maurus* in his proper Sphere might shine,
> And these proud numbers grace great *William*'s sign:
> * *This is the Man, this the* Nassovian, *whom*
> *I nam'd the brave Deliverer to come.*   144

The poem then ends with four more lines of narrative, telling of the travellers' arrival at Exeter. 'Maurus', it will be remembered, was Dryden's name for Blackmore in the epistle *To my Honoured Kinsman, John Driden,* and also in the Prologue to *The Secular Masque.* But Gay, as though to leave no doubt about the identity of 'Maurus', actually quotes the last couplet in the above passage from one of Sir Richard's best known epics, and adds a footnote, thus: *Prince Arthur, Book 5. (The reference to 'great William' in the preceding line is to William III, who was thus to be posthumously rewarded by Blackmore for knighting him in 1696.)

This *Epistle* of Gay's must have been first published in 1716; for although the journey it commemorates was made in the summer of 1715,[1] and the narrative itself in all probability sketched out shortly afterwards, Pope's letter to Jervas proves that the text, as we know it, was printed at some date after the publication of Blackmore's abuse of the Dean on March 8, 1716, and before November 14, 1716, when the letter was written. Confirmation is seen in Lintot's accounts,[2] whose practice it was to pay his authors shortly before publication; for these show that he paid Gay £10 15s. for the 'Epistle to the Earl of Bur-

---

[1] Faber, p. xxxvi.   [2] J. Nichols's *Literary Anecdotes*, VIII, p. 296.

lington' at some time between December 22, 1715 and May 4, 1717, the immediate dates of other settlements with him. Thus as the eighteen lines, above quoted, read like an interpolation, being quite unlike and unconnected with anything else in the poem, and as they break the story only four lines before the end, it is highly probable that Gay's attack on Blackmore was an eleventh hour insertion in a more or less completely narrative poem. The oldest surviving edition of Gay's *Epistle to Burlington* was published together with 'The Fifth Edition' of his earlier *Epistle to a Lady*, in an undated pamphlet entitled *Two Epistles*; but whether it was the first edition, or not, is another matter, which, having nothing to do with the argument, cannot be discussed in this place.[1]

Though the claim for Gay's authorship of *Verses on England's Arch-Poet*, based on Pope's letter to Jervas, can no longer be maintained, the poem might still perhaps be speculatively attributed to him as a friend of Pope and Swift, and a known contributor to the earlier volumes of their *Miscellanies*; on this point too, therefore, a word must be said. The published correspondence of Pope and Swift makes it quite certain that the final volume of their *Miscellanies* (which was suggested and compiled by Pope alone) consisted for the greater part of Swift's work. On November 4, 1732, the Dean wrote to Motte,[2] saying that 'almost six-sevenths of the whole verse part in the book' was his, and he later claimed a slightly higher proportion.[3] Pope, in his 'Advertisement', speaking of the contents of the whole book, prose and verse, says: 'There are in this Volume, as in the former, one or two small pieces by other Hands'—other, that is, than his and Swift's, in whose names the whole set was produced. Little more than two months before this last volume was published, Gay, writing from Amesbury, where he was staying with the Duke and Duchess of Queensbury, to Swift in Ireland (July 24, 1732), tells him of a piece of news he had obviously only just heard: 'Last post I had a letter from Mr. Pope, who informs me he hath heard from you and that he is preparing some scattered things of yours and his for the press. I believe I

---

[1] The Bodleian copy of *Two Epistles*, for example, ends with two leaves of book advertisements, which *appear* to date from 1720. They may, of course, have been added, in 1720, to unsold copies of the pamphlet; for whether the pamphlet was printed in 1716 or not, it is undated, and would therefore still be saleable as a new book in 1720.

[2] Benjamin Motte was the publisher of the three previous volumes of the Swift-Pope *Miscellanies*, and part-publisher, with Gilliver, of this final volume. See Ball, IV, p. 360.

[3] *Ibid.*, IV, p. 367.

shall not see him till the winter . . .'[1] As Gay had nothing further to say about Pope's forthcoming anthology, it is clear from these words that he had neither made, nor thought to make, any contribution to it; and in consequence, his authorship of *Verses* can henceforth be completely and finally dismissed.

With the exception of Swift and Pope, no author is known to have written any poem in the verse section of the 1732 volume of *Miscellanies*; and there are grounds for thinking that the 'one or two small pieces by other Hands' were confined to the prose section and the work of those friends whom we know, from statements made elsewhere by Swift and Pope, to have been Arbuthnot and Parnell[2]—with the sole addition of one piece of prose by Matthew Pilkington,[3] a misguided Irish parson befriended by Swift for a short time. Now, whatever may be known about Arbuthnot's prose writings, there are not more than two or three poems extant which can with certainty be called his. The consequence is that his verse cannot be recognized by any characteristic style. And even if it were as correct as it is customary to attribute to him, wholly or in part, every anonymous poem dealing with scientific or medical subjects, which emanated from that small group of intimates known as the Scriblerus Club,[4] he still could not be credited with any poem in this volume, because it contains none of that kind. It would seem, therefore, that a recent tentative suggestion,[5] that the *Verses* may have been written by Arbuthnot, is very far from probable, especially as the only evidence adduced was one small joke against Blackmore, which Arbuthnot made in a letter to Swift (December 11, 1718), to the effect that Sir Richard's Pegasus needed no spurring.[6] There is, moreover, no evidence on record of any real ill-feeling between the two doctors, Arbuthnot and Blackmore, much less a quarrel of the bitterness which the poem postulates, and of which (one would think) it could hardly be the sole expression; and there is nothing else even appearing to connect Arbuthnot with the *Verses*. As for Parnell, his contribution seems to have been limited to his collaboration with Pope and Arbuthnot in the *Origine of Sciences*; and he could certainly have had nothing to do with this attack on Blackmore, because several of the epics it mentions were not written till years after his death in 1718.

There is, however, a little more information available about the poetical section of the 1732 volume of *Miscellanies*. Pope's corres-

---

[1] Ball, IV, p. 325.   [2] Spence, p. 201.   [3] Ball, IV, p. 309.
[4] The regular members were Pope, Swift, Gay, Arbuthnot, and Parnell.
[5] Faber, p. xxv.   [6] Ball, III, p. 22.

pondence with Bathurst[1] shows that he was directly concerned with the edition of *Miscellanies. In Four Volumes* (published July 3, 1742) in which the original four *Miscellanies* were for the most part reprinted, with much rearrangement of matter, some revision and deletion of text, and 'several additional pieces'. The verse, for example, is now collected in one volume, the fourth, which reveals that Pope suppressed one of his own pieces formerly included, and included two others of his, one never before printed and the other dating only from the preceding year. And in this volume Swift's pieces are for the first time indicated by marking with an asterisk, both in the text and the 'Contents',[2] all the poems which were written by *other* people; a feature which was repeated in subsequent editions. As in no instance have these indications been proved wrong, they may be taken as generally correct; though that is not to say that Swift may not have collaborated in a few of the starred pieces. Some light is therefore reflected back on those poems in the 1732 volume which reappeared in the 1742 edition. Thus, as *Verses on England's Arch-Poet* is starred both in the text and 'Contents', it may safely be assumed it was *not* written by Swift—an assumption with which his latest editor, Mr Harold Williams, evidently agrees, seeing that, like all his predecessors, he excludes it from the canon. So much, then, for Gay, Arbuthnot, Parnell, and Swift: remains Pope.

The case for Pope's authorship of the *Verses* attacking Blackmore is based first of all on a number of general arguments which can be briefly stated thus: (*a*) Pope was the prime and sole mover in the production of the last of his and Swift's *Miscellanies*; he proposed the scheme, collected the material, edited and published it, and is the only person known to have had this poem in his hands; (*b*) all his life Pope was in the habit of including numbers of his own anonymous pieces (prose as well as verse) in anthologies of his editing,[3] and very frequently would have nothing more to do with such pieces afterwards; (*c*) some one within a very small circle must have written the *Verses*; but, as shown above, all its members can be eliminated as possible candidates for authorship except Pope. These arguments, however, do not stand alone, but are corroborated by the witness of oppor-

---

[1] *Gent. Mag.*, Dec. 1855, pp. 586–8.

[2] The note on the 'Contents' page reads: 'N.B. Whatever are not mark'd with a Star are Dr. Swift's.'

[3] Different anthologies, or editions each varying from the previous one, which Pope is known to have edited, and in which he included anonymous work of his own, were published in 1712, 1714, 1717, 1720, 1722, 1726, 1727, 1728, and 1732. See *ante*, pp. 27 ff. for 'Pope's First Miscellany'.

tunity (as seen in his editorship of the volume), motive, occasion, and character; not to mention a certain amount of internal evidence, presently to be discussed.

The first fact of significance to claim consideration is the existence of a long-standing quarrel between Pope and Blackmore, with its sorry but not unamusing tale of attack and counter-attack, in which Pope was assailed on religious, and Blackmore on literary, grounds. As early as the *Essay on Criticism*, 1711, Pope, youthfully indignant at Blackmore's attacks on Dryden in *A Satyr against Wit* and elsewhere, had cited him as one of the crowd of envious detractors which a great man has always to contend with; and, after speaking of what Dryden had to endure in his lifetime from such people, went on—

> Might he return, and bless once more our Eyes,
> New Blackmores and new Milbournes must arise.

In which he coupled another name with Blackmore's (the Reverend Luke Milbourn had offensively criticized Dryden's *Virgil*) as his master had done more than once before him.[1] When the couplet was first published in 1711, Sir Richard's name was only hinted at, thus, 'New *Bl*——*s*'; but in the second edition and for several years later Pope altered this to 'New *S*——*s*' (Shadwells), presumably because he and Blackmore had become acquainted about that time. So at least it would appear, seeing that by April 19, 1714 Pope was sending his 'humble service' to Sir Richard by a mutual friend, John Hughes.[2] In any case, down to 1716 Pope's complaint against Blackmore seems to have been little more than academic. But with Sir Richard's abuse of Swift above mentioned (March 8, 1716), Pope became incensed enough to make a personal matter of it, as his letter shows: and within about three weeks had begun to make public fun of the pompous old poet. His earliest witticisms about him are to be found in the first of the famous 'Emetic' lampoons on Curll, which appeared on or about March 29 (it should not be forgotten that in addition to Curll's offences against Pope, he was also the publisher of Blackmore's attacks on Swift); and that was followed by the second lampoon about the end of November, in which the baiting of Blackmore assumes almost the proportions of a major theme[3]; both lampoons being included by

---

[1] 'Trust Maurus with thy life, and Milbourn with thy soul'—*To my Honoured Kinsman, John Driden* (ll. 86–7); and 'Blackmore and Milbourn are only distinguished ... by being remembered to their infamy'—Preface to *Fables*.

[2] Warton, VII, p. 372.

[3] Both lampoons are discussed and reprinted in Pope's *Prose*, I, pp. xciv ff., 257, 273.

Pope in the prose section of this same miscellany. Between the first and second lampoons, however, Curll in revenge had piratically published Pope's regrettable *Version of the First Psalm* (discussed in a previous chapter); and the whole quarrel finally boiled over when Sir Richard, in a second volume of *Essays* (published March 26, 1717), railed against 'the godless author [who] has burlesqu'd the First Psalm of David in so obscene and profane a manner'. Pope, who—as we know now—had never meant the skit for publication, and was already more than a little ashamed of it, or rather of the misconstruction[1] almost universally placed on it, never forgot or forgave him. Three months later, Blackmore's name reappeared at full length in the *Essay on Criticism* in the collected *Works*, June 3, 1717.

In the meantime, Arbuthnot writing to Swift (June 26, 1714) had reported that 'Pope has been collecting high flights of poetry, which are very good; they are to be solemn nonsense'.[2] This was doubtless the beginning of the *Art of Sinking*, one of the projects discussed by the Scriblerus Club about this time, and left undeveloped. Pope afterwards added to these 'high flights', carried the work through, and published it early in 1728, in the so-called 'Last Volume' of *Miscellanies*. And it is scarcely any exaggeration to say that in the *Art of Sinking* scores of lines from Blackmore's interminable epics are quoted to illustrate every possible literary lapse and every ridiculous aspect imaginable of the 'Profund'; the 'great Author', Sir Richard himself, being promoted 'father of the Bathos, and indeed the Homer of it'.

Ten weeks later came *The Dunciad* (May 18) in which Blackmore's 'endless line' is squinted at in Book I, while in Book II, besides a couple of other scoffing references to him he has ten lines all to himself: Pope is describing the Public Games consequent on the enthronement of King Dunce, and thus announces the winner in the competition of the *Brayers*:

> But far o'er all sonorous *Bl[ackmore]*'s strain,   235
> Walls, steeples, skies, bray back to him again:
> In *Tot'nham* fields, the brethren with amaze
> Prick all their ears up, and forget to graze;
> Long *Chanc'ry-lane* retentive rolls the sound,
> And courts to courts return it round and round;   240
> *Thames* wafts it thence to *Rufus'* roaring hall,
> And *H[ungerfor]d* re-ecchoes, bawl for bawl.
> All hail him victor in both gifts of Song,
> Who sings so *loudly*, and who sings so *long*.   244

---

[1] See *ante*, pp. 156 ff.   [2] Ball, II, p. 160.

To the last line just quoted Pope later added a lengthy footnote, which, because it is virtually a prose counterpart of the *Verses*, and has the same peculiar insistence on the number of the 'Books' in each of Blackmore's epics as is shown in the footnotes to the *Verses*,[1] is of real importance to the present argument. It runs as follows:

'A just character of Sir Richard Blackmore, Kt. . . . whose indefatigable Muse produced no less than six Epic poems: Prince and King Arthur, 20 Books; Eliza 10; Alfred 12; The Redeemer 6, besides Job in folio, the whole Book of Psalms, The Creation, 7 Books, Nature of Man, 3 Books, and many more. 'Tis in this sense he is stiled afterwards, the *Everlasting Blackmore* . . .'

When to all this are added Pope's jibes at him in at least four of the *Imitations of Horace*, and one or two other allusions in other places, it is obvious that the *Verses* fits more neatly and convincingly into the Pope-Blackmore feud than into any other contemporary setting; which setting, moreover, would also have to be such as would allow Pope to know of the poem in MS., and be the first to print it. It should also be remembered that in 1732 Blackmore had been dead three years; and though Pope may have been willing to publish one of his old pieces on the old theme, it does not at all follow that he would have included such untopical matter from any one outside what may be called the 'Miscellanies' circle; and all the others within it have previously been eliminated.

The poem itself looks like another of Pope's high-spirited, irresponsible effusions in which he indulged his wildest fancy, or gave free rein to his peculiar humour, from time to time. For besides being cast in a favourite metre, it has the characteristic acrobatic rhymes and the old impolite words found in so many of his 'unofficial' pieces, while between the lines of the easiest-going verse the scathing ridicule of his subject drives pitilessly on as usual to end with overwhelming effect. In particular, the Hudibrastic rhymes seem to have been struck in the same mint that coined such pairs as: conundrum—grows und'r 'em; step some—Epsom; rump yet—strumpet; Miles Davies—vous-avez; the news saw—Ragusa, and scores of others as intentionally absurd and bizarre scattered throughout Pope's lighter pieces. Indeed, it is difficult to think of any one at that time (except possibly Swift) as lavish of versified absurdities as was Pope, the most correct poet in Christendom! But neither the grimmer Swift nor the lighter-hearted Gay (even if they had been possible candidates in this case) played the

---

[1] See *ante*, p. 249.

clown in just Pope's manner or to anything like the same extent.

Again, amongst Pope's 'bad poets', and one of his frequent butts though of an earlier century than Blackmore, was Thomas Sternhold, the Elizabethan versifier of the Psalms[1]; and here in *Verses* it would appear to be Pope, who, by making Blackmore out-Sternhold Sternhold, kills two birds with one stone and his accustomed neatness and thrift. It would appear to be Pope also because none of his contemporaries worried themselves about Sternhold and Hopkins at that period; only Pope's supersensitive ear for correctness of versification and his genuine love of his craft kept him scornful and intolerant of poor writing all his life. Lastly, the joke about the use of an author's works for toilet purposes was an old one with Pope, who had printed it as early as 1712, toyed with it again in 1716, and was to make use of it once more as late as *circa* 1735 in an epigram now published for the first time on a subsequent page.[2]

The cumulative effect of all the foregoing probabilities may carry— if not conviction—at least justification for the inclusion of *Verses on England's Arch-Poet* amongst the attributed poems in the Pope canon. The piece was obviously written between 1723, the date of Sir Richard's last poem, *Alfred*, and 1729, the year of his death. It may therefore be provisionally dated 1727, the year in which Pope quoted him so extensively in the *Art of Sinking*.

II. EPITAPH AND EPIGRAM

The final volume of the *Miscellanies* of Swift and Pope, in which the foregoing *Verses On England's Arch-Poet* first appeared, was published on October 4, 1732, and was thus the last miscellany in English to be edited by Pope—his subsequent collection of Latin verse, *Selecta Poemata Italorum*, 1740, being in another category. The *Miscellanies* volume, however, differs from his former compilations of the kind, insomuch that nearly the first three-quarters of it consists entirely of prose, while the poetry, which totals only twenty-two pieces in all, is relegated to the last hundred pages.

Shortly after publication, Swift said that he had written 'almost six-sevenths of the whole verse part in the book',[3] and, a little later, emended this proportion to 'seven-eighths'.[4] The latter figure is approximately correct, to judge from the space taken up by his

---

[1] For Pope's caricature of Sternhold's style in the First Psalm, see *ante*, pp. 156 f.
[2] See *post*, p. 323.   [3] Ball, IV, p. 360.   [4] *Ibid.*, IV, p. 367.

poems; for although they are only ten in number, most of them are long and occupy altogether eighty-seven pages out of the allotted hundred. Twelve pieces are thus left, eleven of which were reprinted in the 1742 volume of *Miscellanies* alluded to above,[1] where they are each marked with an asterisk to show that they were *not* written by Swift; the missing piece (the epigram, 'When other Ladies...') having been earlier withdrawn from the reprints of the *Miscellanies* by Pope for use in his *Epistle to a Lady*, 1735.

'Pope's Last Miscellany' thus includes twelve poems of which Swift was not the author. Of these, five are indubitably Pope's: *On the Countess of B[urlington] cutting Paper*; *To a Lady with the Temple of Fame*; *On a Certain Lady at Court*; *Epigram* ('When other Ladies to the Groves go down'); and the epitaph-couplet beginning, 'Here Francis Ch[artre]s lies'. Four more—all of them short epigrams—have for many years been included in Pope's works, hitherto without evidence, but, as the present writer shows elsewhere,[2] with virtual exactness; these four are, *Epigram On the Toasts of the Kit-Cat Club, Anno 1716*; *Epigram* ('You beat your Pate, and fancy Wit will come'); *Epigram from the French* ('Sir, I admit your gen'ral Rule'); and lastly, *Epitaph* ('Well then, poor G[ay] lies under ground') which is discussed on a later page.[3] Three pieces are thus left, namely, *Verses on England's Arch-Poet*, already shown to be almost certainly Pope's; and two others, an *Epitaph* (*of By-Words*), and an *Epigram* ('Peter complains, that God has given'), now to be considered.

First, then, all the general arguments,[4] which, as we saw, pointed to Pope as the author of *Verses*, apply no less forcibly to his authorship of the two remaining pieces; and therefore, though those arguments are not repeated here, they form part of the evidence in each case, and should constantly be borne in mind in the following discussions. That being so, we may safely assume at the very start, that, as with *Verses* so with these two poems, it is extremely improbable (to say the least) that either of them was written by Swift, Gay, or Arbuthnot; while as regards Parnell, Pope told Spence[5] in effect that he had included every poem of his dead friend worth publishing in his edition of Parnell's *Poems* in 1722; and he subsequently refused to allow any more to become known. Consequently, except as a collaborator[6] with Pope and Arbuthnot in the prose *Essay ... Concerning the Origine of Sciences*,

---

[1] See *ante*, p. 254.
[2] In Pope's *Miscellaneous Poems*, 'Twickenham Edition', Vol. VI, in preparation.
[3] See *post*, pp. 327 f.   [4] See p. 254.
[5] Spence, p. 290.   [6] *Ibid.*, p. 201.

and, just possibly, one or two other literary projects of the old Scriblerus Club, Parnell may also be ruled out as a 'contributor' to this
volume. And there is no other person inside—or even outside—Pope's
intimate circle of friends for whose authorship of these two scraps of
verse the smallest iota of evidence exists.

Nevertheless it should be remarked that in the past the *Epitaph* has
not infrequently been ascribed to John Gay, though not until some
years after his death: it being first credited to him by mere assertion in
A Supplement to Dr. Swift's and Mr. Pope's Works, Dublin, 1739, in which
volume, as we have recently been warned, 'the attributions are not to
be relied on.'[1] The piece was first included in Gay's works by Bell in
1773,[2] together with the preceding poem, *Verses On England's Arch-
Poet*; and, like that poem, was unaccompanied by any comment, explanation, or evidence, to show why it was ascribed to Gay. Other
editors of the poet have since followed Bell, both in making the attribution and in concealing, or not revealing, whatever reasons they may
have had for so doing. His most recent editor, however, dismisses the
poem to an appendix of doubtful pieces with the remark, 'The *Epitaph
on Bye-Words* is not at all in Gay's manner'.[3] Thus, as it has never been
ascribed to any one else, this final elimination of any claim for the
last of its possible authors, except Pope, together with the above-
mentioned circumstances in which the *Epitaph* was first published,
seems to leave the student no reasonable alternative but to consider
the case for Pope's authorship.

The poem as it was first printed in 1732 runs thus:

EPITAPH [of By-Words.]

Here lies a round Woman, who thought *mighty odd*
Every Word she e'er heard in this Church about God.
To convince her of *God* the good Dean did endeavour,
But still in her Heart she held *Nature* more *clever*.
Tho' he talk'd much of Virtue, her Head always run
Upon something or other, she found better *Fun*.
For the Dame, by her Skill in Affairs Astronomical,
Imagin'd, to live in the Clouds was but *comical*.
In this World, she despis'd every Soul she met here,
And now she's in t'other, she thinks it but *Queer*.

On reading this ribald yet serious verse, it is evident to a perceptive

[1] Griffith, i, ii, p. 405.
[2] *The Miscellaneous Poems of . . . Gay*, Vol. iv, 1773.
[3] Faber, p. xxv.

ear that it is 'not at all in Gay's manner', but, on the other hand, very much in Pope's, particularly when he is writing in a light-hearted mood. This becomes apparent when the *Epitaph* (*of By-Words*) is compared with some of Pope's 'unofficial' poems, such as, for example, the Scriblerus Club invitation,[1] or those other anonymous lines of his, generally known as the *Epitaph On Himself*, but originally called simply *Epitaph*.[2]

Now the last-named piece, like the 'By-Words', epitaph, was never publicly acknowledged by Pope, though it was attributed to him more than once during the last few years of his life, both in manuscripts, and elsewhere. It has, however, been universally accepted as his since his literary executor and editor, Warburton, included it in the canon in 1751. It was the seeming frivolousness of those lines, *On Himself*, which caused Dr Johnson (obsessed with thoughts of death, as he was) to deprecate Pope's 'attempts to be jocular upon one of the few things that make wise men serious.'[3] Here also, in the *Epitaph* (*of By-Words*), the author is being 'jocular' upon 'serious' things—amongst them being the purity of the English language, the preservation of which was a profoundly serious thing to Pope; but, it seems, to no other poet of his period then alive, except of course his beloved Swift. It is therefore noteworthy that 'the good Dean' (who cannot be any one but Swift) is not only brought into an epitaph concerned with the language, but is also quizzed by the author of it with the same playful fondness that was Pope's—and only Pope's—habitual attitude to him. And when one remembers the allusion to the Dean's sermons in the *Receipt for Stewing Veal*,[4] or the *Lines on Swift's Ancestors* (which Swift called 'Mr. Pope's Roguery'), or indeed any one of a dozen similar references in verse and prose, it cannot be denied that this too was penned in the same spirit. Swift, as we have seen, was staying with

---

[1] See *ante*, p. 223.

[2] The Epitaph is now reprinted for the first time from the earliest printed text yet discovered, in *The Publick Register*, Jan. 10, 1741:

EPITAPH

UNDER this Marble, or under this Sill,
Or under this Turf, or e'en what they will;
Whatever an Heir, or a Friend in his stead,
Or any good Creature shall lay o'er my Head;
Lies He who ne'er car'd, and still cares not a Pin,
What they said, or may say of the Mortal within.
But who living and dying, serene still and free,
Trusts in God, that as well as he was, he shall be.

[3] Johnson, IV, p. 239. [4] See *ante*, p. 229.

Pope at Twickenham during the summers of 1726 and 1727; and both friends, as we know, were keenly interested in questions of a literary or linguistic character. There is Swift's famous letter in *The Tatler* on 'the Corruption of our English Tongue',[1] for example, and his later *Proposal for Correcting, Improving and Ascertaining the English Tongue*,[2] on the one side; and, on the other, Pope's *Essay on Criticism*, the *Art of Sinking*, and numerous passages in his correspondence on literary style and diction, and so forth. With two such men, having such interests at heart, and living together for several months at a time, it would be strange if they did not talk about them. It is therefore not improbable that the conversation turned one day on the use and misuse of certain words and phrases then much in fashion, and that Pope afterwards knocked these lines together in a jocose mood to illustrate those words to which, or to some particular meaning of which, one or other of them had objected. It is surely not without significance, that, with the exception of the words 'God' and 'Nature' (which obviously no philosophic poet could avoid using, but which fashionable use, by opposing them to each other as in the *Epitaph*, had reduced to little better than cant terms), Pope had *never* used any of the italicized 'by-words' in his poetry at the date of the publication of the poem in 1732.[3] Even by the time he died he had only used 'queer' and 'mighty odd' once each, and possibly 'clever' once (the line in which it occurs may be Swift's),[4] but neither of the other offending 'by-words'. As Pope, therefore, was an author who practised what the *Epitaph* preached; and as his *Essay on Criticism*, and *Art of Sinking*, etc. prove that he also liked this sort of preaching, the only reasonable conclusion seems to be that in this *Epitaph* (*of By-Words*) he again preached what he practised.

The remaining *Epigram*, which follows, enjoys the distinction of being the only verse in 'Pope's Last Miscellany' that has never been attributed to, or claimed by, any author. It has rarely, if ever, been reprinted outside the successive editions of the Swift-Pope *Miscellanies*, and is to-day practically unknown.

EPIGRAM

> *Peter* complains, that God has given
> To his poor Babe a Life so short:
> Consider *Peter*, he's in Heaven;
> 'Tis good to have a Friend at Court.

---

[1] *The Tatler*, No. 230, September 28, 1710.   [2] Published 1712.
[3] According to Abbott's *Concordance*.   [4] Hor. Sat. II, vi, l. 11. See Butt, p. 248.

For one student at least this verse is as characteristic of Pope's manner as the four short pieces of the same kind mentioned above,[1] which
he included with it in 1732, and which have long since been regarded
as his work. And as all the general arguments,[2] which, as we saw,
pointed to Pope as the author not only of those four, but also of the
Verses On England's Arch-Poet and the *Epitaph* (*of By-Words*), apply
equally well to this *Epigram* on Peter; it is difficult to accept all the
other pieces as genuine Pope, and in the same breath deny to this one
the probability—if no more—of his authorship.

If only the identity of 'Peter' could be established beyond cavil, it
might throw further light on the problem. This final volume of the
Miscellanies was published on October 4, 1732; but some ten months
earlier[3] Pope had begun to make satirical comments in his poems on
the notorious Peter Walter (or Walters, or Waters), an unscrupulous
and extremely wealthy scrivener, many of whose victims were
amongst the nobility, at the court or in parliament. Between 1731 and
1738, at least a dozen separate passages about the man's financial
activities—in most of which he is referred to simply by the name
'Peter', as in the *Epigram*—can be found scattered up and down Pope's
Satires and Moral Essays; a fact which may seem to suggest that the
two Peters were one and the same, and to that extent corroborate the
evidence for Pope's authorship of the *Epigram*. On the other hand,
unless the *Epigram* hints at the ultimate result of Peter's frauds, its difference from the usual matter of Pope's allusions to him might point to
a different date, if not a different man. Unfortunately, however, there
is nothing to show when the *Epigram* was written; for although some of
the verse Pope collected for his last miscellany was written not long
before it was published, much of it was years old, one piece having
been written as early as 1715[4] and another in 1716,[5] while some of the
prose was actually in print in 1713.[6] Thus, seeing that Peter Walter
was born about 1664, it would appear that the earlier the *Epigram* can
be dated, the less improbable would be his fatherhood of a 'Babe' at
the time it was written, and the more probable the identification of
him with our 'Peter'. If, on the contrary, the *Epigram* was a late composition, its allusion to 'Peter' must apparently remain unidentified;
in which case it would only add one more to the many unsolved
allusions in Pope's satirical work, and would not, of course, affect the

[1] See *ante*, p. 259.   [2] See *ante*, p. 254.
[3] In the *Epistle to . . . Burlington*, published December 14, 1731.
[4] *To a Lady with the Temple of Fame.*   [5] *On the Toasts of the Kit-Cat Club.*
[6] *Dr. Norris's Account.*

evidence stated in the general argument[1] for his authorship of this piece, together with the others. And, except for the fact that Pope later used a similar opening phrase in another epigram—'My Lord complains that Pope . . .',[2] which obviously echoes 'Peter complains that God . . .'—there is nothing more that can usefully be said about the poem at the moment.

Little remains to be added to the story of 'Pope's Last Miscellany'. We have seen that—even more absolutely than with the three preceding volumes—the project was his from beginning to end, that the verse he had included was written by himself and Swift alone, that his poems were unusually few and small, and that Swift's calculations of his own share possibly suggest that besides being puzzled to account for it, he was—at least for the time being—not a little ruffled to find it so disproportionately large.

Unluckily, none of the correspondence which passed between the two friends while the miscellany was being prepared for the press has survived—or rather, has been placed on record. But Swift's last letter[3] before the hiatus, in answer to one from Pope broaching the scheme and asking about possible contributions, is full of information about his work, and implicitly gives Pope free range over all his uncollected 'papers' in prose and verse—in much the same way (he intimates) as his 'Will' would eventually be found to do. If, after receiving this letter, Pope drew largely on his friend for the verse of their last joint *Miscellanies* (for which he has at times been censured), it is not very surprising; and still less so when we know in addition that he could not have had by him much uncollected or unallocated verse of his own at that time. For it should be remembered that Swift was primarily an ecclesiastic, and an author only in his spare time; that his most important work was prose; that he never wrote for money,[4] and, moreover, had never bothered himself to collect and publish his 'Works'. In marked contrast, Pope was a professional poet whose serious work was at once the inspiration and support of his life. Thus, apart from some half-dozen *Epistles* and nine *Epitaphs* which were almost certainly destined from their inception for 'Volume II' of *The Works* (where less than three years later they all appeared), Pope seems to have contributed to his last miscellany practically all the verse he had at hand just then in desk or drawer—always excepting, of course,

---

[1] See *ante*, p. 254.
[2] In the epigram, *On lopping Trees in his Garden*.
[3] Dated June 12, 1732; see *Letters*, ii, 4to, 1741, p. 121.
[4] See *ante*, p. 232 n.

those poetical 'Frolicks' (as he once called them) with which he was determined never to let his name be connected, however remotely. And that he had done his best for the miscellany under the circumstances, is suggested by an analysis of the prose section of the book; for this is found to be not only treble the size of the verse section, but to include a number of his early scattered prose pieces[1] (original copies of which are now very rare, and as regards one piece, non-existent), which together make Pope's prose contributions nearly equal to Swift's in bulk, and—as some think—more than equal in interest.

But even if some degree of criticism of Pope's compilation of this miscellany was implied, in the above-quoted letters to Motte, by Swift's remarks on the preponderance of his work in the verse section, there is no evidence that he either made a grievance of it, or raised the matter with Pope, then or later. And as the incident in no way affected their friendship, it may be supposed that Swift soon afterwards reminded himself that when Pope had made his suggestions for a fourth volume, he had left everything in his hands, and had even gone so far as to divulge—quite unnecessarily—the terms of his will concerning the disposition of his 'papers' after his death. His excuse to Motte, therefore, to the effect that his memory was not very clear about what had been said by Pope and himself at the beginning, may have been meant only to cover up some recrudescence of his illness. More probably, however, it was an attempt to justify the dissatisfaction he seems to have experienced on first glancing through the volume—but whether because (as he complained to Motte) the printing of his 'part' was 'very incorrect', or because Pope's part was less than he expected, is far from certain. All this was on the surface, however; deep down must have been the realization that in the give and take of friendship he was far more in Pope's debt than was Pope in his. Thus it was that their letters to each other showed no diminution of affection. Far otherwise, in fact, for barely seven months after the publication of 'Pope's Last Miscellany', Swift could in all sincerity end a long letter to him in words like these: 'You will observe in this letter many marks of an ill head and a low spirit; but a Heart wholly turned to love you with the greatest Earnestness and Truth.'[2]

---

[1] These include the several lampoons on Curll and Dennis, and *God's Revenge against Punning* (for all of which see Pope's *Prose*, I, N. Ault); the Scriblerus Club papers written in collaboration; and what was probably Pope's also, *A True and Faithful Narrative* (Griffith, I, p. 208).

[2] *Letters*, II, 4to, 1741, p. 137. Letter dated May 1, 1733.

CHAPTER XVI

THE 'CHARACTER' OF CLOE

CLOE:

A Character.

"Yet Cloe sure was form'd without a spot"—
Nature in her then err'd not, but forgot.
"With ev'ry pleasing, ev'ry prudent part,
Say, what can Cloe want?"—She wants a Heart.
She speaks, behaves, and acts just as she ought;
But never, never, reach'd one gen'rous Thought.
Virtue she finds too painful an endeavour,
Content to dwell in Decencies for ever.
So very reasonable, so unmov'd,
As never yet to love, or to be lov'd.
She, while her Lover pants upon her breast,
Can mark the figures on an Indian chest;
And when she sees her Friend in deep despair,
Observes how much a Chintz exceeds Mohair.
Forbid it Heav'n, a Favour or a Debt
She e'er should cancel—but she may forget.
Safe is your Secret still in Cloe's ear;
But none of Cloe's shall you ever hear.
Of all her Dears she never slander'd one,
But cares not if a thousand are undone.
Would Cloe know if you're alive or dead?
She bids her Footman put it in her head.
Cloe is prudent—Would you too be wise?
Then never break your heart when Cloe dies.

These famous lines, now widely known only as a part of the poem, *Of The Characters of Women: An Epistle to a Lady*,[1] were originally published as a separate poem, entitled, *Cloe: A Character*, in *The Works . . . Vol. II. Part II. Containing all such Pieces . . . as were written since the former Volumes*, which, though dated 1738, seems not to have published until May 1, 1739.[2] In the four years that followed, the piece was printed at

[1] The poem was first printed without these lines in 1735.
[2] R. Straus's *Robert Dodsley*, p. 321.

least four times as a separate and complete entity; and it was not until a few weeks before Pope's death that it was inserted in the second epistle in *Epistles to Several Persons* (1744)—a volume which, strictly speaking, was never published,[1] and is to-day of the extremest rarity. In Spence's notes about Pope's last days, he tells how a few copies of this mysterious edition became known to certain of the poet's friends; and reports Pope saying:

> 'Here am I, like Socrates, distributing my morality among my friends, just as I am dying'.—This was said on his sending about some of his Ethic Epistles, as presents, about three weeks before we lost him.[2]

William Warburton, who had helped Pope to prepare this volume, or at least had contributed some notes to it, became on the poet's death his literary executor and editor; and in his collected edition of *The Works*, 1751, *Cloe: A Character* vanishes as a separate poem, and is to be found only in the second of the *Ethic Epistles*—now called *Moral Essays*—where, as lines 157–180, it has ever since remained. But neither Pope between 1739 and 1744, nor Warburton later, in his successive editions of the poet's *Works*, had anything to say about the identity of the lady since declared to be portrayed in these allusive lines.

The usual statement, still current after a hundred and fifty years of repetition, is that the Cloe of these verses was drawn from Henrietta Howard, Countess of Suffolk, who was for some years what might almost be called the 'official' mistress of George II, both before and after his accession to the throne in 1727. Nevertheless, a fresh scrutiny of all the evidence has suggested that the tradition cannot any longer be accepted.

In the first place, it should be remembered that this identification of Cloe was not put forward publicly until thirty years after the lady's death, and more than half a century after Pope himself had died. For it was Joseph Warton, who, in a note in his edition of the poet's *Works*, made the direct but unsupported assertion: 'This highly-finished portrait was intended for Lady Suffolk'[3]—a statement which has been confidently quoted again and again by successive editors ever since. Only comparatively recently have a couple of manuscript jottings (one, if not both, of eighteenth century date) been used to strengthen Warton's statement. Horace Walpole, whose opinion in such matters

---

[1] Griffith, I, ii, p. 473.   [2] Spence, p. 318.
[3] Warton, III, p. 222.

was not always reliable,[1] was responsible for the first—it being a marginal note in his copy of the *Epistle*, which remained unpublished and apparently unknown until 1876. From it we learn that he 'suspected' that Cloe was 'meant' for Lady Suffolk[2]; his only reasons being, first, that 'some touches' were like her—a point to which we shall return; and secondly, that Cloe's place in the epistle 'preceding the Queen's character' seemed significant—though he entirely omitted to explain in what its significance consists. That, fortunately, does not matter, for his second reason for thinking Cloe was Lady Suffolk seems to have been invalidated in advance by Pope himself, who ended his note on the 1744 additions to the *Epistle, To a Lady* (one of which was this 'character' of Cloe), with the statement: 'nor can we answer that these [new characters] are exactly inserted': it being obvious, that, if their position in the epistle is uncertain, any argument based on position is futile.

The remaining piece of evidence which is sometimes quoted in support of the traditional identification is a scribbled note of uncertain date made by Edmund Malone in a scrapbook collection of all kinds of literary odds and ends, where gossip and fact jostle each other on every page, which he began to assemble in the last quarter of the eighteenth century for a projected edition of Pope's works. The note says:

> The lady who counts the figures on an Indian Screen—was Lady Suffolk—from Mr Cambridge, who knew Pope—He was very little, he says, & his bust is extremely like him.[3]

It appears, however, that Cambridge's acquaintance with Pope was of the slightest, since no one else seems to have noticed it, and Cambridge himself apparently saw nothing to remark about one of the most remarkable men of the age, except a couple of facts of common knowledge. It should also be pointed out that Malone does not say that Cambridge claimed to have obtained his information from Pope, who, from all we know of him, was hardly likely to have admitted—or confided—such a secret to a young man and comparative stranger. Thus, seeing that, some years after Pope's death, Cambridge and Walpole became neighbours and friends at Twickenham, and that both, moreover, were great gossips with a perceptible inclination to scandal,[4] it is at least conceivable that Malone's bit of hearsay about the identity of Cloe was derived ultimately from Walpole's not

---

[1] See *post*, p. 345.   [2] Fraser, p. 33.   [3] Bodleian MS. Malone 30, f. 27.
[4] A. Dobson, *Eighteenth Century Vignettes*, III, pp. 200 f.

too well-grounded 'suspicion' that she was meant to be Lady Suffolk.

According to the popular legend, this masterly 'portrait of a lady' was Pope's malicious revenge on his old friend, the Countess of Suffolk, for her failure, or neglect, to influence the new king on his accession in favour of their common friends, Swift and Gay in particular, and, as is sometimes suggested, the whole political Opposition in general.[1] But that legend is demonstrably wrong as regards Pope's attitude to the lady; for although neither Swift nor Gay profited by the new régime at court, and although the former bitterly blamed the Countess[2] for their continued lack of preferment, Pope never blamed her. Indeed, it would appear that Swift's disappointment (whether for his own sake or Gay's, is not always clear)[3] at Lady Suffolk's non-performance was quite unwarranted by the actual circumstances, and was one of the less estimable incidents of his latter years. For although Gay was an old friend of Mrs Howard (as she was then),[4] Swift had not known her much more than a twelvemonth when George II came to the throne. But the degree of Swift's or Gay's disappointment is beside the point, except that, normally, Pope would have espoused their cause as promptly and as heartily as his own. Our present concern is to establish the fact that Pope's friendship for the Lady was sincere; and there is abundant evidence in their correspondence to show, that, if he can be said to have taken sides in the matter at all, it was with the lady, whom he repeatedly defended against Swift's strictures, as Swift more than once acknowledged.[5]

But there are many other arguments which together make the traditional identification virtually impossible. There is, for instance, the literal fact that the 'character' of Cloe contains not the slightest allusion either to the Court, or to politics, as might justly have been expected had Lady Suffolk's failure to influence them on his friends' behalf been the motive and occasion of the poem. There is, besides, the inescapable and immovable objection that Lady Suffolk never complained of Pope's portrait, and that their friendship remained unchanged after its publication in the spring of 1739.

An attempt has frequently been made to support the traditional identification by a reference to the one known occasion, as far back as 1723, when Mrs Howard was addressed as 'Chloe'[6] by Lord Peter-

---

[1] Irving, p. 229. [2] See especially *Letters*, II, 4to, 1741, p. 103.
[3] Compare, for example, EC, VII, p. 212 and p. 254.
[4] She became Countess of Suffolk in 1731.
[5] EC, VII, p. 212; and Ball, IV, p. 183.
[6] The spelling of the name, whether Cloe or Chloe, has no significance.

borough in the now famous song: 'I said to my heart, between sleeping
and waking.'[1] That she was then so addressed by him is true; it is also
true that in those intervening years many ladies must have been
similarly addressed by versifying gentlemen, because ever since the
Restoration 'Cloe' had been a favourite name with the poets. Furthermore, if Mrs Howard can be said to have had a pet-name or nickname
amongst her friends, it was certainly not 'Cloe', but 'the Swiss'[2] (her
apartments being also called 'the Swiss cantons'), probably because
of her 'caution and neutrality'. And not only is Pope never known, in
speech or print, to have adopted Peterborough's earlier, once-used
name for her, but, more conclusive still, in the two years immediately
preceding the publication of *Cloe: A Character*, he had, in two separate
Imitations of Horace,[3] publicly bestowed the name 'Chloe' on a different lady, about whom one thing (if only one) is certain—that she
was *not* the Countess of Suffolk. That being so, and quite apart from
the question of friendship, it is improbable in the last degree that Pope,
after using the name 'Chloe' to designate the same person for two
years in succession, should apply it to some one else in the following
year; for the name had neither then, nor since, become a recognized
generic label like 'Magdalen' or 'Diana'.

Again, the general unlikeness of the character of *Cloe* to the known
personal character of Lady Suffolk is—with a master portrait-
painter like Pope—a further argument against the old identification.
Even Elwin and Courthope, who subscribed to it, felt obliged to admit
that the suggestion, that Cloe had numerous lovers, does not fit the
Countess of Suffolk.[4] As for Cloe's great failing, her 'want of heart', all
who knew Lady Suffolk at all well concurred in thinking her, if anything, rather exceptionally endowed in this respect. That she was a
woman of ready sympathies and genuine kindness is implicit in many
of Pope's letters and explicit in not a few. Writing to Robert Digby,
for example, he actually couples her with his dearest of friends,
Martha Blount, as two ladies who have 'hearts'[5] in the sense of the
poem. Many other people could be quoted to the same effect, amongst
them being the Duchess of Queensbury (than whom Gay had no
truer or warmer-hearted friend) who, writing to Lady Suffolk, declared: 'You were as much his friend as I'.[6] There is also Lady Eliza-

---

[1] This song, however, was not so popular at the date of Pope's 'Character' of
Cloe, as is commonly supposed—if we may judge by the rarity of contemporary
reprints of it.   [2] See Suffolk, *passim*.

[3] Hor. Od. IV, i, l. 20; and Ep. I, vi, ll. 42–3; see Butt, p. 238 n.

[4] EC, III, pp. 107 f.   [5] *Letters*, 4to, 1737, p. 176.   [6] Irving, p. 297.

beth Germain who championed her kindness and sincerity against Swift's censures, in a letter of the frankest statement.[1] And, to make an end, the lady herself might be allowed to go into the witness box on her own behalf, with a few words from a letter to her dear Lady Hervey, which she little dreamt would ever be made public: 'I find . . . I want your head and hand to answer your last; but I do not want a heart, for I have one truly sensible for my friends, and more capable of feeling than expressing tenderness.'[2] It should, moreover, be added that the numerous affectionate allusions to Lady Suffolk by her friends were unprompted tributes, and not called forth to defend her against the 'Character' of Cloe, which had not even been printed when most of them were written.

Now the 'Chloe' of Pope's *Imitations* is thought to have been a 'Miss Foley', for whose hand, it appears, his penniless young friend, 'dear Murray' (later, Earl of Mansfield) had recently been an unsuccessful suitor.[3] In the 1737 poem, Pope wrote that when Venus shall have made Murray rich, Chloe is to 'lend her face' for a statue of the goddess, with which his gardens were to be adorned.[4] In 1738, however, Murray had not only been rejected by the lady, but was so depressed by his loss that Pope felt it necessary to advise his young friend to busy himself with other matters and interests, and not so unworthily—

> Sigh while his Chloe, blind to Wit and Worth,
> Weds the rich Dulness of some Son of earth.[5]

It is probably not a mere coincidence that Pope has drawn the Cloe of the 'character' and the Chloe of the *Satires* as not only sharing a very 'prudent' outlook on life, but as having the same grave imperfection in common—a want 'of heart', which, as we have seen, is not known to have been a failing of Lady Suffolk.

But although there is no evidence that Pope ever intended the 'character' of Cloe as a portrait of Henrietta Howard, and much to show that it was not so intended, he did once make a thumb-nail sketch of her in the well-known lines:

On a certain Lady at Court

> I know the thing that's most uncommon,
>   (Envy be silent and attend!)
> I know a Reasonable Woman,
>   Handsome and witty, yet a Friend.

[1] Ball, IV, pp. 388 f.   [2] Suffolk, I, p. 323.   [3] See Butt, p. 238 n.
[4] Hor. Od. IV, i, l. 20.   [5] Hor. Ep. I, vi, ll. 42–3.

Not warp'd by Passion, aw'd by Rumour,
      Not grave thro' Pride, or gay thro' Folly,
An equal Mixture of good Humour,
      And sensible soft Melancholy.

'Has she no Faults then (Envy says) Sir?'
      Yes she has one, I must aver:
When all the World conspires to praise her,
      The Woman's deaf, and does not hear.

First printed anonymously in the final volume of *Miscellanies*, 1732 (from which this text is taken), the poem was first publicly attributed to Pope by Warburton in *The Works* of 1751, and the 'certain Lady' first publicly identified as Lady Suffolk by Warton at the end of the century, neither editor adducing any evidence. But, happily, corroboration of both statements can now be put on record owing to the discovery of two contemporary transcripts amongst Lord Oxford's papers[1] both of which are headed, *On Mrs. Howard by Mr. Pope*. But that is not all, for further proof of Pope's authorship has been put forward in the preceding chapter, 'Pope's Last Miscellany',[2] where evidence is cited to show that no one but Pope and Swift contributed verse to the 1732 volume, and that this piece was marked as 'not by Swift' in the 1742 edition of *Miscellanies*. Additional proof of the 'certain Lady's' identity is to be found in a letter from Pope to Swift, dated September 14, 1725, which contains virtually a prose counterpart of this then unpublished poem. Pope is writing to persuade Swift to pay a visit to him in England, and after speaking of other inducements, goes on to say:

If you come to us . . . I can also help you to a Lady who is as deaf tho' not so old, as yourself; you'll be pleas'd with one-another I'll engage, tho' you don't hear one-another . . . What you'll most wonder at is, she is considerable at Court, yet no Party-woman, and lives in Court, yet wou'd be easy and make you easy.[3]

To which Swift replied on September 29:

The Lady whom you describe to live at Court, to be deaf and no party-woman, I take to be Mythology. . .[4]

It thus becomes obvious that the two poems, *On a certain Lady at Court* and *Cloe: A Character*, cannot both be portraits of the same person; and

[1] Harl. 7316; and Portland, xviii.   [2] See *ante*, p. 253.
[3] *Letters*, ii, 4to, 1741, p. 32.   [4] *Ibid.*, p. 34.

as Lady Suffolk's known deafness (together with all the other evidence) identifies her beyond cavil with the 'certain Lady', it follows that she was not the original of *Cloe*.

When we are no longer biased by the former identification of Cloe, and Pope is at last acquitted of having so cruelly caricatured an old friend, it becomes possible to recognize how contrary to the poet's real character such an attack on Lady Suffolk would have been, and, with that realization, how completely a number of venerable, related problems disappear.

We again recall that glorious summer of 1726, with Swift for the first time for twelve years in England, a guest of Pope's at Twickenham,[1] where many of the best and brightest spirits of the time foregathered, and talk, incessant talk, flowed sparkling on like the river at the garden foot; where the Dean became acquainted with Pope's old friend, but new neighbour, at Marble Hill, Henrietta Howard, and in the exchange of much visiting and junketing cultivated a friendship with her which even embraced her lap-dog, Fop (to which pet, as we shall see, he appears to have helped Pope to concoct 'An Heroick Epistle')[2]; where plans for future works were talked over by the three writers, Pope, Swift, and Gay, in garden or grotto; and where the happy friendliness of the whole circle, which was centred in Pope's villa, taught Swift how to dream,[3] and recaptured for Pope himself something of the magic of that golden year of his early manhood[4] about which he wrote some nostalgic lines not wholly inapplicable to Twickenham in 1726:

> How oft in pleasing Labors of y[e] day
> Long summer suns rolld unperceivd away;
> At night we met each finding like a friend
> Something to blame & something to comend . . .

And when Swift had returned to Ireland in the autumn, and Pope's alarming accident had brought his friends flocking round him once more, Mrs Howard was there again amongst the chief of them, partaking of the 'poetical soop' and contributing to the 'Cheddar letter'— as we have seen in a previous chapter.[5]

No longer biased by tradition, memory is once again allowed to remind us of something even more in danger of being forgotten—that the person nearest and dearest to Pope's heart during his whole adult life, his beloved Martha Blount, was also a close friend of Lady Suf-

---

[1] See *ante*, p. 224.
[2] See *post*, pp. 342 ff.
[3] *Letters*, II, 4to, 1741, p. 62.
[4] See *ante*, pp. 68 ff.
[5] See *ante*, p. 227.

folk as early as 1727,[1] and almost certainly much earlier; and also that we have Pope's own assurance that Martha was 'of all the Women he knows, . . . the last that would be entertain'd at the Expence of Another'.[2] And with that opportune reminder, it becomes incredible that Pope would either have hurt Martha through her friend by publishing the poem in 1739, or have aggravated and perpetuated that injury—practically on his death-bed—by deliberately inserting such a merciless attack on her dear Lady Suffolk in his last revision of the last poem he ever addressed to Martha, *Of the Characters of Women.* Moreover, there is indisputable evidence that the mutual friendship of all three, Henrietta, Martha, and Pope, continued unchanged and unclouded after the publication of *Cloe: A Character*, on May 1, 1739, as their correspondence shows in a number of places—notably and most happily in a passage in Pope's letter to Martha dated December 27, [1739], as follows:

> Pray tell my Lady Suffolk in ye first place that I think of her every night constantly, as the greatest Comforter I have, under her Edder-down-Quilt: I wish Mr Berkley [whom she married in 1735] lay as easy, who I hear (& am sorry for it) has had the Gout.[3]

That, surely, is as little the voice of a satirist gloating over his recent victim, as is the gift of a comforting eiderdown a believable return for an old friend's perfidious act barely eight months earlier.

The elimination of the Countess of Suffolk from the affair, however, leaves the label blank under this picture of Cloe; for there is no known lady of the period whom the 'character' will even approximately fit. The difficulty of finding the original of the portrait is, however, not surprising in view of the poet's own words. When, about two months before he died, Pope inserted this 'character' of Cloe with others in his last revision of the epistle, *Of the Characters of Women*, he asked Warburton (as his literary executor and editor) to call attention to 'ye authors Tenderness in using no *living Examples* or *real Names* of any one of ye softer sex' in this epistle to Miss Blount.[4] Thus, remembering that there has never been any complete agreement about the originals of the other 'characters' which Pope added to the epistle in 1744 (for Cloe is the only one whose identity has been unanimously accepted!), it would appear that his statement to Warburton was in the main correct, and, therefore, that these female 'characters' were not exact portraits of this or that particular woman, but composite representations

[1] Suffolk, i, p. 233.
[2] *Of the Characters of Women*, 1735.
[3] Mapledurham, 6.
[4] Egerton, 1946, f. 96 v.

of types of *woman*, obtained by combining the traits, habits, and foibles of several different individuals—in fine, by employing a method not dissimilar to that of most novelists.

Thus it must have been with *Cloe*. Miss Foley may have (unwittingly) supplied some of the details of the portrait, as suggested above, while other details would have been drawn from other women. It is not disputed that some particular mannerism may have been taken from Lady Suffolk herself—for Walpole, as we have seen, claimed no more than that 'some touches' were like her. It is even possible that Warton's anecdote was correct in fact, though not in the interpretation he obviously put on it, when (without citing his authority) he annotated the penultimate couplet of the 'character' of Cloe, by saying that it—

> alludes to a particular circumstance: Pope, being at dinner with her, heard her order her footman to put her in mind to send to know how Mrs. Blount, who was ill, had passed the night.[1]

Because it could be reasonably opposed to Warton's interpretation that the overheard request need not have been due to indifference, but—as a matter of common experience—to conscientiousness. There can be few people, who, suddenly remembering at an inopportune moment some impending task or belated duty, have not asked to be reminded of it later, lest a treacherous memory should delay, or further postpone, its tactful or timely observance. Again, as every one testified that Mrs Howard—whose lot it was to be placed at the very cross-roads of court and society gossip and news—was the discreetest of women, it may be that Pope thought of her as he penned the line: 'Safe is your Secret still in Cloe's ear'; but again it may not, for other women besides her have been 'prudent'.

But a description of this personal trait, or a note of that trick of behaviour, neither is, nor is necessarily intended to be, a portrait recognizable by contemporaries; and half a century had to elapse, before Lady Suffolk's real character became so dimmed and dulled by time, that it could at last be plausibly falsified to fit the picture. The pity is, that, despite a complete lack of direct evidence for it, the mistaken identification has not only belied the lady's character down to the present day, but unfortunately has seemed to justify the popular misconception of Pope as a faithless friend.

[1] Warton, III, p. 222.

CHAPTER XVII

'THE SIX MAIDENS'

Amongst the manuscript treasures at Longleat, and now bound in the thirteenth volume of the 'Portland Papers', is a poem on a separate sheet of paper in Pope's handwriting but without title or signature. The poem has never been printed hitherto, and seems to have survived only in this copy. At the head of the manuscript, faintly written in pencil are the words, 'Believed to be Pope. J E J'; and the sheet is endorsed 'From the Duchess of Portland's Papers.—Longleat.' Thus, as the Duchess, who in her youth was well known to the poet, was the daughter of his friend, Edward Harley, second Earl of Oxford, from whom this and other autograph poems of Pope's came into her possession; and as Pope's hand-writing is also vouched for by the British Museum authorities, the authenticity of the document can be accepted without any reserve.

The facts that the poem is in Pope's hand and is found with other autograph poems of his do not of course absolutely prove his authorship. But proof seems not far off when it is realized, that, except for the very rare appearance in his letters of a few lines from other authors, who are usually named and always quoted for definite reasons, there is believed to be no unsigned poem in Pope's autograph in existence, of which he is not the author. And lastly, when, as in the present instance, the writing itself reveals the poet in the act of composition or correction (it is not certain which) deleting, altering, adding, and, further, shows that the first and second thoughts were written by the same hand, Pope's authorship becomes a practical certainty.

Except for the adoption of a phrase from the first line as the title, the poem as Pope left it runs exactly as follows:

'The Six Maidens'

A Tower there is, where six Maidens do dwell;
This Tow'r it belongs to the Dev'l of Hell;
And sure of all Devils this must be the best,
Who by six such fair Maidens at once is possest.

So bright are their beauties, so charming their eyes,
As in spite of his Fall, might make Lucifer rise;
But then they're so blithe & so buxome withall,
As, tho ten Devils rose, they could make them to fall.

Ah why, good Lord Grantham, were you so uncivil
To send at a dash all these Nymphs to the Devil?
& yet why, Madam Dives, at your lot should you stare?
'Tis known all the Dives's ever went there.

There Mordaunt, Fitzwilliams, &c. remain;
(I promis'd I never would mention Miss Vane.)
Ev'n Cart'ret & Meadows, so pure of desires,
Are lump'd with ye rest of these charming Hell-fires.

O! sure to King George, 'tis a dismal disaster,
To see his own Maids serve a new Lord and Master.
Yet this, like their old one, for nothing will spare,
And treateth them all, like a Prince of the Air.

Who climbs those High Seats oh his joy shall be great!
Tho strait be the passage, & narrow the Gate;
And who now of his Court, to this place w^d not go,
Prep—— the Devil and his Angells also?

In this poem, as in not a few of his other anonymous pieces, Pope
the irrepressible is once again playing with fire; and had the piece got
abroad with his name attached, the consequences might well have
been serious. For the persons lampooned, as well as the occasion and
the approximate date, are still recognizable after two hundred years
and more. The poem is, without the slightest doubt, a squib on Frederick, Prince of Wales, and his supposed intrigues with the six Maids
of Honour to his mother, Queen Caroline; the 'Tower' being of course
Windsor Castle, and Lord Grantham the Lord Chamberlain to the
Queen's household.

Corroboration of personalities and date is to be found in hint and
allusion in many places, but with remarkable publicity in *The Pall
Mall Miscellany*, the first edition of which was published on February
5, 1732. In this most topical and popular of miscellanies (it had
reached a fourth edition by the end of the month) is an anonymous
poem entitled, *The Six wanton Maids; or, the Amours of P. Alexis. A New
Ballad*, which unquestionably deals with the same people as Pope's

stanzas. The same six Maids of Honour are indicated, though, as the ballad is printed, their names are only hinted at by initial letters (or, at times, first and last letters); but, that there should be no mistake, their names are made doubly obvious by being placed at the ends of the lines as rhyme words; while the Prince himself figures as Alexis or P[rince] Alexis, as in most of the contemporary lampoons (*e.g.* 'Alexis was the Shepherd's Name, Of Royal Parents born. . .').

There is no evidence to suggest that Pope, who openly professed a 'disesteem of Kings', had any friendly regard for the Prince—or, indeed, any personal relations whatever with him—between the end of 1728 when he first came to England, and October 1735 when Pope was 'surprised by a favour of his royal highness, an unexpected visit of four or five hours' at his house at Twickenham.[1] But he seems, in the meantime, to have begun to regard the Prince with less and less enmity the nearer his Royal Highness drew to the Opposition party in parliament, and the wider grew the resultant breach between him and the King. Late in the following year, 1733, as shown in a subsequent chapter,[2] Pope wrote another poem in which the Prince (not to mention the rest of the royal family), though still shown to disadvantage, is not quite so bedevilled as in *The Six Maidens*. But it was not until the princely visit to Twickenham that any personal intercourse began to obtain between them; after which Pope presented the Prince with a dog, complete with epigram engraved on his collar, and later made a flattering allusion (hitherto unnoticed) to the 'Royal Youth' in a 'new' poem entitled, *Bounce to Fop*.[3] And it seems to have been still later that the Prince responded with his gift of urns or vases ('a choice of six small ones . . . or two large ones') for the poet's garden.[4]

At what stage in this progressive acquaintance Prince Frederick made his well-known challenge to Pope is not known; and from the accounts given it is impossible to tell. For who shall decide whether the dialogue that follows sounds the easy conversational tone of growing familiarity, or still retains the more formal note of exploratory approach? The story is best told in Walpole's brief record (there are other but less effective reports of the encounter) as follows:

'Oh! a story of Mr. Pope and the Prince:—"Mr. Pope, you don't love princes." "Sir, I beg your pardon." "Well, you don't love kings then!" "Sir, I own I love the lion best before his claws are grown." '[5]

[1] EC, VIII, p. 351.   [2] See *post*, p. 316.   [3] See *post*, p. 342.   [4] Ruffhead, p. 198.
[5] Letter to H. Mann, September 13, 1741. Walpole, I, pp. 102 f.

Pope's authorship of *The Six Maidens*, then, although the poem was never printed, is seen not as an exceptional, isolated, or even uncharacteristic act on the poet's part, but as a stage in the development of an acquaintance which could never have been expected by either party to arrive at the intimacy of real friendship. For when all is said, their association derived more from political necessity than from any unity of ideals, or even common principles of conduct.

It remains to add that as far as the Prince was concerned, there was in 1732 ample enough justification for such an attack, had Pope published this poem; for it was in that year, according to the public prints, that Miss Vane gave birth to a child of which the Prince of Wales was the acknowledged father. Indeed, as early as October 30, 1729, when the Prince was but twenty-two, Swift had written (but not published) some lines satirically addressed to the Poet Laureate, Eusden, which seem to have been prophetic:

> Now sing his little Highness Freddy,
> Who struts like any King already.
> With so much beauty, shew me any maid
> That could refuse this charming Ganymede.[1]

And in his 'Rapsody', *On Poetry*, published in 1733, he recognized what the Prince had already achieved in that way, and looked forward to greater things to come:

> Our eldest Hope, divine *Iülus*,
> (Late, very late, O, may he rule us.)
> What early Manhood has he shown,
> Before his downy Beard was grown!
> Then think, what Wonders will be done
> By going on as he begun.[2]

Swift and Pope often confided in each other about their work on hand, and knew what the other was doing; and it was notorious that they thought alike on many subjects; on the other hand in their miscellaneous verse they differed greatly, Swift very frequently, and Pope only rarely, touching on politics. Thus, while both seem to have had much the same opinion of the Prince of Wales, at least in these early days, Pope's treatment of the theme was quite unlike the Dean's, being social satire rather than political squib.

The scandal was at its height in 1732, when *The Six Maidens* was written, and the name of Miss Vane, or 'Vanella', was on everybody's lips. That in itself would explain why Pope, when quizzing the rest of

---

[1] *Directions for a Birth-day Song*; Williams, ɪɪ, p. 466.　　　[2] Lines 429–34.

the Maids of Honour, left her out so comically in his parenthesis—
'(I promis'd I never would mention Miss Vane)'. Nevertheless, while
few people of the early eighteenth century—or of any other period, for
that matter—were any better than they should have been, there is
little reason to suppose the other Maids were any worse; it is, however,
obvious that they suffered for—if not with—Miss Vane. For that
reason it is satisfactory to know that Pope refused to add to their
troubles, and that, however much or little warrant there was for the
scandal, it was at least neither a creature of Pope's imagination, nor
(happily) of his fostering, seeing that after writing these half dozen
stanzas of raillery, he so resolutely suppressed them that they have
remained, to all intents and purposes, unknown till the present day.

CHAPTER XVIII

ATTERBURY'S 'LAST WORDS'

IN spite of Dr Johnson's disparagement, Pope's epitaph on his old friend, Francis Atterbury, one time Bishop of Rochester, is in many ways extremely interesting. It challenges attention in the first place, by the unusual form in which it is cast, and, secondly, by the sympathy and insight revealed in its lines. And if, after reading it, its tragic undertones linger on in one's memory longer than some more famous pieces of the kind, that is probably due rather to the genuineness of the emotion it displays, than to its poetical merit—though that does not acquit Johnson of being unusually obtuse when he dismisses the epitaph with the brief remark: 'The contemptible *Dialogue* between HE and SHE should have been suppressed for the author's sake.'[1]

Though the Doctor did not know it, the piece had actually been suppressed—and very effectively too—by Pope himself as long as he was alive; but apparently not for the reasons which roused the critic's disdain. The epitaph claims a place in the present work, because two distinct but related problems are connected with its first and second printing, which, as their solution lets a little new light into one of the 'close corners' of Pope's mind, have a biographical as well as a bibliographical interest.

Atterbury, it will be remembered, died in exile in France on February 15, 1732; and Pope, writing to another old friend, John Caryll, on March 6, tells him of 'the death of our poor friend abroad, wᶜʰ has suggested to me many reflections on human Views and Infelicities.'[2] One of the results of these reflections was doubtless this epitaph, which, as first printed in 1735, runs thus:

XII.

For Dr. FRANCIS ATTERBURY,
Bishop of Rochester,

Who died in Exile at Paris, in 1732, [his only Daughter having expir'd in his Arms, immediately after she arrived in France to see him.]

---

[1] Johnson, IV, p. 239.
[2] Add. 28618. The word 'Views' is illegible; it might be 'Vowes'.

DIALOGUE.

SHE.   YES, we have liv'd—one pang, and then we part!
       May Heav'n, dear Father! now, have *all* thy Heart.
       Yet ah! how once we lov'd, remember still,
       Till you are Dust like me.

HE.

              Dear Shade! I will:
       Then mix this Dust with thine—O spotless Ghost!
       O more than Fortune, Friends, or Country lost!
       Is there on earth one Care, one Wish beside?
       Yes—*Save my Country, Heav'n,*
                 —He said, and dy'd.

An explanation of this highly unconventional epitaph is probably to be found in the two last letters Pope received from Atterbury. The earlier is dated 'Montpelier. November 20, 1729', and in moving terms tells of the recent death of his daughter:

> . . . I believe my cure had been perfected, but the earnest desire of meeting One I dearly loved, called me abruptly to Montpelier; where after continuing two months. . . I was forced at last to take a long journey to Toulouse; and even there I had miss'd the person I sought, had she not, with great spirit and courage, ventured all night up the Garonne to see me, which she above all things desired to do before she died. By that means she was brought where I was, between seven and eight in the morning, and liv'd twenty hours afterwards, which time was not lost on either side. . . For she had her senses to the very last gasp, and exerted them to give me, in those few hours, greater marks of Duty and Love than she had done in all her life time, tho' she had never been wanting in either. The last words she said to me were the kindest of all; a reflection on the goodness of God, which had allow'd us in this manner to meet once more, before we parted for ever. [1]

The last letter is dated 'Paris. November 23, 1731', about three months before he died; and in it, after alluding to his own death which at nearly seventy, he says, could not be far off ('Whenever I go, you will lose a friend who loves and values you extremely'), he goes on to ask for news from England; and then in the last paragraph bursts out with—

After all, I do and must love my country, with all its faults and

[1] Warburton, VIII, pp. 140 f.

blemishes. . . My last wish shall be like that of father Paul, *Esto perpetua!*[1]

There can be no doubt, that, when Pope heard of Atterbury's death, these two letters recurred to his mind, and (so it would seem) virtually dictated the dramatic form and content of the epitaph that eventually followed. But though presumably written about March 6, the *Dialogue* was neither inscribed on the monument, not was it allowed to escape into print; it was probably composed in part for his own consolation, and then later put on one side until such time as the second volume of his *Works* should be published. But before that could happen, or, more precisely, in 1733, Pope wrote his *Epistle to . . . Cobham* (the first 'Moral Essay')[2]; and it appears that when, towards its close, he was thinking of his friend's patriotism, the lines he had recently written on Atterbury's love for his country recurred to his mind, and as they were unpublished and unknown, and moreover extremely apposite to the poet's immediate purpose, he adapted them for the conclusion of the Epistle, thus:

> And you! brave *Cobham*, to the latest breath
> Shall feel your ruling passion strong in death:
> Such in those moments as in all the past,
> 'Oh, save my Country, Heav'n!' shall be your last.

Then, as now, it was normally the fate of small poems to await publication in an edition of their author's 'Collected Poetical Works', while major poems of length and importance were for the most part printed singly as and when written. It thus happened that conditions of publication were in a great measure responsible for Pope's first 'Moral Essay', 1733, becoming known to the public before the epitaph on Atterbury, though written later.

When, in 1735, Pope was preparing 'Volume II' of his *Works* for publication, he reprinted the *Epistle to Cobham* as the first of the 'Ethic Epistles, To Several Persons' (as the group was then called); and in the sixteen-page section devoted to 'Epitaphs' in the quarto edition he included—apparently in a fit of forgetfulness—the Atterbury *Dialogue* on page 15 as the twelfth and last of them (page 16, which faced the first page of *The Dunciad*, being left blank); and with this arrangement the volume appears to have gone to press. Between printing and publication, however, he cancelled the last leaf of the 'Epitaphs' sec-

---

[1] *The London Magazine*, Dec. 1734, pp. 635 f.

[2] The poem is dated 1733, the year it was written and printed, but it was not actually published until January 16, 1734.

tion, with the result that in all the copies of the quarto examined by the present writer, the section ends with 'Epitaph XI' (the famous couplet on Newton) at the foot of page 14, followed by the stub of the cut-out leaf (pages 15–16) which still shows where the Atterbury epitaph had for so short a time been placed. One sole copy of the cancelled leaf seems to have survived, and this has been inserted comparatively recently in the British Museum copy of the 1735 quarto,[1] in its original position.

Now the folio and quarto editions of *The Works,* ... *Volume II,* 1735, purport to be the same book, both in contents and arrangement; nevertheless, as must have been frequently remarked before, the last of the quarto 'Epitaphs' (No. XI, the Newton couplet) is not found in the folio, where the corresponding section ends on page 12 with 'Epitaph X' ('On Mr. Gay').[2] And the only reasonable hypothesis to cover all the known facts is that the folio likewise underwent some change between printing and publication. It is not improbable therefore, that, as originally set up and printed, the Atterbury *Dialogue* followed the Newton couplet in the folio also, in which case they must, of course, have occupied the same leaf; and that when the Atterbury piece was excluded, the Newton couplet of necessity went with it. Some copies of the folio may show a stub at that place, but it is not likely, as the leaf was probably a single leaf at the end of the section.

But obviously these bibliographical details are not the whole of the story. For when a famous poet, like Pope, publishes more or less simultaneously a much heralded second volume of his *Works* in folio and quarto, the one excluding, and the other including, a certain poem—which poem, moreover, had been published elsewhere years before,[3] and was afterwards always incorporated in his works both by himself and later by his editors—something remains to be said by way of explanation.

On a review of all the evidence, there can be little doubt that what brought about this discrepancy between folio and quarto was a sudden, eleventh-hour realization by Pope, that, in a collection of his most important recent works, barely a score in number, he was about to present a startled world with two poems having the same ending.

---

[1] See C. D. Sherborn, *Athenaeum,* April 13, 1907.

[2] In both editions the 'Epitaphs' run: I Trumbal; II Dorset; III Harcourt; IV Rowe; V Corbet; VI Digby; VII Kneller; VIII Withers; IX Fenton; X Gay; to which only the Quarto adds, XI Newton; as noted by Griffith, I, ii, pp. 281, 287.

[3] Newton's epitaph was first published in *The Present State of the Republick of Letters. For June, 1730. Vol. V.* 1730.

How that would have delighted Grub-street! At any cost—no matter what the trouble and expense of cancellation may be—that must be avoided. Worse still, was the thought, that, in addition to pleasing his enemies, there was at the same time the question of offending his friends. With the epitaph having obviously been written first (for Atterbury had died in February, 1732), it would be the worst of gaucheries thus to prophesy publicly in the epistle that his much admired Lord Cobham would, on his death-bed, be reduced to use his 'latest breath' merely to repeat, parrot-like, the bishop's dying remark. Nor would it be any palliative to suggest that the epistle was composed—as well as printed—before the epitaph; for when Cobham read the epistle in manuscript some three months before it was published, he had written to Pope about the compliment at the end, first acknowledging it with a little appropriate hesitation, then very definitely and proudly making it his own, in the following words:

> Stowe, Nov. 1, 1733.
>
> Though I have not modesty enough not to be pleased with your extraordinary compliment, I have wit enough to know how little I deserve it . . . But I am afraid I shall not pass for an absolute patriot. However, I have the honour of having received a public testimony of your esteem and friendship, and am as proud of it as I could be of any advantage which could happen to me. . . Thank you; and believe me to be most sincerely yours,
>
> Cobham.[1]

After that, how could Pope cheapen his compliment by admitting that it had been paid to another the year before? Small wonder, therefore, if he eliminated the minor piece even at the sacrifice of uniformity in the quarto and folio volumes; or if he continued for the rest of his life to refuse it a place in the later editions of his works, when other poems were being added to them from time to time.

Thus it was that, except for the cancelled leaf of the 1735 quarto (if not the folio also), the epitaph on Atterbury remained unprinted and unknown until 1751, when—Pope and Cobham having died also—it was at last included by Warburton in 'Volume VI' of his 'complete' edition of *The Works of Alexander Pope Esq.*

---

[1] Ruffhead, p. 275.

CHAPTER XIX

THE END OF DENNIS

IF time robs us of our friends, it also delivers us from our enemies. Less than two years after the death of his old friend, Atterbury, Pope heard of the pitiable end of his still older enemy, Dennis, whose persistent hostility to him had been such an important factor in his life and work. The usual account of their interminable quarrel is—at least as regards its main action—well-founded; but it begins in mystery and ends in misrepresentation, and calls for some restatement at both extremes. An attempt to explain the origin of their antagonism has already been made elsewhere[1] by the writer; what remains to do in the present chapter is to retell the close of the story in the light of much new evidence.

That the conclusion of the famous quarrel was due to something more than Dennis's death has long been known; for all Pope readers since the middle of the eighteenth century have been familiar with a poem, entitled, *A Prologue By Mr. Pope, To a Play for Mr. Dennis's Benefit, in 1733, when he was old, blind, and in great Distress, a little before his Death*. This piece was first attributed to Pope by Warburton in 1751, the year in which it is generally supposed to have been first printed. It had, however, been published anonymously ten years earlier,[2] in Pope's lifetime and therefore, presumably, with his consent, under a less expansive title, as follows:

PROLOGUE,
For the Benefit of Mr. Dennis, *1733*.

> As when that Hero, who in each Campaign
> Had brav'd the *Goth*, and many a *Vandal* slain,
> Lay Fortune-struck, a Spectacle of Woe!
> Wept by each Friend, forgiv'n by ev'ry Foe:
> Was there a gen'rous, a reflecting Mind,
> But pitied *Belisarius*, old and blind?
> Was there a Chief, but melted at the Sight?
> A common Soldier, but who clubb'd his *Mite*?

---

[1] See Pope's *Prose*, I, pp. xii ff.
[2] In *The Publick Register; or, The Weekly Magazine*. No. III, January 17, 1741.

Such, such Emotions should in *Britons* rise,
When prest by Want and Weakness, *Dennis* lies;
Dennis, who long had warr'd with modern *Huns*,
Their Quibbles routed, and defy'd their Puns;
A desp'rate *Bulwark*, sturdy, firm, and fierce,
Against the *Gothick* Sons of frozen Verse;
How chang'd from him, who made the Boxes groan,
And shook the Stage with Thunders all his own!
Stood up to dash each vain Pretender's Hope,
Maul the *French* Tyrant, or pull down the Pope!
If there's a *Briton*, then, true bred and born,
Who holds Dragoons and Wooden Shoes in scorn;
If there's a Critick of distinguish'd Rage;
If there's a Senior, who contemns this age;
Let him to-Night his just Assistance lend,
And be the Critick's, *Briton*'s, Old Man's Friend.

The first of the many remarkable things about this poem is that it should have been written at all; for it poses the question—Why did Pope, who had exchanged attack and counter-attack with Dennis as late as—if not later than—1729,[1] and who, since 1718, had steadily refused to write prologues and epilogues for friends and acquaintances alike (always excepting Gay[2]), suddenly produce a piece of this sort for his oldest and most inveterate enemy? The need of an explanation led to a search through the news-sheets of the period; but though these do not throw much light on the question (indeed, they rather darken the mystery if anything), they do supply some new and interesting information about the occasion itself. For example, although the function attracted a lot of attention one way and another, nothing was heard of it in the public prints until four days before it took place, when a bare announcement was made in two dailies[3] simultaneously, thus:

On Tuesday the 18th Inst. will be presented a Comedy, call'd, The Provok'd Husband . . . For the Benefit of Mr. John Dennis.

Both papers reprinted this notice the next day, and the *Journal* again on Monday; besides which a longer advertisement giving more par-

---

[1] See *The Dunciad* A, I, l. 104; II, ll. 231, 271-7; III, l. 167, and elsewhere; and Dennis's *Remarks upon . . . the Dunciad*, and also (if Pope is correct), *Pope Alexander's Supremacy*.

[2] See *ante*, pp. 209-10.

[3] *The Daily Journal*, and *The Daily Post*, for Friday, Dec. 14, 1733.

ticulars appeared on Saturday and Monday elsewhere[1]; but none says anything about a Prologue, or mentions Pope's name. Then, on the day itself, the first two papers mentioned above printed what amounts to a detailed programme of the performance, in the following manner:

> For the Benefit of Mr. John Dennis.
> By the Company of Comedians of His Majesty's Revels,
> At the New Theatre in the Haymarket, this present Tuesday,
> being the 18th of December, will be presented a Comedy, call'd
> The Provok'd Husband: Or, A Journey to London . . .
> [The cast follows and includes 'Mr. Cibber' as 'Count Basset']
> With a New Prologue.
> To which will be added, an Impromptu Revel Masque,
> called The Festival . . .[2]

Two days later, the success of the 'benefit' performance was reported in these words:

> There was an exceeding crowded Audience of Persons of Distinction last Tuesday Night at Mr. Dennis's Benefit, and his Royal Highness the Prince of Wales was pleased to send twenty Guineas as a present to that Gentleman.[3]

But in addition to announcements, advertisements, and news reports, several Grub Street versifiers rushed to supply poetical comment on certain aspects of the occasion, two of them in anticipation of the appointed day. The first (and the more important for our purpose) contains the only mention of Pope's name in any contemporary report or notice of the affair, and this only in so equivocal a fashion that it is impossible to say exactly what the verse means.

> Epigram. Occasion'd by the Interest that has been made,
> for a splendid Appearance of Ladies, at the Haymarket Theatre,
> on Tuesday next, for the Benefit of Mr. Dennis.
>
> Where gen'rous *Morals* curb vindictive *Wit*,
> Till *P—e* forgives, what angry *D——s* writ;
> And, hem'd with *Beauties*, in the *Critick's* Cause,
> Half the gay Town, to grace his Circle, draws:
> Pleas'd, we revolve the Scene, with just Surprize;
> And *hail* the *Golden Age*, that seems to rise:

---

[1] *The Daily Post-Boy,* for Dec. 15 and 17.
[2] *The Daily Journal* for Dec. 18.
[3] *The General Evening Post* for Dec. 18–20.

When *Lambs* wou'd Thorns, from wounded *Lyons*, draw,
And smile—*assistant* to the *pressive* Paw![1]

As regards Pope, the suggestion seems to be that he had not only 'for-given' his old enemy, but was proposing to bring 'Half the gay Town' with him to Dennis's 'benefit'.

The second piece (of little merit and no bearing on our inquiry) made its first appearance in *The Daily Courant* for December 17, where its title ran thus:

The following Lines were occasioned by the free Gift of a Benefit to Mr. Dennis, by the Company of his Majesty's Revels.

Unask'd, though pitying Players grant . . .

This tribute was reprinted in several other papers, one of which,[2] in turn, printed an answer, entitled, *Verses occasioned by those on the free gift of a benefit to Mr. Dennis . . . in the Daily-Courant Dec. 17*. Two days later still, there appeared in two papers simultaneously[3] a poem of fourteen lines, addressed to James Thomson, the poet, and signed 'J.D.', which, though it purports to have been written by Dennis, was shortly afterwards stated to be the work of Richard Savage. As first printed, its title and its opening and closing lines run thus:

VERSES, To Mr. *Thomson*, on occasion of the Part which
that Gentleman took, in the Concern for
Mr. *Dennis*'s last Benefit.

While I reflect thee o'er, methinks, I find
Thy various *Seasons*, in their Author's mind! . . .

'Spring', 'Summer', and 'Autumn' are then successively likened to Thomson's character and work, but not 'Winter', which is declared to be the image of Dennis himself; and the piece ends with these lines:

Shatter'd by Time's bleak Storms, I with'ring lay,
Leafless, and whit'ning, in a cold Decay.
Yet shall my propless *Ivy*,—pale and bent,
Bless the short Sunshine, which thy Pity lent.[4]

This poem was reprinted in a number of papers during the next fort-night, and was still appearing here and there, when, on Tuesday, January 8, 1734, *The St. James's Evening Post* announced:

[1] *The Daily Journal* for Dec. 15.
[2] *The Grub-street Journal* for Dec. 20.
[3] *The General Evening Post*, and *The Daily Journal*, for Dec. 22.
[4] *The General Evening Post*, Dec. 22, 1733.

On Sunday Night last died, that celebrated Critick Mr. John
Dennis, in the 85th Year of his Age. He had a Benefit Play given
him about three Weeks ago by the Players at the Hay-Market.

Several other obituaries appeared elsewhere the same day, and still
more during the rest of the week, some in praise, others in disparagement, but most of them non-committal; and of them all not more than
two or three mention the recent 'benefit', and these only in the briefest
possible manner, like the above. Next, Aaron Hill's *Verses on the Death
of Mr. Dennis*, in which the critic's excellences are found to outweigh
his faults and no allusion is made to the 'benefit', appeared in the
newspapers,[1] and, as usual, was reprinted in the magazines and other
places. And that, in turn, was followed the same year (1734) by *The
Life of Mr. John Dennis* with a title-page semi-jocularly stating—'Not
written by Mr. Curll'[2]; after which, except for an occasional reference
by Pope and others, Dennis may be said to have finally vanished from
the eighteenth-century scene.

This anonymous *Life*, whatever it may have contributed to the
story of his works and days, adds little to our knowledge of Dennis's
last 'benefit'. Indeed, all it has to say is contained in the following
paragraph, which tells how—

within a few Months of his Death, when falling into great Infirmities
both in his Person and Purse, he met with an unexpected Relief
from the Religious Society of Players in the *Hay-market*, who on the
18th of December last, acted the *Provoked Husband*, or a *Journey to
London*, for his Benefit, which put about a hundred Pounds in his
Pocket. Some Gentleman, who it seems writes Verses in Imitation
of *Milton*, we have not yet learnt his Name [it was, of course, James
Thomson], was very generous in supporting his Interest in this
Affair, and another Gentleman was as generous in writing a Copy
of Verses, in Mr. Dennis's Name, to thank him, which he himself
never saw; but hearing them mention'd, after they were printed,
and getting a Friend to read them to him, he swore *by G—, they
could be no one but that Fool* S[avage]'s . . . Thus did this poor Gentleman maintain his Humour to the last.[3]

At this stage it should be emphasized that, in spite of a quite considerable amount of public attention and interest, which, as we have

---

[1] First printed in *The Daily Journal* for Jan. 15.

[2] It was Curll's inevitable 'Lives' which only the previous year had made
Arbuthnot call him 'one of the new terrors of death'; Ball, IV, 378.

[3] *The Life of Mr. John Dennis*, pp. 57–8.

seen, attached to Dennis's benefit, there was no hint, announcement or comment of any kind regarding a prologue to the performance, written or spoken, in any of the contemporary notices, excepting only the bare mention of one in the Tuesday's programme-advertisement given above. And what makes this omission still more puzzling is that it occurred at a time when prologues and epilogues, printed at full length, were a frequent and welcome feature of the periodical press.[1] Furthermore, when it is remembered that Pope was then at the zenith of his fame and universally recognized as the greatest living English poet, the complete absence of his name (except once as a prospective patron) from every known reference to the 'benefit', while at the same time lesser names like Thomson and Savage appeared repeatedly, becomes one of the most puzzling of the Pope problems still unsolved.

Now the growth of a legend is an interesting phenomenon at any time, but especially so when the separate stages of accretion can be distinguished, as in the story of the Pope-Dennis 'reconciliation'. Thus, if we may judge from contemporary accounts, so far from the 'benefit' giving rise to the full-blown legend which has come down to us, nothing exceptional or noteworthy happened to make the performance memorable, or was remembered twelve months later; and several more years had to elapse before an anonymous *Prologue* was published in 1741, claiming some connection with the long by-gone occasion. But this belated printing is no proof that the verse had been spoken at the performance, for the 1741 title neither says it was spoken, nor states (as was customary) the name of the speaker. As we have seen, Pope died in 1744 without acknowledging the *Prologue*, and neither Ayre's *Memoirs* in 1745, nor the *Biographia Britannica* in 1750, mentions it or its occasion, and it was not until 1751, when Warburton gave the piece to Pope in the long and detailed title already given, that the legend began to grow.

The first development is found in *The Lives of the Poets*,[2] 1753, thus:

> When he [Dennis] was near the close of his days, a play was acted for his benefit. This favour was procured him by the joint interest of Mr. Thomson, Mr. Martin, Mr. Mallet, and Mr. Pope.

---

[1] For example, the present writer counted nine printings of at least five different prologues and epilogues in only a portion of the periodical press for December 1733 and January 1734; amongst them being a 'Prologue and Epilogue spoke . . . at the Benefit of Mrs. Wilks' early in December.

[2] Commonly called 'Cibber's Lives of the Poets' (i.e. Theophilus Cibber), but, with the exception of three 'Lives', wholly written by R. Shiels, and largely revised by Cibber. See D. Nichol Smith, in Raleigh's *Six Essays on Johnson*, pp. 124 f.

The play was given by the company then acting at the little Theatre in the Hay-market, under the direction of Mr. Mills sen. and Mr. Cibber jun. the latter of whom spoke a prologue on the occasion, written by Mr. Pope.[1]

This story was repeated, with some modification and expansion, in Baker's *Companion to the Play-House*, 1764, which says that the 'benefit' was—

procured thro' the united Interests of Messrs. Thomson, Mallet, and Pope, the last of whom, notwithstanding the gross Manner in which Mr. Dennis had on many Occasions us'd him, . . . interested himself very warmly for him, and even wrote an occasional Prologue to the Play, which was spoken by Mr. Cibber, jun.[2]

A new edition of *The Companion* in 1782, newly entitled *Biographia Dramatica*, repeated the 1764 story, but added the first of the sneers at Pope's 'generosity', as well as an apocryphal glimpse of Dennis in the theatre on the 'benefit' night, close on half a century after the event, as follows:

. . . Yet our admiration of Mr. Pope's generosity will be somewhat abated, when we recollect that this boasted prologue was designed throughout as a sneer on Dennis. His vanity, however, was so strong, or his intellects were become so enfeebled, that he did not perceive its tendency, though he stood behind the scenes and heard it delivered. Indeed as Count Basset says, this was an act of most 'unmerciful mercy' in the author of the Dunciad, whose charity, on the present occasion at least, was dispensed with a cynic hand.[3]

Next, the *Biographia Britannica*, which in 1766 had again omitted all mention of the story, makes amends in its new edition of 1793, and, citing the 1753 and 1782 accounts (given above), together with Warburton's title of the *Prologue*, as its authorities, elaborates the legend a little more, brings back 'Mr. Benjamin Martin' into it again; ousts Pope as chief helper in favour of 'Mr. Thomson, who had taken the most active part in that affair'; includes for the first time the *Verses* (supposed to be 'written by Mr. Savage', though purporting to be by Dennis) thanking Thomson for all he had done; and, to end with, copies the recently inserted sneer at Pope whose 'benevolence was not so pure as could be wished' . . . With this account, published exactly sixty years after the occasion, the legend of Pope's *Prologue, For the Benefit of Mr. Dennis, 1733,* reached its fullest development, and

---

[1] Vol. IV, pp. 237 f.   [2] *The Companion*, Vol. II.
[3] *Biographia Dramatica*, Vol. I.

in this form was more or less closely repeated in later editions or new works. One example will suffice, namely, Genest's well-known work, *Some Account of the English Stage (1660–1830)*, 1832, which merely reprints the account from *Biographia Britannica*, 1793, practically word for word, and is sometimes cited as the authority for the whole story!

The strongest argument against the authenticity of all these later accretions to the legend is found in the fact that there was no word or whisper of any of them between Dennis's 'benefit' in 1733, and the first attribution of the *Prologue* to Pope nearly twenty years later. Moreover, as shown in the following chapter, from the time that Colley Cibber became Poet Laureate, late in 1730, the *tempo* of the old Pope-Cibber quarrel quickened—at least on Pope's side,—and in his satirical allusions to the father, Pope not infrequently included the son, 'Cibber jun',[1] whom we have met as the alleged speaker of the *Prologue* on the night of the benefit. It would thus have been only human (and the Cibbers were very human) for the son to have blown upon Pope's concealed authorship by way of retaliation, either on his father's behalf or his own. And that he did not reveal Pope's secret for so many years (if ever) seems to argue, not that he wished to save Pope from annoyance, but that he knew nothing about the *Prologue*— which, in turn, would appear to confirm the evidence of the newspapers that the *Prologue* was either not spoken on the benefit night, or was anonymous. Whether Shiels alone was responsible for the article on Dennis in the *Lives* (which, as shown above, first brought 'Cibber jun.' into the tale), or whether 'Cibber jun.' had any hand in it, is not —and probably never will be—known. But any unsponsored report made for the first time twenty years after the event needs very definite documentation to be preferred to the many and unanimous witnesses in immediate print—and trustworthy evidence is exactly what is lacking in support of these later additions to the legend.

Students, observant of a hint of Warburton's, have long supposed that Pope alluded to this *Prologue* in his *Epistle to Arbuthnot*,[2] which was written in the following year, 1734. For when Warburton printed the *Prologue* in 1751,[3] he appended to its sixth line a footnote which ended by quoting the couplet from the *Epistle*, thus:

With so much mastery has the Poet executed, in this benevolent irony, that which he supposed Dennis himself, had he the wit to see, would have the ingenuity [to] own:
>   This dreaded Sat'rist, Dennis will confess,
>   Foe to his pride, but *Friend* to his Distress.

---

[1] See *post*, p. 319.   [2] *Epistle to Arbuthnot*, ll. 370–1.   [3] Vol. VI, p. 66.

And the usual interpretation is, that, since the poet was referring to himself as the 'Sat'rist', it was by supplying the *Prologue* for Dennis's 'benefit' that Pope showed himself to be 'Friend to his Distress'.

But leaving that point for the moment, the chief conclusion to be drawn from the foregoing pages is that, whether Pope was instrumental in taking 'half the gay Town' with him to Dennis's 'benefit' or not, his name was certainly not connected with the 'New Prologue' at the time, even supposing it was the one he had written. For, it may be repeated, the 'benefit' took place at one of the busiest and most important periods of his career, at a time when his fame dwarfed that of every other living writer, when, as mentioned earlier, anything from his pen was news as well as literature, and when such a piquant situation as Pope trying to conciliate his ancient enemy, Dennis, would have been admiringly canvassed or acidly commented on wherever friends or foes chanced to meet. It would therefore seem that the only alternative to Pope's anonymity in the matter would be a universal conspiracy of silence, which—as it did not include the occasion itself, or the rest of Pope's works and acts—is absurd. This desire for anonymity (whatever the reason for it) was further manifested in the first printing of the *Prologue* in 1741, when Dodsley was allowed to publish it in his new magazine only if he omitted Pope's name; for Dodsley was a young publisher whom Pope liked and helped from time to time, and this unlucky venture of his (it did not last six months) might have had more chance of success, had Pope not felt it essential to withhold his name from his occasional contributions to it.[1]

Returning now to the couplet from the *Epistle to Arbuthnot*: there is, of course, little point in a poet alluding to matters incomprehensible to all his readers. If, therefore, we accept the foregoing evidence, that, on the occasion of Dennis's benefit, Pope thought it imperative to conceal his connection with the *Prologue*, it is extremely unlikely that he would have publicly—if tacitly—admitted his authorship of it in this couplet only a few months later, and then, for the rest of his life, unwaveringly refuse to acknowledge it. Yet Pope's couplet must have had some meaning for somebody; and, on a review of all the known facts, it seems virtually certain that the poet was alluding to certain earlier activities of his on Dennis's behalf, of which a glimpse is caught in his correspondence with Aaron Hill.

In 1731, during one of Dennis's earlier periods of distress, there was some talk of republishing several of his works by subscription. This

---

[1] Pope contributed four anonymous poems to the first three numbers of *The Publick Register*.

project seems to have reached Pope's ears very quickly, if, indeed, he was not partly responsible for it; for on January 26, 1731, when writing to Hill he remarked in passing, 'If I could do Mr. *Dennis* any humane Office, I would, tho' I were sure he would abuse me personally To-morrow.'[1] To which Hill made answer, that a man as popular as Pope might secure Dennis a great subscription, and continued: 'This would merit to be called a *Service*'.[2] And Pope in reply wrote on February 5 as follows:

> I nam'd Mr. *Dennis*, because . . . he was uppermost in my Thoughts, from having endeavour'd (*before* your Admonition) to promote his Affair, with Lord *Wilmington*, Lord *Lansdown*, Lord *Blandford*, and Mr. *Pulteney*. &c. who promis'd me to favour it. But it would be unjust to measure my Good-will by the Effects of it on the Great, many of whom are the last Men in the World who will pay Tributes of this sort, from their own un-giving Nature; and many of whom laugh at me when I seriously petition for Mr. *Dennis*. After this, I must not name the many whom I have fruitlesly sollicited: I hope yet to be more successful. But, Sir, you seem too iniquitous . . . when you fansy I call'd such Things *Services*. I call'd 'em but *humane Offices*: Services I said I *would* render him, *if I could*. I *would* ask a Place for Life for him; and I *have*; but that is not in my Power: If it was, it would be a *Service*, and I wish it.
>
> I mention'd the *Possibility* of Mr. *D[ennis]*'s abusing me for forgiving him, because he actually did, in Print, lately represent my poor, undesigning Subscriptions to him, to be the Effect of Fear, and Desire, to stop his Critiques upon me.[3]

Unfortunately, that particular scheme, it appears, was not so zealously supported by Dennis's friends as by his quondam enemy, and was heard of no more. But although it failed, Pope's efforts on behalf of the old critic had been sincere enough, and protracted enough, to prove him beyond all cavil or sneer a 'Friend to his Distress'. And, whether Dennis ever did 'confess' it or not, quite a lot of people—including those who had laughed at Pope's efforts to help him—must have remembered, on reading the couplet, the service to which it alluded.

It appears, then, that there are two things about the *Prologue*, and two only, which can be said to be virtually established: the first being Pope's authorship of it, for which we have the testimony of his literary executor, and much internal evidence besides; and the second, the

[1] *Letters . . . to . . . Hill*, 1751, p. 39.   [2] *Ibid.*, p. 44.   [3] *Ibid.*, pp. 8 f.
u

date of composition, which, as the subject of the poem and its last couplet together indicate, can have preceded the occasion it purports to celebrate by only a matter of days. The rest is little more than a deduction from the facts: for whether Pope was asked to write a prologue, or volunteered to furnish one on condition that his name was kept secret; or whether, prompted by the occasion, he simply sat down one day and wrote it in an absurd mood and an odd half-hour for a strictly limited circle of friends (as he had done with other verses so often before)—we shall probably never know. Whatever the impulse, it would not have been surprising if some touches of harshness or rancour, effects of their long and bitter animosity, had been perceptible in these lines—or between them. But where Pope's detractors, having unquestioningly assumed the legend to be true, have found in the *Prologue* chiefly sneers at the old man's misfortune, an unbiased reader may see only evidence of Pope's genuine (if tardily evoked) goodwill, tempered here and there characteristically enough by a little kindly banter. He will also remember that Dennis's death, which, following so soon after his 'benefit', might seem to add to the poignancy of the whole affair, could not have been foreseen by Pope, any more than by others. It was only natural, therefore, when he set himself to write the *Prologue*, that his thoughts should hark back to his first experiences of Dennis's bullying attacks on his work, his family, and himself, to such effect, that, in mood and style, and even phraseology, the poem echoes his versification of those early eager years, as seen in the *Prologue to Cato*, for example, and, more particularly, the lines on *Argus* whose very cadences are repeated more than once.

In conclusion, then, the story of the poem, which takes cognizance of all the known evidence, and most nearly approximates to the truth, may be summarized thus: The *Prologue, For the Benefit of Mr. Dennis* was no exceptional phenomenon either as a conciliatory move on Pope's part, or as a specimen of his unofficial and anonymous verse on topical or contemporaneous affairs, many examples of which are to be found elsewhere in the present work. Secondly, the piece was written on the occasion of Dennis's 'benefit', and not improbably was offered to the management in some roundabout way that did not reveal Pope's connection with it; after which it was either spoken at the performance as the work of 'an unknown hand', or for reasons not manifest, withdrawn before it could be printed or spoken—for only thus, or thus, does it appear possible for the *Prologue* to have escaped newspaper report and popular gossip alike, and remain for years unknown to all but (possibly) a few of Pope's intimates. Thirdly, the desire, or necessity, which induced Pope to conceal his name in 1733, was still operative when he refused the *Prologue* a place in the second volume of his *Works* in 1735, and again and again in the subsequent octavo reprints, and still operative when, in 1741, he forbade Dodsley to ascribe the lines to him on their first printing; the total result being that the secret outlasted Pope's life. And finally, when the poem at length became known as Pope's, and, in addition, was furnished with a long explanatory title, *then* it was, and not before, that people began to get busy with gossip, invention, and moral judgements, and little by little so expanded and twisted the story of Dennis's last benefit, that Pope's good-humoured sympathy—whether publicly or privately expressed—has ever since been misjudged, and his amiable gesture regarded as little or nothing more than a heartless triumph over a fallen foe.

CHAPTER XX

POPE AND CIBBER

I. FICTION—AND FACT

CIBBER's piecemeal story of the quarrel between him and Pope, how it began and why, and by whom it was continued, has always been accepted hitherto as a more or less truthful statement, if, perhaps, a little highly coloured. And because Pope never directly alluded to the cause of the quarrel, so far as is known, and rarely commented on its prosecution, his silence has only too often been regarded as a tacit confession that he had no case to present, and, therefore, a corroboration of Cibber's tale. The recent identification by the present writer of Pope as the author of a poem which arose out of the quarrel has led on to a fresh examination of the relevant facts, with results that call for a restatement of the whole conflict.

As is generally known, the year 1717 saw the performance at Drury Lane of a comedy, nominally by John Gay, entitled *Three Hours after Marriage*,[1] and, shortly afterwards, the publication of the play.[2] The title-page displays no author's name; but it is followed by an 'Advertisement', signed by Gay, acknowledging 'the Assistance I have receiv'd in this Piece from two of my Friends; who . . . will not allow me the honour of having their names join'd with mine'. The secret of his collaborating friends—who, of course, were Pope and Arbuthnot—was not well kept[3]: their names were guessed before the play was published, and widely known afterwards. For although the comedy was withdrawn after the seventh performance (in spite of much support),[4] it created a great stir, and for various reasons managed to offend a number of people. The 'Marriage' of the title, which is supposed to have taken place immediately before the curtain rises, is that of an elderly pseudo-scientist, Dr Fossile, and a young woman of the town who has deceived him into thinking her a maid. The play is full of farcical incidents, the most bizarre occurring in the third act, in which two former lovers of the bride, who have contrived to be deposited in a museum in the doctor's house, one disguised as a mummy, the other as a crocodile, 'come alive' after he has locked her

[1] Produced January 16, 1717.   [2] Published January 21, 1717 (*The Daily Courant*).
[3] See *ante*, p. 25.
[4] See Irving (p. 156), who argues that the play was not a failure, as is generally supposed.

(as he thinks) alone in the same room. Although there were many other things in the play—such as the satirizing of Dr Woodward, Arbuthnot's professional rival, and of John Dennis, Pope's old critic and enemy—to which exception was perhaps not unreasonably taken; it was the scene in the museum that attracted most attention and ridicule, and was ultimately the cause of the quarrel between Pope and Cibber—according to Cibber, whose artfully artless tale runs in effect as follows.

On February 7, 1717, a fortnight after *Three Hours after Marriage* had been withdrawn, Cibber, at the command of the Prince of Wales, put on a revival of *The Rehearsal* 'which had lain some Years dormant', and in which 'the Part of *Bays* fell to [his] share'. And it being in the tradition of the stage to allow that character to 'gag' at will about current theatrical matters, Cibber says he merely followed the custom 'as usual', with results which he goes on to describe thus:

I, Mr. *Bays*, when the two Kings of *Brentford* came from the Clouds into the Throne again, instead of what my Part directed me to say, made use of these Words, viz. 'Now, Sir, this Revolution, I had some Thoughts of introducing, by a quite different Contrivance; but my Design taking air, some of your sharp Wits, I found, had made use of it before me; otherwise I intended to have stolen one of them in, in the Shape of a *Mummy*, and t'other, in that of a *Crocodile*'. Upon which . . . the Audience by the Roar of their Applause shew'd their proportionable Contempt of the Play they belong'd to . . . Surely to have used the bare Word *Mummy*, and *Crocodile*, was neither unjust, or unmannerly; Where then was the Crime of simply saying there had been two such things in a former Play? But this, it seems, was so heinously taken by Mr. *Pope*, that, in the swelling of his Heart, after the Play was over, he came behind the Scenes, with his Lips pale and his Voice trembling, to call me to account for the Insult: And accordingly fell upon me with all the foul Language, that a Wit out of his Senses could be capable of . . . When he was almost choked with the foam of his Passion, I was enough recover'd from my Amazement to make him (as near as I can remember) this Reply, viz. 'Mr. *Pope*—You are so particular a Man, that I must be asham'd to return your Language as I ought to do: but since you have attacked me in so monstrous a Manner; This you may depend upon, that as long as the Play continues to be acted, I will never fail to repeat the same Words over and over again.'[1]

[1] *A Letter*, pp. 18–19.

It was Cibber's insistence, he says, on repeating this gag in all subsequent performances of *The Rehearsal* (they were probably not many), that was the cause of Pope's animosity against him, and, ultimately, of his elevation to the throne of the Dunces. But Cibber's account was not written until 1742, and, presumably, from memory at that[1]; which may explain in part its divergences from a contemporary report of the affair in a letter from Montagu Bacon to James Montagu, first printed in 1909,[2] as follows:

> I don't know whether you heard, before you went out of town, that *The Rehearsal* was revived. . . Cibber interlarded it with several things in ridicule of the last play, upon which Pope went up to him and told him he was a rascal, and if he were able he would cane him; that his friend Gay was a proper fellow, and if he went on in his sauciness he might expect such a reception from him. The next night Gay came accordingly, and, treating him as Pope had done the night before, Cibber very fairly gave him a fillip on the nose, which made them both roar. The Guards came and parted them, and carried away Gay, and so ended this poetical scuffle.

The strange thing about the affair is that no account of the frail diminutive Pope confronting the sturdy Cibber seems ever to have reached the newspapers, though they were at that moment avid of news or gossip about the extraordinary farce and the most famous of its three authors; while, on the contrary, Gay's battle of fisticuffs with the actor-manager is recorded in more than one sheet, with the victory usually given to Gay. Here, then, is another reason why Cibber's story of the cause of the quarrel can no longer be wholly trusted; and, if not, it automatically follows that the rest of the pamphlet, of which it forms part, becomes likewise suspect—a point to which we shall return. In the meantime it should be noted that the pamphlet in question is entitled—*A Letter from Mr. Cibber, to Mr. Pope, Inquiring into the Motives that might induce him in his Satyrical Works, to be so frequently fond of Mr. Cibber's Name*, 1742.

The foregoing is all the evidence on which has been built up the legend about the beginning of the Pope-Cibber quarrel. And from the same sources is derived the allegation, that, with no further transgression on Cibber's part, Pope from that day onwards carried on a literary vendetta against the Cibber family, never forgiving or for-

---

[1] 'My Memory, from which Repository alone, every Article of what I write is collected . . .' *Apology*, p. 267.

[2] Paston, I, p. 197.

getting his ridiculous grievance year after year, until at last his good-humoured, inoffensive victim was compelled (as he said) by 'several Persons of Quality' to counter-attack in his *Letter*. Thus Cibber, confessing one small sin against his persecutor, gained credence for his story, and so contributed his share to the early propagation of the fable of Pope's fundamental malevolence of character, still current in some quarters.

For a few students, however, the accepted story has always seemed a little inadequate—too much like the parable of the carelessly flung pebble that precipitated the avalanche—because it wholly fails to explain why such disproportionate retribution was already hanging in such delicate equipoise above the house of Cibber. Something had been left out of the tale—forgotten perhaps, or suppressed—wanting which the rest loses its meaning. Nevertheless, on re-reading *A Letter*, it appears that although Cibber has wilfully concealed the truth in one part, he has after all revealed it in another—quite unconsciously, for his way of telling his story shows him to have been incapable of understanding its significance or even perceiving that it had any at all. The clue is to be found in that queasy tale, to which most of Pope's biographers more or less fastidiously allude, of a certain evening he had spent in Cibber's company some two years before the 'mummy and crocodile' incident.

The story itself, which constitutes the most important attack on Pope in the whole *Letter*, is stated to be a requital in kind for a line he had written no less than eight years previously—'And has not Colly still his Lord, and Whore?'[1] With that as an excuse, Cibber proceeds to record with obvious gusto, how, late in 1714 or early in 1715, when Pope 'had not translated above two or three Books of *Homer*', he and two friends (Lord Warwick and 'another Gentleman') had met the young poet one evening, apparently at Button's Coffee-house, all probably a little drunk, and thereupon had conspired together to play a trick on him—if, indeed, they had not arranged it all beforehand. Thus it came about (so Cibber's tale goes) that Pope was 'slily seduced' by the 'noble Wag' and the other 'Gentleman', with 'myself as a Laugher', to a certain 'House of Carnal Recreation' near the *Hay-Market*, with the express intention of making fun of 'the celebrated Mr. Pope' in such a situation. Cibber, who at that date was a man of forty-four or so, and an actor of more than twenty years standing, in marked contrast to Pope's very youthful and frail twenty-six, seems soon to have felt some compunction about the

[1] *Epistle to Arbuthnot*, l. 97.

affair, and strangely takes credit to himself for having then rescued
him from the place 'without hazard of his Health'. Warwick had
'staid tittering without'; and, on Cibber giving him 'an Account of the
Action within' (in the course of which Pope is likened to 'a terrible
Tom Tit'), he promptly cursed and blamed him for 'spoiling the
Sport'. To this, Cibber claims to have replied 'with great gravity',
that to save the poet from 'danger', so that the rest of his *Homer* might
be completed, was more important to the nation than 'our Evening
Merriment'.[1]

One can imagine something of the mortification of such a sensitive
and constitutionally delicate creature as Pope at the moment when he
realized he had been betrayed by his friends, and that the whole business from first to last had been contrived solely to make a laughing-
stock of him—and had succeeded. It can only have been paralleled by
that other moment, nearly thirty years later, when, at the very peak of
his fame, he first learnt that Cibber's sniggering travesty of this youthful indiscretion had been published to the wide world in his despite.

Unfortunately, however, the matter did not end there. The old
actor's scandalous story had a success that was immediate and possibly greater than he expected. The town hummed with excitement.
Never within living memory had the quarrels of authors been so
shocking—or so entertaining—according to individual opinion; and,
as may be imagined, Pope's enemies, at Court and in Grub-street
alike, were overjoyed at Cibber's disclosure, although the incident
was more than a quarter of a century old. Proof of this wide-spread
interest is seen in the numerous pamphlets, pictures, poems, and newspaper articles, which the publication of Cibber's *Letter* (but especially
'the story of the Tom-Tit') instantly evoked. The *Letter* itself is dated
at the end 'July 7, 1742', but apparently was not issued until the latter
part of the month; yet the August number of *The Gentleman's Magazine*
alone lists the publication of no less than six 'Pamphlets occasioned by
it', either for Pope, or against him. In addition to this literary warfare,
the end of July also witnessed the deployment of a pictorial attack on
Pope, when a number of different caricatures of Cibber's 'rescue' of
him began to be displayed for sale in the windows of the print shops.

Of the four engravings of this subject in the British Museum, the
first to appear was probably the one entitled: *The Poetical Tom-Titt
perch'd upon the Mount of Love. Being the Representation of a Merry Description in M*^r *Cibber's Letter to M*^r *Pope. Publish'd according to Act of
Parliam*^t*, July 31. 1742. Price 6d.* The engraving ($9\frac{1}{8} \times 7\frac{1}{4}$ ins.) shows a

[1] *A Letter*, pp. 47–9.

bedroom interior, with Cibber pulling a very diminutive Pope away from a very large 'Damsel', and a man peeping in at the back. Below the picture, but within the plate-mark, are the following lines:

> Does not Satiric Pope your Laughter move
> Thus pertly perching on the Mount of Love?
> How much had British Poetry to fear
> Till 'twas retriev'd by Colley's kindly Care?
> What Greater Good from Cibber cou'd we hope
> Who gave us Homer by his saving Pope?

A second and larger engraving of the same date has the title: *An Essay on Woman, by the Author of the Essay on Man: Being Homer preserv'd, or the Twickenham Squire caught by the Heels.* This example has a special interest for our present inquiry, being full of pictorial detail relating (as we shall see) to earlier stages of the Pope-Cibber quarrel.[1] Moreover, it must have been extremely popular, for there seem to have been at least three issues of it with different titles, one of them curiously revealing a slight anti-Cibber bias, thus—*Homer preserv'd by Colley's brazen Face; or the Twickenham squire laid by the Heels.* The largest[2] of all the various known engravings issued in this concerted attack on Pope (there may be others not yet recorded) was published on August 9, 1742, with the legend, *And has not Sawney too his Lord and Whore? Vide Cibber's Letter.* This, too, had a variant: a tiny reproduction in reverse ($2\frac{3}{4} \times 4\frac{1}{2}$ ins.), which was obtained by cutting away the sides of the large picture, and re-engraving the central portion on a small scale, apparently for use as a frontispiece to some later editions of Cibber's *Letter*, in which it is found.

Whether or not Cibber himself played any active part in this extension of the battlefield is not known. That he was interested in it is deducible from the relish with which he continued to repeat his story of Pope's 'gallantry'. Thus in a little-known anonymous attack on

---

[1] In this engraving, for instance, three pictures are seen hanging on the wall of the room behind the sofa; one is entitled 'Three Hours after Marriage', and shows a lady, a crocodile, and a mummy; another called 'The Terrible Tom-Tit', reveals a tiny bird treading a large hen; and the third, a small officer beating a tall grenadier, the title being, 'Captain don't hurt yourself'. On the floor in the foreground lies a copy of '*The Nonjuror*', and Pope's wig. The engraving also shows a nobleman entering the room saying, 'Zounds Colley you have Spoild Sport'; and Cibber replying, 'My Lord, I have Sav'd Homer.' In the lower margin are two epigrams, one signed 'Sawney', the other, 'Colley'.

[2] This print, which is said to be by the famous engraver, Gravelot, measures no less than $13\frac{1}{8} \times 10\frac{3}{8}$ inches.

Pope, published the following month, entitled, *The Difference between Verbal and Practical Virtue*, to which he contributed 'A Prefatory Epistle from Mr. C—b—r to Mr. P.', he remarks how elated he is that the Town has acknowledged his 'Victory' over Pope, and is obscenely 'waggish' again (to use his own later expression) on the same old theme. He returned to the attack in *Another Occasional Letter . . . to Mr. Pope*, 1744, and reverts yet once more to the 'Tom-Tit' episode, openly bragging that everybody tells him he had 'made [Pope] as uneasy as a Rat in a hot Kettle for a Twelve-month together'. And again, as before, Cibber's taunts about Pope's 'tenderness' (which, he says, only proves 'how little a Stroke' as that story could hurt him) incidentally show him as incapable as ever of understanding the measure of his original offence against Pope.

Nevertheless, although no direct evidence of Cibber's responsibility for these scurrilous prints has yet been found, the gratuitous inclusion, in the second engraving described above, of details referring to his earlier encounters with Pope, and the use of the little engraving in subsequent editions of his first *Letter . . . to Mr. Pope*, suggest that at least those two plates were probably produced with his collusion. And that could still be true, even if Theophilus Cibber was the originator of this pictorial onslaught on Pope, as was broadly hinted in a long letter in a contemporary periodical.[1] But whoever began it, father or son, both together or neither, there can be no doubt, first, that the ultimate responsibility rests on Cibber senior alone, as the author of the *Letter* which provided Pope's enemies (on their own showing) with this new ammunition; and, secondly, that Pope held him strictly accountable in consequence. In fine, all the available evidence seems to indicate that it was due to these two related offences of Cibber—his early unforgettable betrayal of the young poet and his late unforgivable exposure of the incident—and *not* because of any absurd 'gags' about mummies and crocodiles, that he was finally raised to the throne of the Dunces.

As we shall presently see, Pope emphatically denied Cibber's story 'as to the main point'—a denial which, with other evidence in support, suggests that the climax of the tale, as told by the old man nearly thirty years later, was a mischievous exaggeration, if not a complete invention. This suspicion seems to be further strengthened by the grossest detail of the story, for this was almost certainly inspired (if that is the word) by Pope's satirical allusion to him some three months earlier in *The New Dunciad* (published March 20, 1742), where he

[1] *The Universal Spectator* for October 16 and 23, 1742.

speaks of the Laureate as reposing in the lap of the goddess, 'Dulness', the passage being—

> Soft on her lap her Laureat son reclines.[1]

It is possible, therefore, that it was this allusion to Cibber (which was actually his first appearance in *The Dunciad* in his official rôle as Poet Laureate) that finally provoked him to produce the *Letter* of 1742. For although cause and effect seem at first sight hardly commensurable, it is only reasonable to suppose that the cumulative effect of Pope's previous attacks went to swell the resentment he felt at this latest reference to his poetical inadequacy as the official court poet. At least there is no other evidence to account for the publication of the *Letter* at that particular time.

Now Cibber has often been praised, by others besides himself, for his refusal to answer Pope's recurrent attacks prior to 1742. (In passing, we may note that, as is shown later, his silence was in fact not as unbroken as is generally supposed.) And from time to time the question has been asked: What, except his magnanimity, could have made him refrain for nearly thirty years from using this shattering weapon of the 'Tom-Tit' episode to rout, or at least profoundly embarrass, his persistent enemy? No one, however, seems to have asked in return the correlated question: What made Pope—who, whatever else he was, was no fool, and, in addition, knew all there was to know about Cibber's weapon—foolish enough to attack him, not once but repeatedly throughout that period, at the risk of provoking him to use it? Yet the two questions are inseparable, and, being so, admit of only one possible reply: there was no such weapon in existence—none, that is, until Cibber was constrained by his friends to concoct his *Letter* of 1742. In other words, the events of that indecorous evening (however deep and lasting their effects on Pope) were not sufficient *in themselves* to have been regarded subsequently by either participant as a possible weapon, whether of attack, or counter-attack, or intimidation. Thus it came about, as the *Letter* itself reveals, that when, in his search for something with which to stop Pope's pen, Cibber set himself to review all their various contacts in the past, he could not help being reminded sooner or later, of that long-forgotten 'Evening Merriment'; whereupon he seems suddenly to have realized how easily and plausibly it could be falsified into a weapon of unspeakable offence against the most famous moral poet of the day—and acted accordingly.

So far only Cibber's account of the unseemly episode has been con-

[1] *Dunciad* B, IV, l. 20; see also Sutherland, p. xxxiii, n. 3.

sidered, for Pope seems rarely to have talked about it. But, later in life, he did once speak of his early gallantry in general and Cibber's story in particular, his confidant being Spence, who has reported his statement as follows:

> The story invented by Cibber was an absolute lie, as to the main point. [I] was invited by Lord W. to pass an evening with him: and was carried by him, with Cibber and another, to a bagnio; but nothing happened of the kind that Cibber mentions, to the best of my memory, and I had so few things of that kind ever on my hands, that I should have scarce forgot so material a circumstance. [1]

What a different picture that presents to Cibber's lurid painting, and also (it must be admitted) to Pope's own portrait of himself in his *Farewell to London In the Year 1715*! Yet there is much reason to believe it the truest picture of the three. It has been frequently remarked by Pope's biographers that for two or three years from 1714 onwards, when he began first to be much 'about town', he adopted the pose (most incident to young men) of rake and bon-vivant; and tried hard to persuade his friends and himself that he was the very devil of a fellow. His letters, as well as his unofficial poems, during this brief period, speak as though he was living in a perpetual whirl of dissolute gaiety, the letters even boasting at times that he was drunk while in the act of writing them. [2] As he once remarked to Spence long afterwards: 'It is vanity which makes the rake at twenty . . .'[3] But even while he posed in this way, he seems always to have been conscious, deep down, of his mental and spiritual—not to mention physical— unfitness to sustain such a role; and in the midst of his most extravagant pretensions sees himself in cold truth as—

> The gayest Valetudinaire,
> Most thinking Rake, alive. [4]

Still more significant, however, is the inference to be drawn from the very charge Cibber brought against him; for the habitual propriety of Pope's daily life and conduct would seem to be unequivocally established, if Cibber, with every wish and resolve to vilify the poet's character in the eyes of the world, could neither remember, nor discover from the gossip of town, or court, or city, anything more shameful to charge him with, at fifty-four years of age, than this one ancient peccadillo of his early manhood. Even if Cibber's story had proved to be true 'as to the main point', it could have meant no more at that date

[1] Spence, pp. 338 f.
[2] Mapledurham, 10 and 32.
[3] Spence, p. 203.
[4] *A Farewell to London*, ll. 39–40.

than that Pope had for once adopted what was (according to contemporary newspaper comment on the exposure) the customary conduct of 'most unmarried Men at Five and twenty.'[1] But either way,
whether fiction or fact, it is deplorable in the extreme that the young
poet, in what would normally have been the glorious morning of life,
should thus have been gratuitously conspired against and tricked into
a false situation, simply that his companions might (as Cibber himself openly admitted) make a mock of the mockery Nature had made
of him.

Taking all the evidence into consideration, then, it appears that
whatever shame or embarrassment Pope may have felt in 1742 on
Cibber's exposure of his early gallantry, what in 1715 he had been
most conscious of, at the end of the affair in question, had possibly less
to do with sexual morality (for we should not forget that he was the
child of his century), than with a sense of betrayal, frustration, and
wounded pride, which the laughter of his companions could only have
fanned into helpless rage. It is no matter for wonder, therefore, if after
the humiliation of that evening he held Cibber as the older man in
especial abhorrence. The dissipated young Lord Warwick was posting
hard to an early grave anyhow—and arrived at it six years later at the
age of twenty-four; and of the other shadowy 'Gentleman' nothing is
known except possibly his name.[2] Cibber the 'Laugher' remained—to
cross Pope's path and that of his friends from time to time, and (as
though to keep Pope's resentment alive) all too frequently to their
disadvantage.

Here at last would seem to be the explanation why the text of *Three
Hours after Marriage* reveals (in those lines in which Cibber was made
to satirize himself both as despotic actor-manager and plagiarizing
dramatist) that the animosity of Pope and, apparently, of his friends,
against him, was in existence *before* the 'mummy and crocodile'
incident happened, which Cibber later declared was the beginning of
the quarrel; and this is a further reason for discrediting his tale. Thus
it was, by post-dating the quarrel and giving it such a ridiculous origin,
Cibber contrived to evade in great measure his responsibility for it;
and so confused the issue that Pope's attacks on him, culminating in
the last *Dunciad*, have for two centuries seemed to many people un-
justifiably excessive, if not actually uncalled-for.

[1] See *The Universal Spectator*, August 7, 14, 21, 1742; and *Gent. Mag.* August 1742.
[2] This was 'Mr. Commissioner Vaughan', according to W. H. Dilworth's *Life of
Pope*, 1759.

II. THE ACTOR-MANAGER

Pope's hatred of Cibber was justified (if hatred can ever be justified) not only by the deep injury from which it originally arose, but also by Cibber's numerous subsequent acts of provocation, which ended only with Pope's life. Pope rarely spoke of them, and Cibber left them unmentioned in his attacks on Pope from 1742 to 1744, when he was so busy enumerating, and protesting against, Pope's frequent allusions to him in his works; which together probably explain why they have been largely overlooked by scholars ever since.

To establish the unsuspected fact, that Pope was more sinned against than sinning in his relations with Cibber, it is necessary to take a rapid survey of their exchange of hostilities, concealed or open. But two remarks should be prefaced to the summary: first, that Pope regarded his friends' interests as his own, and as readily defended them; and secondly, that, as other people, besides Pope and his circle, had reason to complain of Cibber's autocratic management of Drury Lane Theatre, of which he was part licensee for so long, his treatment of Pope's friends may not always have been as discriminative as they probably supposed.

One of the effects of his direction of the theatre, as the principal and most assertive of its three managers, may be seen in the arbitrary withdrawal of *Three Hours after Marriage* on the seventh night after a rather uproarious but far from unsuccessful week; for it seems, when all reports have been considered, to have been an invidious, if not unwarrantable, decision on his part. An explanation may lie in a recent suggestion[1] that all the three managers—Wilks and Booth as well as Cibber—were hostile to the play from the start; the evidence cited being a pamphlet with the title, *A Letter to Mr. John Gay, Concerning His late FARCE, Entituled, A Comedy*. This attack, which was published in February, contains a dedication to the Drury Lane triumvirate beginning with this statement: 'Gentlemen, Since you had so much good Nature as to admit a *Play* into your House against your Judgments ...'

But the idea, that, in producing the comedy, the managers acted against their better judgement, seems to be unconsciously confuted in a letter from Pope to Martha Blount written only a month or so before the first night. He is telling her the latest news about Gay, in the course of which he says: 'He will have a Play acted in 4 or 5 weeks, wᶜʰ we have driven a bargain for.'[2] Normally, those words would sug-

[1] Irving, p. 159.   [2] Mapledurham, 10.

gest that Pope and Gay were in a position more or less to dictate terms; and that, in the complete absence (as far as we know) of any sort of compulsion, should mean that the managers originally wanted the play at least enough to make them accept a bargain more advantageous to the authors than to themselves. Which of the two statements is correct, cannot be finally decided on the evidence available; but Pope's would appear to be the more probable, being evidence at first hand and contemporaneous, besides occurring in a private letter to a person whom there would be no motive in misleading on such a point; and because, furthermore, it would help to explain the curious retention in the dialogue of the two or three quizzes at actor-managers in general and (unmistakably, one would have thought) Cibber in particular. But whatever was initially agreed, and however it was arrived at, the production of the play led, as we know, to friction and thence to that aggravation of the already existent quarrel—Cibber's notorious gag. And it is not unamusing to note that that source of irritation was probably provoked, if not almost excused, by a passage in the first act of this ill-starred comedy. For Cibber, while rehearsing its successor (whether by royal command, or not) must have remembered a scrap of dialogue in which he himself had so recently taken part as Plotwell, the actor-manager, and in which he had actually been admonished about the vice of gagging by another character, Mrs Phoebe Clinket, a writer of plays, thus—

> *Clinket.*   The part, Sir, lies before you. You are never to perplex the
> drama with speeches extempore.
> *Plotwell.*   Madam, 'tis what the top-players often do.

And Cibber, being himself a natural 'gagger', as well as a top-player, with a subject made to his hand, and an ideal opportunity for using it, the much-blamed 'mummy and crocodile' gag became, if not inevitable, as least not surprising.

The next incident in the Pope-Cibber quarrel was again brought about by Cibber, without Pope having made any public reply to the actor's persistent repetition of the offensive gag. Before the year was out Cibber produced at Drury Lane his adaptation of Molière's *Tartuffe*, which, under the title of *The Non-Juror*, satirized the Jacobites, and those Tories who sympathized with the rising of 1715. The play was especially obnoxious to Pope and many of his friends, by reason of its attack on the Roman Catholics—the character of the 'treason-hatching Jesuit', Doctor Wolf (which rôle Cibber reserved for himself) being particularly offensive. Nevertheless, the play was very successful in the theatre, and, though much censured outside because of its politics, was so popular at court as to have brought Cibber not only an immediate two hundred pounds from the King,[1] but, in due course, the laureateship, which, he said, was also 'given me for having writ the *Nonjuror.*'[2]

One point about the play seems to have escaped notice: three of Pope's best-known poems figure anonymously in *The Non-Juror*, the volumes containing them being brought on to the stage. In Act I, Scene i, 'Maria takes a book from the table and reads'; and when asked what it is, she does not answer, but reads aloud, with some interruption and conversation, four couplets from *The Rape of the Lock.*[3] Again, in Act II, Scene i, Maria 'enters with a book' which, on being addressed by Charles, she hands to the maid, saying, 'Here, take this odious *Homer,* and lay him up again; he tires me . . . so many volumes . . .' She then rather strangely expresses a wish to read it 'in the Greek'; and the dialogue continues:

> *Maria.*   How could one do to learn Greek; was you a great while about it?
> *Charles.*   It has been half the business of my life, madam.
> *Maria.*   . . . Then you think one can't be mistress of it in a month or two?

Seeing that the third volume of Pope's *Iliad* (there were three more to come) had been published barely six months previously, and that the most frequent taunt against his translation was that he knew so little Greek, it is difficult to believe the passage was quite guiltless of intentional offence. Finally, in Act V, Scene i, 'Enter Doctor with a book', who, indicating it, explains that he 'had just dipped into poor Eloisa's passion for Abelard . . .' There is no comment on, or other allusion to, Pope's poem; and it is perhaps just possible that the Doctor's 'book' was a copy of Hughes' prose translation of *Letters of Abelard and Heloise,* published four and a half years earlier,[4] but hardly probable, seeing that Pope's more popular poem had appeared only six months previously[5] and was then in 'everybody's' hands. Except for the conventional, anonymous, 'curtain couplet' at the end of the acts, there is no other contemporary poem or poet quoted or alluded to in the play; and as only one of the three references to Pope's poems can be said to be disparaging, and as Cibber must have had some pur-

---

[1] *A Letter,* p. 24.   [2] *Apology,* p. 305.
[3] Canto II, ll. 9–14, 17–18.
[4] Published July 28–30, 1713; see *The Post Boy* of that date.
[5] In *The Works,* 1717.

pose in bringing them on the stage three times, their repeated display may possibly have had a political significance—the suggestion being that Pope's works (and, therefore, the poet himself) would naturally be popular in houses where disaffection to the Hanoverian succession and the Government was rife. Whatever the reason, or reasons, it is certain that Pope warmly resented what he called 'the great success of so damn'd a Play as the Non-Juror',[1] and practically as certain that he replied to it with an anonymous pamphlet, entitled, *A Clue To the Comedy of the Non-Juror . . . In a Letter to N. Rowe, Esq*[2]; which gravely poked fun at the play by pretending to prove it was a 'Jacobite Libel against the Government'.

For some years after that exchange there seems to have been no further passage at arms between them; but Pope's dislike of Cibber, now as natural to him as the breath he drew, would have been kept alive beyond any possibility of extinction by events arising out of the actor-manager's dictatorial direction of Drury Lane Theatre. Many people, from literary aspirants to successful authors, had cause to complain of his impertinent behaviour to them; and instances of his high-handed conduct were cited in the public prints as late as *The Laureat: Or, The Right Side of Colley Cibber*, 1740. Such treatment as Elijah Fenton received at his hands, in the long postponement, and insolent final rejection, of *Mariamne* in 1722 (as related with some indignation by Dr Johnson[3]), must have set Pope fuming again; for Fenton was a friend of his, and at that time in constant communication with him about his work on the *Odyssey* translation. Two years later, Gay's *Captives* was produced at Drury Lane, a play in which Pope was to some extent concerned, if in nothing more than supplying the anonymous *Epilogue*[4]; and it is difficult to imagine Pope and Gay and Cibber in theatrical conjunction at that period without further (but unchronicled) 'incidents' taking place. It may therefore be significant in this connection, that Pope, when writing to Swift the next year, 1725, had reason to say: 'My name is . . . hated by all bad poets, from Hopkins and Sternhold to Gildon and Cibber',[5]—the last named being the only one of the four then alive. As Pope at that date is not known to have attacked Cibber since writing the *Clue* (which Cibber called his 'jest' about *The Non-Juror*[6]), it seems certain that

---

[1] *Correspondence*, I, 1735 (ii), p. 111.

[2] Published February 15, 1718. For evidence of Pope's authorship see *Pope's Prose*, I, pp. cxix ff.

[3] Johnson, III, p. 113. [4] See *ante*, pp. 210 ff.

[5] The letter is dated October 15, 1725; see *Letters*, II, 4to, 1741, p. 39.

[6] *A Letter*, p. 26.

something must have been said or done by Cibber during the ensuing seven and a half years, if Pope's remark to Swift, semi-jocular though it is, is to become intelligible. Before leaving this point, we should also note a later reference to these strained relations, in an undated letter (probably of November 1, 1729) from Pope to Mallet, who had written about the possibility of procuring the performance of his tragedy. In the course of his reply Pope remarks:

> You'll find it easier to write a good play than to produce it on the stage without displeasing circumstances. You judge very naturally, that I can have no great influence over Cibber, &c. If I had, he should never have hindered some plays from the public. [1]

Next comes Pope's famous *Art of Sinking*, [2] with its well-known references to Cibber. In the first Cibber is included in the 'Parrot' class of writers 'that repeat another's words in such a hoarse odd voice as makes them seem their own' (a broader allusion to his plagiarisms than the hint that had been ventured in *Three Hours after Marriage* ten years earlier). The second mentions him as an exponent of 'the pert style' of prologue-writing. The third occurs at the end, in the satirical *Project for the Advancement of the Stage*, in which 'the Most Undaunted Mr. C–ll–y C–bb–r' joins with Booth and Wilks to 'continue to Out-do even their own Out-doings'. [3]

Towards the end of 1727, Cibber had been offered *The Beggar's Opera* for production at Drury Lane—and had rejected it. It was then sent to his rival, Rich, who produced it on January 29, 1728, at the playhouse in Lincoln's Inn Fields, where it had an unprecedented success. As Cibber is often asserted to have been an excellent judge of theatrical matters, it would seem that he either was singularly unlucky in his dealings with Pope and his friends, or from time to time allowed his feelings to cloud his judgement. For Fenton's rudely rejected play brought the author 'near a thousand pounds' [4] at Rich's theatre; and

---

[1] EC, x, p. 80.

[2] In *Miscellanies. The Last Volume*, dated 1727 but published March 7, 1728 (*London Evening Post*).

[3] This misquotation is a quiz at Cibber's phrase in praise of Mrs Oldfield's acting: ' 'Tis not enough to say she *here Out-did* her usual *Out-doing*' (see *The Provok'd Husband*, 1728, 'To the Reader'), which soon became a popular joke. Thus, although the main part of Pope's *Project* was probably published in 1720 (see J. R. Sutherland, R.E.S., xx, 1944, p. 170), this particular allusion to Cibber is unquestionably dated by the joke as a 1728 addition.

[4] Johnson, iii, p. 113.

now Gay's opera at the same place did so well as to become a popular joke—it made Gay rich and Rich gay.

It is not surprising therefore to find several allusions to Cibber in *The Dunciad* on its first appearance a few months later,[1] the most significant being the passage which alludes to his imperious management of Drury Lane. Pope, describing the dismal future for mankind under the reign of the King of Dulness, artfully sees it only as an intensification of the state of affairs then obtaining, and tells how—amongst other depressing conditions—

> Beneath his reign, shall Eusden wear the bays,
> Cibber preside Lord-Chancellor of Plays.[2]

But even if Cibber's rejection of *The Beggar's Opera* had been due to nothing more than misjudgement, few people in the circumstances would condone his subsequent attempt to imitate it. In his *Apology for his Life*, he made it his boast that he used no notes or other written memoranda, but entirely relied on his memory.[3] That may possibly account for the wrong dating of certain acts of his, by which they are placed in a less sinister light than that in which they must originally have appeared to Gay and Pope. Thus in the course of that narrative, after speaking of 'the vast Success of that new Species of Dramatick Poetry, the *Beggars Opera*' (but failing completely to mention his previous rejection of it), he continued: 'The Year following, I was so stupid, as to attempt something of the same kind'[4]—something, he went on to say in effect, that should make use of, adopt, or steal, the form and design of Gay's novel 'ballad-opera', but, by presenting a picture in direct contrast to his, contrive to make as much money out of 'Virtue and Innocence' as Gay was making out of 'vulgar Vice and Wickedness'—which piece of inverted plagiarism was carried out and entitled *Love in a Riddle*. Cibber's phrase, 'the Year following', makes his reported actions sound almost innocuous; whereas, the fact is, that he must have been writing his imitation of *The Beggar's Opera* for Drury Lane in the latter part of 1728, that is, at the very same time that Gay was busily engaged on his 'Second Part' of the opera (entitled, *Polly*) for Lincoln's Inn Fields, with the result that the two plays arrived at their theatres 'neck and neck' at the beginning of December. News of Cibber's undertaking had, however, leaked out before this, and the newspapers had begun to comment on his coming

---

[1] *The Dunciad* was published May 18, 1728.
[2] *Dunciad* A, III, 319–20.   [3] See *ante*, p. 300 n.
[4] *Apology*, p. 141.

'entertainment' as early as September. Then, when it became known that *Polly*, after having been held up for a while, was finally banned for no given reason on December 12, with the result that Cibber was thus assured of having no rival opera competing with his during the season, the papers became very out-spoken in protest, some going so far as to say, or intimate, that he had used his influence with the Lord Chamberlain to that end. Only two days after the prohibition of *Polly*, it was announced in *The Country Journal* that—

> We hear that the Sequel to the BEGGAR's OPERA, which was going into Rehearsal at the Theatre in *Lincoln's-Inn Fields*, is suppressed by *Authority*, without any particular Reasons being alledged; . . . It is hoped from *this Circumstance*, that the celebrated Mr. CIBBER's *Opera* (which we are assured is perfectly *inoffensive*) will now be acted with great Success. [1]

Cibber himself described the charge that was made against him, in these words:

> Soon after this Prohibition, my Performance was to come upon the Stage . . . Great Umbrage was taken, that I was permitted, to have the whole Town to my self, by this absolute Forbiddance of what, they had more mind to have been entertain'd with . . . The Report, it seems, that had run against me, was this: That, to make way for the Success of my own Play, I had privately found means, or made Interest, that the Second Part of the *Beggars Opera*, might be suppressed. [2]

Love in a Riddle was produced at Drury Lane on Tuesday, January 7, 1729, and, whatever Cibber's transgressions may or may not have been in the past, poetical justice was done on that occasion—to judge by paragraphs in several newspapers, including *Fog's Weekly Journal* for January 11, 1729, which printed the following report:

> On Tuesday Night last, a ridiculous Piece was acted at the Theatre in Drury-lane, which was neither Comedy, Tragedy, Opera, Pastoral, or Farce; however, no Thief or Robber of any Rank was satyriz'd in it, and it could be said to give Offence to none but Persons of Sense and good Taste; yet it met with the Reception it well deserv'd, and was hiss'd off the Stage.—However, it may serve to bind up with the rest of *Keyber's* [3] Works.

And not content with that account, it also printed in the same issue a

---

[1] *The Country Journal: Or, The Craftsman.* Saturday, December 14, 1728.
[2] *Apology*, p. 143.
[3] A facetious spelling of Cibber, used by some papers.

short poem, entitled, 'To Mr. *Keyber*, on his Elaborate Performance of *Love in a Riddle*', deriding alike both the play and the acting of 'Friend Colly'. *The Country Journal* of the same date takes the tale a little further, and tells how not even the presence of the Prince at the theatre the next night (Wednesday) could save the play:

> The second time of acting . . . there was such an extraordinary Disturbance, occasioned by the general Disapprobation of the Audience, that they would not suffer the Performance to be continued, till Mr. *Cibber* assured them that it should not be acted any more than that Night.

Although there is no contemporary evidence on record that Cibber denied the newspapers' implication that he was in some measure responsible for the banning of *Polly*, he emphatically did so in his *Apology* eleven years later, when he bitterly complained of 'the Murder of my Play' which 'a strong Party' would not allow to be heard for 'clamour', so that he was obliged to withdraw it after the second performance. He vaguely hints at the persons composing the party, but declares he 'never endeavour'd to discover' who they were.

III. THE POET LAUREATE

In September 1730, the laureateship fell vacant on the death of Laurence Eusden, and the name of his successor at once became the subject of much speculation and talk. On November 19, Pope published anonymously in *The Grub-street Journal* a mock-learned treatise, *Of the Poet Laureate*, in which he gravely discusses 'the ceremonial of the Laureate', his 'qualifications' and 'privileges'; and then, after briefly mentioning Dennis and Tibbald[1] as possible candidates, he ironically stresses at some length Cibber's suitability for the office in most respects. It has been suggested, on little or no evidence, that Gay had entertained some hopes of the appointment; and it is true that his name was mentioned in that connection in one or two of the newspapers. But his suspense—if it ever existed—was very quickly ended by the following piece of news which appeared in *The Evening Post* for December 3–5, 1730:

> Thursday [December 3], Colley Cibber, Esq; the famous Comedian and Comic-Author, was at Court, and had the Honour to kiss his Majesty's Hand (on his being appointed Poet-Laureat in

[1] *i.e.* Theobald.

the room of the Rev. Mr. Laurence Eusden, deceas'd) and was graciously received.

It would scarcely be an exaggeration to say that a howl of derision greeted this news in many parts of the town; and very soon verses and epigrams appeared in a number of papers, to celebrate or (still oftener) to satirize the occasion. Amongst the more vigorous and out-spoken of the attackers was *The Grub-street Journal*, and amongst the epigrams it published during the ensuing months are several which are generally agreed to be Pope's.

It is noteworthy, that, from the date of Cibber's election to the Laureateship onwards, Pope's derisive allusions to him take on a quality and frequency before unknown, and (apart from hints of fresh personal provocations) are chiefly explicable by the cumulative effect of Cibber's past offences—with the addition of what must have amounted to a recurrent exasperation of a new kind. Pope's abnormal sensitiveness to bad poetry, as previous pages show, was such that per-sistent writers of it filled him with a sort of aesthetic fury which was none the less real because so few people understood it. The laureate's official 'Birthday Odes' and 'New Year Odes', in spite of their being amongst the worst of their kind, were not only regularly displayed in the news-sheets and journals, but were also usually set to music and performed with much pomp and circumstance at court. They thus constituted, both for Pope and other people who had not his personal resentment against the laureate, a twice-yearly incentive to ribald comment. It is not surprising, therefore, with Pope's old grievance against Cibber still unassuaged, to find that six out of his sixteen *Imitations of Horace* written between 1732 and 1738 contain one or more satirical references to him, or his son, or both together. And to these allusions of Pope's, it appears, must now be added a reprisal in kind—a little-known 'Ode' of fourteen stanzas, which seems to have been consistently overlooked by all Pope's editors hitherto, and reprinted only twice since his death. The text which follows is that of the original broadside in every respect, except the six words completed within square brackets.

An ODE for the NEW YEAR. Written by
Colley Cibber, Esq; Poet Laureat.

God prosper long our gracious K[in]g,
Now sitting on the Throne,
Who leads this Nation in a *String*,
And governs all but *One*.

This is the Day when, right or wrong,
  I *COLLEY BAYS*, Esq;
Must, for my Sack, indite a Song,
  And thrum my *Venal Lyre*.

Not he, who rul'd great *Judah*'s Realm,
  Ycleped *Solomon*,
Was *wiser* than *ours* at the Helm,
  Or had a *wiser Son*.

He rak'd up Wealth to glut his Fill,
  In Drinking, Whores, and Houses,
Which wiser *G[EORG]E* can save, to fill
  His Pocket, and his Spouse's.

His Head with Wisdom deep is fraught,
  His Breast with Courage glows,
Alas! how mournful is the Thought,
  He ever shou'd want Foes?

For at his Heart he loves a Drum,
  As Children love a Rattle,
If not in Field, in Drawing-Room,
  He daily sounds to Battle.

The Q[uee]n I also pray God save,
  His Consort, plump, and dear,
Who, just as he is *Wise* and *Brave*,
  Is *Pious* and *Sincere*.

She's courteous, good, and charms all Folks,
  Love's one as well as t'other,
Of *Arian* and of *Orthodox*,
  Alike the *Nursing Mother*.

Oh! may she always meet Success
  In ev'ry Scheme and Job,
And still continue to caress
  That honest Statesman *BOB*.

> God send the P[rin]ce, that Babe of Grace,
> 　　A little Whore and Horse,
> A little Meaning in his Face,
> 　　And Money in his Purse.
>
> Heav'n spread o'er all his Family
> 　　That broad *Illustrious Glare*,
> Which shines so flat in ev'ry Eye,
> 　　And makes 'em all *so stare*.
>
> All marry *gratis*, Boy, and Miss,
> 　　All still increase their Store,
> *As in Beginning was, now is,*
> 　　*And shall be evermore.*
>
> But oh! ev'n Kings must die of Course,
> 　　And to their Heirs be civil;
> We Poets too, on winged Horse,
> 　　Must soon ride to the Devil.
>
> Then since I have a Son, like You,
> 　　May he *Parnassus* rule;
> So shall the *Crown*, and *Laurel* too,
> 　　Descend from F[oo]l to F[oo]l.

The recognition of this 'Ode' as Pope's derives first and foremost from a definite statement by Horace Walpole[1] in his manuscript notes on *The Dunciad*, where Book IV, line 98:

> Or give from fool to fool the Laurel crown.

is annotated thus:

> In an anonymous Ode written by Pope for Cibber is this conclusion,
> 　　So shall the Crown and Laurel too
> 　　　　descend from fool to fool.

Belated though the identification is, there can be little doubt that this is the 'Ode' to which Walpole alluded; but it is not quite so certain whether his knowledge that Pope wrote it was inferred from the *Dunciad* parallel, or obtained more directly. The latter, however, would seem to be suggested by the fact that Walpole's note does not

---

[1] Fraser, pp. 93 f.

cite the parallel to authenticate the *Ode*, but quotes the *Ode* to illustrate *The Dunciad*. In other words, Walpole is not claiming the *Ode* for Pope, but accepting his authorship of it as an unquestionable fact. And, happily, other evidence in support of his statement is not lacking.

There is now no doubt, for example, about Pope's predilection for the form and manner of the old street ballad for anonymous comment on topical affairs, when mocking humour rather than trenchant satire seemed to be called for. Several instances of his use of it have been noted or discussed in previous pages and elsewhere,[1] none of which was ever publicly acknowledged by the poet. And this *Ode*, in spite of its title, is another example, and an extremely characteristic one, of his handling of the ballad metre, which he once admitted (with the implication that the poems were left unacknowledged) having used on several occasions.[2] Moreover, in the last stanza the writer couples ridicule of Cibber with contempt for his son in the distinctive manner in which Pope (and he alone?) sometimes combined them. Thus Pope wrote to Duncombe: 'I think of players as I always thought of players, and of the son [Theophilus] as I thought of the father [Colley].'[3] And in the first edition of *The Dunciad* we find:

> Mark first the youth who takes the foremost place,
> And thrusts his person full into your face.
> With all thy Father's virtues blest, be born!
> And a new Cibber shall the Stage adorn.[4]

Furthermore, in the final version of the same poem, the sixth line of the First Book,

> Still Dunce the second reigns like Dunce the first,

is annotated to afford 'full proof' that Cibber's son is 'exactly like him, in his poetical, theatrical, political, and moral Capacities'.

The Ode likewise reflects Pope's political views at that period, and also his opinion of the Court; for, as we have seen, although his animosity against the Prince of Wales was fast disappearing, friendly terms were not established between them before October 1735, when the Prince first visited him at Twickenham.[5] But the poem chimes with Pope's authorship of it in a dozen places, and, very significantly, *not* with the known work of any other writer then alive. Cibber's 'Venal Lyre', for instance, is strongly reminiscent of the famous line

---

[1] See *ante*, pp. 11, 186–90; also *Pope's Own Miscellany*, pp. xlvi ff.

[2] Spence, p. 285.

[3] The letter is dated November 23, 1734; Warton, VII, p. 380.

[4] *Dunciad* A, III, 131–4.   [5] See *ante*, p. 278.

about Gildon's 'venal Quill'[1]; and the phrase 'at his heart' (l. 21) meaning 'at heart', was something of a favourite of Pope's: 'at her heart' appears in the *Epistle To a Lady* (l. 68), and *Epistle To Miss Blount* (l. 56), and the locution occurs in a number of other places in his works. Again, the same keen observation which Pope always showed in his verbal sketches from the life is present in the *Ode*: the prayer that the Prince might be granted, amongst other things, 'A little Meaning in his Face' (l. 39), recalls Sir Plume's 'round unthinking Face' in *The Rape of the Lock* (III, 125); and similarly the glare 'Which shines so flat in ev'ry Eye', reminds one of the 'pert flat eyes' of the phantom More in *The Dunciad* (A, II, 39); and also the line, 'Each sire imprest and glaring in his son' (A, I, 98). Indeed, the 'glare' and 'stare' of that stanza seem to betray Pope's pen in a very personal manner. Possibly because of his physical disabilities and diminutive size, Pope seems always to have been peculiarly sensitive to people staring. The earliest of his 'literary' quarrels was with Dennis whose 'stare tremendous' he alluded to—whether as grievance or attack—on several occasions; and stares and glares must have been his lot all his life. It is not without relevance to note that the lines:

> . . . stately, staring things,
> No wonder some Folks bow, and think them *Kings*.[2]

were written or at least published, within a month or two of the ascribed date of the *Ode*; and there are numerous other allusions to 'stares' and 'staring eyes' up and down his work in prose and verse, not to mention the reference to 'the whole Art of Staring', in *The Critical Specimen*, 1711, recently attributed to him.[3]

Altogether, then, with corroboration from so many sides, it would seem that Walpole's note on Pope's responsibility for *An Ode for the New Year* can be regarded as correct. But so well kept was the secret of its authorship that Pope's name was never publicly associated with it; and the *Ode* dropped out of sight, and was forgotten by everybody for nearly one hundred and thirty years. It thus escaped being reprinted until 1860, when it appeared in *Notes and Queries*, in a short article signed with the Greek letter β, in which it was suggested, without any evidence being adduced, that, on Eusden's death, Gay 'aspired to the office of the laureate'; and that disappointment at Cibber's election provoked 'Gay and his friends' to retaliate with this composite poem

---

[1] See *ante*, p. 101.

[2] *Fourth Satire of Donne*, 210–11; published November 5, 1733.

[3] See Pope's *Prose*, I, pp. xi ff. and p. 15.

in which 'both the hand and the kindly nature of Gay are discernible'.[1] The article, however, attracted no attention, and the *Ode* was again lost sight of until 1926, when it was once more reprinted, this time in Gay's *Poetical Works*, by Mr G. C. Faber, who placed it amongst the 'Doubtful Pieces' with a reference to the *Notes and Queries* article and a cautionary comment: 'But whether Gay wrote this singularly cruel attack on the Royal Family is perhaps more than doubtful',[2] and a further note saying: 'There seems very little evidence for the ascription to Gay'.[3] As Gay's 'kindly nature' and 'singularly cruel attack' seem to cancel out; and as the solemn ascription of the piece to Cibber, in the heading, was clearly part of the joke and never intended to deceive for more than a moment (for no laureate would have used the ballad form for the official odes), the attribution to Gay may appear to have as little actuality as the attribution to Cibber, and may now perhaps be allowed to lapse—as indeed it must, if the date presently to be assigned to the *Ode* is correct, for the simple reason that he had died twelve months previously.

Copies of the original broadside are extremely rare, only two[4] being known to the present writer; but although these two were printed from the same setting of type (as far as the poem is concerned), they are of different issues, as is shown by the band of printer's ornaments across the top of the sheet, in the details of which the two impressions have not the slightest resemblance to each other. The two copies are otherwise identical in every respect, including the lack of imprint and date, so that it is impossible to say which was the first issue. Fortunately, however, the approximate date of composition is deducible from internal evidence. In the first place, the poem cannot have been written before December 3, 1730 (when Cibber was made Laureate), or later than April 27, 1736 (when the Prince was married); and within those limits three further references combine to indicate that it was written at the close of 1733. The first of them occurs in the sixth stanza, and especially its last two lines:

> If not in Field, in Drawing-Room,
> He daily sounds to Battle.

Between our immovable limits, 1730 and 1736, these lines can only allude to the beginning of the 'War of the Polish Succession', which broke out in October 1733, with Louis's attack on the Emperor who at once appealed to England for aid. Sir Robert Walpole, however,

[1] *Notes and Queries*, 2nd Ser., x, p. 1.
[2] Faber, p. xxxi.   [3] *Ibid.*, p. 653.
[4] B.M. C.40.m.10 (176); and Texas University Library, AK/C482/A730o.

was resolved to preserve England's neutrality, and had much difficulty in restraining George II from joining in the fray. One historian states that, for a time, 'The King, excited by these events, would hear and talk of nothing but war.'[1] Secondly, and as unmistakably, the wish expressed in the tenth stanza—'God send the Prince . . . Money in his Purse',—alludes to the political agitation, which began in 1733, for an increased allowance for the Prince. And thirdly, the beginning of the twelfth stanza—'marry *gratis*, Boy, and Miss,'—appears to refer to the Prince of Orange's visit in November 1733 to woo the Princess Royal, and his extremely parsimonious entertainment by George II.[2] It is perhaps also worth adding that the last stanza—if it hints at Cibber's abdication from the theatrical world in favour of his son—is likewise congruous with the ascribed date of the *Ode*; for Cibber had made over his share in the patent of Drury Lane Theatre to his son not long before, and was now (that is, late in 1733) on the point of retiring officially from the stage, if he had not already done so, as some have maintained.[3] Thus all the available evidence points to Pope as the concealed author of the mock *Ode for the New Year*; and as he also had (as has been shown) motive enough and to spare, it will be difficult henceforth to refuse the poem a place in the canon of his works amongst the unacknowledged pieces of occasional verse.

In the exhaustive catalogue of Pope's 'attacks' on him which Cibber so meticulously compiled for his notorious *Letter*, the fact that he failed to mention the above *Ode* as yet one more example of Mr Pope's frequent fondness of Mr Cibber's name is ample proof that he never knew from whom that particular buffet came. But there were other verses written about him, which, as they seem never to have been associated with Pope's name, likewise escaped being catalogued in Cibber's list. About the year 1734, the retired actor-manager, with much unaccustomed leisure on his hands, was becoming well known as a frequenter of the fashionable spas and watering places, each in their season—Bath, Scarborough, Tunbridge Wells, etc.—where he seems to have contracted a typically eighteenth-century variety of exhibitionism, namely, the writing of poetry on window-panes. In that year *The Bee*[4] printed a poem entitled, *Wrote on a Window in the Long Room at Scarborough, by the Poet Laureat*, which was reprinted later in *The Scarborough Miscellany for the Year 1734*, with the caption *To Miss Eger—n singing in the Long Room. By C—y C—r*, and the same statement

---

[1] See D.N.B., 'George II'.
[2] Hervey, pp. 230 ff.
[3] See D.N.B., 'Colley Cibber'.
[4] *The Bee*, Vol. VII, No. lxxxii, p. 163.

about the window. At Bath he spoilt another window-pane with some complimentary but uncouth verses addressed to the celebrated Beau Nash.[1] Pope also was fond of Bath, if not of Cibber; and his reactions to this window-scratching craze of the Laureate's have survived amongst the Portland Papers[2] at Longleat, in the form of two epigrams in his own handwriting on a single sheet, as follows:

I

Occasioned by Cibbers Verses in praise of Nash.

O Nash! more blest in ev'ry other thing,
But in thy Poet wretched as a King!
Thy Realm disarm'd of each offensive Tool,
Ah! leave not this, this Weapon to a Fool.
Thy happy Reign all other Discord quells;
Oh doe but silence Cibber, & the Bells.
Apollo's genuine Sons thy fame shall raise
& all Mankind, but Cibber, sing thy praise.

II

Another

Cibber! write all thy Verses upon Glasses,
The only way to save 'em from our A—s.

Of the first it may be remarked in passing that Nash had found it 'necessary to forbid the wearing of swords'[3] in the assembly rooms, and that 'Upon a stranger's arrival at *Bath*, he is welcomed by a peal of the Abbey bells',[4] which, as people were very frequently arriving in the season, explains Pope's heart-felt cry and his characteristic coupling of the two nuisances. This epigram is here printed from Pope's autograph—as well as identified as his—for the first time; but an incorrect

---

[1] The text of Cibber's lines which follows is taken from F. D. Senior's *Life and Times of Colley Cibber*, p. 123.

> Let Kings their power by lineal birth inherit,
> Nash holds his empire from his public spirit.
> If Populi with Dei Vox we join,
> This place at least he rules by right divine.
> Learn Britons hence the needfull use of Kings,
> From Freedom bound general wellfare springs.

[2] Portland, XII, f. 255.
[3] O. Goldsmith's *Life of Richard Nash*, 1762, p. 37.   [4] *Ibid.*, p. 41.

transcript of it without attribution, said to be found in the Malet collection at the British Museum, has recently been published.[1]

The second epigram seems never to have been printed hitherto; but Ruffhead (presumably on Warburton's authority) gives in a footnote a fragment of an undated letter which Pope wrote to Hugh Bethel from Bath, 'where a certain princess at that time resided'.

'Cibber', says he, 'is here to celebrate her; and he writes his verses now, in such a manner, that no body can use them as they were wont to do; for no body will, on certain occasions, use a pane of glass.'[2]

This fragment appears to put the seal of Pope's authorship on the couplet, especially as he made much the same joke elsewhere more than once—as has been remarked earlier in a comment on the foible of Pope and Swift for this kind of humour.[3] All things considered, there can be little doubt that both pieces are Pope's.

The quarrel with Cibber lasted out Pope's life. And though for some time after these two epigrams were written, the laureate's offensiveness to Pope seems to have been limited to the punctual effusions of his office—reputedly the worst irregular odes ever regularly concocted—their mutual dislike flared up again into open animosity during Pope's last years. But the main culminating stages of their quarrel have of necessity already been considered while we were tracing its obscure origins; and, in consequence, may be excused repetition in their proper chronological place here at the end of the story. And now that the end of the story becomes understandable in the light of its beginning, it may seem to most readers that Pope's final vengeance—the elevation of Cibber to the throne of the Dunces —so far from being disproportionate to his original offence, as it formerly appeared, was a fitting, if tardy, climax to the fluctuating fortunes of this minor 'Thirty Years' War' (1714–44).

---

[1] Senior, p. 123.   [2] Ruffhead, p. 390.   [3] See *ante*, p. 131.

CHAPTER XXI

POPE'S 'OTHER' EPITAPHS

ALEXANDER Pope has been praised beyond any other of our poets as a writer of epitaphs. Dr Johnson, no mean performer himself, admitted even while sharpening his pen to criticize them that Pope excelled in such writings; and Bishop Warburton, Pope's first editor, roundly asserted: 'These little compositions far exceed anything we have of the kind from other hands,'—judgements in which succeeding generations have perhaps on the whole concurred. But in addition to the well-known examples in the section of Pope's *Works* entitled 'Epitaphs' (which now total sixteen, and comprise the fourteen published and acknowledged by the poet in his lifetime, and the two added in 1751), Pope wrote almost as many more, grave or ribald, cynical or merely funny, which for the most part he never publicly acknowledged, and which, in consequence, are all less familiar than the famous sixteen, and some of them practically unknown. As was pointed out in an earlier chapter,[1] Pope had a vein of irresponsible fun in his composition, which, though it may in great measure have been lost sight of and forgotten, explains as nothing else can many an un-Pope-like verse of which he was certainly the author, and not a few apparent strokes of malice of which he was as certainly not guilty, yet for which he has been unjustly censured these two hundred years. The present work provides an excuse (if such were needed) to examine a few of these little-known epitaphs, and inquire into their causes and consequences, in tardy justice to his character, if not for the entertainment they may incidentally provide.

One of the famous sixteen epitaphs—that on Sir Godfrey Kneller, the painter—has an amusing pendant, or prelude rather, in another, on his lady, which seems to have been printed only three times, and has never yet appeared in any edition of Pope's poems. The stories of the two epitaphs are inextricably mixed up together, and cannot be better told than in Pope's own words taken from his letters to the Earl of Strafford, as follows:

> I will tell y^r l^{d}ship the story as shortly as I can . . . Sr Godfrey sent to me just before he dy'd. He began by telling me he was now convinc'd he could not live, and fell into a passion of tears . . .

[1] See *ante*, pp. 8 f.

[After reporting some conversation about God's will, Pope continues:] The next word he said was this—*By God, I will not be buried in Westminster*. I asked him why? He answered, *They do bury fools there*. Then he s^d to me, My good friend, where will you be buried? I said, Wherever I drop; very likely in Twitnam. He reply'd, So will I; then proceeded to desire I w^d write his epitaph, wch I promised him. It would be endless to tell y^r l^dship ye strange things he suggested on that head; it must be in Latin, that all foreigners may read it: it must be in English too, &c. . . . Then he desir'd me that I would take down my father's monum^t, *For it was ye best place in ye church to be seen at a distance*. This (as y^r l^dship may well imagine) surprised me quite. I hesitated and s^d I fear'd it w^d be indecent, and y^t my mother must be asked as well as I. He fell crying again, and seem'd so violently moved, that in pure humanity to a dying man (as well as to one I thought *non compos*), I w^d not directly persist in denying it strongly, but begg'd him to be easy upon ye whole, and said I would do for him all that I could *with decency*. These words, and that reserve, I can swear to.[1]

Kneller died in 1723; and by July, 1725, his widow (a 'huge lady') had resolved on additions to his scheme of a Twickenham monument, which would have affected a pew belonging to Lord Strafford as well as the Pope memorial standing at its head. Hence Pope's letters to him, from which these excerpts are taken. The next stage was as follows:

A *monition* (I think they call it) from ye Drs Commons was publish'd here [*i.e.* at Twickenham] last Sunday, wherein that pious widow desires their leave to pull down ye tablet I set up at ye head of y^r lordship's pew, to fix there a large one of Sr G. and herself with both their figures. If y^r lordship should really chance to take no great pleasure in beholding my name full before y^r eyes . . . yet at least . . . it cannot incommode you so much as a vast three-hundred-pound pile projecting out upon you, overshadowing my Lady Strafford with ye immense draperies and stone petticoats of Lady Kneller, and perhaps crushing to pieces your lordship's posterity! This period sounds very poetical; and yet Reeves seriously tells me . . . that the main wall at y^r pew will be greatly in danger of falling by ye addition of such a tomb.[2]

Alarums and excursions of all kinds followed and the battle grew very

---

[1] From the letter dated, 'Twitnam, July ye 6' [1725].

[2] From the first letter of the group, undated. [July 1725.]

confused; and at its height Pope sent Strafford this 'Epitaph, wch over and above my promise to Sr G. may serve for my lady's, and justly celebrates her pious design of making as large a figure on ye tomb as Sir G. himself.'

EPITAPH

One day I mean to Fill Sir Godfry's tomb,
If for my body all this Church has room.
Down with more Monuments! More room! (she cryd)
For I am very large, & very wide.[1]

It is satisfactory to learn that the case went in favour of Pope. The monument to his father was not disturbed and remains in its place to this day, the only change being that in due course it has received the name of his mother and, lastly, of the poet himself. Nothing more is heard of Kneller's monument, or Pope's promised epitaph, until April 21, 1730, when *The St. James's Evening Post* made the following announcement: 'A curious Monument is putting up in Westminster-Abbey, . . . in Memory of . . . Sir Godfrey Kneller Bart. upon which the following Inscription (made by Mr. Pope) will be engraved . . .' Whereupon the well-known epitaph is printed for the first time.

.   .   .

Pope's admirable and deeply felt tribute to his beloved John Gay was in its various versions the most popular of all his works, judging from the number of times and places of its printing during his life. But Pope has also been credited (though without evidence until recently[2]) with the authorship of a semi-jocular epitaph, 'On G—', which has been misunderstood more consistently, and done his memory more disservice, than almost anything he has written. It was first published anonymously by him in the 1732 volume of his and Swift's *Miscellanies*, where the lines run as follows:

EPITAPH

On *G——*

Well then, poor *G—* lies under ground!
    So there's an end of honest *Jack*.
So little Justice here he found,
    'Tis ten to one he'll ne'er come back.

[1] From the letter of 'July ye 6'. This and the foregoing quotations are taken from Pope's autographs, now in the possession of Mr D. F. Hyde, New York.

[2] That is, until September 1944, when the present chapter was in part first printed in *The National Review*.

The collection—Pope's last miscellany—in which this epitaph first appeared, has already been discussed in a previous chapter,[1] and the general arguments there advanced to prove Pope's authorship of a number of pieces in it (of which this epitaph is one) need not be repeated here. Other evidence, however, touching this piece in particular, remains to be considered.

After its first anonymous publication, this epitaph was marked as *not* by Swift in the re-arranged edition of his and Pope's *Miscellanies*, 1742, only to be irresponsibly ascribed to him in several subsequent anthologies. Then, in 1775, it was printed for the first time—but for no given reason—under Pope's name in *The St. James's Chronicle* for September 21–23; and thus, four years later, in 'Johnson's' *English Poets*, it came to be incorporated, again without proof, in the Pope canon, where it has ever since been as arbitrarily retained by practically all his editors. In the same way, most of the editors have identified 'G—' with John Gay—forgetting, or not mentioning, that the epitaph was published on October 4, 1732, exactly two months before Gay's death on December 4; and that, strictly speaking, it is not an epitaph at all. Consequently, it follows that if Pope was the author, he is straightway acquitted of having spoken so heartlessly of his dead friend; and that if 'G—' was not Gay, that old libel is even more completely exploded.

Nevertheless, there is evidence that tradition was right for once—though only partly right. It was correct in its identification of author and subject, but not of date and occasion. In addition to the 'general' evidence, earlier advanced,[2] for Pope's authorship of this piece (among others), the present writer has located at the British Museum[3] a contemporary transcript among the papers of Pope's great friend, the Earl of Oxford, which is entitled 'Mr. Gay's Epitaph by Mr. Pope.' Moreover, internal evidence supports both conjectures, for the 'honest Jack' of the second line is paralleled a number of times in Pope's letters, it being probably his favourite epithet for Gay, whose honesty and integrity he never tires of praising: 'like Gay . . . inflexibly honest'[4]; 'a man of a most honest heart, so honest an one, that . . .'[5]; 'Poor Gay is gon before and has not left an honester Man behind him',[6] and so on.

But still more convincing, perhaps, is the witness of occasion. Consequent on the success of *The Beggar's Opera* in February, 1728, Gay

[1] See *ante*, pp. 258 ff.   [2] See *ante*, p. 254.
[3] Harl. 7316, f. 90.   [4] Ball, vi, p. 130.
[5] *Letters*, 4to, 1737, p. 266.   [6] Add. 28618. Letter dated Dec. 14. 1732.

wrote a 'Second Part', *Polly*, the performance of which was banned by
the Lord Chamberlain on December 12, 1728, as we have seen.[1]
The 'book', however, was published early in 1729; and Gay's friends
at Court thereupon became so solicitous for its success, that the chief
of them, the Duchess of Queensbury, was actually 'forbid the Court',[2]
and, on quitting it, took the Duke with her. Gay, about the same time,
was deprived of his apartments in Whitehall, and several others of his
friends were 'turned out of their places'.[3] Altogether a pretty little
scandal, but the death of all Gay's prospects at Court. Thus, apparently early in March, Gay wrote to Pope, half-regretfully, half-
humorously—

> I have no continuing City here. I begin to look upon myself as
> one already dead; and desire . . . that you will, if a Stone should
> mark the Place of my Grave, see these Words put on it:
>> Life is a Jest, and all Things show it;
>> I thought so once, but now I know it.
> With what more you may think proper. If any Body should ask, how
> I could communicate this after Death? Let it be known, it is not
> meant so . . .[4]

Pope's response, it is now practically certain, was this mock epitaph on
(what may be called) Gay's 'court' death. For Gay appears to refer
directly to the words, 'Well then, poor *G*— lies underground!' when,
writing to Swift (March 18), he says: 'Mr. Pope tells me that I am
dead, and that this obnoxiousness is the reward of my inoffensiveness
in my former life.'[5] It has been suggested that when Gay lost his
quarters in Whitehall, he may have taken temporary lodgings in
rooms such as are now termed 'semi-basement', which would have
added further point to Pope's lines, but for which no evidence exists.
But however that may have been, it could not have affected the evidence we have, which all points to one conclusion, namely, that this
epitaph of Pope's, contrary to general supposition, was neither an
unfeeling jest on his friend's death, nor the least offence to him while
still alive, but only yet another of Pope's semi-humorous comments on
contemporary life.

. . .

There is an inscription by Pope still extant in the churchyard of
Stanton Harcourt, which somehow escaped the official collection of
'Epitaphs', and, moreover, was not included in *The Works* until 1751.

---

[1] See *ante*, p. 314. [2] Ball, IV, p. 69. [3] *Ibid.*, p. 73.
[4] *Memoirs*, II, pp. 117 f. [5] Ball, IV, p. 70.

The monument commemorates what Pope calls the 'true and tender story' of the death on Thursday, July 31, 1718, of a pair of village lovers killed in each other's arms by lightning in the nearby harvest fields. The facts are beyond question, and by all reports the storm seems to have been one of the worst of the century. For example, *The Weekly Journal* of Saturday, August 2, reports:

> Such a dreadful Tempest of Thunder and Lightning began betwixt twelve and one of the Clock last Thursday morning . . . that the like has scarce been known in the Memory of Man . . . 'Tis to be fear'd that we shall hear of some bad Accidents . . . but at present we only learn that the greatest Part of a Village near Dagenham in Essex has been destroyed.

Those fears were justified. By the following week news had come in from many districts: hailstones 'full eight inches about' at Lowestoft; 'barns full of wheat . . . burnt up' elsewhere, and buildings wrecked and houses flooded; a farmer and a carter killed near Salisbury, where also 'five Horses were in a Moment struck dead'; and there were other deaths in other places. But while scarcely a newspaper lacks its 'Accounts of Damages done', no mention has been found in them of the Stanton Harcourt couple; and they would have had no more than brief, local fame, had not Pope been in the district. The poet was staying in the old Harcourt house that summer, finishing off the fifth volume of *The Iliad*; and the circumstances of the lovers' deaths, almost at his very door, made a deep impression on him. Gay was visiting him at the time, and apparently they collaborated in a long letter describing the accident in much detail. Copies of this once famous letter, very similar in matter and phraseology were sent by Pope to Martha Blount on August 6,[1] and to Lady Mary W. Montagu on September 1[2]; another copy was sent by Gay on August 9[3] to 'Mr. F—' (probably Fortescue)[4]; and about the same time Pope and Gay together sent the same letter—presumably—to Lord Bathurst, for although their transcript is not on record, he replied to Pope on August 14, sending 'my thanks to Mr. Gay and you for your melancholy novel you sent me of the two unhappy lovers . . .'[5] In addition to these Pope sent a short description of the accident to Caryll[6] (September 3) and Atterbury[7] (September 8), of which, more later. All the long 'August' letters extant, and the one to Lady Mary, include a

---

[1] Mapledurham, 3. [2] Warton, VIII, p. 363. [3] *Letters*, 4to, 1737, p. 243.
[4] Ayre says 'Fenton', and dates the letter August 3. (See *Memoirs*, II, p. 108.)
[5] EC, VIII, p. 325. [6] Add. 28618, f. 51. [7] Atterbury, II, pp. 63 ff.

six-line epitaph on the lovers; but on whose initiative it was written and who wrote it are not at all clear.

The wife of Simon Harcourt (son of Pope's host), writing from Cockthrop in the neighbourhood, on August 16, and speaking about the accident to the 'sweethearts', said that 'they are both buried in a grave, and my Father tells Mr. Pope and Mr. Gay, that he thinks they ought to make an Epitaph upon them'.[1] Ten days earlier, however, Pope writing to Martha Blount had said: 'I have prevailed on my Lord Harcourt to erect a little Monument over them, of plain Stone, and have writ the following Epitaph which is to be engraved on it'.

> When Eastern lovers feed the fun'ral fire,
> On the same pile the faithful fair expire;
> Here pitying heav'n that virtue mutual found,
> And blasted both, that it might neither wound.
> Hearts so sincere th'Almighty saw well pleas'd,
> Sent his own lightning, and the Victims seiz'd.

And he similarly claimed the initiative and the authorship of these lines in his letter to Lady Mary. On the other hand, Gay, in his letter to his and Pope's friend, William Fortescue, is sometimes said to claim —though he does not do so explicitly—part authorship when he wrote:

> My Lord Harcourt, at Mr. Pope's and my request, has caus'd a stone to be plac'd over them, upon condition that we should furnish the Epitaph, which is as follows; *When Eastern lovers . . .* [quoted in full, as above]. But my Lord is apprehensive the country people will not understand this, and Mr. Pope says he'll make one with something of scripture in it, and with as little poetry as Hopkins and Sternhold.

On the foregoing evidence a variety of opinions might seem possible. Nevertheless it appears, that, in spite of the fact that Gay's letter to 'Mr. F—' was the only version of the letter which Pope allowed to be printed in his lifetime, the initiative in the matter was again—as so often before—Pope's, and, to judge by their previous collaborations, his the master-pen in both letter and epitaph.

But whatever part Gay may have had in the first epitaph, it is certain that the second one (which Harcourt persuaded or bullied Pope to write) was written by Pope alone. And it is not unamusing to find that although he joked about it with Gay in private, he submitted the first version of twelve lines to Bishop Atterbury on September 8, for

[1] Harcourt, II, p. 184.

his 'opinion both as to the doctrine and to the poetry' (for, after all, it was the poet's first epitaph to be actually engraved on the stone). The bishop replied on September 12, at exhaustive length, the result being that Pope deleted two lines to which he had objected, but took no notice of the rest of the criticisms. The epitaph was thereupon inscribed with only one other correction of the text (not suggested by the bishop), on a memorial tablet on the outside wall of the church, where it stands to this day—now badly in need of renovation.

The first printing of this 'godly' epitaph has hitherto been thought to be the version in *Court Poems*, 1719; but there had been at least three earlier publications of it, the first of which appeared in the third number of a new newspaper, *The White-hall Evening-Post* for September 20–23, 1718. In this version, while the poetry is identical with the inscription on the stone, the preliminary prose statement has several variants which were obviously earlier. And as the 'first edition' of the whole has never been reprinted, this may seem to be the place and time to put it on record. The first printing ran as follows:

Chipping Norton, Sept. 21, 1718.

Sir,—Stanton Harcourt being in this Country, and Mr. Pope being here when the Accident happen'd, he wrote the enclosed Epitaph; which being on a remarkable Occasion and new, I send you for your new Paper.

Near this Place lie the Bodies of John Hewett and Mary Drew, an industrious young Man, and virtuous Maiden of this Parish, who being at Harvest-work (with several others) were in one Instant killed by Lightning, the last Day of July 1718.

> Think not by rig'rous Judgment seiz'd,
>   A Pair so faithful cou'd expire;
> Victims so pure Heav'n saw well pleas'd,
>   And snatch'd them in Cælestial Fire:
> Live well, and fear no sudden Fate;
>   When God calls virtue to the Grave,
> Alike 'tis Justice, soon or late,
>   Mercy alike, to kill or save.
> Virtue unmov'd can hear the Call,
> And face the Flash that melts the Ball.

In addition to these two epitaphs on the Stanton Harcourt lovers, Pope wrote yet another, a ribald couplet, which had survived unpublished and unidentified at Mapledurham until the recent bicentenary of the poet's death, when it was printed for the first time in the article

above-mentioned.[1] When the couplet, which occurs in Pope's autograph in an undated letter to the elder of the Blount sisters, is related,
as it must be, to the Stanton Harcourt accident, it no longer appears
the pointless indecency it has hitherto been supposed, but is seen to be
a typical example of Pope's punning humour, not without parallel
in the present volume.[2] Having been on the spot from the beginning,
he possibly began to think, after a few days, that enough fuss had
been made of the whole affair; possibly Harcourt had been too
exigent or too critical in such a comparatively unimportant matter
as a village churchyard epitaph, while the immortal *Iliad* (the *raison
d'être* of Pope's presence there) and the ancient world awaited the
poet in the study; possibly the ladies of the Harcourt family had
sentimentalized the affair too sweetly—whatever the provocation or
impulse, Pope's irrepressible sense of humour at last broke through
and restored sanity with a smile and a slightly improper third epitaph.
And as Martha Blount had already received her long, romanticized
narrative containing the first epitaph, he sent a copy of the ribald
couplet to Teresa, who, whatever her faults (and they were not so
apparent in 1718 as later), would more readily understand his last
cynical reaction to the whole affair.

To Mrs Teresa Blount

Madm. Since you prefer three hundred pound to two true
Lovers, I presume to send yu the following Epitaph upon them,
wch seems to be written by one of your Taste.

> Here lye two poor Lovers, who had ye mishap
> Tho very chaste people, to die of a Clap.[3]

(The reference to the 'three hundred pound' is obscure; but Pope
appears to be quizzing Teresa for her lack of sentiment and preoccupation with money—as is shown in their letters of 1717–18, and
in the deed executed by Pope in her favour on March 10, 1718.)

.   .   .

On May 17, 1736, Pope wrote to Mrs Knight, the sister of his dead
friend, Craggs:

Madam, Though I forget all the town at this season, I would not
have you think I forget your commissions; but (to put it upon a
truer foot) I can't forget a person I so really loved and esteemed as
the subject of the enclosed inscription. It is now as I think it ought
to be, and the sooner it is engraved the better.[4]

---

[1] See *ante*, p. 327 n.   [2] See *ante*, p. 137.
[3] Mapledurham, 57.   [4] EC, IX, p. 455.

Elwin and Courthope, who did not know of any printed copy of this 'inscription', suggested that it might be the anonymous epitaph on the tomb of her husband, John Knight, in Gosfield church; but advanced no evidence in support of it. Their suggestion, however, is in all probability correct. It is, at least, certain that exactly two months later, four newspapers[1] more or less simultaneously announced:

Yesterday a curious fine Monument was erected in the Church at Gossfield in the County of Essex, to the Memory of John Knight, Esq; and his Lady, on which is the following Inscription, viz.

Johanni Knight,
De Gossfield in Com. Essex Armig.
Qui obiit Oct. 2d 1733.
Anna Craggs
Jacobi Craggs Regi Georgio J.A.
Secretis Soror
Memoriæ, &c. amori sacrum
Conjugi suo charissimo H.S.P.

O fairest Pattern to a failing Age,
Whose publick Virtue knew no Party Rage,
Whose private Name all Titles recommend,—
The pious Son, fond Husband, faithful Friend.
In Manners plain, in Sense alone refin'd,
Good without Show, and without Weakness kind;
To Reason's equal Dictates ever true,
Calm to resolve, and constant to pursue.
In Life with every social Grace adorn'd;
In Death by Friendship, Honour, Virtue mourn'd.

That Pope should have sent an inscription written at her request to Mrs Knight, who lived at Gosfield, to be engraved on a tomb; and that Mrs Knight two months later should have completed the erection of a monument in Gosfield church to her husband's memory, on which is engraved a poetical epitaph written in Pope's style and embodying two or three phrases he used elsewhere more or less about the same period—such an extraordinary series of coincidences of place, time, person, occasion, inscription and style, together make his authorship of the epitaph virtually certain.

Moreover, George Vertue's diary at Welbeck contains a transcript

---

[1] These were *The Daily Gazetteer*; *The General Evening Post*; *The London Evening-Post*; and *The St. James's Evening Post*,—all published on July 17, 1736.

of these lines, both Latin and English, under the year 1739, with the following comment:

> In the church at Gosfield—is a monument of Marble statues erected by Mrs. Knight, in memory of Mr. Knight and her self . . . at no small expence the work of M. Rysbrake—these lines by Mr. Pope. she soon married again . . . and since that has ordered it to be enclosed as it is with a wainscot screen to shutt up this Monument from her sight when she goes to church, tho' seldom.

There is now on the monument a third inscription (unfortunately added too late to have given Vertue any pleasure) which reads:

Anne Craggs,
married
1st to James Newsham, Esq:
2dly to John Knight, Esq:
3dly to Robert Nugent, Esq:
created Earl Nugent in 1775.
She died the 22d of November 1756,
Aged 59.

The dates of the various deaths and marriages are omitted; but when it is recalled that Mrs Knight married Nugent within a year of her persuading Pope to write the epitaph on her second husband, it is not surprising to find the poet next year making a tart but (as usual) carefully generalized comment to the world at large on 'widows' and epitaphs:

> But random Praise — . . .
> Each Widow asks it for the Best of Men,
> For him she weeps, and him she weds agen.[1]

The suggestion has already been considered in a previous chapter[2] and virtually established, that, if Pope did allude to any particular person in this couplet, it was not (as has sometimes been stated) Mrs Rowe, the widow of the playwright, but Mrs Knight. And this identification, supported as it is by Horace Walpole's corroboration, would seem to add the last touch of conviction to the case for Pope's authorship of the epitaph. It remains only to note that, unlike the foregoing problem, the difficulty of determining the first printing of the poem amongst four newspaper versions of the same date is in this case more apparent than real. As we have seen,[3] both natural law and the custom of the trade ensured that morning papers were normally published earlier than evening papers; it may therefore be taken as certain that

---

[1] *Epilogue to the Satires*, ii, ll. 106, 108–9.   [2] See *ante*, p. 151.   [3] See *ante*, p. 197.

the 'first edition' of this recovered epitaph of Pope's is that which is found in *The Daily Gazetteer* for July 17, 1736.

.   .   .

But fame as the first epitaph-writer of the period had its drawbacks. Pope found that he was continually being pestered, often beyond the limits of good manners, and sometimes of endurance, to write epitaphs in praise of the dead he had never known. In the *Epilogue to the Satires*, II, 1738, he alluded not a little bitterly to this constant solicitation, of which we have already caught a glimpse—

> Find you the Virtue, and I'll find the Verse.
> But random Praise—the Task can ne'er be done,
> Each Mother asks it for her Booby Son,
> Each Widow asks it for the Best of Men,
> For him she weeps, and him she weds agen.
> Praise cannot stoop . . .

It is of course only human to wish the best for one's dead: it is no less human under such importunity to grow irritable, unsympathetic, or flippant in self defence. There is one epitaph, now practically unknown, which is reported to have been spoken extempore by Pope after 'repeated importunities', and which may well be authentic, seeing that it is also vouched for by no less responsible a person than William Stukeley (1687–1765), clergyman, antiquarian, doctor, and friend of Sir Isaac Newton and Warburton (Pope's literary executor). In his manuscript diary, now in the Bodleian, he made the following entry under January 1, 1760:

A gentleman desir'd Mr Pope to give him an epitaph for his da^r *Lætitia* of 3 years old. He gave him this.

EPITAPH

> See here, nice Death, to please his palate,
> Takes a young Lettuce for a sallad.

In conclusion, it may be noted that a slight variant of this epitaph, similarly ascribed to Pope, was printed in *The Fugitive Miscellany*, I, 1775, and again in *The Flower-Piece*, 1780; since when it appears not to have been reprinted until the present day.

CHAPTER XXII

POPE AND HIS DOGS

NEW facts about Pope's life and new interpretations of old facts more and more discredit the hoary tradition of his demonic nature—as many previous pages have shown. One more example, hitherto only glimpsed in passing, may be cited, namely the slowly dawning recognition of the poet's innate humanitarianism. For this has been due in no small measure to a recent biography[1] which rightly stressing Pope's sympathetic advocacy of the brute creation against man's brutality, has helped to spread abroad a truer appreciation of his character. No apology therefore will be expected—or, indeed, offered—for the apparent triviality of these final pages, especially as the story of Pope and his dogs is the story also of a long but little-known poem on the last and best-loved of them, now newly attributed to him with evidence and argument.[2]

Amongst the earliest letters extant in Pope's autograph, untouched and unamended, is one of a group sent to his old friend, Henry Cromwell, dated October 19, 1709; in the course of which, after saying of a certain man who had maligned him to Wycherley—'if I were to change my Dog for such a Man as the aforesaid, I shoud think my Dog undervalu'd; (who follows me about as constantly here in the Country, as I was us'd to do Mr W[ycherley] in the Towne.)', he continued thus:

> Now I talk of my Dog . . . I will give you some account of him . . . You are to know then, that as 'tis Likeness that begets Affection, so my Favorite Dog is a Little one, a lean one, and none of the finest Shap'd. He is not much a Spaniell in his fawning; but has . . . a dumb surly sort of Kindness, that rather shows itself when he thinks me ill-us'd by others, than when we Walk quietly & peaceably by ourselves. If it be the chief point of Friendship to comply with a Friend's Motions & Inclinations, he possesses this in an eminent degree: he lyes down when I sitt, & walks where I walk, wch Is more than many very good Friends can pretend to, witness Our Walk a year ago in St. James's Park.—Histories are more full of Examples of the

[1] Sitwell, pp. 101–2.

[2] The substance of this chapter appeared on the bicentenary of the poet's death, in *The Nineteenth Century and After*, May 1944, pp. 212–21.

Fidelity of Dogs than of Friends. but . . . I will only say for the honour of Dogs that the Two most ancient and esteemable Books . . . (viz: the Scripture and Homer) have shown a particular Regard to these Animals. [1]

Whereupon he briefly instances 'Toby' in the Apocrypha as the more remarkable 'because there was no manner of reason to take notice of the Dog besides the great humanity of the Author'. He then goes on to say that 'Homer's Account of Ulysses's Dog Argus, is the most pathetic imaginable', and after further talk transcribes his little poem, *Argus* (to be found in all editions of his works), which re-tells rather than translates the touching story in the *Odyssey*. Other observations on canine character, breeds, and behaviour follow—with which he concludes his 'Discourse of Dogs' for the time being, only to resume it in a later letter.

There is abundant evidence that the Pope family owned a succession of dogs, the first of which dates back beyond the poet's infancy. In the above letter he recalls how one of them lived to be twenty-two; and seems to imply that, like the normal country household of the period, the Popes kept more than one at a time. Indeed, his first letter to Cromwell, written in verse more than two years earlier than his 'Discourse', bears this out, for it ends with what he called 'news', the last piece being—

> One of our Dogs is dead and gone,
> And I, unhappy! left alone. [2]

The effect of such an upbringing obviously persisted, so that even in middle age he could still write, apropos of a future visit, that 'not to have Mr. Newsham and his dogs' would be 'a diminution to my happiness'. [3]

Thus Pope grew up into manhood, 'with dogs well-bred' (if a misquotation may be allowed), and familiar with them and their ways, whether lap-dog, house-dog, or field-dog. For example, he noticed how on waking in the morning they would 'give themselves the rowsing shake'; and how, if Shock thought his mistress slept too long, he would leap on to the bed 'and wake his Mistress with his Tongue'. He marked the loose-jointed shambling gait of a puppy as it 'daggled through the town', as well as its playful endeavour to 'fetch and carry in its mouth' whatever pleased its passing fancy. He described the ideal country house as one in which he finds everybody willing to be

---

[1] Rawl. letters, 90, f. 17.   [2] *Miscellanea*, I, p. 82.
[3] Bowles, x, p. 103. Letter dated Aug. 23, 1731.

pleased and please, and 'even the very Dogs at ease'; and observed with genuine amusement how the excitable creatures will insist on participating in any household crisis or disturbance, such as the advent of a rat, when—

> . . . from the Hall
> Rush Chaplain, Butler, Dogs and all:
> A Rat! a Rat!

Similarly with field-dogs, he noted how, when accompanying their master out of doors, they would bound before him 'panting with hope'; and how, as the result of training—

> . . . well-bred Spaniels civilly delight
> In mumbling of the game they dare not bite.

In strong contrast to such pleasing glimpses, he also sketched 'the gaunt mastiff growling at the gate', and 'the snappish cur (the passengers' annoy) close at my heels'. All these vivid little pictures, and as many more, show Pope to have been a keen observer of dogs and their ways.

Such minute and sensitive descriptions—apart from their literary merit—are possible only to those with a lively interest in dogs. With Pope this interest was inseparably merged, very early, and for life, in a genuine fondness for their companionship. Their friendly presence was always welcome, for more reasons than one, but chiefly because it fulfilled a spiritual need that was none the less real for being unconscious. His dogs accepted him as he was, without pity and without impertinence, not perceiving that he was in any way different from other men. Thus he always felt 'safe' with them, as never even with his friends, except possibly Gay and Swift.

It is not surprising, therefore, that in his ceaseless advocacy of a more humane treatment of animals (in which he may be said to have led the modern world[1]), dogs should so frequently figure. Three such passages out of many will suffice. In his early essay, *Against Barbarity to Animals*, he quotes 'the excellent Plutarch' with approval for saying that horses and dogs should be cared for, not only while they are of use to us, 'but even when their old Age has made them incapable of

[1]It is not widely realized even now, that in his humanitarianism Pope was born so long before his time. For although its origins may be traced back to the miseries of his puny frame and physical infirmities, which in his impressionable youth induced a fellow feeling for all small or weak creatures in pain, his zealous interest in their well-being, early and late, anticipated by nearly a hundred years the first of the various humane crusades, on which the early Victorians (who for the most part did not think much of Pope or his poetry) prided themselves.

Service'.[1] From his writings of middle life, his indictment of John Ward may be cited, whose 'amusement was to give poison to Dogs and Cats, and see them expire by slower or quicker torments'.[2] And, shortly before he died, Spence recorded, and commented on, his ardent denunciation of vivisection on hearing Dr Hales praised as 'so worthy and good a man', which began thus—

'Yes, he is a very good man; only I'm sorry he has his hands so much imbrued in blood.'

'What, he cuts up rats?'

'Ay, and dogs too!'—[With what emphasis and concern he spoke it.]—'Indeed, he commits most of these barbarities, with the thought of being of use to man: but how do we know that we have a right to kill creatures that we are so little above as dogs, for our curiosity, or even for some use to us?' . . .[3]

Truly Pope's 'concern' for dogs was somehow different from his all-embracing pity and tenderness for other animals: it had a personal quality born of the understanding which long familiarity had given him; it was the solicitude not only of a good man but a good friend. He loved dogs, that is unquestionable; but even more he loved this dog and that dog, Shock and Fop, Bounce and the legendary Argus, not to mention all those companions of his youth who were—and for him always remained—distinct and separate individuals with characters and names of their own; though for us they are no more than nameless playful shadows leaping about the path of the dreaming poet in the Forest, or recumbent at his feet as he sat scribbling verses by the fireside.

Of all Pope's dogs, perhaps the best loved, certainly the best known, was Bounce—if indeed there were not two of that name. The poet's half-sister, Mrs Rackett, once told Spence, that, after the publication of *The Dunciad* in 1728—

My brother does not seem to know what fear is. When some of the people that he had put into his Dunciad, were so much enraged against him, and threatened him so highly: he loved to walk out alone, and particularly went often to Mr. Fortescue's at Richmond. Only he would take Bounce with him . . .' [At this point Spence adds a note: 'Bounce was a great faithful Danish dog belonging to Mr. Pope.'] 'When my brother's faithful dog, and companion in

[1] *The Guardian*, May 21, 1713. (Pope's *Prose*, I, pp. 197 ff.)

[2] *Moral Essay*, III, 1732, l. 20 n.

[3] Spence, pp. 293 f. (see also Ruffhead, pp. 514 f.).

these walks, died; he had some thoughts of burying him in his garden, and putting a piece of marble over his grave, with the epitaph: O RARE BOUNCE! and he would have done it, I believe, had not he apprehended that some people might take it to have been meant as a ridicule of Ben Jonson.'[1]

The question now arises: Was this Bounce the Bounce of Pope's last years? If Mrs Rackett, or Spence, or Spence's editors did not confuse dogs, names, sexes, or dates—apparently not; for *this* Bounce was a male dog, was Pope's guardian in 1728, and was dead and buried some time before 1742–43, the date of the above conversation; whereas the Bounce of 1736 was, as will be seen, a bitch who lived till 1744. If, however, there was some slip of memory, tongue, pen, or print, it is just possible there was only one Bounce, a bitch, Pope's dog from about 1727 to 1744—and even then she would not be as old as the dog he knew in his youth. Either way there are difficulties; but on the whole it seems most probable that Pope had two large dogs in succession, both being called Bounce; in which case it was the second Bounce that became famous.

The earliest printed reference to Bounce on record was made by Pope's old enemy, Curll, in 1735, when he wrote of visiting Pope's house in his absence, and taking 'a full view of our Bard's Grotto, ... Gardens, Statues, Inscriptions, and his Dog BOUNCE'—which unfortunately throws no light on our problem. Next year, however, George (later Lord) Lyttelton, writing to Pope from Bath (December 22, 1736),[2] begins his letter thus:

> Dear Sir,—My cold is gone, and I am now so much recovered, that I grow very impatient to get away from Bath. . . . But to shew you how much I am master of my passions, I will be quiet here for a week or ten days longer, and then come to you in most outrageous spirits, and overturn you like Bounce, when you let her loose after a regimen of physic and confinement. I am very glad that his Royal Highness has received two such honourable presents at a time, as a whelp of *her's*, and the freedom of the City.[3]

Pausing a moment to linger over the pleasing picture of the 'little man' (as Pope's friends called him) being knocked down by his big dog's gambols and *not minding it a bit*—rather liking it, if anything, or Lyttelton would never have threatened to do the same—one cannot

[1] Spence, pp. 267–9.
[2] *Memoirs . . . of . . . Lyttelton*, I, pp. 129 f. (date of letter misprinted, '1739').
[3] This was conferred on him on December 17, 1736.

help contrasting this picture with the popular idea of the poet. Here
too, as a pendant to the above letter, it should be noted that about this
time, or not long after, Pope commemorated the Prince's acceptance
of Bounce's puppy with the following epigram (which was included in
his *Works* two years later):

*Engraved on the Collar of a Dog which I gave to
his Royal Highness.*

I am his Highness' Dog at *Kew*;
Pray tell me Sir, whose Dog are you?

What seems not generally known is that an offer to the Prince of *two* of
Bounce's puppies had been tentatively made some seven months
earlier, in a poem which, for that reason and others presently to be
considered, can now with virtual certainty be attributed wholly or
mainly to Pope.

On May 4, 1736, Thomas Cooper, one of the publishers whom Pope
was at that time employing, brought out in London a handsome
poetical pamphlet of twelve folio pages, entitled, *Bounce to Fop. An
Heroick Epistle from a Dog at Twickenham to a Dog at Court*; and about the
same time Dean Swift's publisher, Faulkner, issued the same poem in
Dublin—each pamphlet claiming to be a reprint of the other. But
whereas the London edition had on the title-page the words, 'By Dr.
S——T', the Dublin copy had no ascription. This poem, which seems
not to have been reprinted for the last hundred years or more and is
to-day practically unknown, now follows; the text being that of the
London pamphlet, except that it copies the MSS. (of which more
later) in omitting a couplet after line 40, and substitutes 'And' for
'When' in the preceding line.

BOUNCE TO *FOP*

AN HEROICK EPISTLE

From a Dog at *Twickenham* to a Dog at Court.

To thee, sweet *Fop*, these Lines I send,
Who, tho' no Spaniel, am a Friend.
Tho, once my Tail in wanton play,
Now frisking this, and then that way,
Chanc'd, with a Touch of just the Tip,
To hurt your Lady-lap-dog-ship;
Yet thence to think I'd bite your Head off!
Sure *Bounce* is one you never read of.

Fop! you can dance, and make a Leg,
Can fetch and carry, cringe and beg,   10
And (what's the Top of all your Tricks)
Can stoop to pick up *Strings* and *Sticks*.
We Country Dogs love nobler Sport,
And scorn the Pranks of Dogs at Court.
Fye, naughty *Fop!* where e'er you come
To f—t and p—ss about the Room,
To lay your Head in every Lap,
And, when they think not of you—snap!
The worst that Envy, or that Spite
E'er said of me, is, I can bite: 20
That sturdy Vagrants, Rogues in Rags,
Who poke at me, can make no Brags;
And that to towze such Things as *flutter*,
To honest *Bounce* is Bread and Butter.

While you, and every courtly Fop,
Fawn on the Devil for a Chop,
I've the Humanity to hate
A Butcher, tho' he brings me Meat;
And let me tell you, have a Nose,
(Whatever stinking Fops suppose)   30
That under Cloth of Gold or Tissue,
Can smell a Plaister, or an Issue.

Your pilf'ring Lord, with simple Pride,
May wear a Pick-lock at his Side;
My Master wants no Key of State,
For *Bounce* can keep his House and Gate.

When all such Dogs have had their Days,
As knavish *Pams*, and fawning *Trays*;
[And] pamper'd *Cupids*, beastly *Veni*'s,
And motley, squinting *Harvequini*'s†. . .   40
Fair *Thames* from either ecchoing Shore
Shall hear, and dread my manly Roar.

See *Bounce*, like *Berecynthia*, crown'd
With thund'ring Offspring all around,

† For *Harvequini*'s, read *Harlequini*'s.

x

Beneath, beside me, and a top,
A hundred Sons! and not one *Fop*.

Before my Children set your Beef,
Not one true *Bounce* will be a Thief;   50
Not one without Permission feed,
(Tho' some of I[lay]'s hungry Breed)
But whatsoe'er the Father's Race,
From me they suck a little Grace.
While your fine Whelps learn all to steal,
Bred up by Hand on Chick and Veal.

My Eldest-born resides not far,
Where shines great *Strafford*'s glittering Star:
My second (Child of Fortune!) waits
At *Burlington*'s Palladian Gates: 60
A third majestically stalks
(Happiest of Dogs!) in *Cobham*'s Walks:
One ushers Friends to *Bathurst*'s Door;
One fawns, at *Oxford*'s, on the Poor.

Nobles, whom Arms or Arts adorn,
Wait for my Infants yet unborn.
None but a Peer of Wit and Grace,
Can hope a Puppy of my Race.

And O! wou'd Fate the Bliss decree
To mine (a Bliss too great for me)   70
That two, my tallest Sons, might grace
Attending each with stately Pace,
Iülus's Side, as erst *Evander*'s,*
To keep off Flatt'rers, Spies, and Panders.
To let no noble Slave come near,
And scare Lord *Fannys* from his Ear.
Then might a Royal Youth, and true,
Enjoy at least a Friend—or two:
A Treasure, which, of Royal kind,
Few but Himself deserve to find.   80

Then *Bounce* ('tis all that *Bounce* can crave)
Shall wag her Tail within the Grave.

§ Son of Æneas: reference to the Prince of Wales.   * *Virg. Æn.* viii.

And tho' no Doctors, Whig or Tory ones,
Except the Sect of *Pythagoreans*,
Have Immortality assign'd
To any Beast, but *Dryden*'s‡ Hind:
Yet Master *Pope*, whom Truth and Sense
Shall call their Friend some Ages hence,
Tho' now on loftier Themes he sings
Than to bestow a Word on *Kings*,　　　　　90
Has sworn by *Sticks* (the Poet's Oath,
And Dread of Dogs and Poets both)
Man and his Works he'll soon renounce,
And roar in Numbers worthy *Bounce*.

‡ A Milk-white Hind, immortal and unchang'd. Ver. 1. Of the *Hind* and *Panther*.

Here Fop begs for a word. Briefly, she belonged to the Countess of Suffolk, formerly Mrs Howard, near neighbour and friend of Pope's at Twickenham. When Swift came to England in 1726 and 1727, he stayed at Pope's house and, as we have seen,[1] accompanied him on visits to Mrs Howard, with whom he became very friendly. Writing to her on July 9, 1727, Swift speaks of 'your dog Fop'; and the dog is mentioned by name elsewhere in his mistress's correspondence several times between 1727 and 1730. Nothing is known of Fop's death; but Walpole says that Pope 'wrote the Epitaph in [the Countess's] Garden on her Dog Fop'[2] (apparently one of the 'lost works' of Pope); Fop, however, would seem to have been still alive in 1736 when *Bounce to Fop* was first published.

This 'Heroick Epistle' has in the past been separately ascribed to Swift and to Gay, and simultaneously included in some old editions of their works. The Swift tradition derives originally from the words 'By Dr. S—T' on the title-page of the first London edition, both the text and the attribution being immediately afterwards copied by the magazines. There is no other contemporary evidence that points to Swift, though Walpole subsequently made the unsupported statement that it was the Dean's in a note of which the earlier part is mostly not verifiable and the later part demonstrably wrong.[3] All the other evidence points away from him. For instance, Faulkner, Swift's friend, editor, and publisher, who issued the anonymous Dublin edition of the *Epistle*, consistently excluded the piece from the Swift canon; as indeed have all Swift's editors from Scott onwards, the most recent of

[1] See *ante*, p. 273.　　　　[2] *Reminiscences*, etc., 1924, p. 102.　　　　[3] *Ibid.*

whom thinks it may be Pope's.[1] Furthermore, whoever was responsible for the London title-page (and, in passing, it should be remembered that numerous pamphlets, in verse and in prose, were fathered on the Dean, which he never wrote), Pope himself, later that same year (1736), included this poem, without ascription and docked of its last twelve lines, in his and Swift's *Miscellanies*, where no new poem except his and Swift's were admitted after 1732. Moreover, in 1742, in the rearranged edition of the *Miscellanies* (in the preparation of which Pope had much to say[2]), the piece was marked by an asterisk in the 'Contents' expressly to indicate that it was *not* by Swift. Lastly, Swift's continued absence from England from 1727 onwards is a further argument against his sole responsibility for the poem, which alludes to incidents and facts unlikely to have been known to him in Ireland: such, to mention no more, as the various recipients of Bounce's puppies, and the suggested offer to the Prince of two of them.

Gay, in marked contrast, was not credited with Bounce's *Epistle* until 1773, when it was first included in his works, in Bell's edition, without comment.[3] But Gay died in 1732, before several events mentioned in the poem could have happened (including Pope's invention and publication of Hervey's nickname, 'Lord Fanny'); and Gay's latest editors independently deny his authorship of the poem, thinking it more in the manner of Pope than of Gay.[4]

The case for Pope is a different matter altogether. Nevertheless, the only contemporary testimony of his connection with *Bounce to Fop* yet recorded, is that found in Lord Oxford's copy of the London folio, now in the Bodleian, on whose title-page, after the words, 'By Dr. S——T', the Earl has written 'much altered by Mr. Pope'. And Oxford, as an old friend of both poets, and the owner of one of Bounce's puppies as well as the preserver of the earlier manuscript version of Bounce's *Epistle*, was in a better position than most to know the facts of the case. On the other hand, internal evidence abundantly testifies to Pope's authorship. The poem is concerned with his own dog Bounce and is written with a gusto possible only to an inveterate dog-lover such as we now know Pope (but *not* Swift) to have been. The piece also contains attacks on one of Pope's latest enemies, Lord Hervey, which he (but again *not* Swift) had every incentive to make. These are seen in the intentional 'misprint', *Harvequini*'s for *Harlequini*'s, and its correction (in the MS. version it is spelt 'Hervey queenies', and not corrected); and also in the line, 'And scare Lord *Fannys* from his Ear'

---

[1] Williams, III, p. 1135.   [2] See *ante*, p. 254.
[3] *Miscellaneous Works*, IV, pp. 120–4.   [4] Underhill, II, p. 234; and Faber, p. xxv.

('his' being the Prince's), which actually echoes Pope's earlier couplet on the same person: 'Not *Fannius* self more impudently near, When half his Nose is in his Patron's Ear' (*Fourth Satire of Donne*, 1733).

Another striking parallel is found in the first edition of *The Dunciad*, Book III (published May 18, 1728), as follows:

> As *Berecynthia*, while her offspring vye
> In homage, to the mother of the sky,
> Surveys around her in the blest abode
> A hundred sons, and ev'ry son a God.
>
> (ll. 123–26)

> See *Bounce*, like *Berecynthia*, crown'd
> With thund'ring Offspring all around,
> Beneath, beside me, and a top,
> A hundred Sons! and not one *Fop*.
>
> (*Bounce to Fop*, ll. 45–48)

One other parallel is especially interesting. Pope had—what Swift certainly had not—a fondness for what may be called the pathetic parenthesis, a form which will probably be remembered best in Thomas Gray's later use of it in the famous *Elegy*: 'He gain'd from Heav'n ('twas all he wish'd) a Friend.' Thus, in Pope's early poem on *Argus*, where the aged dog recognizes his master, Ulysses, we find:

> Him when he saw he rose and crawl'd to meet
> ('Twas all he could) and fawn'd, and kiss'd his feet.

Again, nine years later, in *The Iliad*, xvi, 632:

> To Phœbus then ('twas all he could) he pray'd.

And then, in 1726, in *The Odyssey*, xvii, 362–3, again about Argus:

> Yet (all he could) his tail, his ears, his eyes
> Salute his master.

And now, here in the *Epistle*, we hear Bounce speaking with the very voice of *her* master:

> Then Bounce ('tis all that Bounce can crave)
> Shall wag her Tail within the Grave.

The echoes of phrase and manner in the foregoing passages, together with all the preceding evidence, present an overwhelming case for Pope's authorship, whole or part, of *Bounce to Fop*—a case which is further strengthened by an earlier version of the poem found only in manuscript. The present writer has been able to locate and collate a contemporary transcript amongst the Oxford family papers at Welbeck Abbey, the text of which does not include the couplet on 'Lord Fanny', for instance, or name more than two of the five noble recipients of Bounce's puppies—Oxford himself being one of those who had not yet been so honoured. A second manuscript copy, found amongst the 'Portland Papers' at Longleat, is verbally identical with the Welbeck text, and is likewise one of the Oxford family papers.

If, therefore, a hypothesis covering all the known facts may be ventured: it would appear that the idea of the poem dates from 1726 or, more probably, 1727, when Swift was staying with Pope (and Bounce) at Twickenham; and when on visits to Mrs Howard with Pope, he met Fop as well; and that, one day, some chance remark by host or guest on the different natures of the two dogs led on to a comparison of the rustic Bounce and the court Fop, and thence possibly to the notion of a letter from one to the other; on which (as seems to have happened before[1]) impromptu lines were bandied to and fro in jocular rivalry and jotted down by Swift or Pope indifferently—lines which became the basis of the poem to be largely rewritten by Pope years later. Some such natural origin would at least provide a colourable excuse for the appearance of Swift's name on the title page of the London folio, and would account for Oxford's acceptance of Swift's original co-operation in the writing as well as Pope's extensive alterations.

Thus the poem would seem to have passed through three stages, the earliest being the Swift-Pope collaboration in a first draft now vanished; the second, Pope's subsequent expansion of the joint draft, which has survived in the Oxford transcripts only, where it is entitled *Bounce and Fopp*, and contains matter about the second Bounce almost certainly outside Swift's cognizance; the third and final stage being the text of the 1736 folio, which is Pope's still later revision of the poem on the eve of publication.

Bounce was the last of Pope's dogs; and her death so nearly coincided with that of her master as to make them one story, and a not unfitting close to the present volume. During the six years that followed the printing of her *Epistle*, Bounce 'kept House and Gate' at Twickenham; and it seems to have been during this period, that—like other celebrities of the time—she sat for her picture. In a little-known portrait of Pope by Richardson[2] preserved at Hagley, she is depicted

---

[1] See *ante*, pp. 242–3.

[2] See frontispiece, where the complete picture is reproduced for the first time.

in the foreground as 'a large brown hound . . . looking lovingly up at him'.[1] In the summer of 1742, however, failing strength or increasing infirmities of either the master or the dog led to Bounce's being committed to the care of the poet's friend, Lord Orrery. But, in spite of separation, Pope's continuing concern for the dog's well-being is revealed in a letter to Orrery (July 23, 1742) in which, after praising his friend's humanity not only to mankind but also to animals 'and in particular to dogs', he goes on to say, 'Yet I will not allow you should retard the satisfaction I was sure to receive in hearing of your own, till you could also acquaint me of Bounce's safe arrival in Somersetshire'[2] (Orrery's house being at Marston in that county).

Within eighteen months of the separation, when Pope was rapidly failing, what looks like a chance remark seems to show that his thoughts would often fly to Bounce and her 'offspring' on the most unlikely occasions. One 'Sunday Night', in January 1744, so it is said, on receiving an inquiry, by note or messenger, asking whether he was well enough to be taken on the morrow to Marchmont's house to meet him and Bolingbroke, Pope replied:

My dear Lords,—Yes, I would see you as long as I can see you, and then shut my eyes upon the world as a thing worth seeing no longer. If your charity would take up a small bird that is half dead of the frost, and set it a-chirping for half an hour, I will jump into my cage, and put myself into your hands to-morrow at any hour you send. Two horses will be enough to draw me (and so would two dogs, if you had them)[3] . . .

—The quick semi-humorous irruption of the parenthesis suggests a sudden mental vision of the contrast between his own small weight and tiny frame and the size and strength of Bounce and her 'tallest Sons'. And, as we have seen when writing to friends, Pope was always inclined to 'throw out what came uppermost'.

Barely three months later, the event which Pope had been dreading happened, and, not improbably, helped to hasten his own end. Early in April, 1744, Pope heard from Orrery of the dog's death, and in the course of a letter, dated April 10, replied:

I dread to enquire into the particulars of yͤ Fate of Bounce. Perhaps you conceald them, as Heav'n often does Unhappy Events, in

[1] *Chronicles of the Eighteenth Century*, M. Wyndham, I, 1924, p. 47.
[2] EC, VIII, p. 503.   [3] Marchmont, II, pp. 291 f.

pity to the Survivors, or not to hasten on my End by Sorrow. I doubt not how much Bounce was lamented: They might say as the Athenians did to Arcite, in Chaucer,

> Ah Arcite! gentle Knight! why would'st thou die,
> When thou had'st Gold enough and Emilye?

Then, with a whimsical but wholly characteristic touch, he adapted the imperfectly remembered lines to his own sad loss, and penned what seem to have been the last lines of verse he ever wrote:

> Ah Bounce! ah gentle Beast! why wouldst thou dye,
> When thou had'st Meat enough, and Orrery?

Seven weeks later, Pope too had entered the Elysian fields, where (for one reader at least), like 'the poor Indian' in the *Essay on Man*,

> His faithful dog shall bear him company.

THE END

APPENDICES
&
INDEXES

APPENDIX A

BIOGRAPHICAL NOTES

[Concerning persons discussed in the text, with particular regard to their connection with Pope]

ADDISON, Joseph (1672–1719). Poet, essayist, and Whig statesman. He is best known to-day for his contributions to *The Tatler*, *The Spectator*, and *The Guardian*, which made him the acknowledged arbiter of morals and manners. His review of Pope's *Essay on Criticism* led to their acquaintance, and Pope shortly afterwards wrote the Prologue to his play *Cato*. His friends, political followers, and toadies, frequented Button's coffeehouse, forming there what Pope called Addison's 'little Senate', which on the whole was inimical to the young poet. He countenanced, if not participated in the rival translation of the *Iliad* by Tickell, which resulted in the famous Pope-Addison quarrel and the 'Atticus' lines (see Chap. VI). Addison was M.P. for Malmesbury from 1709 till death; married the Countess of Warwick (1716); retired from office with pension (1718); and quarrelled with Steele (1719).

ARBUTHNOT, John (1667–1735). Physician and author; M.D. St Andrews, 1696. He settled in London, date unknown, but prior to 1704 when he was made F.R.S.; was appointed physician in ordinary to Queen Anne 1709–14; wrote *History of John Bull*, 1712, about which time he was introduced to Pope by Swift, forming with them and Gay the Scriblerus Club, which often met at his lodgings, 1713–14. He collaborated with Gay and Pope in the farce, *Three Hours*

after Marriage, 1717; contributed to the Swift-Pope *Miscellanies*, 1727–8; continued in intimate friendship with Pope, who wrote his famous *Epistle to Dr. Arbuthnot* in 1734.

ARGYLE, John Campbell, second Duke of (1678–1743). Soldier and statesman. He entered the army 1694; succeeded to dukedom 1703; was created Earl of Greenwich 1705, and Duke of Greenwich 1719. He warmly promoted the Act of Union in 1705, and crushed the Jacobite rebellion, January 1716. He was a friend of Pope, who stayed with him occasionally between 1717 and 1739, and who addressed several poems to him (see Chap. X).

ATTERBURY, Francis (1662–1732). Bishop of Rochester and Dean of Westminster, 1713. How he and Pope became acquainted is not known, but he was a member of the Scriblerus Club in 1713, and Pope and he became firm friends. His strong Jacobite sympathies led him to correspond with the Pretender, 1717. He was imprisoned in the Tower, 1722, and at his trial (at which Pope gave evidence in his favour) he was found guilty of conspiracy to restore the Stuarts, and banished, 1723; he went first to Brussels and then to France, where he died. Pope wrote, and suppressed, an epitaph in dialogue on him and his daughter, who had predeceased him (see Chap. XVIII).

BLACKMORE, Sir Richard (1655?–1729). Court physician, knighted by William III, 1697; published many long poems 1695–1723, as well as medical, theological and political works, much of his verse being written in his coach on his professional rounds, for which Dryden ridiculed him as one who 'Writes to the rumbling of his chariot wheels'. After an early acquaintance with Sir Richard, Pope quarrelled with him for attacking Swift (1716); and when the knight in return accused Pope of blasphemy for writing what seemed to be a burlesque of the 'First Psalm', Pope continued the quarrel on his own behalf, and made fun of him from time to time in his works both prose and verse, but chiefly in *The Dunciad*, and a 'new' poem called *England's Arch-Poet* (see Chapter XV).

BLOUNT, Martha (1690–1762). Friend of Pope from youth onwards. She and her sister Teresa were daughters of Lister Blount of Mapledurham, and grand-daughters of Anthony Englefield of Whiteknights, neighbour and friend of the Pope family at Binfield, at whose house Pope probably made their acquaintance. She was educated at a ladies' school in Hammersmith, and later in Paris. Gay described 'the two lovely sisters' in 1720 as 'The fair-hair'd Martha, and Teresa brown'. Unfounded rumours at various times made Martha indifferently Pope's mistress or wife; but for either relation there is 'no evidence of the slightest validity' (see Sherburn, pp. 291–7). Pope bequeathed to her practically all his property as residuary legatee.

BLOUNT, Teresa Maria (1688–1759). Elder sister of Martha, and likewise a friend of Pope until a growing enmity (1718–20) finally led to a complete estrangement about 1721, after which she practically passed out of Pope's life.

BOLINGBROKE, Henry St John, First Viscount (1678–1751). Tory statesman, and moral philosopher. He was a friend of Pope prior to his attainder and flight to France in 1714; and Pope courageously acknowledged his indebtedness to the exile in the Preface to *The Iliad*, 1715. On being pardoned in 1723, Bolingbroke returned to lead the opposition to Walpole's government; and settled down at Dawley Farm near Twickenham. Pope's admiration of him grew to be only a little less than idolatry; and he has been called 'the father of the *Essay on Man*, the *Moral Essays*, and the *Imitations of Horace*'. He attended Pope's death-bed, but afterwards his loyalty to Pope fell short of Pope's early loyalty to him.

BOYLE, John, Earl of Orrery. See Orrery.

BOYLE, Richard, Earl of Burlington. See below.

BURLINGTON, Richard Boyle, third Earl of (1695–1753). Statesman and patron of literature and art. He was a connoisseur of architecture, especially the work of Palladio, in whose style he rebuilt Burlington House at Chiswick. From 1715, if not earlier, he was an intimate friend of Pope; and became one of the three 'publishers' of *The Dunciad* in 1728. Pope addressed his epistle, *Of Taste*, to him; and some charming stanzas to Lady Burlington on 'cutting paper'.

BURNET, Thomas (1694–1753). Youngest son of Bishop Burnet; as a young man he was 'notorious for debauchery and wit', but subsequently reformed. In 1715, as a follower of Addison and a frequenter of Button's coffee-house, he joined in the general attack on Pope, without personal provocation, writing against him in several numbers of his periodical, *The Grumbler*. The same year he also produced, in collaboration with George Duckett and with Addison's concurrence, two editions of a squib called *Homerides*, and another work with the same title in 1716—these attacks being specially directed against Pope's *Iliad*. He thus qualified for his place in *The Dunciad*. He became a judge in 1741 and was knighted in 1745.

CAMPBELL, John, second Duke of Argyle. See Argyle.

CARYLL, John (1666?–1736). A worthy and wealthy Roman Catholic squire of West Grinsted, Sussex; remembered now only as an intimate friend of Pope. They probably became acquainted at the house of Caryll's relative, Anthony Englefield, Pope's neighbour in the Forest, at some date before 1710, in which year Pope's famous correspondence with him began. These letters (in a transcript by members of the Caryll family) are now preserved in the British Museum. It was at the instance of Caryll (whose relative, Lord Petre, had cut off a lock of Arabella Fermor's hair, and thus started a quarrel between the two families) that Pope wrote *The Rape of the Lock* in 1712.

CIBBER, Colley (1671–1757). Actor, dramatist, and Poet Laureate. He went on the stage in 1690, and succeeded best in comedy. His first play, *Love's Last Shift*, was produced 1695–6. He became joint-licensee of the Haymarket Theatre, 1710, and of Drury Lane, 1712; brought out *The Non-Juror* (adapted and translated from Molière) attacking the Jacobites, 1717. His autocratic management of the theatre caused much resentment; he refused *The Beggar's Opera* in 1729; was appointed Laureate in 1730; and wrote his *Apology* for

his life in 1740. His quarrel with Pope began about 1714–15 and continued intermittently till Pope's death; his most virulent attacks taking the form of public 'Letters', the first being *A Letter from Mr Cibber to Mr Pope*, 1742, in return for which Pope raised him to the throne of the Dunces.

CIBBER, Theophilus (1703–1758). Actor, dramatist and pamphleteer; son of Colley Cibber (above). He made his first appearance on the stage in 1721; and succeeded his father as part licensee of Drury Lane, 1731–2. He had only a relatively small part in the production of *The Lives of the Poets . . . By Mr Cibber and other Hands*, 1753, which was mainly compiled by Robert Shiels.

COBHAM, Sir Richard Temple, Viscount (1675–1749). Soldier and Whig statesman, patron of literature. He fought under Marlborough, 1708, and captured Vigo, 1719. He opposed Walpole's Excise Bill (1733); was later dismissed from his regiment; and after Walpole's fall was made Field Marshal (1742). His friendship with Pope began about 1725 and lasted till death. He is best known today as having rebuilt Stowe, and laid out its famous gardens on lines of which Pope, a frequent visitor there, highly approved. Pope's first *Moral Essay* was addressed to Lord Cobham in 1733.

CROMWELL, Henry (1659–1728). A distant connection of the Protector's family, with an estate in Lincolnshire. He lived much in London—man about town, poetaster, critic, elderly rake, and friend of the youthful Pope. The originals of their correspondence are preserved in the Bodleian. Their friendship lasted from 1708 to 1712 when it practically ceased, probably because Cromwell had become friendly with Pope's most implacable enemy, Dennis.

CURLL, Edmund (1675–1747). Bookseller and pamphleteer. The most notorious publisher in the history of English literature, his imprints range from 1706 to 1746. Unscrupulous and uncontrollable in his methods of obtaining copy, and as ready—if not more ready—to publish pornographic, seditious, or scandalous matter, as to publish reputable literature, he made money by pirating authors' works while they were alive, and by selling unauthorized 'lives' of them when they were dead. Pope first became his victim in 1714, and, though he revenged himself on Curll in various ways, was still being victimized in 1741.

DENNIS, John (1657–1734). Critic, dramatist, and poet, irascible and domineering in manner, but an honest and intelligent critic on the whole. He is remembered to-day for his criticism to some extent, but principally because of his interminable quarrel with Pope, the cause of which is unknown but probably sprang from a mutual antipathy. He bitterly attacked most of the major works of Pope from *An Essay on Criticism*, 1711, to *The Dunciad*, 1728; his criticism, in the case of Pope, being largely vitiated by personal abuse. Pope occasionally retaliated; his chief weapon being ridicule, his humorous *Narrative of Dr. Robert Norris Concerning the . . . Frenzy of Mr. John Denn—*, 1713, probably hurting the humourless old critic most of all. His last years were spent in straitened circumstances which Pope twice attempted to relieve without his knowledge (see Chap. XIX).

DODSLEY, Robert (1703–1764). Poet, dramatist, and one of the most famous booksellers of the eighteenth century, his best-known publications being his *Select Collection of Old Plays* (12 vols., 1744) and his *Collection of Poems* (which began with three but ended with six vols., 1748–58). He was befriended by Pope in his early days as publisher, with financial assistance as well as the publication of various editions of the poet's works, both single and collected.

DYER, John (1700?–1758). Painter and poet. He studied art under Richardson and became 'an itinerant painter'; visited Italy 1724–6, and published *Grongar Hill* and *The Country Walk*, his best known poems, in 1726. *The Ruins of Rome* did not appear till 1740, about which date he took orders and settled for a time in Leicestershire. Later, he held the livings of Coningsby and Kirby, completing *The Fleece* at the former place in 1757, the year before his death. It is not known that Dyer and Pope ever met; but they knew some of the same people, and Dyer's verse was certainly influenced by Pope, whom he also followed in the frequent use of colour-words in description.

GAY, John (1685–1732). Poet and dramatist, and, from about 1711 onwards, Pope's dearest and most intimate friend—not even excepting Swift. He held posts as secretary to various people, the Duchess of Monmouth, Lord Clarendon, Pulteney, etc., finally being domiciled with the Duke and Duchess of Queensberry till his death. One of the original members of the Scriblerus Club, he collaborated with Pope in various literary projects, the farce, *Three Hours after Marriage*, 1717, in which Arbuthnot also had part, being the best known example. He is said to have made more than £1,000 by the publication of his *Poems*, 1720, only to lose it the same year in the 'South-Sea Bubble'. *The Beggar's Opera* (1728) and *Fables* (1727), and, probably, *Trivia* (1716) are his most famous works. He was buried in Westminster Abbey and Pope wrote his epitaph.

GILDON, Charles (1665–1724). Author, critic, and compiler of miscellanies 1694–1701. With no known provocation by Pope, Gildon attacked him in *A New Rehearsal*, 1714 (for which there is evidence suggesting he was paid by Addison), and in other publications, including the *Memoirs of Wycherley*, 1718. The cause of his persistent animosity to Pope is unknown, but at least it is certain that Pope's rejoinders were neither so numerous nor so virulent as Gildon's attacks.

HARLEY, Edward, second Earl of Oxford. See OXFORD.

HARLEY, Robert, first Earl of Oxford. See OXFORD.

HORNECK, Philip (d. 1728). Attorney and party writer; Solicitor to the Treasury (1716–28). He was the author of a periodical called *The High-German Doctor* (1714–15), which repeatedly and unprovokedly attacked Pope and his friends. To these acrimonious assaults Pope made few and curiously unmoved rejoinders, which, of course, may only have irritated Horneck the more, as showing Pope thought him not worth serious attention.

HOWARD, Henrietta, Countess of Suffolk. See SUFFOLK.

HUGHES, John (1677–1720). Poet and dramatist; first editor of Spenser; contributor to *The Tatler*, *The Spectator*, and *The Guardian*; friend of Addison and Blackmore; he is said to have had some instruction in painting in early life. His acquaintance

with Pope probably began at Button's coffee-house about 1712–13; but in 1714 he wrote an anonymous epigram on the publication of Pope's *Iliad* by subscription, which included a covert sneer at its success. His collected *Works*, first published in 1735, revealed his authorship of the epigram, which, if Pope had not known its author's name earlier, might account for an otherwise puzzling change of tone in Pope's allusions to him from that date onwards. He unsuccessfully solicited Pope to write a Prologue for his last play, *The Siege of Damascus*; and died of consumption about the time of its first performance.

JACOB, Giles (1686–1744). Legal hack-writer, poetaster, and compiler of the *Poetical Register* and other works of reference. He burlesqued Pope's *Rape of the Lock* in 1717, attacked *Three Hours after Marriage*, and otherwise offended Pope, thus earning for himself a niche in *The Dunciad*.

JERVAS, Charles (1675?–1739). Portrait painter, and translator of *Don Quixote*. He studied under Kneller, and for a period in Italy; was appointed 'Principal Painter' to George II, and became the fashionable portraitist of the day. He painted many of Pope's friends, and Pope himself more than once. His house in Cleveland Court, St James's, was Pope's London residence for several years from 1713 onwards; it was there that Pope took lessons in painting from him in 1713–14; and it was still being used by Pope as his London address as late as 1725. Their friendship was life-long; and Jervas bequeathed £1,000 to Pope if he should outlive Mrs Jervas—which he failed to do. Jervas's *Don Quixote* was published posthumously in 1742.

KENT, William (1684–1748). Architect, sculptor, painter, and landscape-gardener. He practised painting in London as early as 1703, before going to study in Italy; was brought back to England in 1719 by Lord Burlington, who became and remained his patron, and gave him house-room for life. Pope and Kent, having many tastes in common, became intimate friends, and it is said that 'Pope both instructed and was instructed by Kent', which is certainly true of gardening. Kent painted Pope's portrait, and made many engravings for his books, notably *The Works*, Vol. II, 1735. In the Pope-Burlington correspondence still unpublished, Kent's 'sweetness of manners' is alluded to, and he is often styled 'the Signior'.

KNELLER, Sir Godfrey (originally Gottfried Kniller), (1646–1723). Portrait-painter; he came to England from Germany, 1675; painted a portrait of Charles II, 1678, and nine other reigning sovereigns. Most of the important people of his day sat to him for their portraits. Pope, with whom he was very friendly, was painted by him more than once; and wrote his epitaph when he died.

LEWIS, Erasmus (1670–1754). Political servant of Robert Harley, Earl of Oxford, and, after the Earl's fall from power, steward. He was the trusted friend of Swift, Pope, Gay, and Arbuthnot, and an occasional member of the Scriblerus Club. He is mentioned in several of Pope's lighter pieces. Lord Bathurst, another of his friends, used to say that Prior was his verse-man and Lewis his prose-man.

LINTOT, Barnaby Bernard (1675–1736). Bookseller. One of the earliest of Pope's publishers, his imprint is, except for the *Essay on Criticism*, found on the title-pages of all Pope's principal poems from *The Rape of the Lock* (1712–13) to the completed *Homer* (1725), including 'Pope's First Miscellany' (see Chap. II) and the collected *Works* (1717). Disagreement between Lintot and Pope arose over the publisher's high-handed conduct of the publication of *The Odyssey*; as a result of which he ingloriously appears in *The Dunciad*, 1728, and business relations between them were interrupted for some years, and were not resumed until 1736, shortly before Lintot's death.

MANSFIELD, William Murray, first Earl of (1705–1793). Barrister (1730), Lord Chief Justice (1756–88). He first attracted public attention by a speech in the House of Commons about the Spanish depredations in 1738. It is not known when he and Pope first became acquainted; they were, however, on friendly terms in 1737. Pope alluded to him at least twice in his *Imitations of Horace*; and inscribed one of them to his 'dear Murray' in 1738; indeed, Warburton declared that Pope loved him 'with the fondness of a father'. He was one of Pope's executors; and the owner of Pope's portrait of Betterton—which the family still possesses.

MONTAGUE, Lady Mary Wortley (1689–1762). Daughter of Evelyn Pierrepont, afterwards Duke of Kingston; married Edward Wortley Montague, 1712. About three years later she made the acquaintance of Pope, who became deeply attached to her. Curll pirated some of her poems in 1716, for which crime Pope administered the famous emetic to him. Later that year she accompanied her husband to Constantinople and on her return (1718) introduced into England the practice of inoculation for small-pox. She and Pope corresponded from 1716 to 1721, Pope's letters being both ardent and tinged with a playful extravagance which suggests that his gallantry was not meant to be taken too seriously. At some date between 1721 and 1726, and for reasons unknown, Lady Mary and Pope became the bitterest of enemies, and began to attack each other in poem and pamphlet in the most shameful manner and without any inhibitions. She passed much of her later life abroad, finally returning to England on Wortley's death, the year before she herself died.

MOORE-SMYTHE, James (1702–1734). Playwright and man about town. He included some unpublished lines of Pope's in his comedy, *The Rival Modes*, 1727, with the author's permission, and, when that permission was (for reasons unknown) afterwards withdrawn, insisted on retaining them; thereby angering Pope and gaining a place in *The Dunciad* as a phantom poet. With his friend Welsted he retaliated with *One Epistle to Mr Pope*, 1730; and this in turn provoked Pope to write a number of searing epigrams on him in *The Grub-street Journal*.

MURRAY, William, first Earl of Mansfield. See MANSFIELD.

OLDFIELD, Anne (1683–1730). Actress, distinguished both for comedy and tragedy. On Vanbrugh's introduction she was engaged at Drury Lane (1692); made her name in the part of Lady Betty Modish (1704); played at the Haymarket (1705–10), but returned to Drury Lane in 1711, where she remained till her death. Pope's dislike of her, which is evident from his occasional remarks, has long been a puzzle to students of the period. Some fresh light is thrown on the

problem by an early epigram hitherto unprinted (see Chap. VII, ii).

ORRERY, John Boyle, fifth Earl of (1707–1762). Author, friend and correspondent of both Swift and Pope in the latter part of their lives, performing many kind services for them. Amongst other things, he supplied Pope with minerals from Kerry for the celebrated grotto; and he took Pope's dog, Bounce, into his care when her master could no longer keep her. He wrote *Remarks on the Life and Writings of Jonathan Swift*, 1752.

OXFORD, Edward Harley, second Earl of (1689–1741). Collector. He was a friend and correspondent of both Pope and Swift, and allowed the former to deposit letters and papers in his library from time to time for safe keeping. He added greatly to his father's great library, especially priceless MSS. now in the British Museum.

OXFORD, Robert Harley, first Earl of (1661–1724). Tory statesman. He held many high offices, chiefly under Queen Anne. He was created Earl of Oxford and Mortimer, 1711; ousted from royal favour by Bolingbroke and dismissed from office, 1714; impeachment dismissed, 1717. Friend of Pope, Parnell, and Swift, he attended many meetings of the Scriblerus Club, while still in power, by invitation; and, when he was in retirement and forsaken by former friends, Pope loyally addressed one of his most moving Epistles to him. He began the great Harleian collection of books and MSS.

PARNELL, Thomas (1679–1718). Poet and cleric. He came to England from Ireland, 1711; contributed occasional papers to *The Spectator* and *The Guardian*, 'probably publishing more than he owned'; became an intimate friend of Pope, Swift, and the first Earl of Oxford, and, as an original member of the Scriblerus Club, collaborated in some of the papers there projected, including *The Origin of Sciences.* He helped Pope with *The Iliad,* especially with the collection and preparation of the notes; and Pope after his death prepared and published his poems, dedicating the volume to their common friend, Lord Oxford.

PHILIPS, Ambrose (1675?–1749). Poet and dramatist, and fellow of St John's College, Cambridge (1699–1708). He published four *Pastorals* in 1708, which with two more he contributed to Tonson's *Poetical Miscellanies,* VI, in 1709—the volume that also contained Pope's four *Pastorals.* His *Pastorals* were contemporaneously preferred to Pope's, being praised in five papers in *The Guardian;* whereupon Pope contributed an anonymous sixth paper, comparing both sets and lavishly praising Philips's for wrong reasons. When the anonymous author became known, Philips threatened Pope with personal chastisement. He was a member of Addison's 'little senate' at Button's coffee-house. His poems about children directly inspired the coining of the epithet 'Namby-Pamby'.

ROWE, Nicholas (1674–1718). Dramatist, first editor of Shakespeare's plays, and Poet Laureate. He was an early friend of Pope, warm-hearted, vivacious, and gay, and they visited each other in their homes. Pope wrote an Epilogue for Rowe's *Jane Shore* (1714), and the following year a Prologue to his *Lady Jane Gray,* only recently identified. Rowe is mentioned in several of Pope's lighter pieces and praised elsewhere in his work. Pope wrote his epitaph in two versions, the first (1719) was printed in Pope's works but not engraved on the stone; the second (1743) was not acknowledged or printed by Pope but appears on the monument in Westminster Abbey (see Chap. VII).

ST JOHN, Henry, first Viscount Bolingbroke. See BOLINGBROKE.

SMYTHE, James Moore. See MOORE-SMYTHE.

SPENCE, Joseph (1699–1768). Anecdotist and friend of Pope; Professor of Poetry at Oxford (1728), and Regius Professor of Modern History (1742). He took notes of the conversation of Pope and his friends with the design of writing Pope's 'Life', but gave up the idea on Warburton's statement that he himself intended doing so. His manuscripts were used by several of Pope's biographers before they were published in two editions simultaneously in 1820, one edited by Singer, the other by Malone.

STEELE, Sir Richard (1672–1729). Dramatist, essayist, and politician. He originated the three most famous periodicals of the period, *The Tatler,* 1709, *The Spectator,* 1711, and *The Guardian,* 1713, to all of which Addison largely contributed and in the conduct of which largely shared. Steele was elected M.P. for Stockbridge, 1713, after which his interests and activities became increasingly political. He made Pope's acquaintance (probably through Caryll's good offices) in 1711, after which they became warm friends. Besides writing essays for *The Guardian,* Pope contributed several poems to Steele's *Poetical Miscellanies,* 1714. Later, their paths diverged more and more, and with no loss of goodwill, they were seeing little of each other at the time of Steele's death.

SUFFOLK, Henrietta Howard, Countess

of (1681–1767). Mistress of George II. She was a daughter of Sir Henry Hobart, Bart., and wife of Charles Howard, later Earl of Suffolk (1731); Lady of the Bedchamber to the Princess (afterwards Queen) Caroline, and Mistress of the Robes in 1731. Pope, who had known her at least as early as 1716, was largely responsible for the design of her garden, when her house was being built at Marble Hill, Twickenham (1724), and he remained her friend all his life. Her house became the meeting place of many of his friends; Gay, Swift, Arbuthnot, Peterborough and others; and Martha Blount paid many visits there. She retired from the court in 1734 and married the Hon. George Berkeley in 1735. Her correspondence was edited by Croker in 1824.

SWIFT, Jonathan (1667–1745). Dean of St Patrick's, Dublin; poet and satirist. Swift's acquaintance with Pope began about 1712, and in the autumn of 1713 he was busying himself to gain subscriptions to Pope's *Iliad*. He joined Pope and Gay and Arbuthnot in setting up the Scriblerus Club (1713–14). On the death of Queen Anne and all his political hopes, he retired to his deanery in Ireland, where he remained for the next twelve years, his friendship with Pope deepening rather than dying during the separation. In 1726, and again in 1727, Swift made long summer visits to England, Pope being his chief host both years. Thereafter they never met again, but exchanged long and intimate letters until Swift's increasing illness stopped even their correspondence; Pope's last surviving letter to his old friend being dated March 22, 1741.

TEMPLE, Sir Richard, Viscount Cobham. See COBHAM.

THEOBALD, Lewis (1688–1744). Scholar and dramatist. The origin of the long quarrel between Theobald and Pope is uncertain; the former may have begun it if, as Pope thought, he was partly responsible for *A Complete Key to . . . The What D'ye Call It* (1715), which attacked the farce Pope had helped Gay to produce. But Theobald subsequently praised Pope's *Iliad* (1717), and Pope subscribed for four copies of the other's miscellany *The Grove*, 1721. Next, however, the edition of *The Works of Shakespeare*, 6 vols., which Pope published in 1725, was followed in 1726 by Theobald's attack on it, deplorably entitled—*Shakespeare restored; or, a Specimen of the many Errors as well committed as unamended by Mr. Pope, in his late Edition of this Poet*. And, there being other irritants too, it is not surprising that Theobald was enthroned king of the Dunces in 1728.

TICKELL, Thomas (1686–1740). Poet, and Fellow of The Queen's College, Oxford; friend and literary executor of Addison, and contributor to *The Spectator* and *The Guardian*. He wrote with Addison's approval, if not at his instigation, a poetical translation of the first book of the *Iliad*, and published it within a day or two of Pope's first volume (Books I–IV) 1715. He thus occasioned one of the most famous quarrels in the history of literature—that of Pope and Addison; *not*, as might have been expected, between Pope and himself; for Pope never seems to have borne him any ill-will. New light is thrown on this quarrel in Chapter VI of the present volume.

TONSON, Jacob (1656?–1736). Bookseller; set up business in 1677; published much of Dryden's work, published also for Addison, Rowe, Steele, and other of Pope's friends, and enemies. He was Pope's first publisher, printing three of his poems in *Poetical Miscellanies*, VI, 1709, but no separate work before Pope's *Shakespeare*, 6 vols., 1725, and none afterwards.

WARWICK, Edward Henry, Earl of (1697–1721). Young man about town, 'finely accomplished', according to Dr Young, but profligate. He made Pope's acquaintance about 1714; warned him of Addison's enmity against him in 1715 (Addison married his mother the Countess of Warwick the following year); Warwick thus also helped to precipitate the Pope-Addison quarrel. He died of his excesses at twenty-four.

APPENDIX B

A LIST OF ABBREVIATIONS
[Used in the Notes, &c.]

A LETTER = *A Letter from Mr. Cibber to Mr. Pope.* 1742.

ADD. = British Museum Additional MSS.

ADDITIONS = *Additions to the Works of Alexander Pope, Esq.* 2 vols., 1776.

APOLOGY = *An Apology for the Life of Mr. Colley Cibber, Comedian,* 1740.

ATTERBURY = *The Epistolary Correspondence.* Ed. J. Nichols. 5 vols., 1783–90.

B.M. = British Museum.

BALL = *The Correspondence of Jonathan Swift.* Ed. F. E. Ball. 6 vols., 1910–14.

BIOG. NOTES = Biographical Notes.

BOWLES = *The Works of Alexander Pope, Esq.* Ed. W. L. Bowles. 10 vols., 1806.

BURNET = *Letters of Thomas Burnet to George Duckett, 1712–22.* Ed. D. Nichol Smith. 1914.

BUTT = *Alexander Pope. Imitations of Horace.* Ed. J. Butt. (Twickenham edn., Vol. IV), 1939.

CARRUTHERS = *The Life of Alexander Pope.* By R. Carruthers. 2nd edn., 1857.

CORRESPONDENCE = *Mr. Pope's Literary Correspondence.* 5 vols. (published by Curll), 1735–37.

D.N.B. = *Dictionary of National Biography.*

DEVONSHIRE MSS. = Autograph Letters and Papers of Pope, at Chatsworth.

DUNCIAD A = *The Dunciad, Variorum.* 3 books, 1729.

DUNCIAD B = *The Dunciad, In Four Books.* 1743.

EC = *The Works of Pope.* Ed. W. Elwin and W. J. Courthope. 10 vols., 1871–89.

EGERTON = British Museum Egerton MSS.

FABER = *The Poetical Works of John Gay.* Ed. G. C. Faber. 1926.

FRASER = *Notes on the Poems of . . . Pope, by Horatio Earl of Orford.* Ed. Sir W. A. Fraser. 1876.

GENT. MAG. = *The Gentleman's Magazine.*

GRENVILLE = *The Grenville Papers.* Ed. W. J. Smith. 4 vols., 1852–3.

GRIFFITH = *Alexander Pope: A Bibliography.* By R. H. Griffith. 1 vol. in two parts, 1922, 1927.

HARCOURT = *The Harcourt Papers.* Ed. E. W. Harcourt. 14 vols., 1876–1905.

HARL. = British Museum Harleian MSS.

HERVEY = *Memoirs of the Reign of George II.* By John, Lord Hervey. Ed. R. Sedgwick. 3 vols., 1931.

IRVING = *John Gay*. By W. H. Irving. 1940.

JOHNSON = *The Lives of the English Poets*. By S. Johnson. 4 vols., 1781.

LANG, LEAF AND MYERS = *The Iliad of Homer*. Translated by A. Lang, W. Leaf and E. Myers. 1897.

LANSD. = British Museum Lansdowne MSS.

LETTERS, 4to, 1737 = *Letters of Mr. Alexander Pope*. (Pope's authorized edition), 1737.

LETTERS II, 4to, 1741 = *The Works . . . In Prose*. Vol. II (containing the rest of his Letters), 1741.

LETTERS . . . TO A LADY = *Letters of the late Alexander Pope, Esq. To A Lady*, 1769.

LETTERS . . . TO . . . HILL = *A Collection of Letters . . . to the late Aaron Hill*, 1751.

M.L.N. = *Modern Language Notes*.

MALONE = *Life of Edmond Malone*. By J. Prior. 1860.

MANWARING = *Italian Landscape in Eighteenth Century England*. By E. W. Manwaring. 1925.

MAPLEDURHAM = Mapledurham MSS. (Pope's autograph letters to the Misses Blount, numbered as in the bound volume.)

MEMOIRS = *Memoirs of the Life . . . of Alexander Pope, Esq*. By W. Ayre. 2 vols., 1745.

MISCELLANEA = *Miscellanea. In Two Volumes*. 1727. (A Curll production.)

MISCELLANIES = *Miscellanies*. By Pope and Swift. 4 vols., 1727–32.

MARCHMONT = *Marchmont Papers*. Ed. Sir G. H. Rose. 1831.

NICHOLLS = *The Correspondence of Thomas Gray and the Rev. Norton Nicholls*. Ed. J. Mitford. 1843.

O.E.D. = *Oxford English Dictionary*.

PASTON = *Mr. Pope*. By George Paston (i.e. E. M. Symonds). 2 vols., 1909.

POLWHELE = *The History of Devonshire*. By R. Polwhele. 3 vols., 1793–1806.

POPE'S OWN MISCELLANY = *Pope's Own Miscellany*, Being a reprint of *Poems on Several Occasions*, 1717. Ed. N. Ault. 1935.

POPE'S PROSE = *The Prose Works of Alexander Pope*. Ed. N. Ault. Vol. I. 1936.

PORTLAND = Portland Papers (many vols.) at Longleat.

R.E.S. = *Review of English Studies*.

RAWL. = Bodleian MS. Rawlinson letters. 90. (The Pope-Cromwell correspondence.)

REMINISCENCES = *Reminiscences Written for . . . Mary and . . . Agnes Berry*. 1805. (Reprint 1924 used.)

ROSCOE = *The Works of Alexander Pope, Esq*. Ed. W. Roscoe. 10 vols., 1824.

RUFFHEAD = *The Life of Alexander Pope, Esq*. By O. Ruffhead. 1769.

SENIOR = *The Life and Times of Colley Cibber*. By F. D. Senior. 1928.

SHERBURN = *The Early Career of Alexander Pope*. By G. Sherburn. 1934.

SITWELL = *Alexander Pope*. By Edith Sitwell. 1930.

SPENCE = *Anecdotes . . . of Books and Men. Collected from the Conversation of Mr. Pope . . .* By J. Spence. Ed. S. W. Singer. 1820.

STOWE = British Museum Stowe MSS.

STRAUS = *The Unspeakable Curll.* By R. Straus. 1927.

SUFFOLK = *Letters to and from Henrietta, Countess of Suffolk.* 2 vols., 1824.

SUTHERLAND = *Alexander Pope. The Dunciad.* Ed. J. Sutherland. (Twickenham edn, Vol. v), 1943.

UNDERHILL = *The Poetical Works of John Gay.* Ed. J. Underhill. 2 vols., 1893.

WALPOLE = *The Letters of Horace Walpole.* Ed. P. Toynbee. 16 vols., 1903–5.

WARBURTON = *The Works of Alexander Pope, Esq.* Ed. W. Warburton. 9 vols., 1751.

WARD = *The Poetical Works of Alexander Pope.* Ed. A. W. Ward. 1869. (Reprint 1930 used.)

WARTON = *The Works of Alexander Pope, Esq.* Ed. J. Warton. 9 vols., 1797.

WHITLEY = *Artists and their Friends in England, 1700–1799.* By W. T. Whitley. 2 vols., 1928.

WILLIAMS = *The Poems of Jonathan Swift.* Ed. H. Williams. 3 vols., 1937.

WORKS, 1717 = *The Works of Mr. Alexander Pope.* 4to, 1717.

WORKS, II, 1735 = *The Works of Mr. Alexander Pope.* Vol. II, 4to, 1735.

WORKS = Pope's *Works* in various editions, 8vo and 12mo, 1736–44.

APPENDIX C

BIBLIOGRAPHY OF THE POEM
To Mrs. M.B. on her Birth-day

'A' TEXT
(14 lines, beginning—'Oh be thou blest')

Pope's autographs: Mapledurham MSS. 4, 1723; Portland Papers, XIII, 1725; B.M. MS. Stowe 964, 1725.

Contemporary transcripts: B.M. MS. Harl. 7316; B.M. MS. Add. 28101.

The British Journal. November 14, 1724.

The Whitehall Evening-Post. November 12–14, 1724.

Miscellany Poems, Vol. I. 5th Edn., 1726.

The Christian Poet. 1735.

Letters of the late Alexander Pope, Esq. To a Lady. (Written 1723), 1769.

'B' TEXT

(20 lines, containing a version of the six lines first printed
in Moore-Smythe's comedy, *The Rival Modes*, 1727)

Miscellanies. The Last Volume. 1727 (published March 7, 1728), and later editions.
The Works . . . With Explanatory Notes and Additions. Vol. 1. Dublin. 1736.
Miscellanies. The Fourth Volume, Consisting of Verses. 1742, and later editions.

'C' TEXT

(10 lines, beginning—'With added days')

Contemporary transcripts: B.M. MS. Harl. 7316; Portland Papers xviii.
The St. James's Chronicle. September 28–30, 1775.
Additions to the Works of Alexander Pope, Esq. Vol. 1. 1776.

'D' TEXT

(6 lines, beginning—'With added days')

Letters of Mr. Pope, and Several Eminent Persons. 1735.
Mr. Pope's Literary Correspondence. Vol. 1. 1735; (and 3rd edn. 1735).
Letters of Mr. Alexander Pope. 1737.
The Works . . . Vol. VI. Containing . . . Letters. 1737; (and 2nd edn. 1737).
The Works . . . Vol. IV. Part II. Containing . . . Letters. 1742.
The Works of Alexander Pope, Esq. Ed. W. Warburton. Vol. viii. 1751.

'E' TEXT

(20 lines, beginning—'Oh be thou blest'; and containing the 6 lines beginning—'With added years')

*The Works . . . Vol. II. Part II. Containing . . . Pieces . . . Written since the former
Volumes.* 1738.
A Choice Collection of Poetry. 1738.
The Works . . . Vol. II. Containing his Epistles, &c. 1739.
The Gentleman's Magazine. June 1739.
The Works . . . Vol. II. Part I. Containing his Epistles &c. 1740; and 1743.
The Works of Alexander Pope, Esq. Ed. W. Warburton. Vol. vi. 1751.

INDEX OF FIRST LINES

[Most of the poems listed below are new candidates for the Pope canon on the evidence submitted in the foregoing pages (a dagger † marking those now printed for the first time). Of the few familiar pieces amongst them several have long been accepted as Pope's, but hitherto without evidence of his authorship—such evidence being now submitted for these also.]

GENERAL INDEX

PRINTED IN GREAT BRITAIN
BY THE BROADWATER PRESS LTD
WELWYN GARDEN CITY
HERTFORDSHIRE